ASIAN AMERICANS IN DIXIE

THE ASIAN AMERICAN EXPERIENCE

Series Editors
Eiichiro Azuma
Jigna Desai
Martin F. Manalansan IV
Lisa Sun-Hee Park
David K. Yoo
Roger Daniels, Founding Series Editor

A list of books in the series appears at the end of this book.

Asian Americans in Dixie

Race and Migration in the South

Edited by
KHYATI Y. JOSHI
AND JIGNA DESAI

UNIVERSITY OF ILLINOIS PRESS
URBANA, CHICAGO, AND SPRINGFIELD

Brief portions of Chapter 1 are reprinted by permission of the
publisher from *Bengali Harlem and the Lost Histories of South Asian
America* by Vivek Bald, Cambridge, Mass.: Harvard University Press,
Copyright © 2013 by the President and Fellows of Harvard College.

Chapter 2, Racial Interstitiality and the Anxieties of the "'Partly
Colored': Representations of Asians under Jim Crow," by Leslie Bow
is reprinted from the *Journal of Asian American Studies*. Feb. 2007.
10.1: 1–30.

Library of Congress Cataloging-in-Publication Data
Asian Americans in Dixie : Race and Migration in the South / edited
by Khyati Y. Joshi and Jigna Desai.
pages   cm. — (The Asian American Experience)
Includes bibliographical references and index.
ISBN 978-0-252-03783-2 (cloth : alk. paper)
ISBN 978-0-252-07938-2 (pbk. : alk. paper)
ISBN 978-0-252-09595-5 (ebook)
1. Asian Americans—Southern States.
I. Desai, Jigna. II. Joshi, Khyati Y., 1970-
F216.2.A85   2013
305.895'073075—dc23   2013015155

For Hetal

and

For Rakesh and Seema

CONTENTS

ACKNOWLEDGMENTS

We acknowledge those who have helped bring this volume to fruition. First, we thank our contributors whose patience and intellectual efforts are demonstrated on the subsequent pages. Our gratitude to you for having faith in the volume and us; we have enjoyed the journey together and learned much along the way from all of you.

We thank Derek Krissoff for thinking this project worthwhile from the onset. Our gratitude also extends to the anonymous reviewers whose lively and insightful comments have improved this manuscript immeasurably. We are further indebted to vibrant Vijay Shah for his enthusiasm, ideas, and support. We would also like to thank the production staff (Dustin Hubbart and Jennifer Clark) at the University of Illinois Press and copy editor Nancy Albright and indexer Sheila Bodell for their professionalism, helpfulness, and diligence. It brings us great joy to have the book be a part of the Asian American Experience book series.

Thank you to our programs, departments, and colleges at the University of Minnesota and Fairleigh Dickinson University, which have provided the support that has permitted us to complete this manuscript. Thank you to our chairs Regina Kunzel and Vicki Cohen for recognizing this scholarship as critical to our intellectual endeavors and contributions.

Our gratitude to our Asian American Studies colleagues Leslie Bow, Floyd Cheung, Elena Creef, Shilpa Dave, Pawan Dhingra, Jennifer Ho, Karen Ho, Jane Iwamura, Ann Kalayil, Erika Lee, Jo Lee, Madhavi Mallapragada, Anita Mannur, Sharmila Rudrappa, Tom Sarmiento, Jaideep Singh, Cathy Schlund-Vials, Eric Tang, Pam Thoma, and the many others who always create an intellectual community within the Association for Asian American Studies for the myriad of conversations that sustain us.

From Jigna: You can take the girl out of the South, but not the South out of the girl. Thank you to Khyati for her ebullience, fortitude, and organization in confronting edited volumes. Without her vision and zeal, this collection would not exist. Though I deeply resented my family in the seventh grade for moving me from the ethnic enclaves of New Jersey to the freshly paved suburbs of Atlanta, I marvel, now, at how Asian American my Atlanta has become and appreciate how it has become home for so many of us. The heavy and humid nights, the chirping of crickets, the ever-present sight of kudzu, and the spaghetti of highways are all familiar landmarks in a journey home. To my father and mother who have spent more years in Gwinnett County than in Gujarat, my gratitude for their migrations filled with hope, adjustments, and resilience; I also thank them for their unshaking belief that I can do anything. No matter to which regions my feet wandered, my brother Rakesh and sister Seema always made me leave my heart with them in the South; in addition to their loving support, they have graciously shared their extensive understandings of what it has meant to grow up brown-skinned below the Mason-Dixon line. My appreciation to Ruskin who helps brings the South into our Minnesota home, sharing a penchant for collards and cornbread, as well as conversations about the color line. He helps me process the enthusiasm and disappointments of everyday life into thoughtful optimism for the coming day. His support, love, and labor have greatly enriched this book. And, finally, I thank Rohan and Khayaal for tasting new and fresh experiences of the South with such fervor and excitement that I get to experience things anew.

From Khyati: Unlike Jigna, I knew nothing but the South—and India—until graduate school. I was five when my father and mother, then pregnant with my younger sister, moved us to Atlanta. Thanks to my parents, my sister Hetal, and the rest of my "family"—the Sanghvi, Desai, Shroff, Bhargave, Manocha, Razdan, and Vijay families—I had a place where I felt I could just be me. My parents and those families devoted thousands of hours of loving labor to building Atlanta's Indian American community physically, socially, and spiritually. Today, that community is thriving and growing in ways that few families in the early 1970s could ever have imagined. It, like this book and the professional and personal successes of my second-generation peers from that community, is a testament to what they built, and I am eternally grateful. After leaving Atlanta, I have lived predominantly in the Northeast, where I often identify myself to others as a proud southerner. That's not what most people are expecting, any more than they expect southern "y'all" and accent from this brown-skinned Hindu woman. But you can have feet in two worlds and still be proud of both of them. I am fortunate to have found Jigna, who shares my complex yet fond relationship with the South, as a partner in crime. Everyone should have the opportunity to work with Jigna; she is insightful, encouraging, and supportive, and through thick and thin she keeps her eye on the prize. Finally, I am grateful to my husband John, who is a sounding board for my ideas, and our son Kedhar, for whose future I do the work that I do.

HONEYSUCKLE, GEORGIA

In dark, a flicker.

Last night I dreamt of fireflies,
dew of Georgia day, heat   as pecan sizzle in salted air.

In my minds, a woods.

    Honeysuckle. What cannot be remembered—
            the unquiet wind chafing a plied body.

There are memories you wish to forget   & ones you wish to flame—
    somewhere

       in that pulse we call the present, your face

glows as air under abdomen   of
firefly. In this moment, phosphoresce

    —and sight.

ASIAN AMERICANS IN DIXIE

Discrepancies in Dixie:
Asian Americans and the South

Jigna Desai and Khyati Y. Joshi

The figure of the Asian American is perceived to be discrepant in and antithetical to the U.S. South.[1] Within the American imaginary, the Asian American as perpetual foreigner and alien is always seen as a recent immigrant, and therefore associated with contemporary times,[2] while the South is perceived as an anachronistic and isolated region; this renders the two—the Asian American and the South—allegedly mutually exclusive and incongruous. In these imaginings, the South remains a space quintessentially American but one steeped in an antebellum era of White supremacy, anti-Black racism, and outdated isolation; in supposed contrast stands the figure of the Asian American who is associated with immigration and borders, globalization, and contemporaneity. Even in assertions of the "New South" as a modern, industrial, and cosmopolitan space, there is little mention of Asian migration;[3] instead the "new" refers to two different moments, one beginning after the Civil War and the other indicating the economic boom in which global manufacturing industries became located in the South.[4] In all of these formulations, Asian Americans are mentioned, rarely if at all, when speaking about the South. Consequently, Asian Americans are perceived to be doubly foreign within the context of the South as a U.S. region; they might be perceived to be and to create what we might call "discrepancies in Dixie."[5]

In contrast, historiographical scholarship within Asian American studies has for several decades documented the presence and significance of Asian Americans in the South. Narratives of Asian American historiography often begin with the "Manilamen"—Filipino sailors who jumped ship and traveled to Louisiana over land via Mexico.[6] Additional figures, Chinese coolies, South Asian peddlers and lascars (sailors), Chinese Mississippians, Vietnamese refugee communities in New Orleans, and Indian Gujarati motel owners are peppered throughout the scholarship.[7] However, these figures quickly appear in and disappear from understandings of the South as well as the Asian American Studies "canon."[8] Hence, while they offer some "local" color to Asian American historiography, for the most part, Asian Americans in the South become quirky exceptions to the larger story of Asian America that is configured through its bicoastal, if not Californiacentric, paradigm. Rather than see these historical figures as discrete or random aberrations, we place them in close proximity to each other in order to demonstrate and explore the presence and significance of Asian Americans to the South. This proximity allows us to consider the racialized historical and contemporary *presence*[9] of Asian Americans in the South to trouble our formulations of Asian America, the South, and racial projects within the United States.

By resituating Asian Americans in the South, this anthology considers the discrepancies that are produced by this *dis*-placement. We find the many meanings of *discrepant*—discordant, dissident, disagreeing, and variant—productive in considering Asian Americans *and* the South. The figure of the Asian American disrupts popular discourses about the South in multiple ways: the Asian American demonstrates the shifting meaning of Black and White in a region in which this binary is writ large; is associated with foreignness and globalization in a space assumed to be parochial and isolated; and most generally, troubles more simple narratives of America's own amnesia around his/her presence. It is important to note that the South itself is considered a discrepancy within, rather than an exemplar of, the nation.[10] We seek not to be mired in the debate about Southern distinction, but rather seek to understand how Asian American racial formations within the South participate in regional, national, and transnational racial projects. As Asian Americans and the South are both taken as exceptional and anomalous, we seek to question these logics and expectations, asking how the stakes may change if we see them as a lens into this region and the nation. In other words, we believe that much can be gained when we consider Asian Americans in the South.

The anthology considers the *presence* of Asian Americans in the South in terms of demographics and epistemology. Racial demographics are radically changing within many emerging Asian American communities located in the South. Long studied through the lens of Black-White relations, studies of race in the South are increasingly attempting to contend with the increasing presence of Asian Americans and Latino Americans and their shifting racializations within the context of the contemporary South. We want to emphasize that the significance of Asian Americans to the South is not merely numerical or demographic. As many scholars have argued, historically, the *figure* of the Chinese and Indian coolie has been essential for the discourses of freedom and race during Emancipation in the South, despite the low number of actual Chinese and Indian migrants. Thus, a deliberation on the Asian American *presence*, past and present, can provoke a consideration of Asian American racial formations and migrations in regard to the broader constitutions of race, region, empire, and the nation-state. Consequently, interdisciplinary scholarship on race in the South has considered three important and related points: 1) the impact of the South's history of transnationalism on racial formations; 2) the historical racialization of Whites (e.g., Arabs and Jews) within the context of Black, White, and Asian American racial formations in the South; and 3) the role of Afro-Asian connections in producing Asian American and African American racial formations as relational.

In this manner, Asian American racial formations in the South have been understood in relation to other racial formations regionally, nationally, and transnationally; hence, several of the essays in this anthology attend to the nuanced ways in which Asian American racial formations are located in relation to the hegemony of the Black and White binary. Other essays provoke us to reconsider the isolationist narratives of the South, reintroducing the South as located in a historical web of global networks stretching across the Caribbean, Pacific, and Atlantic. As discrepant subjects, Asian Americans in the South suggest more than a project of recovery and recuperation. Instead, reflecting on the Asian American presence can be a method of reconsidering discourses of race, slavery, empire, citizenship, and the nation-state in broad terms. Therefore, it is not just the contemporary demographics that scholars must reckon with—it is the epistemological presence and absence (erasure, elision, and disappearance) of these racialized figures that requires further exploration as well. We suggest that attention to the presence of Asian Americans in the South demonstrates how multiple social differences (such as gender, ethnicity, and sexuality) as well as citizenship, nativism, and empire have continuously been constitutive of Asian American, Latino, White, and Black racial formations.

The Imagined South

One might ask where and what is the South. Scholars have debated over its meaning, its borders, its histories, its identity, its cultures, its distinction, and its role and location within the context of nation for over a century.[11] The South takes on different meanings based on whether its definition is based on historical, social, or geopolitical parameters. Historically, it is often used to refer to those states that were slave states before 1860 now known as the Old South: Alabama, Arkansas, Delaware, Florida, Georgia, Kentucky, Louisiana, Maryland, Mississippi, Missouri, North Carolina, South Carolina, Tennessee, Texas, and Virginia, as well as the territory of Oklahoma. *Dixie* is a nickname that is often associated with the states that seceded from the nation to form the Confederacy and refers to the states listed above minus Delaware, Kentucky, Maryland, and Missouri. Dixie also is used interchangeably with the terms Old South, Deep South, and the Bible Belt to describe those states that are assumed to share some kind of cultural and religious similarities. The U.S. census designates the South as a geopolitical region that includes Alabama, Arkansas, Delaware, the District of Columbia, Florida, Georgia, Kentucky, Louisiana, Maryland, Mississippi, North Carolina, Oklahoma, South Carolina, Tennessee, Texas, Virginia, and West Virginia.[12]

We use the category of the South to signify a historical, cultural, and geopolitical space that is both understood to be a region of the United States and a
space connected to and part of other transnational spaces such as the Atlantic
world. More specifically, we recognize that the South is conceived as a coherent
region and place as it is associated with a distinctive and authentic Southern
culture and history. This history of slavery, war, Jim Crow segregation, and
White supremacy leads to differences in political economy, social and cultural
development, and racial projects. We point out that certain, but not all, spaces
within this geographic region are associated with the legacies of Southern history and culture(s). This collection utilizes both understandings of the South
as a geopolitical space in looking to specific places (e.g., Georgia, Louisiana,
and Texas) and as a part of our national imaginary in looking to sociocultural
discourses (e.g., Orientalist consumption, redneck humor, Black/White racial
binary, and Christian normativity).

In the dominant American imaginary, "the South"[13] is perceived to be an exceptional space within and to be temporally asynchronous with the nation. This
regional difference is often understood through cultural, racial, and religious
terms. The South is seen repeatedly as the primary site of American racial trauma
and oppression. The region has been framed within narratives of distinction and
exceptionalism so that the Old South of antebellum slavery, lynchings, and Jim
Crow segregation is both romanticized for its quaint White Southern culture and
demonized for its historical and explicit acts of racial violence that, supposedly,
make it like no other region. These narratives inadvertently result in reifying
the dominant paradigm of framing race only through the binary terms of Black
and White while erasing the South's exemplary experiences of race within the
nation-state. The South's "failure" to be modern and American is attributed to
an individual Southerner's own backwardness and inability to transcend her/his
individual racisms specifically, and Southern culture more broadly. Furthermore,
Christian hegemony is also strongly associated with the South. As we discuss
below, the South is perceived to be more religious and oppressive than other
regions; for example, the term Bible Belt is often used synonymously with the
South in most discourses. By rendering the South as explicitly racist and hyper-
Christian, these claims bolster non-Southern identities and spaces as postracial,
secular, and modern in contrast.

The American religious metaphor of the Bible Belt, which associates evangelical Christianity with the South, is both a product of the region's history and an
oversimplification of it. There is, and has always been, more to the South than the
Bible Belt and that term's implicit assumption that White Protestantism had taken
a different shape in the South. Even if the myth overstates the reality, religion does
play a very significant role in the lives of Southern residents; data have shown
not only that there are more churches in the South than in any other region of

the United States, but also that those churches are attended more frequently and by a greater proportion of the population.[14]

Among Southerners, more than a third (37 percent) are members of evangelical churches, and more than a tenth (11 percent) are affiliated with a historically Black church.[15] Even more individuals than those who self-identify as "members" may nevertheless identify with the worship practices and cultural ideas expressed by those churches. Hence, organizational religious practice is strongly ingrained in the everyday practices of Southern culture. Charles Reagan Wilson uses the phrase *Southern Civil Religion* to describe "a common religion of the South which grew out of confederate defeat in the civil war" and that has an identifiable mythology, ritual, and organization.[16] Wilson also asserts that Southern Civil Religion did not stand entirely separate from other Christian denominations.[17] What Wilson identifies as Southern Civil Religion may be more directly named as *Christian normativity* in the South. Christianity is hegemonic within social and cultural practices across the South (and all of the United States); specifically, mainstream culture is dominated by evangelical Protestant churches and moral values.[18] The normative presence of Christianity is encountered in the everyday lives of Southerners both past and present. Although the proportion of adults identifying as Christian is in decline in all regions of the United States, including the South, we nevertheless suggest that the normative power of White Protestant Christianity permeates Southern culture at many levels.[19]

Southern difference is often expressed through both temporal and spatial tropes. As Southern cultural difference is marked as the residue of the antebellum period, this association frequently locates the South in a temporal lag. Hence, these contemporary narratives of Southern exceptionalism also function to scapegoat the South as premodern, backward, and noncosmopolitan, thus the *only* region that has not transcended its history of racial oppression within the modern nation.[20] Geographically, despite its long history of transnationalism through the Atlantic and the Caribbean, the South is assumed to be isolated, rather than transnational, and Southern culture to be insular, rather than transcultural. This is not to say that immigration to the South has historically been as substantial and vibrant as it was to other regions such as the Northeast, West Coast, or Texas and Southwest border areas. But because of its narrative of exceptionalism, the South is seen as removed from larger national and global processes such as late capitalism, migration, empire, transnationalism, and/or cosmopolitanism. Rather than locating the South as part of past and present global networks linking Africa, Europe, the Caribbean, and Latin America to the United States, most constructions of the South emphasize its lack of transnational connectivity and globality. Hence, all Southerners, Black and White, are assumed to be noncosmopolitan and nonmodern, while the region is taken to be disconnected from modern global processes. Despite its long-standing economic, political, social,

and cultural connections with Europe, Asia, Africa, Latin America, and the Caribbean, the South is, nonetheless, associated with parochialism, isolationism,
and xenophobia.[21] In contrast to narratives that see the South as isolated, others
have located the South as globally connected in the past and present.[22]

While the significance of Asian American migration has been mostly ignored
in scholarship on the old and new South, the entry points of migration to the
South via ports and border crossings create different geographies. For example,
early Filipino migration to the South occurred through a geography foregrounding the oceanic circuits of the Pacific Ocean and the Gulf of Mexico, Mexico and
Texas borderlands, and the waterways of French Louisiana, while South Asian
peddlers traversed port towns from New Orleans to Charleston and Savannah.
Hence as scholars have indicated, the emergence and formation of Filipino communities in Louisiana, and other Asian communities elsewhere in the South, can
help reorient Asian American studies and Southern Studies through alternative
geographies and formations that integrate the South with the Atlantic, the Caribbean, Central and South America, and the Filipino diaspora and Pacific world.[23]

Consequently, the trope of isolation coupled with the overemphasis on the
Black/White binary buttresses notions of the South as a nativist and parochial
space. Discussions of migration as well as Asian Americans and Latino Americans
disappear from renderings of the South. It is precisely this overidentification
with nativism that ensures the South an exceptional space within the American
imaginary—one by which America's progressive narrative of modernity can be
measured and compared domestically. Of course, this idea of a nativist space in
the American imaginary has much more to do with the ways in which the South
needs to be understood as fixed within a premodern moment of isolation that
is unlike other places within the nation than it does with any material, social,
cultural, and historical realities.

Early Migration and Racial Formations
within the Transnational South

If we begin with the premise that the South historically is a space of transnationalism, contact, intimacy, and presence rather than isolationism and absence,
how might we understand the Asian American South differently? Race and immigration are certainly writ large in the contemporary South and Southwest;
however, this volume suggests that we also rethink the historical narratives of
the South that discuss it as a space untouched by globalization. It is interesting to
note how this history of transnationalism is often erased in order to render the
South isolated and provincial; the South as a global geopolitical space becomes
abundantly clearer as scholars replace a paradigm of isolationism with that of
transnationalism. It is necessary to understand Asian migration to the South

and its related spaces of the Caribbean, Latin American (including Mexico), and Atlantic worlds[24] within its embedded context of the three major global forces that have shaped modernity: capitalism, colonialism, and nationalism.

If the African diaspora resulted from slavery, Asian migration is conjoined to this history as a source of "voluntary" labor that succeeded slave labor;[25] hence, these histories are inextricably linked. Moreover, examining the multiple and cross-migrations that constitute Asian migrations through and between Asia, the Caribbean, Britain, and the South suggests that the racial formations of Asians in the South are formed within larger contexts than just those of the United States. Studies of Asian migrant communities in the Caribbean and Latin America by scholars, such as Walton Look Lai, Tan Chee-Beng, and Erika Lee, provide us with a means of understanding how the South is part of larger transnational formations, such as the Americas or the Atlantic world, and how these transnational processes form and impact racial formations and migrant communities. Studying the U.S. South, the Caribbean, Latin America, and the Atlantic as a deeply connected space has been a steadily growing project within transnational history and cultural studies.

Asian migration to the South can be understood as indicative of the South's connection to other spaces such as the Americas and Europe, rather than as a regional extension of Asian migration to California. Thus, discussions of Asian migration to the South can be placed in larger transnational historical movements in which South Asians travel the Atlantic world through Britain and other ports as peddlers and lascars,[26] in which the sugar trade raises questions of racialized labor and slavery,[27] and in which Asian migration leads to the formation and transformation of multiracial societies.[28]

Recent research on Asian racialized labor migration before, during, and after slavery reconsiders how (South Asian and Chinese) *coolie* migration is located within the global sugar economy, slavery, and American and British imperialisms. Scholars situate the figure of the coolie squarely at the center of national and transnational discourses about race, slavery, and migration in the age of emancipation.[29] They suggest that prior to emancipation, the option of coolie migration was raised as an economic option to enhance America's competitive edge in the sugar industry; arguing for coolies as a cheaper, more docile, and "more free" form of labor in relation to enslaved Africans, advocates of indentured labor from China posed coolies as a competitive and moral alternative to slavery. Consequently, Southern attitudes toward Asian migration have fluctuated with the changing status of slavery and labor needs in the South. In these debates, various parties conceived of coolies as a coerced or a voluntary form of labor. Coolies were repeatedly wedged into debates of slavery, freedom, and migration; generally, Chinese coolie migration to the South was discussed in relation to domestic debates about slavery and emancipation and in relation to international debates about (South Asian) coolies, empire, and capitalism. Thus, focusing on the coolie is a way of foregrounding how Asian migrant and bonded labor is firmly located within modernity and the global forces of capitalism, colonialism, and nationalism.

Early on, with the exception of Californians and U.S. diplomats to China, no opponents were as vehemently anti-coolie as proslavery Southerners; citing examples from the British deployment of South Asian indentured labor within the Caribbean plantation system, they argued that Chinese indentured migration was worse than slavery and would threaten the Southern economy and the free American way of life through savagery, miscegenation, and the obfuscation of slavery.[30] Through this scholarship, one can see how the political economy of empire and racialized labor migrations (African slavery and Asian indentured labor) are mutually constitutive within this context. By considering the racialization and migration of Chinese coolies in relation to discourses of slavery, for example, scholars make clear that the category of "immigrant" emerges in a dependent and vexed relationship with concepts of free/enslaved and White/Black. Prior to emancipation, it is the figural presence of the coolie, rather than demographic presence of Asian Americans, that is key to understanding these larger discourses of migration, slavery, freedom, and the nation-state in relation to the transnational space of the South. In this moment, coolies were located significantly between Black and White, between slavery and freedom—and were perhaps critical to the perceived line between them. Asian migrants played a significant role within the region linking the Caribbean, Latin American, and Atlantic worlds with the South; the side-by-side participation of Asian and African migrants in struggles for freedom continues to be a growing site of scholarly and activist exploration in these regions.

After emancipation, some Southerners looked to immigration, in addition to free African Americans, as a means of acquiring cheap labor to support primarily the agricultural economy. The Southern states also advocated for reversing the prohibitions within immigration law; for example, the governor of North Carolina in 1900 lobbied for the repeal of the Chinese Exclusion Act when cotton growers complained of labor shortages.[31] A desire to reformulate a racialized underclass of subordinate laborers created a resurgence of interest in European and Asian migration to the South, this time, with greater Southern support. "Coolies represented a vexing anomaly whose contested status would reconstruct American identities after emancipation. Where would coolies fit in a race-obsessed society that no longer bounds Blacks to enslaved labor or allowed racial barriers to citizenship rights?"[32] Coolie labor advocates whitened the figure of the coolie in order to render him a voluntary immigrant who was continued to be perceived as being dangerous to dissolving the line between colored and White. In 1867, sugar and cotton planters brought over one hundred Chinese laborers, some from Cuba, to Louisiana to work the plantations with emancipated African Americans.[33] This resurgence of interest resulted in the migration of several hundred additional Chinese laborers to Louisiana, Mississippi, Arkansas, Alabama, and South Carolina toward the end of the nineteenth century in widely dispersed areas.[34] Chinese did not necessarily seek to migrate to the South—"a destination that they dreaded even worse than Cuba or Peru."[35] These were not seen as successful ventures and Asian labor migration to the South ceased soon after this initial migration of laborers. Historians have long pointed out that most immigrants in the latter half of the nineteenth and the first half of the twentieth century went to places other than the South because of the expanding economic opportunities of the Northeast and Midwest and because of the inhospitality and nativism of the South. However, Chinese coolies were sought-after plantation labor; because they were a cheaper source of labor compared to Black slaves, there remained a lot of anxiety about their participation in the labor market. "Only 'one power alone could conquer' the 'immorality of the Chinamen and Indians,' but 'these are the races of all others most difficult to convert to Christianity.'"[36] One plantation owner is said to have remarked, "I believe they are completely destitute of moral principle. They are all heathens and won't become Christians."[37] Consider the interplay of race and religion inherent in the owners' viewpoint. Slaves, while Black, were seen as preferable to coolies because slaves converted to Christianity more readily. By contrast, there was a fear of coolies that did not exist about slaves—a fear that related back to their unwillingness to adopt their employers' religious viewpoints. Non-Christians were less acceptable, and the only path to full acceptance (within the other, race-based social constraints of the time) was through conversion to Christianity. In summary, racism, xenophobia, and Protestant Christian supremacy continued to flourish despite a need for additional labor and the scarcity of immigrants in many Southern communities. While anti-immigration fervor targeted European and Asian migrants, religious and racial ideologies about the Oriental and Mongol races more strongly fortified anti-Asian immigration sentiment in the post–Civil War era.

The long-standing vitality of evangelical Protestantism as the cornerstone of Southern religious and civic culture can easily obscure an equally long-standing history of religious diversity. The region is, and has always been, a nexus of global flows of population and commerce, particularly with respect to trans-Atlantic trade. Different religions' adherents migrated to the South in precolonial and colonial times. Thus, in addition to the spiritual traditions of the region's indigenous Native Americans, it was home to the Protestant Christianity of northern European traders, the Catholicism of French migrants, the animist traditions of African and Caribbean migrants, and the Hinduism and Islam of South Asian sailors and traders. Scholars have often remarked upon the ways in which some of these practices have been integrated into various nondominant forms of Christianity.

Afro-Asian South

Moving away from Whiteness, we consider the relationship between Asian Americans and African Americans in the South. As discussed earlier, Asian Americans have often been measured against, aligned with, and outside of Whiteness in many ways. Usually characterized as a subfield, Afro-Asian Studies pursues the multiple dimensions and modalities of the "encounters" between African Americans and Asian Americans; however, seldom has the South been specifically demarcated as a space for these numerous and strong interactions. This collection provides numerous examples of how the South has facilitated and been the space of such encounters.

The interactions between African Americans and Asian Americans were shaped by the broader national discourses of Orientalism and anti-Black racism. The specter of the coolie within debates about emancipation and slavery created anxieties about race, labor, and citizenship among Whites and African Americans. In arguing against Asian migration, both Whites and Blacks often posed the heathen aliens (Chinese and Hindoos) as unable to assimilate into America. In decrying segregation in the South in *Plessy v. Ferguson* and voicing the minority opinion, Supreme Court Justice John Harlan sought to name the injustice of segregation by contrasting the privileges denied to the African American with the supposedly inappropriate and undeserved privileges garnered by the Chinaman who could ride with the White citizen in the streetcar.[38] Both Whites and Blacks employed an Orientalist difference to pose Blacks as more capable than Asians of inclusion into the nation and citizenship. Hence, some Black discourses of Orientalism defined and framed Blackness as more American in relation to Asian American religious and racial difference. Many different examples of *African American* deployments of Orientalism within Black discourses, popular periodicals, Christian and feminist discourses, and literary narratives have emerged as scholars seek to understand the mutual constitution and inextricable histories of Asianness and Blackness within Afro-Asian interactions; it is notable that many of these examples emerge from within the space of the South.

Many African Americans realized that policies and processes that oppress based on race, ethnicity, and religion could reflect or impact negatively their own attempts to claim rights; claims to assimilation and Christianity could most certainly backfire. Going beyond anti-Black racism and Orientalism, Afro-Asian studies suggests a more dynamic and heterogeneous discourse with multiple forms, politics, and modalities of Asian and African encounters in the South.[39] Certain aspects of Afro-Asian studies emphasize the points of connection and solidarity as a counterdiscourse to these endeavors. Bill Mullen suggests that Afro-Orientalism is a "signifying discourse on race, nation, and global politics constituting a subtradition in indigenous U.S. writing on imperialism, colonialism, and the making of capitalist empire."[40] As a basis for cross-racial solidarities,

Afro-Asian can be "employed as an important site where a crude opposition between Blacks and Asians can be contested, where the parallel courses of Western imperialism through Asia and Africa can be explored, where the experiences of African Americans and Asian Americans as slaves and indentured servants in the Americas, respectively, can be compared, and where cross-racial, cross-ethnic, and trans-Pacific political solidarity that is not based on racial identification can be sought out."[41]

Examples of Afro-Asian encounters can be found within past and contemporary Southern Black texts. In the novel *Dark Princess* (1928), W. E. B. DuBois links struggles against segregation with those against imperialism through the figure of an African American activist protagonist and an anti-imperialist Indian princess. As Desai discusses, the novel articulates DuBois's complex internationalist, anti-imperialist, antiracist, Marxist politics focusing not only on the infamous color line between "darker peoples" and Whites in the United States and transnationally, but also on the racial hierarchies among people of color that impede political anti-imperialist solidarity.[42] DuBois furthers his query of the role of the African American proletariat in the internationalist movement against capitalism in a vision that is not Afrocentric but is simultaneously national and international. To achieve this, *Dark Princess* explicitly ends in the South in an attempt to connect to the Africa and Asia it faces, searching continually for connection and inspiration between African diasporic and Asian liberation struggles. Desai posits Mira Nair's film *Mississippi Masala* as a contemporary example of how recent migrations have led to similar narratives of Afro-Asian encounters.

Essays in this collection implicitly and explicitly further discussions through studies of past and contemporary Afro-Asian interactions. Historically, Bald addresses the relationships between Indian migrant peddlers and African American women in early-twentieth-century New Orleans, and Bow contemplates Asian American racial interstitiality within the Black/White binary in the mid–twentieth century. Within contemporary communities, Brandzel and Desai examine how Asianness is deployed as a mark of cosmopolitan inclusion in relation to African Americans at Virginia Tech; Vu locates the White supremacy and racism faced by Vietnamese Americans in relation to the racism experienced by African Americans in Houston; and Nguyen probes the Afro-Asian encounters between Vietnamese Americans and African Americans in post-Katrina New Orleans. We hope that this collection will encourage and engender other illustrations of Afro-Asian imaginings and solidarities between Asian Americans and African Americans in the South.

Immigration, Labor, and the State in the Twentieth Century

In the nineteenth and twentieth centuries, the United States relied heavily on its history of dominance and colonialism of Mexico, in addition to its history of slavery and Asian migration, to satisfy its labor demands within agricultural, railroad, and other industries. Hence, Asian and Latino racial formations are also bound together due to a shared legal, economic, and social status within histories of dominance and colonialism that constitute both Asia's and Mexico's relationship with the United States for the last two hundred years. During the nineteenth century, many Mexican laborers worked in places that had been recently colonized and had historically been part of Mexico as the United States seized land in California, the Southwest, and Texas. While usually considered in isolation from each other, it is abundantly apparent that Asian and Latino histories of migration, labor, racial ideologies, and state management are conjoined; specifically, it is often the case that they are racialized constitutively, meaning that racial ideologies often compare and contrast the groups, pitting them against each other and assigning values of desirability and belonging.

Latino and Asian labor and migration histories inform and shape each other through state management of labor, mobility, citizenship, and capital. As Asian migration and settlement became less attractive, the passing of the Chinese Exclusion Act in 1882 led to a dearth of migrant labor for building the railroads and the subsequent recruitment of Mexican workers by the railroad companies. Mexican migrants, unlike their Asian counterparts, were characterized by greater mobility between the United States and their country of origin. This mobility and flexibility was in part supported by the nation-state and capital, neither of whom sought Mexicans as citizens or permanent laborers. Asian and Latino immigration became increasingly linked, though differently managed, as the demand for cheap racialized labor expanded in the twentieth century. Hence, when the patrolling of the United States–Mexico border was established in 1904, it was not so much for the surveillance of Mexican migration, but the prevention of Chinese and other Asian laborers entering through Mexico. The border patrol is one example of a modern state technology for managing the migration of racialized populations across borders that was developed to target Asians and then extended to other racialized groups. In light of nativist and eugenic sentiments, new quota systems put into place by the Immigration Acts of 1921 and 1924 continued to limit immigration based on nations of origin for Asian and European immigrants, but did not apply to Mexican migrants. Nevertheless, Mexican migrants were also subject to increased management and regulation through taxes, labor contracts, and literacy requirements. Policies and technologies of regulation denied permanent residency and citizenship to the vast majority of Mexican migrants, facilitating the state to control the flow of migration whenever the demands for labor increased and deporting or expelling migrants en masse when demands decreased. Such was the case of the Mexican Repatriation between 1929–1939 when nearly half a million Mexican workers were forced to repatriate. In contrast, the Bracero Program (1942–1964) marked the formal intensification of the state's regulation and management of the racialized (Mexican) migrant labor system as demands by agriculture and railroad industries increased due to war, Japanese internment, and other factors. The program expedited the mobility of Mexican migrant labor and return migration while preventing citizenship within the context of the rising nativism and White supremacy of this period. Nevertheless, facilitating exploitation and opportunity, this controversial guest worker program drew forth and focused the xenophobia and racism against transnational Mexican migrants while simultaneously providing labor to farms throughout California, Texas, and the Southwest as well as the South.

While Asian migrants had already been racialized as foreign and non-American, this period conjoins Latinos and Asians as foreign and unassimilable aliens within social and legal discourses, resulting in the formation and emergence of a new sociopolitical and legal subject—the illegal alien. "The racial formations of Asians and Mexicans in the 1920s were particularly significant because they modified a racial map of the nation that had been marked principally by the contours of White and Black and that had denoted race a sectional problem."[43] As scholars point out, this period demonstrated not only the establishment of new immigration policies and technologies by the state, but also a tremendous contestation about the meaning and metrics of race itself. While nativism, eugenics, and White supremacy thrived, the paradigm for defining and understanding race was repeatedly brought into question. Shifts in racial ideologies in which race was increasingly linked to body (physiognomy) and place (nation) produced new discourses and technologies for defining and identifying citizenship eligibility and racial classification for Asians, Mexicans, and other ethnic groups as we discuss below.

Reconsidering Race, Considering Whiteness

How were Asian Americans located in relation to Blacks and Whites during segregation? How did the racial codes account for a "third race" that was strongly associated with xenophobia and nativism? As Leslie Bow so poignantly points out, how can a binary system account for partial or different racializations? In this section, we discuss some critical moments in Asian, Black, and White racial and ethnic formations within the South; primarily, we turn to how race and ethnicity were decided and assigned legally for a variety of groups to better determine how Asian Americans were relationally read into race. Within the binary racial paradigm already described, the concepts and definitions of Whiteness and Blackness have changed over time (although it could be argued that certain fundamental tenets of the racial paradigm for Blackness, such as the idea that "one drop" of African blood made one Black, have not). We are not interested in simply inserting Asians into the Black/White binary, but questioning the binary and the ways that Asian Americans and others (such as Syrians and Jews) are racialized similarly and differently in relation to Whiteness and Blackness.

Clearly, racial formations of Asian Americans in the South have changed as the broader racial ideologies have been transformed. Scholars (e.g., James Loewen, Susan Koshy, and Leslie Bow) interested in the racialization of Asian Americans in the South have turned, in part, to the Chinese Americans settled in Mississippi prior to 1965 to explore the processes of Asian racialization; several reach the conclusion that these Chinese Americans became White. Racial ideologies within the twentieth century underwent great transformations and legal disputes were a critical site where race was not just interpreted but produced and managed. These twentieth-century court cases demonstrate the mutability of racial ideologies as they articulated Whiteness in terms of biology and blood (grounded in science and pseudoscience) and then in popular perceptions of race (as defined by the "common man" and dominant culture). Shifting between cultural and biological definitions, racialist thinking deployed many differing ideas of race to further racial projects. It is illuminating to look more broadly at the legal debates about the meaning of Whiteness that provide the broader context for this one community. The phenomenon that allowed Asian Americans to go from Black to White within this Mississippi community requires that we examine how racialist thinking produced these categories legally during this time; one method for doing so is to attend how race and ethnicity were constructed in relation to Whiteness for other migrants.

It is important to note that the contours and characterizations of the racial category Asian, like Whiteness, have also changed over time. The answer to the question "Who is Asian?" is different today than during antebellum times. Indeed, the concept of "Asian"—a category of regional origin only used by the U.S. Census Bureau in the late twentieth century—may not have even existed in the nineteenth century, which was dominated by the racial formation of Oriental. Historically, Asian racialization has often fluctuated. Today Asian American is posed as a panethnic racial and political category that encompasses various ethnic groups who have been similarly racialized as Oriental. However, this is not to say that Chinese, Koreans, Indians, Pakistanis, and others, who can all be now categorized as Asian, are identically racialized. For example, even within the context of this collection, it is clear that East Asians such as the Chinese in Georgia and Mississippi (Bow and Bronstein) can be and have been racialized differently from the South Asians in New Orleans (Bald). These studies of earlier communities demonstrate the complexity of the racialization processes for many ethnic groups.

To understand the complexity of the racialization process during the twentieth century for Asian Americans including East Asians and South Asians, the situations of two other racially ambiguous groups—Syrians and Jews—are illustrative. Like South Asians, Syrians and Jews were seen as racially ambiguous: not Black, White or "mongoloid" (Oriental or East Asian), based on a visual inspection. At the same time, these groups carried the perception that their cultures were inassimilable and "fundamentally at odds with the Southern Way of life."[44] Three court cases, each involving a dispute over the granting of citizenship to an individual (a legal process known as "naturalization"), each of which took place in the early twentieth century, demonstrate how skin color, geography, religion, and congressional intent were all factors in the racialization of Syrians in the South. In all three cases, Syrians petitioned the courts for citizenship. In order to become a U.S. citizen at the time, the applicant was required to be "White," a term which was used but not defined in the Naturalization Act of 1790. In Georgia in 1909, Costa Najour was granted citizenship when a court concluded that Syrians were members of the "White race."[45] In making his case for naturalization, Najour relied on "scientific evidence" and asserted that there is a distinction between skin color and race. The court agreed, conveying the message that skin color did not matter if individuals "possessed personal qualifications deemed necessary for naturalization."[46] Importantly, Najour was a light-skinned man. A few years later in South Carolina, when Faras Shahid petitioned the federal court in that state for citizenship, color apparently did matter; Shahid was denied citizenship because of the darkness of his skin.[47] In this case, the court ruled Syrians were not White, they had never been White, and that this was a matter of common knowledge.[48] Thus, one could be both Asian and "White" under certain circumstances, and ascription of lightness increased the eligibility for citizenship while darkness decreased the likelihood.

George Dow was also a Syrian immigrant residing in South Carolina in the early twentieth century. His quest for citizenship highlights the combination of factors that led to the denial of his request. In 1914, Dow was refused citizenship because the judge disagreed with his argument that "scientific evidence" showed Syrians to be "Caucasians."[49] The judge denied Dow's petition for naturalization, ruling "the applicant is not that particular free White person to whom the act of Congress has donated the privilege of citizenship in this country with its accompanying duties and responsibilities." The outcome was unacceptable to many in the Syrian community, who raised funds to support Dow's appeal of the lower court's decision to the federal circuit court. And then on appeal, we see another set of factors impacting the racialization process. In *Dow v. United States*, 226 F. 145 (4th Cir. 1915), citing scientific evidence and congressional intent, the presiding judge held: "At the date of the new acts and amendments . . . it seems to be true beyond question that the generally received opinion was that the inhabitants of a portion of Asia, including Syria, were to be classed as White persons," thereby overturning the lower court's decision to deny George Dow's application for U.S. citizenship. Dow gained citizenship as the Fourth Circuit court concluded Syrians were White because, at the time the law was passed, the Congress's understanding of geography was such that individuals from a certain but unspecified "portion of Asia" were, in fact, "White persons." Thus, whereas the lower court concluded that Dow was not the sort of person Congress meant to be "White," the circuit court reached the opposite conclusion. Clearly, this contradiction, within the scope of a single legal case, demonstrates that Syrians had little control over which racialization processes were in effect and impacted their shifting racial formations. Moreover, while citizenship afforded certain privileges, it did not protect against discrimination. In Georgia, Syrians like other groups such as Jews and African Americans were for many years even after George Dow won his case, the targets of the Ku Klux Klan, thus indicating how Syrians' racial experiences occurred in multiple and often contradictory domains.

Juxtaposing the situation of the Syrians with those of Jews in the South shows how the combination of religion and geography further impacts the racialization process. Jews in the United States had always been entitled to citizenship. Syrians argued that they too were Semites, like the Jews, and therefore they should be considered citizens also. In the South, the idea of racial contamination had roots in religious difference. The judge, while granting citizenship to Najour, also stated in his opinion that "Najour, as a subject of the Muslim Ottoman Sultan, was incapable of understanding American institutions and government."[50] While the Jews were othered based on religion, there was another dimension to the racialization process—that of geography. Most of the Jews arriving to U.S. shores came from Europe; Syrians, even if Christians like Najour, did not. Such implicit and explicit unfavorable comparisons to Protestant Christianity were part of the racial othering process in which Orientalized Muslims were seen as incompatible with democracy, modernity, and citizenship within a White Christian nation.

For Jews in the South, anti-Semitism was predominantly based in religion and class; they were not seen as racially different, or subjected to legal segregation and social exclusion like Blacks. (One major exception was the lynching of Leo Frank, a young Jewish man, after he was convicted of murdering Mary Pheagin in 1913 in Atlanta.) Still, Jews did confront residential restriction, social isolation, and university quotas.[51] Jews could be used as a scapegoat when convenient. For many Southerners, especially staunch segregationists, the Jewish presence was a "problem," as they perceived Jews to be "White niggers" or of inferior blood who were diluting the White race by encouraging race mixing.[52] Echoes of these ideations can also be seen in the experience of Asian Americans in the South. Asian Americans, like Jews, were not Black and therefore entitled to some of the privileges of Whiteness, but were nevertheless not quite White.

Juxtaposing the varied Syrian and Jewish experiences of racialization described above with the experiences of East Asians in the South further illustrates the multidimensionality of the racialization of Asian Americans, and how that racialization collided with the underlying Black/White paradigm. In the much discussed 1927 case of *Gong Lum v. Rice*,[53] the U.S. Supreme Court upheld a lower court's ruling that, as between the categories of White and "colored," Chinese Americans were "colored." When Gong Lum charged that his daughter was denied access and admission to schooling because of her race, he claimed that she was "Chinese" and not colored or mixed blood. As there were no separate schools for "Mongolians," he further argued that his daughter should be able to attend the White schools in preference to the "colored" schools. The Supreme Court denied this claim to Whiteness and affirmed segregation for Chinese Americans as colored. In the educational context of the time, that designation resulted in a denial of privileges enjoyed by Whites, and a grouping of the Chinese with Blacks.

James Loewen's analysis of the Chinese Mississippi community proposes that the Chinese Americans generated a shift in racial formation and classification from ambiguously colored (1920s) to White (1960s) within the span of a few decades.[54] The significance and simplicity of this explanation has been the site of interrogation by recent scholars, who have sought to trouble and complicate this story of racial assimilation and normalization. Despite Loewen's claim that the Chinese "became White," one can see other markers for the continued racialization of Asian Americans as racial Others past the middle of the twentieth century. For example, the famous Southern case of *Loving v. Virginia*, though not explicitly about Asian Americans, shows that in 1959 anxieties about racial mixing, miscegenation, and intermarriage still reference Asian Americans within discourses of Whiteness. The Lovings—Mildred, who was of Black and Native American ancestry and Richard, who was White—were charged with violating Virginia's ban against interracial marriage. The trial judge who sentenced the Lovings to a year's imprisonment for their crime of marrying, argued for the continued separation of races with these words: "Almighty God created the races White, black, yellow, malay and red, and he placed them on separate continents. And but for the interference with his arrangement there would be no cause for such marriages. The fact that he separated the races shows that he did not intend for the races to mix."[55] Despite Loewen's assertion that the Chinese in Mississippi are White, it is also apparent that in 1959, anxiety about racial mixing, miscegenation, and intermarriage continued to dominate discourses of Whiteness. In this formulation, Asianness exceeds and buttresses the Black/White binary in defining racial and ethnic formations in the South, and the concept of the "yellow" and "malay" people as non-Whites, would seem to contradict Loewen's conclusion.

The legal cases discussed above are significant mile markers in twentieth-century U.S. history, and particularly Southern history, because they demonstrate how racialization occurred through the legal system, and also impacted how Asian Americans experienced other economic, political, educational, religious, and cultural institutions. Clearly the dominant Black/White racial binary has affected the racialization of Asian Americans. Asian Americans have been seen as in-between, partially Black and White, mediating middlemen, third race, or as part of a racial triangulation. Though these various arguments take different positions on Asian American racialization, they all suggest that the racialization of Asian Americans is continuously (re)produced in relation to other racial formations such as Latino, Syrian, White, and Black. The essays within this volume examine historical as well as contemporary Asian American racial formations in the South from a variety of perspectives to implicitly and explicitly highlight the ambiguous, complex, and changing racialization of Asian Americans. Scholars in this volume deploy various approaches to suggest no simple or singular historical racial formation of Asian Americans in the South. We propose that these disparate accounts relay the diverse and shifting racializations of Asian Americans in the South historically.

This volume continues the Asian American Studies project of telling a variety of Asian American stories: an Asian American interracial marriage story, an Asian American civil rights story, an Asian American violence story, an Asian American segregation story, an Asian American labor exploitation story, and an Asian American religious story. By doing so, we hope to demonstrate the complex and numerous ways that Asian American racialization is both intersectional and relational (with other groups such as Syrians, African Americans, Whites, etc.), thereby reading Asian Americans into race.

Emerging Communities

The long-standing presence of Asian Americans in the South is often overshadowed by discussions focusing on the recent migrations to the South. Changes in the Southern economy over the last decades of the twentieth century have made the region an "immigrant belt" for Asians and Latinos in unprecedented ways.[56] Recent developments in the revitalization of the South's industrial, agricultural, and technological economies have been preceded by transformative transnational and global processes.[57] Asian and Latino migration to the South has been integral to these developments. Despite these transformations, there is no doubt that anti-immigration policies and practices are strongly entrenched in the South and Southwest—from the Minutemen vigilante border patrols to discriminatory laws and policies, there are many indications of nativism and resistance to Asian and Latino migration in the twentieth and twenty-first centuries. For example, though many Southern states later benefited from migration engendered by the pivotal 1965 Immigration Act, it was poorly supported by these same states. The Senate passed the act with a vote of 76 to 18, with all but two of the dissenting votes coming from Southern Senators.[58] (This vote echoes earlier deliberations about the Chinese Exclusion Act of 1882 that garnered Southern support.) In examining the Congressional deliberations of the 1965 Immigration Act, it is clear that many Southern constituencies were opposed to lifting the immigration restrictions set forth in the Immigration Act of 1924. However, the overemphasis solely on isolationism and nativism poorly illuminates a more complex history of attitudes and perspectives on immigration within the South. Although nativist and anti-immigration activism and ideology have a long history in the South, political and social attitudes toward migration have fluctuated during the last few centuries and should be considered in light of larger Southern interests in such systems as slavery, empire, and race as discussed earlier.

Anti-immigration racism, White supremacy, and nativism continue to thrive in the South; recent policies targeting migrants have proliferated nationally, and specifically, in the South. Modeled on the contemporary Arizona law SB 1070 that allows for the checking of immigration and citizenship status for racialized subjects by law enforcement officers, many other states—including Alabama, Arkansas, Florida, Georgia, Maryland, Mississippi, North Carolina, Oklahoma, South Carolina, Texas, and Virginia—have proposed or passed similar legislation that requires proof of citizenship. This is not to say that only states in the South have proposed such measures, but that a large number of them are located here. Although many of these laws are perceived as targeting Latinos, Asian Americans must be considered as a target of such policies as well.[59]

Since the 1980s, Southern states have been the location of rapidly increasing Asian and Latino immigrant populations. The 1986 Immigration Reform and Control Act again functioned as a method to prevent and criminalize undocumented labor migration. The Act unintentionally shifted previously established migration patterns geographically, deterring Californiacentric Mexican migration to more national dissemination, including the South. Furthermore, with its increase in state surveillance, heavily patrolled borders led to undocumented workers seeking longer and more permanent residencies rather than attempting frequent recrossings. Hence, the 1990s saw a great influx of Mexican (and Asian) migration to the South where agricultural, manufacturing and processing, and service labor were in high demand; within census counts alone, the Hispanic populations increased 200–400 percent within Southern states during this decade.[60]

More recently, the 2010 census[61] clearly shows that some of the fastest-growing areas in the United States are located in the South. The top six states of growth—Texas, California, Florida, Georgia, North Carolina, and Arizona—gained nearly a total of fifteen million people in the last decade and accounted for more than half of the overall increase during this time. These increases continue a trend from recent decades of migration to states in the South, Southwest, and West. While these numbers include all groups, not just Asians and Latinos, past analyses clearly indicate that much of this increase can be attributed to immigration from these two groups: by 1980 over 20 percent of the country's foreign-born residents were in the South, and by 2000 the South was home to over one-quarter of U.S. immigrants.[62] It is important to note that growth was concentrated in large metropolitan areas in the South. In a recent study, the fastest growing metropolitan areas in the nation—Houston, Atlanta, and Dallas–Fort Worth—had growth rates of approximately 25 percent which accounted for over 50 percent of the growth in Texas and Georgia.[63]

The significant increase in Asian migration to the United States spanning the latter half of the twentieth century (1950 and 2000), a thirtyfold increase, reflects the changes in immigration policies during this time. By 2000, the Asian American population in the South increased 106 times, the highest among all regions.[64] Since the 1960s, with the changes in immigration policy, the foreign-born population has quadrupled.[65] Secondary and tertiary migration to the South from other states like California has also increased due to the draw of lower costs of living and greater economic opportunities.[66] Between 2000–2010, the Asian American population in the South increased 43 percent, making Asian Americans the fastest-growing racial group in the nation with a total population of about fifteen million.[67] Sakamoto et al. note in this volume that more Asian Americans now reside in Texas than in Hawaii, and in Atlanta than in San Francisco.

It is important to note that demographic studies often undercount vulnerable groups, such as unauthorized residents and undocumented migrants. Crossing borders without authorization, staying beyond authorized periods, or violating methods of legal entry can classify an individual as "illegally" entering or residing in the United States. Ironically, despite a long history of crossing borders without authorization in response to restrictive immigration laws, Asian migrants remain largely invisible within political and social discourses on illegal immigration. Though Asians constitute a smaller percentage of undocumented migrants than Mexicans (approximately 60 percent) and other Latinos (approximately 15 percent), migrants from the Philippines, India, Korea, and China, nevertheless, comprise nearly 10 percent of the total unauthorized immigrant population of the United States.[68] Recent reports suggest that Asians, especially South Asians, continue to cross the U.S.-Mexico border in increasing numbers; with Indians accounting for nearly one third of non-Mexican unauthorized migrants detained in 2011.[69]

However, experiences of racism and class differences within Asian America continue to be erased so that Asian Americans are constituted as a model minority, pitting them not only against African Americans, but also against Latino Americans in contemporary American discourses. For example, a recent Pew Research Center study on "The Rise of Asian Americans" has the subtitle "Meet the New Immigrants: Asians Overtake Hispanics." Playing on many discourses that evoke an Asian tide, model minority, tiger mom, and perpetually foreign, the online report rejuvenates multiple stereotypes. It is important to note that the Pew study proffers economic statistics and explanations that can be misleading—the study explains that Asian Americans have the highest incomes and most education because they "place more value than other Americans do on marriage, parenthood, hard work, and career success."[70] Consequently, the media coverage of the report pits the figure of the Asian professional against that of the undocumented ("illegal") Mexican. The report has drawn the ire and critique of Asian American Studies scholars and community activists who have noted its heavily biased presentation of information, misleading framing, perpetuation of stereotypes, and fostering of interracial strife and competition. In their letter to the Pew Research Center, the Asian American and Pacific Islander Policy Research Consortium emphasize that data for income has to be calibrated more precisely to acquire an accurate picture of Asian American wealth; for example, an adjustment for household size (per capita) and location shows that Asian Americans earn only seventy-one cents for every dollar for non-Hispanic Whites.[71] Furthermore, such reports do not attend to the highly variable income distribution of Asian Americans wherein certain ethnic and refugee groups (including Hmong, Cambodian, Vietnamese, and Laotian Americans) are much more economically vulnerable with significant rates of poverty that are sometimes higher than those of African Americans. (See Roy Vu and Margeurite Nguyen in this volume for in-depth analyses of Vietnamese American communities in the South.) It is imperative to delve more deeply into Asian American communities to identify and understand the significance of location, class, and economic differences, rather than presume homogeneity; otherwise, it becomes possible to foster ideologies that obliterate the interrelationships between racial groups (Asians and Latinos) and the differences within Asian America.

These documented and undocumented migrants have appreciably remade the landscape of the South with highly visible and vital communities in many rural, suburban, and urban spaces. As a consequence of these migrations, in towns, suburbs, and cities scattered throughout the South are Korean shopping centers, Vietnamese apartment complexes, Hindu temples and Islamic mosques, and Hmong farms. In motels and universities, restaurants and low-income housing, fishing villages and manicured suburbs, Asian Americans span the professional and class spectrum.

Religious Hegemonies

Contemporary migration of Asian immigrants has increased the vitality of religious diversity in the numerous emerging communities located in the South. Samuel S. Hill notes that this religious diversity contributes to "the dismantling of normative religious patterns and conditions."[72] Contemporary Asian American religious communities in the South face the challenge not only of establishing their own ethnoreligious communities, but also of doing so in the entrenched and sometimes hostile presence of Black and White Evangelical Christianity. Asian migrants have arrived in a place not only where Whiteness and Protestantism are normative, but also where they have functioned as an established part of a political and cultural power structure that for centuries has subjugated Blacks and oppressed and marginalized others.[73] Since the Immigration Act of 1965, Asian American religious groups have developed strong communities within the South. The entire Southern landscape is peppered with Buddhist and Hindu temples, as well as gurdwaras, mosques, and Korean churches. These houses of worship and others can be found in small and large towns alike.[74] In some places, rapidly growing Asian Christian communities have achieved the "critical mass" necessary to break off from predominantly White host churches and establish their own separate houses of worship.[75] Often, Asian American religious communities have had to establish and maintain themselves in this hostile terrain by creating and fortifying clearly demarcated ethnoreligious spaces, by exposing and guarding against the normative influence of Christianity, and by slowly adapting social and political structures to accommodate religious diversity and difference through legal, cultural, and media activism. In doing so, these communities have begun to expose and erode, if not dismantle, some of the dominance of White Protestant Christianity in the South.

Increasing decade after decade since 1965, Asian immigration is now impacting the traditional biracial order. The shape of that impact, and the nature of the changes that will result for mainstream Southern culture, largely remain to be seen. Will demographic changes, along with the influence of other social identities such as religion, lead to a loosely organized "triracial" order posited by Bonilla-Silva "white, honorary white, and the collective black?"[76] Will Asian American Buddhist, Sikh, Hindu, and Muslim communities be accepted and be able to participate in the Southern cultural and political citizenship as much as Asian American Christians? In contemporary times, individuals who do not follow Christianity continue to be seen as potentially suspect, particularly in the political culture of the U.S. South.

In answering this question, it is important to consider the rise of Nikki Haley, Governor of South Carolina, and Piyush "Bobby" Jindal, Governor of Louisiana. The South's only two governors of color, Haley and Jindal are both Indian Americans who converted to Christianity before starting their political careers. Haley was raised in a Sikh family and converted to the Methodist faith at age 24. Jindal, raised in a Hindu family, converted to Catholicism in high school. As candidates, and now in office, both frequently assert and make reference to their identity as Christians. Haley and Jindal are the first non-Whites elected governor of their respective states. Was it by "accepting Christ into their lives" that they made themselves acceptable to the South as political leaders? Put more simply, and more broadly, is religion a litmus test for full acceptance into Southern society? Is it a "secret handshake" that Asian Americans can master and "become White"? Or do their ethnic and racial identities cause consternation and are their conversions (Jindal) or "acceptance of Christ" (Haley) questioned just as they were with Indians and Chinese coolies over a century ago? Despite their political victories, will their authenticity and acceptability in Southern culture remain perpetually subject to challenge because of their racial and religious backgrounds?

Asian American Studies and the South

We hope that these sections have made clear what can be gained by locating *Asian Americans* within the South. We would also like to consider what is gained by locating the South within Asian American studies. Scholars have long considered whether or not Asian American studies can be best addressed by a California-centric paradigm. In looking to the South, while California may function as an important point of reference for some (see Bronstein in this collection), it by no means provides the dominant paradigm. While there has been a move to consider the West Coast–centric orientation of Asian American studies by facilitating the rise of the "East of California" paradigm, the framing continues to provincialize and marginalize other sites and spaces within Asian American studies. As Stephen Sumida forcefully argues:

> Working with evidence of Asian/Pacific American history and culture of the South and Midwest reveals certain limitations of a Californic paradigm. . . . The expression "East of California" itself both reinscribes and plays with notions of centrality of the West Coast in Asian American studies. By contrast, not boundedness but the vastness of the places to the east—as well as to the north, south, and west—of California in Asian American studies resists centralization. The seemingly scattered evidence of whatever concerns Asian American studies East of California—and all the better because it seems scattered—speaks of not one but many centers, many points of origin and departure, for narratives that constitute the field.[77]

In fact, the essays in this collection suggest various material and discursive conditions of emergence as well as numerous ports of entry and routes of migration. Although we want to ensure these sites and presences are located and noted on the map of the South and Asian America, in shifting to the South, we hope to do more than pepper the map with new "sightings" of Asian Americans or create a singular narrative about the South. Importantly, we seek to think about the significance of Asian American migration to, racial formations within, and community formations in the South as well as the epistemological and intellectual questions raised about the region and space. What we highlight here methodologically is not the addition of a different region to Asian America by deploying a cookie-cutter paradigm based on a California model, but rather a consideration of how the South as a transnational space raises its own questions, concerns, histories, and arguments for Asian American studies.

This multidisciplinary collection of essays highlights the presence and involvement of Asian Americans in the American South. We explore the intersections of racial formation, immigration, religion, gender, and community formation both past and present. And in doing so, we hope to illuminate the presence of different Asian groups in Southern U.S. history and show how their presence and involvement in their communities are part of Southern life. From a variety of methodologies and approaches, the essays provide analyses of how Asian Americans are located in, adapting to, and transforming the South.[78] The essays in this collection are grouped into three sections: Disrupting Race and Place; Community Formation and Profiles; and Performing Race, Region, and Nation.

In the first section "Disrupting Race and Place," the essays offer divergent ways of understanding the racialization processes of Asian Americans in the South. In "Selling the East in the American South: Bengali Muslim Peddlers in New Orleans and Beyond, 1880–1920," Vivek Bald's insightful analysis presents the complex racializations and negotiations of South Asian sailors who jumped ship in Southern and Northeastern seaports and became entrepreneurs who traded ethnic notions within the larger cultural economy of Orientalism of the time. Leslie Bow's previously published essay, "Racial Interstitiality and the Anxieties of the 'Partly Colored': Representations of Asians under Jim Crow" has revitalized the study of Asian Americans in the South as it critically intervenes in the debates about Asian Americans' near-White status in popular and scholarly discourses; Bow provocatively forwards the idea of "racial interstitiality" as a method of reading the excess of racial formations within the context of the Black/White binary. Finally Amy Brandzel and Jigna Desai in "Racism without Recognition: Toward a Model of Asian American Racialization" turn to Seung-Hui Cho and the violence at Virginia Tech to critically interrogate Asian American masculinity and racial formations in relation to contemporary postracial discourses in the American South since 9/11.

The next section "Community Formation and Profiles" articulates how different Asian American groups remake the Southern landscape. Daniel Bronstein's detailed and rich essay "Segregation, Exclusion, and the Chinese Communities in Georgia, 1880s-1940" examines the impact of various state apparatuses, including exclusion laws, on the little remarked but fascinating Chinese American merchant communities in Atlanta, Augusta, and Savannah, Georgia. Based on the more-detailed 2000 census (rather than the 2010 census),[79] Art Sakamoto, ChangHwan Kim, and Isao Takei in "Moving out of the Margins and into the Mainstream: The Demographics of Asian Americans in the New South" meticulously present the changing demographics and provocatively suggest the beginning of a new stage of Asian American history that is characterized by improved socioeconomic opportunities and a move away from the Asian American strongholds of Hawaii and California. Roy Vu's engaging discussion in "Natives of a Ghost Country: The Vietnamese in Houston and Their Construction of a Postwar Community" identifies the significant factors impacting the emergence and establishment of the refugee Vietnamese American community in Houston, Texas. Khyati Joshi's essay "Standing Up and Speaking Out: Hindu Americans and Christian Normativity in Metro Atlanta" explicitly and importantly focuses on the significance of race, ethnicity, and religion by discussing the how and why a group of Hindus in Metro Atlanta came together to challenge Southern Christian normativity.

The final section focuses on "Performing Race, Region, and Nation." Jennifer Ho's capacious essay "Southern Eruptions in Asian American Narratives" attends to the eruptions of Asian American literature and film about the South as they disrupt multiple narratives about race relations and racial subjectivity. Jasmine Kar Tang in "A Tennessean in an Unlikely Package: The Stand-Up Comedy of Henry Cho" probes the comedy and figure of Southern and Asian American entertainer Henry Cho. Tang utilizes Bow's framework of racial interstitiality (see this volume) to better locate Cho's racial, classed, and gendered performances within the context of White Southern comedy and culture. Finally, Marguerite Nguyen in "Like We Lost Our Citizenship: Vietnamese Americans, African Americans, and Hurricane Katrina" examines newspapers and archival documents to understand how Afro-Asian relations in New Orleans East have shifted before and after Hurricane Katrina.

We hope this collection will soon be one of many that take immigration, transnationalism, and race as central to the study of the South. In the twenty-first century, the migrations of Asian Americans and Latino Americans to the South can no longer be ignored or marked as discrepancies. These improbable Southerners have already arrived and are radically remaking the landscape.

Notes

1. Recent articulations often refer to the region as the U.S. South (as opposed to the global South). Others distinguish between the Old South, Jim Crow South, Deep South, and the New South. We simplify our use to the "South" in order to encompass the broadest meaning of the term in the American imaginary.

2. In the South, both White Americans and African Americans often see Asian Americans as perpetually foreign. See Khyati Y. Joshi, *New Roots in America's Sacred Ground: Religion, Race, and Ethnicity in Indian America* (New Brunswick: Rutgers University Press, 2006), 95–96. For a more general discussion of how the "citizen" is opposed to the foreignness of the Asian American, see Lisa Lowe, "Heterogeneity, Hybridity, Multiplicity," *Immigrant Acts: On Asian American Cultural Politics* (Durham, N.C.: Duke University Press, 1996); and Mia Tuan, *Forever Foreigners or Honorary Whites? The Asian Ethnic Experience Today* (New Brunswick: Rutgers University Press, 2001).

3. For a brief discussion, see Carol Schmid, "Immigration and Asian and Hispanic Minorities in the New South: An Exploration of History, Attitudes, and Demographic Trends," *Sociological Spectrum* 23 (2003).

4. One could similarly argue that the Latinoization of the Southern states is also unnoted for the most part. Recent collections that specifically address this topic include Heather A. Smith and Owen J. Furuseth, eds., *Latinos in the New South: Transformations of Place* (Burlington, Vt.: Ashgate Publishing, 2006); and Mary E. Odem and Elaine Lacy, eds., *Latino Immigrants and the Transformation of the U.S. South* (Athens: University of Georgia Press, 2009).

5. Philip Deloria's *Indians in Unexpected Places* (Lawrence: University Press of Kansas, 2004) also provides a similar but distinct frame for understanding the perception that people of color are anomalies. Deloria examines how the juxtaposition of Native Americans with mise-en-scènes of modernity creates a disjuncture in the White imaginary. As American Indians are consistently relegated to a premodern era, representations that place them within modern spaces and technologies challenge assumptions about their spatial and temporal locality as reservation-based primitives. Thus, their unexpected locations cause anxiety within White America as they bring to the foreground the location of Native Americans within modernity. Our frame of discrepancy shares that sense of challenging assumptions that underlies Deloria's argument. Unexpectedness emphasizes assumptions—what people imagine and assume. Discrepancy suggests discord and disagreement in a situation in which similarity or sameness is expected. We want to emphasize several different meanings enabled by the use of discrepancy: the perception that Asian Americans are a variation that deviates from the norm because they are out of place (closest to Deloria's definition); the disagreements that underscore debates about Asian migration to the South; the divergence between common perception and historical evidence and presence; the perspective that Asian Americans are antithetical to the South; and the way that Asian Americans deviate from the binary of Black and White.

6. Filipinos were present in the South as early as 1765. Marina Espina, *Filipinos in Louisiana* (New Orleans: A. F. Laborde and Sons, 1988).

7. See R. Visram, *Ayahs, Lascars and Princes: Indians in Britain 1700–1947* (London: Pluto, 1986); Robert Seto Quan, *Lotus among the Magnolias: The Mississippi Chinese* (Jackson: University Press of Mississippi, 1982); Karen J. Leong et al., "Resilient History and the Rebuilding of a Community: The Vietnamese American Community in New Orleans East," *Journal of American History* 94.3 (2007); and Pawan Dhingra, "The Possibility of Community: How Indian American Motel Owners Negotiate Competition and Solidarity," *Journal of Asian American Studies* 12.3 (2009).

8. Of course there are notable exceptions. Lisa Lowe, "The Intimacies of Four Continents," *Haunted by Empire: Geographies of Intimacy in North American History*, ed. Ann Laura Stoler (Durham, N.C.: Duke University Press, 2006); and Moon-Ho Jung, *Coolies and Cane: Race, Labor and Sugar in the Age of Emancipation* (Baltimore: Johns Hopkins University Press, 2006) both interrogate how Asian migration via Chinese or Indian coolie migration was inextricably linked to discussions of slavery, modernity, and notions of America. Leslie Bow (in this volume) forcefully argues that Asian Americans were complexly racialized as Black and White in the Jim Crow South.

9. By *presence*, we mean several things including existence, influence, specter, and significance.

10. People often ask if the South is more racist than the rest of the United States. The claim of Southern exceptionalism, in our minds, mirrors the claim of U.S. exceptionalism. Here we seek to understand what is at stake in such claims to exceptionalism and distinction rather than foster or dispute such claims.

11. Rebecca Mark and Rebecca Vaughn, *The South: The Greenwood Encyclopedia of American Regional Cultures* (Westport, Conn.: Greenwood Press, 2004).

12. See Sakamato, Kim, and Takei, chapter 5 in this volume.

13. Originally just called "the South," then "the American South," and most recently the "New South" and the "U.S. South." These shifts indicate an increasing engagement

with placing "the South" in dialogue with broader discourses on globalization, political economy, and the "global South." See Jon Smith and Deborah N. Cohn, *Look Away!: The U.S. South in New World Studies, New Americanists* (Durham, N.C.: Duke University Press, 2004). These changing nominations also attempt to mark social and historical ruptures by creating temporal distinctions between the "Old South" and the "New South." In this way, there is an attempt to temporally distance the South from its own historical past by asserting its transformation and "newness."

14. Frank Newport, "Mississippians Go to Church the Most; Vermonters, Least," *State of the States* (2011). http://www.gallup.com/poll/125999/mississippians-go-church-most -vermonters-least.aspx. Accessed April 10, 2011.

15. Similarly, of all the regions, the South has the smallest concentration of Catholics (16 percent) and unaffiliated people (13 percent). See "The Pew Forum on Religion and Public Life," *US Religious Landscape Survey* (Washington, D.C.: Pew Research Center, 2008), 70.

16. Charles Reagan Wilson, "The Religion of the Lost Cause: Ritual and Organization of Southern Civil Religion, 1865–1920," *Religion and American Culture: A Reader*, ed. David G. Hackett (Oxford, U.K.: Taylor and Francis Group, 2003), 207.

17. However, Robert Bellah asserts American civil religion was not seen as specifically sectarian or explicitly Christian (Robert Bellah, "Civil Religion in America," *Daedalus* 96:1 (1967): 1–21).

18. See Joshi, chapter 7 in this volume.

19. Barry Kosmin and Ariela Keysar, *American Religious Identification Survey (Aris) 2008* (Hartford, Conn.: Trinity College, 2009).

20. For example, in contrast, one can see that the Midwest is perceived to be middle America, and thereby homogenously White, but not racist.

21. Additionally, such histories suggest much more a hemispheric, oceanic approach than one in which a region is isolated or taken merely in relation to other regions within the nation. Hence we attempt to link the local, the national, and the transnational through reading the Asian American South.

22. See Paul Gilroy, *The Black Atlantic: Modernity and Double Consciousness* (Cambridge, Mass.: Harvard University Press, 1993); Lisa Lowe, "The Intimacies of Four Continents"; and James L. Peacock, *Grounded Globalism: How the U.S. South Embraces the World* (Athens: University of Georgia Press, 2007).

23. For discussions of how Manilamen helped to forge multiple transoceanic connections around the world, see for example, Evelyn Hu-DeHart, "Latin America in Asia-Pacific Perspective," *What's in a Rim? Critical Perspectives on the Pacific Region Idea*, ed. Arif Dirlik (Lanham, Md.: Rowman and Littlefield Publishers, 1998), 251–282; "Asian American Studies as Global Studies," paper presented at Re/Siting Asian American Studies: Connecting Critical Approaches in the Field, Rutgers University, February 19, 2010; Kale Bantigue Fajardo, *Filipino Crosscurrents: Oceanographies of Seafaring, Masculinities, and Globalization* (Minneapolis: University of Minnesota Press, 2011); Espina, *Filipinos in Louisiana*; and E. San Juan, "Configuring the Filipino Diaspora in the United States," *Diaspora: A Journal of Transnational Studies* 3:2 (1994): 117–133.

24. See, for example, Lisa Yun, *The Coolie Speaks: Chinese Indentured Laborer and African Slaves in Cuba* (Philadelphia: Temple University Press, 2009).

25. See Susan Koshy, Introduction, *Transnational South Asians: The Making of Neo-Diaspora* (Oxford: Oxford University Press, 2008).

26. See Visram's *Ayahs, Lascars and Princes.*

27. See, for example, Walton Look Lai, *Indentured Labor, Caribbean Sugar: Chinese and Indian Migrants to the British West Indies 1839–1919* (Baltimore: Johns Hopkins Press, 2004); and Walton Look Lai and Tan Chee-Beng, *The Chinese in Latin America and the Caribbean* (The Netherlands: Koninklijke Brill, 2004).

28. See Armando Choy, Gustavo Chui, and Moises Sio Wong's *Our History Is Still Being Written: The Story of Three Chinese-Cuban Generals in the Cuban Revolution* (Atlanta: Pathfinder Press, 2005); and Aisha Khan, *Callaloo Nation: Metaphors of Race and Religious Identity among South Asians in Trinidad* (Durham, N.C.: Duke University Press, 2004).

29. Jung, *Coolies and Cane*; and Matthew P. Guterl, "After Slavery: Asian Labor, the American South, and the Age of Emancipation," *Journal of World History* 14.2 (2003).

30. Jung, *Coolies and Cane.*

31. See Rowland T. Berthoff's "Attitudes toward Immigration, 1865–1914," *Journal of Southern History* 17.3 (August 1951): 331.

32. Jung, *Coolies and Cane*, 7.

33. See Lucy Cohen's *The Chinese in the Post–Civil War South: A People without History* (Baton Rouge: Louisiana State University Press, 1984).

34. Obviously the South itself is not homogenous. Migration to various urban and rural venues created often vastly different experiences. For example, New Orleans as a trading port and entry point of migration is a confluence of varying and complex racial projects and racial formations due to French, Caribbean, Latin American, and Asian migration. This expansive racial code and structure accommodated multiple racial groups in comparison to those located in other spaces within the antebellum and postbellum South. See Guterl, "After Slavery," 229.

35. Jung, *Coolies and Cane*, 120.

36. Ibid., 66.

37. Ibid., 68.

38. Ibid., 219.

39. Vijay Prashad, *Everybody Was Kung Fu Fighting: Afro-Asian Connections and the Myth of Cultural Purity* (Boston: Beacon Press, 2001); and Bill Mullen, *Afro Orientalism* (Minneapolis: University of Minnesota Press, 2004).

40. Mullen, *Afro Orientalism*, xv.

41. Nami Kim, "Engaging Afro/black-Orientalism: A Proposal," *Journal of Race, Ethnicity, and Religion* 1:7 (2010): 6. http://www.catholiccincinnati.org/wp-content/uploads/2011/01/Engaging-Afro-black-Orientalism.pdf. Accessed January 13, 2013.

42. Jigna Desai, *Beyond Bollywood: The Cultural Politics of South Asian Diasporic Film* (New York: Routledge, 2004).

43. Mae Ngai, *Impossible Subjects: Illegal Aliens and the Making of Modern America* (Princeton, N.J.: Princeton University Press, 2005), 8.

44. Sarah Gualtieri, "Becoming 'White': Race, Religion and the Foundations of Syrian/Lebanese Ethnicity," *Journal of American Ethnic History* 20.4 (2001): 32. See also Leonard Rogoff, "Is the Jew White? The Racial Place of the Southern Jew," *American Jewish History* 85.3 (1997).

45. *In re Najour*, 174 F. 735 (N.D. Ga. 1909).

46. Gualtieri, "Becoming 'White,'" 34.

47. Ibid.

48. *Ex parte Shahid*, 205 F. 812 (E.D.S.C. 1913).

49. *Ex Parte Dow*, 211 F. 486 (E.D.S.C. 1914).

50. Gualtieri, "Becoming 'White,'" 37.

51. Rogoff, "Is the Jew White?" 228.

52. Ibid., 227.

53. See *Gong Lum v. Rice*. Accessed July 1, 2009.

54. James W. Loewen, *The Mississippi Chinese; Between Black and White*, Harvard East Asian Series, 63 (Cambridge, Mass.: Harvard University Press, 1971).

55. http://law2.umkc.edu/faculty/projects/ftrials/conlaw/loving.html. Accessed January 5, 2013. Additionally, Georgia, Mississippi, and Virginia are Southern states that had long-standing miscegenation laws for Asian Americans (and "Malays") and Whites.

56. George E. Pozzetta, ed., *The Immigrant Religious Experience* (New York: Garland, 1991); and David Reimers, "Asian Immigrants in the South," *Globalization and the American South*, eds. James Cobb and William Stueck (Athens: University of Georgia Press, 2005).

57. See Kathryn McKee and Annette Trefzer, "Global Contexts, Local Literatures: The New Southern Studies," *American Literature* 78.4 (2006); Reimers, "Asian Immigrants in the South"; and Alfred Hornung, "Unstoppable Creolization: The Evolution of the South into a Transnational Cultural Space," *American Literature* 78.4 (2006).

58. James Frank Hollifield, *Immigrants, Markets, and States: The Political Economy of Postwar Europe* (Cambridge, Mass.: Harvard University Press, 1992).

59. The relationship between Latino and Asian American communities in the South is a prime topic for research. While we find this a significant topic that would engender fruitful conversations about race, immigration, and class in the new South, it is beyond the scope of this collection. Here, we modestly consider the significance of Asian American presence to the South. Importantly, many of the essays in the collection implicitly and explicitly locate Asian American racial formations in relation to the Black and White racial binary.

60. Raymond A. Mohl, "Globalization, Latinization, and the *Nuevo* New South," *Other Souths: Diversity and Difference in the U.S. South, Reconstruction to Present*, ed. Pippa Holloway (Athens: University of Georgia Press, 2008), 413–414.

61. At the time of writing, more specific ethnic and racial information about Asian American populations in the South from the 2010 census had not been released.

62. Carl L. Bankston III, "Immigrants in the New South: An Introduction," *Sociological Spectrum* 23.2 (2003).

63. U.S. Bureau of the Census, *Estimates of the Resident Population by Race and Hispanic Origin for the United States and State, 2008* (Washington, D.C., 2009).

64. U.S. Bureau of the Census, *Historical Census Statistics on Population Totals by Race, 1790 to 1990, and by Hispanic Origin, 1970 to 1990, for the United States, Regions, Divisions, and States* (Washington, D.C., 2002).

65. See http://www.census.gov/population/www/documentation/twps0029/tab14.html. Accessed January 5, 2013.

66. See Sakamoto et al., chapter 5 in this volume.

67. This discussion focuses on those reporting as single-race Asians on the census for 2010. We have not aggregated the increases due to multiracial-identified Asian Americans here.

68. Michael Hoefer, Nancy Rytina, and Bryan C. Baker, "Estimates of the Unauthorized Immigrant Population Residing in the United States: January 2009." Department of

Homeland Security's Office of Immigration Statistics. January 2010. http://www.dhs.gov/
xlibrary/assets/statistics/publications/ois_ill_pe_2009.pdf. Accessed September 5, 2012.

69. Ravi Kumar, "New Guys on the Border: Nepalis Join the Trek to America," Global-
Post. http://www.globalpost.com/dispatch/news/regions/americas/120730/South-Asians
-Nepali-immigrants-Latin-America-US-border?page=full. July 31, 2012. Accessed Sep-
tember 5, 2012.

70. Pew Research Center, "The Rise of Asian Americans," June 19, 2012. http://www
.pewsocialtrends.org/2012/06/19/the-rise-of-asian-americans. Accessed September 4, 2012.

71. Asian American and Pacific Islander Policy Research Consortium, "Letter to Pew Research Center," June 22, 2012. http://www.aapiprc.com/home-1/pressreleases/pewopenletter.
Accessed September 4, 2012.

72. Samuel S. Hill, "Introduction," *Religion in the Contemporary South: Changes, Continuities, and Contexts*, eds. Corrie E. Norman and Donald S. Armentrout (Knoxville:
University of Tennessee Press, 2005), viii.

73. Indeed, some argue that the Civil Rights movement was a turning point for the
South's Catholic and Jewish communities as well because it allowed them to take a place
in the Southern power structure by virtue of their shared opposition to Black equality.
The Ku Klux Klan has targeted Catholics, Jews, Blacks, and immigrants historically.

74. See Pluralism Project, www.pluralism.org. Accessed January 5, 2013.

75. Raymond Brady Williams, *Christian Pluralism in the United States: The Indian Immigrant Experience, Cambridge Studies in Religious Traditions* (Cambridge: Cambridge
University Press, 1996), 9.

76. Eduardo Bonilla-Silva, "From Bi-Racial to Tri-Racial: Towards a New System of
Racial Stratification in the USA," *Ethnic and Racial Studies* 27.6 (2004).

77. S. H. Sumida, "East of California: Points of Origin in Asian American Studies,"
Journal of Asian American Studies 1.1 (1998): 95–96.

78. Although this project is broadly conceived and inclusive, the collection is not and
cannot be comprehensive. There are, of course, topics, ethnic communities, histories, and
perspectives that remain outside of the scope and purview of this volume.

79. It is important to note that the "long-form" version of the census questionnaire,
which requests socioeconomic information such as income and education, was not col-
lected by the 2010 Census for the first time in many decades. There have been a few recent
surveys since 2006 that have included these variables, but they are too small to appreciably
change any of the reported results, especially for Asian Americans (Sakamoto in personal
correspondence).

PART I

Disrupting Race and Place

CHAPTER 1

Selling the East in the American South
Bengali Muslim Peddlers in New Orleans and Beyond, 1880–1920
Vivek Bald

Over the past two decades, while South Asian American Studies has begun to coalesce as a field, the broad historical narrative of South Asian immigration to the United States has changed little. Most of the work in the field has focused on the decades of migration and settlement that unfolded after passage of the 1965 Hart-Cellar Immigration Act. This work was initially centered on the immediate beneficiaries of the 1965 Act—the doctors, engineers, and other professionals who arrived by the thousands over the course of the 1970s and '80s. Since the mid-1990s, scholars have turned their attention to newer migrations from the subcontinent and to a "South Asian America" that is conceived much more broadly along differing lines of class, gender, religion, sexual orientation/identification, generation, and regional and national origin. Pre-1965 histories are only now becoming the focus of renewed interest and inquiry. For years, scholarship on this period has centered primarily on Punjabi migration, settlement, and activism on the North American West Coast in the two decades between 1904 and 1924. Work on the period follows the lives of Punjabi farm and mill workers in British Columbia, the Pacific Northwest, and California; focuses on the expatriate nationalist politics of the San Francisco–based Ghadar Party; and charts both the violence and the lobbying efforts of anti-Asian citizen groups, labor leaders, and politicians on the West Coast that led up to the federal government's barring of Indian immigration and naturalization. Scholars focusing on this period have produced crucial work, and newer research on the Ghadar Party and West Coast migration now promises to expand what we know and how we think about these histories.[1]

However, another early history of South Asian migration to the United States, far from Pacific shores, has remained hidden, its traces scattered across a series of disparate archives for over a century. In the 1880s, Bengali Muslim peddlers began arriving in New York—passing through immigration at Castle Gardens on the Southern tip of Manhattan and then Ellis Island after its facilities opened in 1892.

These men did not stay in New York, nor did they follow the patterns of migration that became common after 1965, to the cities of the North and Midwest. Instead, they headed for New Jersey's beach boardwalk towns—Asbury Park, Atlantic City, Long Branch—and then turned southward to New Orleans, Charleston, and a series of other cities below the Mason-Dixon line. They came in small numbers at first, but many of the earliest arrivals married and settled within local communities of African descent, establishing a network that was firmly rooted in the U.S. South. Bengali peddlers not only moved throughout the region to a constellation of Southern cities, they traveled outward from New Orleans across the Caribbean and the Gulf of Mexico to Cuba, Belize, Honduras, and Panama. Their network expanded and flourished over the years that anti-Asian xenophobia grew to a fever pitch on the West Coast and Jim Crow was imposed in the South, and it continued to operate, albeit in different and diminished ways, even after Indian exclusion was formalized through the Asiatic Barred Zone provision of the 1917 Immigration Act.

Recovering the history of this peddler network enlarges the existing picture of early South Asian migration both geographically and conceptually. It challenges our understanding of when immigration from India to the United States began: which groups were migrating to the United States; where they were headed upon arrival in the United States; if, when, and where they were settling; and for what purposes. The choices that Bengali peddlers made and the paths they traveled prompt us to consider the importance of the Southern States in South Asian American historiography. Moreover, the lives they fashioned give us a glimpse of the interstices within which some South Asian migrants continued to work during the exclusion period. In the pages that follow, I explore the history and context of this forgotten migration. First, I consider the context in which Bengali peddlers were able to operate: a fashion for "Oriental" goods and entertainments that swept the United States in the late nineteenth and early twentieth centuries, in which fancies and fantasies of "India" took a central role. Then, I examine a series of archival sources—ships' logs, marriage and birth records, Census enumerations, and local news items—to piece together the record of this peddler network, from its origins in West Bengal to the U.S. South and beyond. The documents reveal a history that is important for the same reason it has thus far remained invisible—because these migrants followed a different and unexpected path, one that diverged sharply from later, normative patterns of South Asian immigration to the United States. Most chose not to settle permanently, and those who did stay integrated into working-class African American communities.

Fancies of India

How was it that at a time of heightened anti-immigrant sentiment in the United States—and at a time when Asian immigrants were being singled out by xenophobic politicians and citizens—a group of Muslim migrants from India was able to establish a peddler network that extended through New York, New Jersey, and New Orleans and across the U.S. South? The answer to this question lies in what the men were selling. At the most literal level, they were selling a range of compact and readily transportable "Oriental goods": embroidered cotton, silk kerchiefs and tablecloths, small rugs, wall hangings.[2] Just as importantly, however, these men were selling ideas about, and access to, India and the East. They were selling the exotic. They were selling worldliness and cosmopolitanism to the working- and middle-class customers who bought their wares.[3] The value of the peddlers' wares stemmed from the cache of meanings and status that these goods provided, as a craze for "India" and "the East" overtook elites in New York and Chicago and then spread across geographic and class lines into the growing spaces of American mass consumption, tourism, and leisure that marked the end of the nineteenth century—beach boardwalks, resort towns, and traveling shows.

The fashion for "Oriental" goods and entertainments was not new. John Kuo Wei Tchen has argued that U.S. popular ideas about and attitudes toward China were in fact constitutive of the American national identity as it developed from the late eighteenth through the early twentieth centuries. American ideas about this Far Eastern "Orient" changed over the course of the period, however, progressing through a series of distinct phases as the U.S. relationship to Chinese commodities and labor shifted. In the late 1700s, during a phase of what Tchen terms "patrician Orientalism," the possession of Chinese luxury goods such as porcelain and silk became a marker of social status for America's newly independent "elite and striving elite" classes. The early to mid–nineteenth century saw a broader popularization of the trade in and desire for Chinese things, ideas, and people as U.S. consumer culture rapidly expanded. In this phase of "commercial Orientalism," the middle and working classes joined elites in the clamor for Chinese goods and became the audience for circuses and exhibitions featuring Chinese performers and human "specimens." Finally, by the latter half of the nineteenth century, American ideas about China and the Chinese had turned to "fear and loathing" as an increasingly established population of Chinese immigrant workers came to be regarded as an economic and cultural threat. In this phase of "political Orientalism," Tchen writes, "Chinese laborers . . . became the center of a national political debate" and the target of xenophobia and racial violence.[4]

Period sources suggest, however, that while U.S. attitudes toward China and the Chinese turned xenophobic, the popular trade in the signs, cultures, and objects of "the Orient" showed no signs of abating. Instead, as the nineteenth century came to a close, American Orientalist desires seem to have shifted from China to "nearer" parts of the East; as the fascination with "the Orient" grew more widespread and commodified, India and the Middle East increasingly took center stage.[5] In this case, the phases of "patrician" and "commercial" Orientalism were virtually simultaneous. At the turn of the century, the "patricians" of New York, Chicago, and other major U.S. cities were abuzz over new translations of the *Rubaiyat*—the verses of the seventeenth century Persian poet Omar Khayyam.

Elite women tackled Khayyam's work in their clubs and reading circles. The British composer Liza Lehman penned a musical version of the *Rubaiyat* that made the rounds of theaters and opera houses from New York to St. Louis, Missouri, while the choreographer Isadora Duncan performed her own dance "interpretation" of the poet's work for the matrons of New York society.[6] Performances, music, and imagery based on the Old Testament story of the dancer-temptress Salome became so popular in this period—from Broadway to burlesque halls to Black vaudeville—that the press started referring to the phenomenon of "Salomania."[7] Arab horsemen and acrobats, in the meantime, traveled with Barnum and Bailey's, Forepaugh's, and other U.S. circuses, passing from one small town to the next across the Midwest, South, and Southwest.

Images and ideas of "India" pervaded U.S. popular culture at this time. Southern growers marketed tobacco under brand names like Hindoo, Mogul, and Bengal with labels that depicted Maharajahs, hookahs, and dancing girls. Tin Pan Alley songwriters churned out show tunes, such as "My Hindoo Man," "Down in Hindu Town," and "Down in Bom-Bombay," that middle-class Americans then sang to amuse themselves in the piano parlors of their homes. While Swami Vivekananda had first introduced Americans to the philosophy of the Hindu Vedas at the 1893 World Parliament of Religions, Vedantism only grew in popularity after a handsome young colleague of Vivekananda, Swami Abhedananda, came to New York in 1897. Within weeks of his arrival, Abhedananda filled a meeting hall in Midtown Manhattan to capacity three times a week, and reports of his "sermons" circulated in newspapers across the country.[8] The sexualized figure of the Indian "nautch" dancer became a staple of American burlesque in these years, and by 1906, the modern dancer Ruth St. Denis was performing in Indian nautch style on Broadway, bedecked with jewels and wrapped in a colorful silk sari.[9] In 1904, the owners of Coney Island's Luna Park turned fifteen acres of the park into a replica of the city of Delhi, filling its "temples," market stalls, and "native homes" with three hundred Indian men, women, and children "imported" to Brooklyn for the summer season.[10] By 1909, even the Wild West showmen "Buffalo Bill" Cody and Gordon "Pawnee Bill" Lillie joined in, touring a "Far East Show" across the U.S. Midwest and South that featured Arabian horsemen, a troupe of Sinhalese dancers, a "Hindu fakir," and a "nautch dance ballet."[11]

The American desire for "Oriental goods" grew within this context, as "Eastern"-themed entertainments spread. As the nineteenth century came to a close, Victorian propriety and restraint were giving way to mass consumerism, while the United States became an increasingly far-reaching imperial power. In this moment, historian Kristin Hoganson has argued, "Oriental goods" came to convey a range of different meanings. For American men of this era, items like hookahs, animal skins, rugs, and weapons from "the Orient" became markers of an imperial white masculinity, their possession and display simultaneously conveying the conquest of far-off lands and conjuring the fantasy world of the Eastern harem.[12]

Meanwhile, the consumption and display of Eastern fabrics, jewelry, decorative items, and interior furnishings became a means through which women of the era could stake a claim to cosmopolitanism, independence, self-definition, and ultimately, a liberated, post-Victorian sexuality.[13] While the sale of oriental goods had once been limited to high-end department stores and suppliers, by the end of the century a broad array of importers and department stores provided such goods to the middle-class market. In New York, this included Macy's, Lord and Taylor's, and A. A. Vantine, a specialty retailer offering everything from rugs and silks to teas, coffees, dinner gongs, teak furniture, and perfumes with names such as "Java Lily," and "Delhi Heliotrope."[14] Oriental goods also began to circulate, via peddlers and gift shops, within the spaces of middle- and working-class leisure and tourism.[15]

From Atlantic City to the Crescent City

The first mention of Bengali peddlers in the United States, dating from 1891, places them in just such a tourist site—in the New Jersey seaside resorts of Atlantic City and Asbury Park. At the turn of the twentieth century, these resorts drew hundreds of thousands of working people from Philadelphia and New York City. The resorts made their money by encouraging and catering to this group's desire to regard itself as class-ascendant; as historian Charles Funnel puts it, "the values expressed in the resort's entertainment were those of citizens vigorously striving for the good life which . . . they imagined the upper middle-class and rich to enjoy."[16] "Oriental" items such as silks, embroidered cloth, and small trinkets and curios were accessible and affordable markers of this good life, and the demand for them in Atlantic City and Asbury Park was significant enough that both resorts not only featured permanent "Oriental gift shops" along their boardwalks but became fertile ground for individual fancy goods peddlers from "the East." By 1891, the number of Bengali peddlers in New Jersey was sufficient to warrant a mention hundreds of miles away; the *Chicago Tribune* published an item describing a population of "very interesting" "dark skinned Hindoo peddlers" who had, in its reporter's words, come to "infest the seaside resorts of the Jersey coast in summer."[17]

Shipping and census records confirm the presence of Bengali peddlers in New Jersey at this time, but they do not suggest that these men were settling in significant numbers in the area. The records point further south to New Orleans, Charleston, and elsewhere. Indeed, ships' logs show that the Indian peddlers who entered the United States through the port of New York in the 1880s and '90s came to follow a regular pattern tied to the seasonal movements of American tourists. A group of peddlers arrived from India once a year, in the early weeks of the summer resort season, and made their way to New Jersey's beach boardwalk towns. On June 4, 1888, for example, five Indian Muslim merchants, listed as Sohboth Aly,

Abdoul Majack, Abdoul Zafah, Abdoul Barz, and simply Abdoul arrived at Castle Gardens; seven such merchants—Abad Ally, Shaik Abdool Huq, Mushareef Ali, Abdool Luteef, Muhioadeen Alli, Mobarak Alli, and Mohamed Musa—arrived at Ellis Island on June 9, 1894, and twenty-one arrived on June 15, 1895. Over the next two decades, similar groups of Indian Muslim "merchants," "traders," "peddlers," and "hawkers" entered the United States at Ellis Island between May 31 and July 15 of each year, always headed for the same handful of addresses in Atlantic City, Asbury Park, and nearby Long Branch.[18] The homes to which they were headed were within working-class African American neighborhoods, where groups of Bengali Muslim "Oriental goods" peddlers lived amid the hundreds of Black seasonal workers—stewards, cooks, chambermaids, bartenders, laundresses, bellmen, and musicians—who came to the area each summer to form the backbone of the resorts' service economy.[19]

While the "Hindoo peddlers" used the same New Jersey addresses over several years, suggesting that at least a small number of Indian men stayed in the area year-round, most of the peddlers were as transient as the resorts' other seasonal workers. Shipping records show that some members of the Bengali network made trips back out of the United States at the end of each summer, most likely to renew stocks of goods and/or shepherd younger traders through from India into the United States. However, the majority of the peddlers, in the words of one observer, came "down South along with the climate-changers and pleasure-seekers and continued their business [there], to move back to the north the next summer." The Bengalis established footholds in a series of Southern cities; the largest number operated out of New Orleans, but others set up in similar locations with bustling ports and tourist markets, most notably Charleston and Savannah. New Orleans's centrality to the network is not surprising. In the late nineteenth century, New Orleans was the second-busiest port city in the country. It was also becoming a year-round destination for tourists and travelers, and gave the peddlers access via train lines to other sites of travel, consumption, and commerce in the South.[20]

The first handful of Bengali peddlers—ten or eleven in all—arrived in New Orleans over the course of the 1880s and '90s. At the time of the 1900 U.S. Census, most were living together in a single joint household on St. Louis Street, on the outskirts of New Orleans's semilegalized sex district, Storyville. The men settled at this address before the 1895 creation of Storyville, when this block of St. Louis Street was part of an area of low-rent apartments, boardinghouses, and brothels that was close to the railway station, the waterfront, and the city's main commercial districts. Over the next decade, the population of Indian peddlers operating in New Orleans increased dramatically; according to the U.S. Census enumerated in April 1910, there were more than fifty of these men living at eight addresses, along the perimeter of Storyville, while another account suggests that hundreds of Bengali peddlers were passing through New Orleans by this time. In 1920, the U.S. Census again recorded about fifty Indian peddlers in the city, but these men had spread out over more than thirteen addresses, stretching northeastward into the heart of the neighborhood of Tremé.[21] In these years after the disruptions of the world war and the imposition of the Asiatic Barred Zone, some of the Bengalis chose to settle within Tremé, where they opened shops in the Black commercial district along North Claiborne Avenue and began to sell clothing and cloth goods to a local African American clientele.[22]

A smaller number of Bengali peddlers appear to have made their way to Charleston around the same time that their kin and colleagues were first setting up in New Orleans. At the turn of the century, the U.S. Census found eight Bengali peddlers living at a series of addresses that cut a straight line through the commercial center of the city. Three of these men had arrived in the United States in 1890, and by 1900, two of them had married local African American women in Charleston. Ahmed Alley was living with his wife Delia in a small bungalow at 97 Smith Street, and John Rudden (likely a mistransliteration of Uddin) was living with his wife Mary just down the block at 77 Smith Street, where two other peddlers, Kamieth Alley and Shaha Box, were boarding with them. The other four peddlers, who had all arrived in 1896, lived a few blocks further south, each within walking distance of Charleston's city center. One was boarding with an African American family of nine, another was renting a back room from a widowed 49-year-old African American woman, and the other two were rooming with the family of a white doctor, whose presence as the only white family on the block suggests he may have been administering to the local working-class Black community.[23] By 1910, the Bengalis had set up a group household at 7 Horlbeck Lane, steps away from Charleston's long, covered City Market, where vendors sold meat and produce, locals and tourists gathered, and the men likely peddled their silk and cotton embroideries. The address 7 Horlbeck Lane comes up repeatedly on different archival documents from this period, suggesting it was home to a more transient population of Indian peddlers than those who had first married and settled in the city.

Records also show that in the opening years of the century, members of the Bengali network who were living in Charleston sought to stabilize their operations by initiating the process of naturalization. Theirs were some of the earliest naturalization proceedings in the United States involving East Indians. Abdul Rohim Mondul, who had arrived in the United States in 1896, filed his intention to naturalize in January 1900 and was admitted two years and one day later in January 1902. Abdul Jobber Mondul filed his intention in September 1901 and was admitted in February 1905. At this time, only two categories of people were eligible to become U.S. citizens—"free white persons" and "persons of African descent"—and Abdul Rohim and Abdul Jobber Mondul, like other Indians would after them, made their claims under the first category. The fact that they were granted citizenship, however, was not a sign of any fixed federal policy categorizing Indians as "free whites." Elahi Baksh Mondul, for example, filed an intention to naturalize in 1905, six years after his arrival in the United States, and when he submitted his formal petition to naturalize in 1908, it was denied, "the petitioner not being a free born white person or of African nativity." This case notwithstanding, either the peddlers believed that the subjectivity and inconsistency of the process could work in their favor, or they found that the simple step of filing an intention to naturalize, and therefore holding "first papers," gave them greater freedom of movement at U.S. borders or on the streets of Southern cities. In the fifteen years that followed Elahi Baksh's denial, at least a dozen more Bengali peddlers filed intentions to naturalize in Charleston's federal district court.

By this time, the Bengali peddler network had gained a well-defined structure and a presence that stretched from the southern Atlantic coast as far west as Fort Worth, Texas. One group of traders had established roots in Southern cities through marriage and/or naturalization and played a key role in introducing newer peddlers into the trade. By 1908, there is also evidence that a number of these more senior traders were receiving boxes of embroidered goods shipped by their kin in Calcutta to the customhouses of Southern ports—New Orleans, Charleston, and Savannah—and then distributing these items to other peddlers to sell on the streets, door to door, and in open air markets. These individual peddlers spread far and wide across the South. The 1910 and 1920 Census found Indian peddlers in New Orleans, Charleston, and Savannah as well as in St. Louis, Missouri, Birmingham, Alabama, Jacksonville, Florida, and Galveston, Texas. Draft registration records provide an even broader picture of this network's spread. After the United States entered the World War in 1917, the federal government required all males between the ages of 18 and 35 to register for a military draft, regardless of their immigration status. Peddlers and others who worked out in the open were particularly vulnerable to having their registration documents checked by police or other officials, and if they were caught without a draft registration card they were subject to deportation or conscription. As a result, a good number of these men appear to have registered with their local draft boards: thirty-five Indian peddlers filed their registration cards in New Orleans, Louisiana, and twenty-seven more in other urban and commercial centers throughout the South—seven in Charleston, South Carolina; six in Jacksonville, Florida; four in Memphis, Tennessee; and between one and three in Chattanooga, Tennessee, Galveston, Texas, Dallas, Texas, Birmingham, Alabama, and Atlanta, Georgia. Many of the Indians who registered for the draft outside Louisiana appear to have been men who had been living in New Orleans and/or New Jersey earlier and had then branched out in smaller groups to work in other cities.[24]

These draft records, which required each registrant to list his place of birth and the name and location of his nearest relative, also point to a specific group of villages in the district of Hooghly, West Bengal, just north of Calcutta, suggesting that the network had been built on ties of region and/or kinship.[25] This is further borne out by the increasingly detailed information found on ships' manifests in the opening decades of the century.[26] Manifests from this period not only confirm that there was a network of interconnected Indian peddler households in New Jersey, New Orleans, Charleston, and elsewhere; they also show that most of the men heading to these households were joining a male relation—a brother, uncle, father, son, or cousin—who was already living there. Just as significantly, the "home" addresses these men listed on ships' manifests were, almost without exception, either in a cluster of neighboring villages in Hooghly—Babnan, Dadpur, Sinhet, Alipur, Chandanpur, Mandra, Bandipur, Bora, Bhadur, Gopinathpur—or in the Collinga Bazar neighborhood of Calcutta.[27] The villages listed here occupy a small swath of land roughly ten miles west of the town of Hooghly, which lies just thirty miles up the Hooghly River from Calcutta. They are part of a region still known for the production of intricately embroidered cloth in the "chikan" style—one of the common types of small "oriental good" that became popular in the United States and Europe at the turn of the twentieth century.[28] The 1912 *Bengal Gazetteer*—the reference published and used by British colonial administrators in India—indeed describes the growth of a small, independent export trade in chikan embroidery originating from this region. The *Gazetteer* notes that Hooghly's chikan embroidery was produced "primarily by Musulman ladies" and describes its popularity "with European ladies," and its export to "Europe, America, and Australia by Calcutta dealers." "Some of the local people," it continues, "also go to America, South Africa, and Australia to trade in *chikan* goods."[29]

The Calcutta addresses that members of the group listed on their documents most probably corresponded to the offices of the network's "dealers" and the spaces through which peddlers themselves passed on their way to the United States. All were on or adjacent to Kerr Lane, a narrow side street off Collinga Bazar. Period sources describe this as an area of inexpensive accommodations, drinking establishments, and sex workers who worked among the sailors of various nationalities who were passing through the port.[30] Parts of the neighborhood, however, were also home to a section of Calcutta's working-class Muslim population. The similarities between Collinga Bazar in Calcutta and Storyville in New Orleans clearly would have been numerous. What is important to note here is that while members of the peddler network that stretched from Bengal to the U.S. South had their origins in the villages of rural Hooghly, their entry into global circuits of trade and their travels to cities such as New Orleans were preceded, mediated, and no doubt conditioned by time already spent in this complex cosmopolitan space within Calcutta.

The Orient in New Orleans

Why did this network set up its main U.S. hub in New Orleans? The answer lies in a series of changes that the city was undergoing at the turn of the century—particularly its growing position as a center of travel and tourism. New Orleans was experiencing a significant political and economic shift as the nineteenth century came to a close. Over the course of the century, an Anglo-American business class with roots in the U.S. Northeast had taken the reins of power from the city's older Francophone Creole elite. By the 1890s, this new business class was attempting to transform New Orleans from a city weighed down by the South's slaveholding past—and by the waning economy in cotton and sugar—into a progressive metropolis and tourist site that would attract a year-round flow of visitors.[31] The development and promotion of the city's two main shopping districts—Canal Street and the French Market—were key to this transformation. Over these years, New Orleans's political and business leaders set about turning Canal Street into a glittering modern commercial thoroughfare, while the nearby French Market was promoted as "an eighteenth century market in a twentieth century city," where visitors could experience a romanticized version of New Orleans's Creole past.[32] In the meantime, New Orleans's boosters worked with regional and national railroads to transform Mardi Gras from a local Catholic, Creole celebration into a national attraction, and city leaders established the Storyville sex district. Historians such as Alecia P. Long and Jasmine Mir have argued that the creation of Storyville was in fact a crucial part of efforts to turn the city into a year-round tourist destination. On one hand, containing the city's considerable sex trade within a clearly bounded area allowed for the development of the rest of New Orleans into a more visitor-friendly city. On the other hand, the delineation of a well-defined "legal" sex district meant the creation of an illicit attraction whose draw for male visitors equaled that of the city's more publicly acknowledged and promoted charms. Indeed, Mir asserts, Storyville's significance went deeper than this; the promotional strategies of the sex district's madams became the blueprint for those of New Orleans's political and business leaders as they tried to forge an image of New Orleans as a city of unbridled pleasure. By the turn of the twentieth century, New Orleans had become a place like no other in the United States, whose very business was "constructing, disseminating, embodying, and selling myths."[33]

Myths of "India" and "the Orient" flourished within this context. Years before Thomson and Dundy staged "The Streets of Delhi" at Coney Island and Buffalo and Pawnee Bill took their "Wild West and Far East Show" across the country, mass spectacles of "the East" had become a regular part of New Orleans's Mardi Gras parades. Although Mardi Gras itself had its roots in eighteenth-century Creole cultural/religious practice, the large-scale themed parades that took over the main streets of the city each year were the nineteenth-century creation of New Orleans's Anglo-American elites. The preeminent Mardi Gras "krewes" of this era, writes Joseph Roach—the Mistick Krewe of Comus, the Krewe of Proteus, the Krewe of Rex, and the Knights of Momus—were all-male white secret societies made up of New Orleans's wealthiest and most powerful businessmen. These Krewes' Mardi Gras processions—in which members dressed up in masks and costumes and rode on floats elaborately designed around a chosen theme—became a means for these men to saturate French Creole Mardi Gras with imagery drawn from English history and literature, and thus to assert their power and ascendancy over New Orleans's older, French-identified establishment and the city's large racially mixed population.[34]

Roach points out that these yearly processions were frequently fashioned around stories and imagery taken from "Milton, Spenser, and Dickens," but what is striking about the records of the Mardi Gras processions of the nineteenth and early twentieth centuries is just how often New Orleans's elite Krewes chose to march under "Indian" and "Oriental" themes. The oldest Krewe, Comus, started this trend in 1868 when its members chose to fashion their costumes, parade floats, and ball around the theme "The Departure of Lalla Rookh from Delhi," drawing on a section of Thomas More's Orientalist narrative poem *Lalla Rookh*. The 1880s and '90s saw a flurry of similar themes: Rex marched under the theme "The Arabian Knights"; Proteus staged "The Hindoo Heavens," "Myths and Worships of the Chinese," and "Tales of the Genii"; Momus staged "The Ramayana," "Aladdin or the Wonderful Lamp," and "The Mahabharata (The Wooing and Wedding of Naila and Dayamanti)." These parades were lavish in style. When the Krewe of Comus paraded under the theme "The Mahabharata" in 1903, its members, hidden behind elaborate Indian costumes and masks, were said to have presented their theme "on a scale of great artistic splendor . . . illustrat[ing] in twenty superb floats the great epic poem of the Hindus." The Krewe of Proteus's pageant for the 1908 Mardi Gras was a "night parade [of] twenty big floats," on which "masked and costumed men" portrayed "Hindu beliefs and Buddhistic and Brahminical customs . . . including allegories of Yasodhara the Fair, the dancers of Indra's temple; The Lords of Light; Parihga and Mano; . . . and The Abode of the Rishis."[35]

These processions marked the Anglo-American elite's embrace of, and mastery over, English Orientalist "knowledge." In this sense, they were a complex display of power by New Orleans's secret societies. On the one hand, the processions were a means by which Krewe members asserted a local form of white supremacy in the act of occupying the city's streets and—as was their practice—hiring groups of New Orleans residents of African descent to walk the ground below and in front of them as they rode high up on their floats. On the other hand, the Oriental pageantry and performance of these processions became a means by which these men symbolically identified themselves with British imperial power—in much the way that the display of Oriental luxury goods aligned elite American women with their counterparts in the imperial metropoles of London and Paris.[36] At the same time, these processions constituted a broad public arena, specific to New Orleans, in which fantastic ideas about India and the Middle and Far East

were circulated, popularized, and naturalized; in their local idiom, they both
reflected and reinforced the broader fashion for the imagery and goods of an
imagined "East."

The public circulation of Orientalist fantasy in the context of Mardi Gras had
a more illicit analogue within the brothels of Storyville. The most commonly
purveyed sexual fantasies in Storyville revolved around the figure of the mixed-
race "octoroon"; elite white male customers sought out light-skinned African
American women and girls through whom they could reenact generations of
sexual power and violence over enslaved Black women.[37] Alongside "octoroons,"
however, a number of Storyville brothels and saloons purveyed the fantasy figure
of the "Oriental dancing girl." The women who worked and performed in this
role—like their contemporaries in burlesques across the country—were most
likely Creole, African American, Jewish, or Southern European women dressed up
in some form of "Oriental" garb and surrounded by decorations meant to evoke
the imagined palaces of Arab, Persian, or Mughal emperors.[38] Storyville's "Blue
Book," which ran advertisements by the District's madams and listed the addresses
and characteristics of individual sex workers, bears traces of this phenomenon.
One of Storyville's madams, Bertha Weinthal, for example, took out a full-page
advertisement when "Mademoiselle Rita Walker" began to work in her brothel,
billing her as "the Oriental Danseuse . . . one of the first women in America to
dance in her bare feet." The Cairo Club on North Franklin Street appears to have
built its main "entertainments" around "oriental dancers."[39] At the same time,
photographs from the period, including those by E. J. Bellocq, show neighborhood brothels thickly decorated with "Oriental" rugs, cushions, tablecloths, and
tapestries.[40] The lavish interiors that Storyville's madams created out of such
items were of a piece with the private parlors and smoking rooms fashioned by
elite men of this era which intermingled images of "eroticized Eastern women"
with Oriental "daggers, swords, and spears."[41]

The public and private circulation of Orientalist fantasies ultimately made New
Orleans a fertile market for the kinds of small goods that Bengali peddlers could
access from India—particularly if the peddlers themselves could play the appropriate role. The success of a "Hindoo peddler" would no doubt have depended
upon his ability to perform an exotic and nonthreatening "Indian-ness"—one
which would have required a particular bearing, style of dress, mode of speech,
and perhaps even some replication of the servility of the imagined colonial subject.
Such a performance would have been crucial to the act of lending authenticity—and
thus value—to the goods these men sold. Like the "oriental dancers" who worked
in brothels and burlesques of this era, these peddlers were performing widespread
and well-entrenched Western fantasies of "the East." A handful of newspaper
reports describing the "Hindoo peddlers" of this era suggest that this enactment
of "Indian-ness" was a central part of the men's appeal. The earliest was the brief
news item that appeared in the *Chicago Daily Tribune* in 1891, describing, with

racial condescension and voyeuristic fascination, "[t]he dark-skinned Hindoo peddlers who infest the seaside resorts of the Jersey Coast." The article went on to detail a deliberate style of purveying goods. "They are invariably courteous," the *Tribune* wrote of the traders, "and their genial shrewdness when trying to effect a sale is most engaging. As a rule they are handsome men, with clean-cut features and intellectual faces. They speak Hindustanee and occasionally Bengali, while their English is excellent."[42] A decade later, the *Daily Herald* of Biloxi, Mississippi, published a longer, less favorable dispatch from one of its correspondents in New Orleans, describing a "colony of East Indians" who wore "black skullcaps and long-tailed frock coats," and presented "an air of Oriental mysticism," as they "prowl[ed] about town peddling rugs and such like." An account of "Hindoo peddlers" who were operating further south in Cuba during this period echoed both of these U.S. newspaper reports. In a travel feature on Havana in August 1901, a correspondent for the *Atlanta Constitution* wrote of an "attractive" group of "Hindoo . . . street vendors"—men who entered "stores and offices and cafes, with gentle persistency begging to show the contents of their packs" and were "so courteous, so graceful, so interesting in their blouses . . . so attractive with their fathomless eyes and shining teeth, brilliant smiles, that we will buy in spite of resolutions to the contrary."[43]

The growing presence of Western tourists in the Caribbean and Central America was another reason for New Orleans's importance as a hub of the Bengali peddler network. As the main gateway for travel and trade between the United States, the Caribbean basin and South America, New Orleans gave the peddlers access to a series of key sites beyond U.S. borders. By the 1910s, peddlers from the Bengali network were regularly making their way to Cuba, Belize, Honduras, and Panama and then traveling back to and through New Orleans. These men often traveled alone or in small groups, but the records of their individual movements trace out a clear set of links between Hooghly, Calcutta, New Jersey, New Orleans, and points further south. Passport, census, and ships' documents, for example, show one member of the network, Solomon Mondul, traveling from Calcutta to Southampton to New York in 1896, living at 1420 St. Louis St. in New Orleans in 1900, traveling from India via Liverpool and New York to Atlantic City in 1906, living in New Orleans in April 1910, traveling from Colon, Panama via Kingston, Jamaica, and New York to Asbury Park in August 1910, living back in New Orleans in 1920, and finally living in Memphis, Tennessee, in 1930.[44] In 1917, Mohamed Issa, another peddler who listed his place of birth as "District Hooghly" traveled from Belize to New Orleans. Issa listed Belize as his "last permanent residence," but stated that he had lived in New Orleans previously and was now intending a three-week stay in the city, at what was then one of the key group residences used by the Bengali peddler network, 1825 St. Ann Street. In 1919, Shaik Mondul—a 30-year-old merchant whose last residence was Tela, Honduras, and who spoke "Bengalese" and Spanish—was recorded traveling from Tela to La Ceiba, Honduras, where he sailed northward through the waters of the Caribbean and the Gulf of Mexico to New Orleans, with a remarkable $3,250 in hand (equivalent to $40,000 in today's currency). From New Orleans, he was to sail back through the Gulf and Caribbean to Panama, and ultimately from Panama to "Bengal, India."[45]

Conclusion: Enlarging the Picture of Early South Asian Migration

The archival traces of this early history of South Asian migration are scattered and fragmentary. We do not have first-person accounts from the peddlers or their wives or children—memoirs, oral histories, autobiographies—and there are few contemporary accounts by other writers describing the peddlers' presence in the South. Ships' manifests, census sheets, and vital records tell us only part of the story, and they are often skewed toward the lives of men. What emerges from these varied archival documents, however—from the movements they do trace and the lives they record—is a picture of South Asian migration to the United States that differs from both that of Punjabi farmers and mill-workers on the West Coast in the 1904–1924 period and of South Asian professionals arriving in the United States in the immediate post-1965 era. On one level, the difference between the early Bengali migration and these other, more iconic histories of South Asian immigration lies in its geographic trajectory. Early Punjabi migrants followed a path through British Columbia southward into Washington, Oregon, and California—as well as directly to California through the port of San Francisco—and then inland to agricultural areas of the state stretching from Yuba City to the Mexican border. The immigrants in the post-1965 era came to a few major cities—the first among them being New York, but also Chicago, Boston, Philadelphia, Los Angeles, San Francisco/San Jose, Atlanta, and Houston—moving into these cities' metropolitan areas and then, often, out to their suburbs.

The Bengali Muslim peddlers who came to the United States at the turn of the century followed a very different path that took them through New Jersey to New Orleans and other parts of the South, and then onward all the way to Panama. This trajectory was structured by a specific set of historical and economic circumstances. If Punjabi immigrants sought out the rich agricultural lands of California and the Southwest after being displaced by British colonial land and taxation policies on the subcontinent, and post-1965 immigrants were drawn to the professional jobs clustered in U.S. metropolitan areas in the post-Fordist era, the path that Bengali peddlers took to and through the United States was determined by the shape of emerging circuits of travel and tourism and by the geography of consumer demand for their "fancy goods" and "notions." Their migration reflected a confluence of global, regional, and local changes in the latter half of the nineteenth century: the advent of steamships, the opening of the Suez and Panama Canals, the growth of leisure travel and consumer culture, the pervasive American fashion for goods and entertainments from the "exotic" East, and the rise of New Orleans as both a tourist site and a gateway to other sites of commerce and travel. New Orleans was also a city with a long history of racial heterogeneity and intermixture. Two decades or more before Punjabi men made their lives within and alongside rural Mexican/o communities in California and the Southwest, these men from Hooghly and Calcutta were able to establish roots in New Orleans, living and in some cases marrying within the city's African American and Creole of Color neighborhoods.

This "other" history of early South Asian migration raises a number of questions—not the least of which is why it has remained "hidden" to us for such a long time. There are a number of factors that likely contributed to the historical invisibility of Bengali peddlers, especially set against the greater visibility of early-twentieth-century Punjabi immigrants: Bengali peddlers seem to have been much smaller in number than Punjabi mill-workers and farmers on the West Coast; as itinerant salesmen who fanned out from New Orleans to other cities, they were both more transient and more dispersed than their counterparts on the West Coast. Early on, West Coast Punjabis established ethnic-religious associations and were involved in organized politics (and thus became more visible in their own day and in the historical record)—a pattern that the Bengali peddler population in the South does not seem to have followed; and whereas Punjabi immigrants became targets of anti-Asian xenophobia and antiradicalism on the West Coast, Bengali peddlers, who filled a specific niche in a translocal tourist economy fueled by Orientalist fashions, appear to have succeeded in quietly carrying on their business. Finally, fewer of these men stayed permanently in the United States, and those who did appear to have integrated into the communities that had provided a home for them. Their children came of age in a South shaped and transformed by the imposition of Jim Crow. Instead of forming ethnic enclaves, those Bengali peddlers who settled in the neighborhood of Tremé—along with their partners, children, and ultimately their descendents—became part of the larger history of Black New Orleans.

The fact that this history has remained invisible or illegible suggests the limits of existing models to account for the complexity and variety of experiences of South Asian (im)migration to the United States. Such experiences become less legible the more they vary from the iconic narrative of twentieth-century immigration to the United States—that in which families leave their homeland behind in search of a "better life" in the United States, settle and reconstitute their communities in well-defined enclaves, accumulate wealth, educate their children, and assimilate into white middle-class neighborhoods and norms, even as they become "hyphenated" Americans. Sojourning laborers—a category that Sucheta Mazumdar and others remind us represented a significant proportion of early-twentieth-century migrants from India, China, Southern Europe, and elsewhere—are unaccounted for in this picture. Such migrants moved often, following the temporary openings and shifting demands of the United States and other economies. They did not establish permanent settlements in the United States, did not "reconstitute" families and communities once they were here. Instead, they forged new forms of affiliation in the places they labored, while operating as part of economic circuits that stretched back to their families and home villages and included the women who labored there in their absence.[46]

The Bengali men who came to the United States to sell Oriental goods were one such group. Along with dancers, acrobats, magicians, and other circus and exhibition performers, they were part of a small number of Indians who were able to enter and work in the United States to fulfill the short-term desires created by the turn-of-the-century craze for "India" and "the East." Although they spent extended periods in the United States, and constituted a significant presence in New Orleans and other parts of the South over the course of more than three decades, most of the men who traveled from Hooghly and Calcutta to the United States between the 1890s and 1920s were gone well before midcentury. Their migration was not one of permanent relocation; for most of these men, U.S. cities were not final destinations but nodes on a global network. And while this network arose in response to Western demand for their goods, it was also built upon a specific, gendered and global, division of labor involving three interconnected groups: the Bengali women who labored in Hooghly villages to produce chikan embroidery and maintain family landholdings while their men were abroad; the men who circulated to and through the United States, performing their Eastern-ness and selling their goods; and the U.S. women of color who performed the labor that was necessary for the Bengali network to become, and remain, rooted in New Orleans.[47]

This early history, then, is important on multiple levels. It expands the South Asian American narrative to include a group of previously unknown migrants who lived and worked in the United States as early as the 1880s. It points to the significance of the cultural and economic context of turn-of-the-century American Orientalism within which they were able to establish a viable commercial network. It directs our attention beyond the East and West Coasts to different trajectories of migration from the subcontinent—trajectories that South Asians followed through the Southern states and into the economic and cultural orbit of the Caribbean and Central America. Perhaps most importantly, this history challenges us to expand our analytical approach to South Asian immigration itself in ways that can account for a broader variety of migrant experiences—so that we can hold in a single frame, for example, the lives and labor of these highly mobile Bengali Muslim men, the African American and Creole of Color women with whom they partnered in New Orleans, and the Bengali women who remained in Babnan, Dadpur, and elsewhere in Hooghly. As South Asian America continues to grow in both size and heterogeneity, it is crucial that we account for such complex relationships between global movement, local rootedness, and geographic and temporal impermanence—relationships that characterize the experiences of many South Asian migrants to this day.

Notes

I would like to thank the editors, Jigna Desai and Khyati Joshi, for their careful readings and guidance in the preparation of this essay. A note on sources: Census, Draft Registration, and Passport records were accessed via the online database Ancestry Library Edition. Ships' records were accessed online via Ancestry and Ellis Island's Arrivals database at Ellis Island.org. New Orleans Birth and Marriage Records were obtained from the Louisiana State Archives, Baton Rouge, La.

1. Joan Jensen, *Passage from India: Asian Indian Immigrants in North America* (New Haven, Conn.: Yale University Press, 1988); Karen Leonard, *Making Ethnic Choices: California's Punjabi Mexican Americans* (Philadelphia: Temple University Press, 1992); Nayan Shah, "Between 'Oriental Depravity' and 'Natural Degenerates': Spatial Borderlands and the Making of Ordinary Americans," *American Quarterly* 57.3 (2005): 703–725; Seema Sohi, "Echoes of Mutiny: Race, Empire, and Indian Revolutionaries on the Pacific Coast," PhD Dissertation, University of Washington, Department of History, 2007; Maia Ramnath, "Two Revolutions: The Ghadar Movement and India's Radical Diaspora, 1913–1918," *Radical History Review* (Spring 2005): 7–30.

2. *Biloxi Daily Herald*, "Not Very Dignified—Amusing Story of an Oriental Who Took a Bicycle Ride," May 5, 1900, 6; S. L. Beckwith, "Havana: A City of Strange Peddlers," *Atlanta Constitution*, August 25, 1901, A9; *Philadelphia Inquirer*, "Burglars Made Rich Haul at the Shore," August 1, 1902, 3.

3. Kristin Hoganson, "Cosmopolitan Domesticity: Importing the American Dream, 1865–1920," *American Historical Review* (February 2002). http://www.historycooperative.org/journals/ahr/107.1/ ah0102000055.html (accessed February 20, 2008).

4. John Kuo Wei Tchen, *New York before Chinatown: Orientalism and the Shaping of American Culture, 1776–1882* (Baltimore: Johns Hopkins University Press, 1999), xxi–xxiii.

5. There were a number of factors that contributed to this shift. One was the relatively low number of immigrants from India and the Middle East in the 1890s United States. In the absence of large-scale labor migration from these parts of "the Orient," their "peoples" and "cultures" were less threatening; they were still largely fantastical and abstract, defined by the exotic tales of European Orientalists and the spectacle of American circus sideshows. At the same time, as a number of scholars have noted, the notion that the people and cultures of India and the Middle East could open westerners up to new worlds of spirituality and sensuality appealed to a millennial generation that was pushing at the restrictions of the Victorian era. Fantasies of India and the Middle East also provided Americans with a sense, however vicarious, of imperial dominion over far-off parts of the globe, at precisely the moment that the U.S. empire was expanding beyond North America. That said, in the realm of mass entertainments and Oriental goods, the lines between India, the Middle East, China, Japan, and the Pacific Islands; between Hindu, Muslim, Sikh, Parsi, and Buddhist; and between Arab and Persian, and so on were blurred. The line between fantasies and commodities from "the East" and immigrant workers from

Asia was, by contrast, clear and distinct; the former remained in vogue even as Japanese and Indian immigrants were added to the Chinese as targets of xenophobic legislation and violence.

6. "In and Out of Women's Clubs," *Chicago Daily Tribune*, March 15, 1897, 9; "The Song Cyclus at Long Branch," *New York Times*, July 24, 1898, 13; "A Concert at Vassar—John D. Rockefeller Provides an Entertainment for the Students," *New York Times*, October 23, 1898, 1; "Newport Society Doings," *New York Times*, September 5, 1898, 7; "What Is Doing in Society," *New York Times*, October 29, 1898, 7; "'In a Persian Garden'—Mrs. Speyer and Others Give the Song Cycle on the Rubaiyat To-Morrow," *Kansas City Star*, November 9, 1898, 12; "What Is Doing in Society," *New York Times*, March 12, 1899, 16.

7. Sara Katherine Rowe, *Salomania: The Reception of Salome Imagery in Turn-of-the-Century America* (Seattle: University of Washington Press, 2001); Toni Bentley, *Sisters of Salome* (New Haven, Conn.: Yale University Press, 2002); Karen Sotiropoulos, *Staging Race: Black Performers in Turn of the Century America* (Cambridge, Mass.: Harvard University Press, 2006), 175–190.

8. "A Teacher of the Vedanta," *The Critic: A Weekly Review of Literature and the Arts*, March 19, 1898, 200; "On Sin and Sinners—Swami Abhedananda of India Discusses the Subject at Mott Memorial Hall," *New York Times*, March 21, 1898, 10.

9. "Bringing Temple Dances from the Orient to Broadway," *New York Times*, March 25, 1906, X2; "Sam T. Jack's Theater" (advertisement), *New York Times*, February 8, 1898, 12. For more on St. Denis and her expropriation of the style and movements of Indian nautch dancers, see Priya Srinivasan, "The Nautch Women Dancers of the 1880s: Corporeality, U.S. Orientalism, and Anti-Immigration Laws," *Women and Performance* 19.1 (March 2009); and Srinivasan, "The Bodies beneath the Smoke or What's behind the Cigarette Poster: Unearthing Kinesthetic Connections in American Dance History," *Discourses in Dance* 4.1 (2007): 7–48.

10. "A New Coney Island Rises from the Ashes of the Old," *New York Times*, May 8, 1904, SM5; "Greater Luna Park," *New York Tribune*, May 8, 1904, A14.

11. The "Two Bills" premiered their "Wild West and Far East Show" at Madison Square Garden in 1909, before taking its massive retinue on the road. "Wild West at Garden—Two Bills, Pawnee and Buffalo, at Every Performance," *New York Tribune*, May 2, 1909, B2; Glen Shirley, *Pawnee Bill: A Biography of Major Gordon W. Lillie* (Lincoln: University of Nebraska Press, 1958), 164.

12. Hoganson, "Cosmopolitan Domesticity," par. 29.

13. Ibid., pars. 5–9; Gina Marchetti, *Romance and the "Yellow Peril": Race, Sex, and Discursive Strategies in Hollywood Fiction* (Berkeley: University of California Press, 1993), 28–32.

14. "Cowperthwait's 'Reliable' Carpets—Special Sale" (advertisement), *New York Times*, December 7, 1898, 12; "W. and J. Sloane—Special Christmas Offering" (advertisement), *New York Times*, December 12, 1898, 4; "Ehrich Bros—Phenomenal Bargains" (advertisement), *New York Times*, December 4, 1898, 15; "Vantines Oriental Furnishings and Decorations" (advertisement), *New York Times*, February 13, 1898, 12; F. James Gibson, "Oriental Rugs," *New York Times Illustrated Magazine*, February 20, 1898, IWM12; "AA Vantine's History and Perfumes." http://experience8.com/aa-vantines-history-and-perfumes-2 (accessed December 30, 2008).

15. This was a trend that was not limited to the United States. According to historian Mark-Anthony Falzon, a community of Sindhi Hindu traders based in Malta grew along-

side the global expansion of European middle-class travel and tourism in the 1840s to the 1910s. The key points in this "Sindworki" network—which ultimately stretched across the Mediterranean, North Africa, the Middle East, the Far East, East and West Africa, and South America—corresponded to the ports of call of European travelers. Sindhi peddlers sold "silk and curio items from the Far East and India" throughout this network, following European travelers from Singapore to Panama, while running larger "oriental goods" shops catering to tourists on the main commercial thoroughfare in Malta's capital city of Valetta. Mark-Anthony Falzon, "Origins and Establishment of the Indian Business Community in Malta," *Bank of Valetta Review* 24 (Autumn 2001): 73–92.

16. Charles E. Funnell, *By the Beautiful Sea* (New Brunswick, N.J.: Rutgers University Press, 1983), 24, 32.

17. *Chicago Daily Tribune*, "Hindoos in America," July 19, 1891, 6.

18. District of the City of New York, Port of New York, *List of Passengers: SS Alsatia*, June 4, 1888; *SS Armenia*, June 9, 1894; *SS Paris*, June 15, 1895; United States, Department of the Treasury, *List or Manifest of Alien Passengers for the Immigration Officer at Port of Arrival: SS St. Louis*, June 12, 1897; *SS Teutonic*, June 2, 1904; *SS Cedric*, June 10, 1904; *SS Sardegna*, June 15, 1904; *SS Arabic*, July 24, 1904. United States, Department of Commerce and Labor, *List or Manifest of Alien Passengers for the Immigration Officer at Port of Arrival* (hereafter USDCL/LMAP): *SS Cedric*, July 13, 1906; *SS Celtic*, May 31, 1908; *SS Majestic*, June 24, 1909; *SS New York*, July 11, 1909; *SS Arabic*, July 20, 1909; *SS Adriatic*, June 24, 1910; *SS Celtic*, June 5, 1911; *SS New York*, June 17, 1912; *SS Oceanic*, July 17, 1912; *SS Olympic*, July 2, 1913; *SS Oceanic*, July 2, 1914; *SS St. Paul*, July 5, 1914.

19. The 1900 Census illuminates one key set of addresses on North Kentucky Avenue in Atlantic City: at number 213 N. Kentucky, 47-year-old Mohomed Rohman was a boarder in a Black household of five from Pennsylvania; next door, at number 215 lived Abdul Gofford, 27; Mohi Odin, 30; Abdul Sethy, 27; and Ali Mubarak, 25. All five of these men were recorded as "East Indian" merchants of "fancy dry goods." Two doors down, at number 219, Mary Hosain, a 21-year-old African American woman from Virginia lived with her mother Kate Hardin and her two sons, Abdul, 3, and Arkedan, 2, and although Mary Hosain's husband did not appear on the census sheet, her children were listed with "East India" as their father's birthplace. United States Department of Commerce, Bureau of the Census (hereafter USDC/BC), *U.S. Census, 1900: Schedule No. 1—Population*, Atlantic City, Atlantic County, New Jersey, 1st Precinct, Ward 3, Sup. Dist. 169, Enum. Dist. 12, Sheet 16. For a description of the racialized division of labor in turn-of-the-century Atlantic City, see Funnell, *By the Beautiful Sea*, 24–34.

20. Tom Murray, *Southern Railway* (St. Paul, Minn.: Voyageur Press, 2007), 39.

21. USDC/BC, *U.S. Census, 1900, 1910, 1920*, Population Schedules for New Orleans, La. (various).

22. Ibid.

23. USDC/BC, *U.S. Census, 1900*, Population Schedule for Charleston, S.C., P1/W11/SD1/ED108/Sh2–3; P1/W4/SD1/ED82/Sh11; P1/W8/SD1/ED96/Sh11; P1/W2/SD1/ED76/Sh9.

24. USDC/BC, *U.S. Census, 1900, 1910*, Population Schedules for Asbury Park, Atlantic City, and Long Branch, New Jersey, and New Orleans, Louisiana (various); United States, Selective Service System, *World War I Draft Registration Cards*, Local Registration Boards of New Orleans, La., Charleston, S.C., Memphis, Tenn., Chattanooga, Tenn., Galveston, Tex., Dallas, Tex., Birmingham, Ala., Atlanta, Ga., Jacksonville, Fla.

25. United States, Selective Service System, *World War I Draft Registration Cards*, Local Registration Boards of New Orleans, La., Charleston, S.C., Memphis, Tenn., Chattanooga, Tenn., Galveston, Tex., Dallas, Tex., Birmingham, Ala., Atlanta, Ga., Jacksonville, Fla.

26. By the 1910s, all "alien" passengers arriving in the country were required to provide authorities with their destination address in the United States, as well as a home address in their country of origin and the name of a friend or relative on each end of their voyage.

27. USDCL/LMAP, *SS Celtic*, May 31, 1908; *SS New York*, October 4, 1908; *SS Majestic*, June 24, 1909; *SS New York*, July 11, 1909; *SS Arabic*, July 20, 1909; *SS Adriatic*, June 24, 1910; *SS Celtic*, June 5, 1911; *SS Baltic*, November 20, 1911; *SS New York*, June 17, 1912; *SS Oceanic*, July 17, 1912; *SS Olympic*, July 2, 1913; *SS Oceanic*, July 2, 1914; *SS St. Paul*, July 5, 1914.

28. Jasleen Dhamija, Crafts Council of India, *Asian Embroidery* (New Delhi: Abhinav Publications, 2004), 264–265; West Bengal State Akademi of Dance, Drama, Music and Visual Arts, *Cultural Directory of West Bengal* (Calcutta: Rabindra Bharati University, 1997), 137.

29. L. S. S. O'Malley and Monmohan Chakravarti, *Bengal District Gazetteer: Hooghly 1912* (New Delhi: Logos, 1985), 187.

30. P. Thankappan Nair, *A History of Calcutta's Streets* (Calcutta: Firma KLM, 1987), 267. See also Kipling's typically fantastical description of this neighborhood: Rudyard Kipling, "On the Banks of the Hugli," in *Wee Willie Winkie—City of the Dreadful Night—American Notes* (New York: H. M. Caldwell Company, 1899), 43–44.

31. Jasmine Mir, "Marketplace of Desire: Storyville and the Making of a Tourist City in New Orleans, 1890–1920," unpublished PhD Dissertation, Department of History, New York University, 2005, 21–23, 27–28.

32. Ibid., 27. A travel feature that ran in U.S. newspapers in 1903 hailed the French Market's "quaint customs," its "kaleidoscope of sights and . . . Babel of sounds" and declared that "the 'best people' of New Orleans still patronize the old Market," particularly "on Sunday mornings [when] the street cars are . . . crowded with fashionably dressed people from the 'up-town' section on their way to the Market for a cup of the famous Creole coffee." "An Eighteenth Century Market in a Twentieth Century City—Progressive New Orleans Cherishes Its Old French Market," *Montgomery Advertiser*, December 27, 1903, 9.

33. Alecia P. Long, *The Great Southern Babylon: Sex, Race, and Respectability in New Orleans* (Baton Rouge: Louisiana State University Press, 2004); Mir, "Marketplace of Desire," x–xi, 1–2.

34. Joseph Roach, *Cities of the Dead: Circum-Atlantic Performance* (New York: Columbia University Press, 1996), 245–259; Kevin Fox Gotham, *Authentic New Orleans: Tourism, Culture, and Race in the Big Easy* (New York: New York University Press, 2007), 42–44.

35. "Carnival at End—Krewe of Comus Give Their Parade in New Orleans," *Montgomery Advertiser*, February 2, 1903, 1; "Parade Knights of Momus Ushe[r]s In the Mardi Gras," *Macon Weekly Telegraph*, February 23, 1906, 2; "New Orleans Greets Rex—Carnival Crowd Not So Large as in Previous Years," *Montgomery Advertiser*, March 3, 1908, 1.

36. On Mardi Gras performance and local social order, see Roach, *Cities of the Dead*, 244–245, 247–249.

37. Ibid., 227–231.

38. Abbott and Seroff point out that in 1890, Sam T. Jack, one of the earliest theater owners to put together a burlesque featuring "Oriental" dancers, used the same poster, text, and promotional images for his "Creole Burlesque Company," and his "Oriental Sensation

Company," the latter of which was purported to feature twenty Egyptian women. In fact, they write "the percentage of 'Louisiana Creoles' in Jack's compan[ies] was probably about the same as the percentage of 'young Egyptian women,' i.e., not many. A later report said that the company was 'made up of many New York City girls.'" Lynn Abbott and Doug Seroff, *Out of Sight: The Rise of African American Popular Music, 1889–1895* (Jackson: University Press of Mississippi, 2002), 154.

39. Al Rose, *Storyville, New Orleans: Being an Authentic, Illustrated Account of the Notorious Red Light District* (Tuscaloosa: University of Alabama Press, 1974), 69, 77–80, 89, 146.

40. E. J. Bellocq, *Storyville Portraits: Photographs from the New Orleans Red-light District, Circa 1912* (New York: New York Museum of Modern Art, 1970); Jay Moynahan, ed., *The Blue Book of New Orleans* (Spokane, Wa.: Chicadee Publishing, 2006).

41. Hoganson, "Cosmopolitan Domesticity," par. 29.

42. "Hindoos in America," *Chicago Daily Tribune*, July 19, 1891, 6.

43. Beckwith, "Havana," A9.

44. British India Steam Navigation Company, Passenger List for *SS Goorkha*, May 31, 1896; District of the City of New York, Port of New York, *List of Passengers* for *SS St. Paul*, June 6, 1896; USDCL/LMAP, *SS Cedric*, April 29, 1906; *SS Tagus*, August 3, 1910; USDC/BC, *U.S. Census, 1900–1930*, Population Schedules (various).

45. USDCL/LMAP, *SS Coppename*, July 9, 1917; *SS Yoro*, November 16, 1919; USDC/BC, *U.S. Census, 1920*, Population Schedule, New Orleans, Louisiana, 5th Precinct, Ward 5, Sup. Dist. 1, Enum. Dist. 82, Sheet No. 15B.

46. Sucheta Mazumdar, "What Happened to the Women," in *Asian Pacific Islander Women: A Historical Anthology*, eds. Shirley Hune and Gail Nomura (New York: NYU Press, 2003).

47. For further discussion of the role of U.S. women of color in the Bengali peddler network, see Vivek Bald, *Bengali Harlem and the Lost Histories of South Asian America* (Cambridge, Mass.: Harvard University Press, 2013), 74–76.

CHAPTER 2

Racial Interstitiality and the Anxieties of the "Partly Colored"

Representations of Asians under Jim Crow

Leslie Bow

> [W]hen you look at the Chinese stores down by the river, you get a totally different picture. The[y]'re right down in nigger town, and what goes on there, God only knows. When those yellow people first came here, nobody really know what to think, but some of them have proved themselves, and we've accepted them, but those that stayed down with the niggers, well *we just let them go.*
> —White informant in Mississippi, 1966, emphasis mine.[1]

In the delta, home of the blues and Muddy Waters, cooks are sizzling catfish and collards and crayfish every day and night. But you don't expect to find those home chefs stir-frying them or steaming them in a giant backyard wok."[2] So begins a feature about the Chow family of Clarksdale, Mississippi, titled "East Meets South at a Delta Table: Chinese-Americans bring the tastes of their ancestors down home." The hook for the reader's attention is based on simple juxtaposition—Crayfish? Woks?—that trades upon a stereotypical belief in the South's lack of cosmopolitanism. The unexpected hybridity nevertheless produces what is perceived to be quintessentially American: immigrant ingenuity and adaptability. Or so we are led to believe as the triumphant Chows descend upon Washington to demonstrate the aforementioned stir-fry on the National Mall.

In their presumed aberration, the Chows are made to represent American normativity albeit through a circuitous route. They are only representable insofar as their eccentricity is both asserted as a point of interest (Chinese who say "y'all") and reinscribed within dominant values and expectations (Ms. Chow is a finalist in the contest to find a new image for Betty Crocker). This progression is subtly reenacted within the feature as well; it introduces the Chows' backstory, how they came to be in Mississippi, as it is enmeshed in Reconstruction-era politics and racialized labor competition only to end with the image of three generations linking hands around the table to say grace. The radical implications of Chinese presence in a region dominated by black-white relations and the sedimented class hierarchies of the plantation system become resolved by the Chows' use as model citizens; they exemplify adaptation, proliferation, and belief in divine providence. A tall order for a piece about cooking, indeed.

Such a portrayal reproduces a dominant narrative governing American racial representation since the Civil Rights Movement: a progressive chronology of racial uplift that buttresses a liberal vision of ethnic incorporation. The use of Asians as evidence of this movement has become ubiquitous in popular culture; hence, the simultaneously laudatory and derogatory designation of Asian Americans as "honorary whites" or "model minorities." Thus, the judgment, "the Chinese in Mississippi play the white man's game better than white folks do," elicited by an African American informant during Robert Seto Quan's research for *Lotus among the Magnolias: The Mississippi Chinese* (1982), prefigures a dominant representation of Asians in the United States.[3] Nevertheless, for this southern community during the era of formal segregation, the ability to "play the white man's game" took on *literal* stakes.

How did Jim Crow accommodate a supposed "third" race, those individuals and communities who did not fit into a cultural and legal system predicated on the binary distinction between colored and white? Put another way, where did the Asian sit on the segregated bus? W. E. B. DuBois's famous pronouncement that "the problem of the Twentieth Century is the problem of the color-line" could not prognosticate on which side of the line an Asian, for example, might fall.[4] The very metaphor admits no middle, or interstitial, space. How could a buffer, a potential DMZ of indeterminate race relations, exist within a context where it was said that even days of the week were segregated?[5] Unlike apartheid in South Africa, segregation in the American South made no provision for gradations of color. Sociologist Max Handman noted in 1930 that American society had "no social technique for handling partly colored races. We have a place for the Negro and a place for the white man: the Mexican is not a Negro, and the white man refuses him an equal status."[6] Brewton Berry's informal, 1963 study of triracial peoples in the South, *Almost White*, speculates that a mixed-blood Indian's racial status under segregation "falls somewhere along a continuum, between nearly white on the one hand and nearly Negro on the other."[7] Yet, how can the space between "partly colored" and "almost white" be maintained within a binary caste system?

James Loewen's influential 1972 study, *The Mississippi Chinese: Between Black and White*, offers one such answer. He argues that when faced with a culture that provided no accommodation for a "third" race, the Chinese engineered a shift in status from colored to white in the course of one generation. The Chinese in Mississippi, Loewen claims, "worked systematically . . . in order to rise from Negro to white status" in the period following World War II, and once crossing over, left "the black world behind without a second glance."[8] While the Supreme

Court ruling, *Gong Lum v. Rice*, had formally established the colored status of the Chinese in Mississippi in 1927, by the time that sociologist Loewen arrived to do fieldwork in 1967 the Chinese were apparently card-carrying white people—or at least they were according to the "W" on their driver's licenses. His book-length study attempts to show what transpired between the years 1941 and 1966, the twilight of formal segregation. What he postulates is an Asian community's shift from reviled caste to what one could call less reviled caste, but what he chooses to call, perhaps for lack of a better word, "white." Loewen attempts to account for the shift not simply by positing acculturation to white norms and values as intrinsic to the processes of Americanization. Rather, he depicts a community who, not content with their social address as "colored," began to engineer a "transition from near-black to near-white" as a response to segregation's racial dichotomy.[9] This narrative—with differing prophecies and conclusions—is repeated in a number of studies of this community. The resulting archive provides empirical evidence of the ways in which cultural ambiguity became resolved.[10]

I want to take Loewen's thesis in a different direction to engage representations of this southern community in ways that suggest why Asian Americans have become such a fruitful site for uncovering national ambivalences about race, class, and equal opportunity. When I cast my gaze on Asians in the South, my intent is not to replicate Loewen's significant work by focusing on the *historical* process of how the shift occurred—which has to do with a certain kind of modeling back of cultural norms including—ironically—the tacit agreement to respect the color line. Rather, I'm interested in what lies in excess of this population's purportedly successful transition. What does it mean to claim "near whiteness" for a population formerly known as "colored"? What becomes erased in its construction, and to what extent do those occlusions disrupt the naturalized teleology of racial advancement that governs American race talk?

The putative status shift of the Chinese in Mississippi represents one resolution to what I call racial interstitiality, the space between normative structures of power. If the context of American apartheid codified what continues to be the dominant narrative of American race relations, the black-white binary, what of the space that lies within its interstices? Edna Bonacich's concept of "middleman minorities," those who "occupy an intermediate rather than a low-status position," speaks to the tri-part class divisions that arose under colonialism as nonnative, diasporic ethnic minorities filled the gap between indigenous peoples and colonial elites.[11] The context of Asians in the South might thus be said to reflect the American version of what Avtar Brah calls "the colonial sandwich": "Europeans at the top, Asians in the middle, and Africans at the bottom."[12] To what extent does the interstitial begin to suture those relations? To what extent does the existence of intermediacy need to be repressed for the smooth functioning of that racial hierarchy? The period of legally enforced segregation only exaggerated and codified the racial hierarchy existing elsewhere within the nation and outside it;

in this sense, southern regionalism is not, to invoke Richard Gray's terms, an aberration to the nation, but a site where the implications of racial classification played out in heightened relief.[13] The emergent status of the Asian under formal segregation thus suggests that what appears to be unaccommodated within a system of relations may serve to unveil the structures and interests that support it—even as such communities did not offer a primary challenge to the system of segregation. Nevertheless, the "partly colored races" are potentially productive sites for understanding Jim Crow's investments and the meanings accrued to "white" and "black"—or, more appropriately, "not white" and "not black."

Loewen has suggested that Chinese transition to "near whiteness" in Mississippi was enabled, among other things, by their willing disassociation from African Americans—and, ironically, from whites as well: "The final step [of status elevation] was for the Chinese to convince Caucasians that they too believed in racial integrity and had no intention of mixing with anyone. . . . [T]he Chinese simultaneously denied that they married Negroes and explicitly vowed that they would never marry whites in the future."[14] The paradox of caste elevation was that it seemed predicated on respecting Jim Crow's primary distinction. Thus, as revealed in my epigraph, the "acceptance" of "those yellow people" depended upon upholding the color line in both directions or suffering the consequences of historical oblivion, of being "just let go." The theoretical implications of his findings for comparative ethnic studies are suggested not simply by the metaphor of racial triangulation as the documentary film that took those findings as a script, *Mississippi Triangle*, suggests. Rather, they suggest a spatial metaphor that emphasizes the condition of being *between* the terms that define a dominant social hierarchy, the condition of interstitiality. Thus, Gary Okihiro's ontological question, "Is Yellow Black or White?" might be reconceived: what does the intermediate space between white normativity and black abjection look like?[15]

Like *The Mississippi Chinese*, a number of works in American Studies have engaged this as an empirical question: Karen Blu's *The Lumbee Problem* (1979); Neil Foley's *The White Scourge* (1997); and Clara Jean Kim's *Bitter Fruit* (2000), to name a few.[16] But, what is particularly suggestive about representations of Asians in the segregated South, and of this Chinese community in particular, is the way in which social status becomes measured within the black-white dichotomy through degrees of distance or proximity. This historical process occasioned by Jim Crow's legal regime underscores the very interplay between likeness and difference inherent within subject formation, as Judith Butler has theorized in regard to gender: "Identifying with a gender under contemporary regimes of power involves identifying with a set of norms that are and are not realizable, and whose power and status precede the identifications by which they are insistently approximated. This 'being a man' and this 'being a woman' are internally unstable affairs. They are always beset by ambivalence precisely because there is a cost in every identification, the loss of some other set of identifications, the forcible approximation of a norm one never chooses."[17] Locating gender as the "forcible approximation" of normative conceptions of male and female offers a ready analogy to race, particularly in the heightened context of race relations under formal segregation. In this case, racial identity must emerge out of a prescribed identification with the "internally unstable" categories, "colored" and "white," forcing the inverse process of identification into relief: that of disavowal. The "near whiteness" of the Chinese in the South—their caste elevation—required a dual engagement: both white identification and black disavowal.

As Toni Morrison has noted, black abjection lies at the foundation of national community. The emergent status of immigrant groups is negotiated not merely through an engagement with the dominant, but through the repudiation of those who lack social power. "A hostile posture toward resident blacks must be struck at the Americanizing door before it will open," Morrison argues. "The public is asked to accept American black as the common denominator in each conflict between an immigrant and a job or between a wannabe and status."[18] A wave of academic studies highlights this dynamic in order to challenge the historicity of European "whiteness" in the U.S.—hence the proliferation of the provocative titles that intend to question any notion of naturalized white identity: to wit, *How the Jews Became White Folks, How the Irish Became White, Are Italians White?*[19] These titles are reflective of what has become known as "critical white studies," works such as David Roediger's *The Wages of Whiteness* (1991), Alexander Saxton's *The Rise and Fall of the White Republic* (1990), Ruth Frankenburg's *White Women, Race Matters* (1993), Ian F. Haney Lopez's *White by Law* (1996), and Mike Hill's *After Whiteness* (2004).[20]

Robyn Wiegman locates three strains of thought within "Whiteness Studies": "[T]he race traitor school (which advocates the abolition of whiteness through white disaffiliation from race privilege), the 'white trash' school (which analyzes the racialization of the permanent poor in order to demonstrate the otherness of whiteness within), and the class solidarity school (which rethinks the history of working-class struggle as the preamble to forging new cross-racial alliances)."[21] One tenet of the latter is that white privilege is the compensation for the labor subordination of the European immigrant working class. Yet it can only be realized through its antithesis, the inverse of Zora Neale Hurston's recognition, "I feel most colored when I am thrown against a sharp white background."[22] The "class solidarity school" establishes how a group's apprehension of and collusion with (a white/black) racial hierarchy is intrinsic to the process of ethnic acculturation. Such scholarship has transfigured the understanding of race: it is conflictual rather than self-evident, juridically legislated rather than organic, state-imposed or legitimated in addition to collectively imagined, contextual rather than timeless. It has provided one answer to the first part of the narrator's musing in Chester Himes's novel, *If He Hollers Let Him Go*: "I began wondering when white people started getting white—or rather, when they started losing it."[23] But to push the borders of inquiry further, it could be claimed that any number of communities feel "most white" when "thrown against" a sharp black background—even those whose whiteness never became naturalized.

In a self-critique of his book, *The Wages of Whiteness*, Roediger has suggested that the "weakness in recent histories of white racial formation" was that they contributed to the "tendency to see racial formation in Black and white."[24] My intent here, however, is not to provide a triangulated "corrective" to critical white studies by emphasizing the role of Asian Americans in the consolidation of whiteness. Rather, if one could say that the Irish, Italians, or Jews represent the "success" of white identification as it translated into both state and cultural recognition *and* an affective though invisibly normative identity, what of those who failed? By "failed," I mean those who remain within the gap between white identification and black disavowal, who may have taken on the prejudices of the elite without ever gaining entry into their society—that is, those who remain, in Handman's terms, "partly colored." In contrast to such European groups, the Asian's supposed caste rise can be characterized only as partial, as a registered incompletion, a "near whiteness."

My intent is not to add to the empirical evidence of in-between status—or to show that there are varying degrees of whiteness. Rather, I want to suggest that this registered incompletion is reflected in the discourses that have sought to represent interstitial status. Looking at the other end of the spectrum, "failure" has different connotations: representations of Asians under segregation reflect the anxious, contradictory, and, I would argue, incomplete attempts to convince of African American disassociation. As Loewen suggests, caste elevation is dependent upon repressing a history of intimacy with African Americans, yet figures of Chinese-black amalgamation are never wholly buried or repressed. Representations of the Mississippi Chinese in particular reveal the fraying edges of accepting whiteness as the ego ideal coupled with the failure to disassociate completely from African Americans, the simultaneity of being oppressor and oppressed.

Casting one's gaze on the interstitial reveals not only the anxieties of the "partly colored," but also of representation itself. I want to focus on these anxieties as they appear within academic and popular cultural depictions of Asians in the South: Jonathan Daniels's memoir, *A Southerner Discovers the South* (1938); the documentary film, *Mississippi Triangle* (1984) by Christine Choy, Worth Long, and Allan Siegel; Ruthanne McCunn Lum's *Chinese American Portraits: Personal Histories 1828–1988* (1988); Choong Soon Kim's *An Asian Anthropologist in the South* (1977); and Judy Yung's *Chinese Women of America: A Pictorial History* (1986).[25] In surprising ways, the class and caste position of the Asian in the South is at times mediated through representations of gender and sexuality, underscoring the interaction between axes of difference. My focus lies on the jarring moments and incommensurabilities that attend depictions of racial status in these portrayals of Asians in the Deep South. Interestingly, the same anxieties of representation evident in early attempts to fix the status of this interstitial community reemerge in subsequent depictions of the postsegregationist moment. The anxieties of the "partly colored" are thus revealed in ruptures to logic, in discursive contradiction, and in the spaces between visual and narrative signification—in short, within the *failures* to convince of idealized status on the part of both interstitial subjects and those who seek to represent them.

Asian Interstitiality

The legal status of the Chinese as "colored" was formalized in the 1927 Supreme Court ruling, *Gong Lum v. Rice*, which assigned members of the "Mongolian race" to "colored" schools. In 1924, Gong Lum brought suit against school trustees in Mississippi district court charging that his daughter, Martha, had been unfairly prevented from attending Rosedale Consolidated High School where the student body was exclusively white. Upon the court's decision in her favor, school officials appealed to the state supreme court, which reversed the decision. In upholding the Mississippi Supreme Court's decision against the plaintiff as the case went before the U.S. Supreme Court, Chief Justice Taft asserted that as a "member of the Mongolian or yellow race," the plaintiff was "not entitled to attend the schools provided by law in the State of Mississippi for children of the white or Caucasian race."[26] "The question here," Taft wrote, "is whether a Chinese citizen of the United States is denied equal protection of the laws when he is classed among the colored races and furnished facilities for education equal to that offered to all, whether white, brown, yellow, or black. Were this a new question, it would call for very full argument and consideration, but we think that it is the same question which has been many times decided."[27] The decision both fixed the intermediate racial status of the Chinese in the South and was the occasion to affirm the constitutionality of *Plessy v. Ferguson* (1896). This use of the Chinese in the affirmation of "separate but equal" is indeed ironic as the dissenting opinion to *Plessy* invoked Chinese privileges under segregation. "A Chinaman can ride in the same passenger coach with white citizens of the United States," wrote Justice Harlan in his dissent, "while citizens of the black race . . . who are entitled, by law, to participate in the political control of the State and nation . . . are yet declared to be criminals, liable to imprisonment, if they ride in a public coach occupied by citizens of the white race."[28]

That seeming privilege notwithstanding, sociologist Robert O'Brien prophesied in 1941, "[A]s the number of Chinese in the Delta increases it will become more difficult to maintain an intermediate position between the Negro on one hand and the whites on the other. . . . [A] study of the relationship of the Chinese, whites, and Negroes [in the Mississippi Delta] seems to point inescapably toward an inferior position of the Chinese in the southern communities."[29] While recognizing the pressures of intermediacy that occasioned such a prophecy, twenty years later, however, others were coming to the opposite conclusion. Despite *Gong Lum* and an earlier association with African American labor, third-generation Chinese Americans were, George Rummel III concludes from fieldwork done in 1964, "trying to live down their previous image" and had formed an "almost exclusive social and economic identification with the dominant white community rather than with the lower-class Negro community."[30] As if to confirm that Asian identification with the dominant culture in the South is articulated via white approximation, filmmaker Rene Tajima Peña interviews a pair of aging Filipina sisters in New Orleans while on the road to find "Asian America" in the 1990s for the documentary, *My America (. . . or Honk if You Love Buddha)*. In the course of recounting their pasts as belles of the French Quarter, the sisters cheerfully assert their white status as it is confirmed on their birth certificates and by their schooling, romantic partners, and the cemeteries that house their ancestors: "Filipinos were not considered a race other than white. Because Spain owned the Philippines. So they were just considered white."[31]

The emergent class status of racialized individuals no doubt generated southern discomfort in a white population confronted with the specter of the Asian professional who had to be interpolated into the elaborate codes of southern etiquette. One catches a glimpse into how the incommensurability between race and class status was reconciled—or rather, failed to be reconciled—within the incidental depiction of "four Chinamen" in Jonathan Daniels's 1938 memoir/travelogue, *A Southerner Discovers the South*. Here, the invocation of sexual deviance queers the testimony about the Chinese status rise and functions as one anomalous moment that cannot be wholly reconciled within the narrative of Chinese American arrival. Daniels describes a casual exchange on a ferry crossing the Mississippi River:

> A fat and effeminate man got out of the sedan in which he rode with
> four Chinamen.
> I looked at him with careful distaste but I asked, "Tell me, what do
> the Chinese do for a living in Mississippi? Do they farm?"
> He looked back at his companions. "Oh, no, they're business men. And
> that one yonder is a preacher, a Presbyterian preacher. Oh, they're fine
> gentlemen." His eyes filled with a pleasant dream. "You ought to see a
> Chinese boy I know. He's just fifteen. I tease him. And he just smiles so
> sweet, so sweet!"
> He mimicked a monstrous coyness. And he pursed, in imitation of
> the China boy's smiling, a mouth like the sessile, fleshy suckers on the
> tentacles of an octopus.
> "I'm sure of it," I said, "Excuse me."[32]

Here, the status of these Chinese Americans as "fine gentlemen" is not only overtly confirmed, but validated circumstantially: they travel in the company of a white man. But, their professional status is marked as grotesque and unnatural as it becomes grafted onto the queerness of the messenger.

Both the aping of femininity by the white man and the aping of gentility by his Chinese companions inspire the curiosity and distaste of the white, middle-class speaker. His response indicates how the "fat and effeminate" man's status as white—and indeed, given his bestial description, as a *man*—is demoted by his presumed homosexuality. His pedophilic desire—he is not quite right—renders him the fit companion of the not quite white. The class status of those formerly known as "colored" becomes queered and thereby challenged: through associative intimacy it is not true gentility, only a "monstrous imitation." In this portrayal, the bourgeois status of the Chinese is only an approximation revealing how social status is multiply mediated: color triangulated by queerness emerges as a class sign. Here, anxiety about the middle-class person of color becomes grafted onto other signs of difference. The "careful distaste" that their professional status inspires, and here is expressed by contiguity, must be distinguished from the violent repercussions suffered by middle-class African Americans and other "partly colored" people in the South.

These representations attest to the ways in which racial ambiguity became adjudicated, disciplined, rationalized or subject to divination in disparate cultural forums; what remains constant from the 1920s through the 1990s are the narratives in which this interstitial community was placed: they were represented as either backsliding into blackness or extolled as exemplary citizens "accepted" by southern whites. As Loewen has suggested, the community's repudiation of African Americans (and those Chinese who were intimate with them) was crucial to its status rise, demonstrating their apprehension of what Ariela Gross has called, "race by association," determining racial status by one's associates.[33] While I do not doubt that those acts of repudiation existed in multiple forms, what I would like to question here is how successful they were. That is, it would seem that the repression of cross-racial intimacy within the discourse of Asian American subjects and those who represent them is itself only approximate.

Eruptions of "Funk" in *Mississippi Triangle*

By the early twentieth century, Chinese Exclusion laws and their gendered precursor, the 1875 Page Act, had severely restricted the immigration of Chinese women to the U.S., truncating the growth of Chinese communities across the country. At the same time, Mississippi's antimiscegenation laws expressly forbade intermarriages between a "white person and negro *or Mongolian*" (emphasis mine).[34] In looking at interracial marriage between Chinese and blacks, then, documentary filmmakers Choy, Long, and Siegel recognized that they had a visceral template for depicting Chinese caste movement: the transition from black to white intermarriage. To introduce this racial chronology, the film *Mississippi Triangle* gives symbolic centrality to the figure of Arlee Hen, an elderly Afro-Chinese woman. The film grants her prominence not only in its frequent return to her narration, but also in her use as a framing device. Beyond her value as an informant imbued with privileged access to the history of Chinese origins in the Delta, the filmmakers clearly found in her a symbol of black/Chinese amalgamation, the embodiment of the original taboo. This proof of intimacy between two "colored" races had to be repressed in order to facilitate Chinese status shift, but to what extent does her representation exceed its intended use?

Both Loewen and the filmmakers acknowledge Hen's exile from the Chinese American community in the Delta. As Loewen notes in a caption to her photo included in the 1988 edition of his book, "[Arlee Hen] was living in Greenville when I did my fieldwork, but because her mother was black, the Chinese community never mentioned her, and I learned of her lonely existence only when Third World Newsreel filmed her just before her death in 1982." As Christine Choy writes, the "discovery" of Hen was policed by the community to the extent that the crew had to concoct an elaborate ruse to gain access to her without the awareness of the community:

> [The Chinese American community] refused to take us to the black-Chinese areas. No one wanted us to talk to the elderly black-Chinese woman who became a major character in the film. So we made an announcement in Greenville that we were leaving town. Word traveled quickly from Jackson, Mississippi to Memphis, Tennessee. All the gossips spread the word. We went down to Jackson, spent the night, and then sneaked back into Greenville. We parked the car in an alley behind the woman's house, and stayed in her home for two days of filming. The Chinese community didn't know we had any relationship with this woman. When they saw the final film they were very upset.[35]

In documenting Hen's communal repudiation, the story lends credibility to Loewen's assertion that the majority of Chinese in the Delta was white-identified and actively disavowed the existence of interracial marriage between blacks and Chinese as part of their bid for acceptance among the white elite. In a subtle parallel, with its hints of skullduggery and doubling back in the dead of night, the story resembles those of Civil Rights activists trying to do their work under threat of violence by white supremacists, only in this case it is Chinese Americans whose disapproval—and implied power—provokes such machinations. What the story also conveys is Hen's significance to the filmmakers who went to such lengths to secure her interview.

The film chooses to use Arlee Hen as a reminder of the ignominious class and color roots of the community. A symbol of black-Chinese amalgamation, Hen exists, in the words of Toni Morrison, as that eruption of "Funk" that disturbs the dearly won near-white status of the pillars of the Chinese community. In Morrison's conception, such eruptions represent the unwelcome reemergence of the residues of a past strategically left behind. Emphasizing the domestic context of upward rise, she critiques those class-conscious African American women who work assiduously to cultivate "thrift, patience, high morals, and good manners" while subduing—however incompletely—the "base" passions that demarcate the line between "colored" and "nigger": "Whenever it erupts, this Funk, they wipe it away; where it crusts, they dissolve it; wherever it drips, flowers, or clings, they find it and fight it until it dies. They fight this battle all the way to the grave. The laugh that is a little too loud; the enunciation a little too round; the gesture a little too generous."[36] For the Chinese, Hen represents one such eruption; racial amalgamation is a class sign that lingers. Nevertheless, the film's staging of Hen's pariah status as proof that the community's racism is somewhat undermined by an alternative assessment of her place in the community: in *Chinese American Portraits: Personal Histories 1828–1988*, Ruthanne McCunn Lum reports that Hen worked in the most prominent Chinese grocery store in Greenville, Mississippi. While focusing on Hen's triple ostracism, McCunn Lum nonetheless notes that "Arlee and her sister, . . . were both accepted by the local Chinese community and never left Greenville."[37] The disjunction bespeaks a potential rupture in the narration of Chinese caste elevation: to what extent is the disavowal of African American intimacy (Hen's "lonely existence") a matter of public self-representation to the outsider, whether filmmaker or scholar?

Throughout the film, she testifies to discrimination against blacks and Chinese perpetuated by whites even though, ironically, one of the film's few "integrated" scenes occurs at Hen's birthday celebration in which, bedridden and frail, she receives black and white well-wishers and congregants led by a black minister. In effect, the party is filmed as if it were a funeral; Hen's supine body lies in state to receive those who pay their last respects. It is as if the tri-racial society can be so sanguine in this scene precisely because she—and what she represents—is likely to die soon. All can afford to be gracious at the demise of those lingering signs of a past intimacy.

The film pointedly addresses southern Asian racism via Hen's actual death in ways that bolster Loewen's thesis on Chinese American crossover—at the same time, I would argue that Hen's use in the film can be said to question it. At the end of film, we see a coffin being lowered into the ground. Hen's voice rises over the image of a field in spring, her words depicted in subtitles for emphasis: "I couldn't be buried in a Chinese cemetery . . . I'm mixed with Negro, you know . . . and I couldn't be buried in a Chinese cemetery." Choosing to end with this image of burial, the film achieves multiple purposes: it signals the "end" of the community as a natural conclusion to the testimony of Chinese Americans, who express the financial insupportability of the small grocery businesses and prophesy the next generation's out-migration. More importantly, what is being buried is evidence of amalgamation now lost to near-whiteness. Choosing to close on these words, the filmmakers succeed in conveying that Hen's ostracism represents a collective repudiation of the community's previous racial status—that past is being buried with her.

Nevertheless, this figure of miscegenation does not remain underground: Hen's voice, and with it the community's "colored" past, pops out of the grave to haunt what the film has previously inscribed, albeit ambivalently, as Chinese American crossover to white norms and values. In refusing to "just let go" of a figure like Hen, the filmmakers ensure that black-Chinese intimacy, the origin of community, is not erased. The film pointedly refuses to mark Hen as an abject figure and sees to it that, even in death, she has the last word. Nevertheless, the only overt testimony of Chinese racism that she makes in the film is given prominence. Thus, the film has it both ways: it documents the crossover at the same time that it tethers the crossover to the community's deliberate repression of the Chinese who, in excess of Loewen's thesis, became black. In allowing for eruptions of "Funk" in biracial Arlee Hen, the film succeeds in marking white status as contingent—it does not dispute the fact that white-identification has occurred, but it does mark that status as tenuous. In addition, the penultimate sequence witnesses three separate racial spheres in the Delta: a white country club and bar, black workers in a fish-processing plant, and a Chinese American wedding. This visualization of the ongoing processes of segregation is certainly ironic in the context of the film's chronological progression depicting Chinese crossover: in effect, it wants to show the Chinese as de facto white people without ever showing them *with* white people.

This absence produces a rupture similar to that in Loewen's study: the "middlemen" have taken on the prejudices of the elite without ever gaining entry into their society. Community reaction to the film reveals a similar slippage indicative of approximate status, the anxieties of interstitiality: when the film premiered in town, Chinese Americans were not happy with it. Rather than being angry about their portrayal as racists mouthing the pieties of a white elite, they were upset that they were not portrayed as white enough. That is, in the peculiar tangle of class-as-race logic, they were not represented as being more prosperous or successful. As Adria Bernardi reports, "Most said they didn't think it portrayed the progress of the Chinese Americans. Some objected because they thought it left the impression that Chinese are linked more closely with the black community than the white. Certainly the scenes in small country stores and interviews with people of Chinese and African American ancestry did not sit well with the Chinese audience, most of whom were successful merchants."[38] This response conveys an inherent duality: on one level, in expressing anxiety about black association as class demotion, the reaction lends credibility to sociological claims of their white, middle-class identification. At the same time, it reveals the degree to which they feel the incompletion of status elevation: the fact that it needs to be publicly validated testifies to its fragility. This vulnerability is likewise uncovered in Robert Seto Quan's fieldwork done over a decade later. "In nearly every conversation, the Delta Chinese of the first two generations spoke of the respect shown them by the whites," he writes. "Such emphasis may mean that some Chinese have doubts as to how the whites feel about them."[39] The fact that white association needs to be publicized and affirmed bespeaks both its desirability and the awareness of its instability. The need for reassurance unveils tenuousness; the claim of status shift, postulated under segregation, remains incomplete.

These discursive ruptures emerge out of an inherent contradiction: the move to document the transference of white status to an "outsider" population proceeds against the common-sense awareness that people of color can never "be" white. This contradiction presented the filmmakers with a visual conundrum: how to depict the community's "whiteness" when confronted with Chinese faces, especially if its achievement means embodying what is normative and, hence, invisible. The disjunction reveals itself in the rhetoric of both researcher and informant. As one college-age, southern Chinese American remarks in an interview with Quan in the late 1970s, "The whites will accept you at every level, but not socially."[40] The contradiction of the statement is readily apparent: if whites do not accept you socially, then they don't accept you. "Near whiteness" is revealed to be an inadequately blunt instrument to define the nuances of social status. Loewen marks the incommensurability between racial classification and equal treatment: "Although they still do not enjoy full equality, the Chinese are definitely accorded white status, affirmed for example by the "W" in the appropriate blank on their driver's licenses."[41] His statement questions the determinants of white classification above and beyond the study's self-conscious examination of its artificiality: in other words, what is the value of "white status" if it does not ensure full equality? That is, "whiteness" (or proximity to it) is not an independent indicator of social status and does not guarantee entry among social elites. Each citizen's constitutional guarantee of equal rights, his presumed abstract universality under the law, does not obviate the material enactments of racial hierarchy attending the citizen's embodiment. Such dissonance in this case points to the disjunction between the state's (or, rather, the oligarchy's) interpellation of the Chinese as "white" as bestowed by a single capital letter on state identification documents and the social practice of whiteness. Thus, even as Chinese American informants attest to the privilege of inhabiting an invisible norm—their ability to avoid being targeted as the objects of racial violence, ridicule, ostracism, or discourtesy, for instance—their testimony reveals ambivalence.

Scholars are themselves not immune from rationalizing their own treatment within an unjust system. In documenting his fieldwork in *An Asian Anthropologist in the South: Field Experiences with Blacks, Indians, and Whites* (1977) and elsewhere, Korean American anthropologist Choong Soon Kim poses the question, "Had a proverbial 'southern hospitality' been extended to Asians?"[42] His answer simultaneously acknowledges racism as it is expressed via social etiquette at the same time that he negates the possibility that he himself has been a target of it: "The early Chinese in the Mississippi delta might have a different answer, but most Asians, including myself, who came to the South recently, would have a positive answer to the question."[43] While one can grant the autonomy of the individual's mediation of his own experience, Kim's affirmation of the courtesies whites show him provokes the same uneasy questioning that underlies those expressed by the Chinese in the Delta: "Despite my observations of racial discrimination exhibited toward others, I wish to emphasize that I have never been subjected to it during my ten years of living in the South. It is true, though, that southerners are more openly ambivalent about foreigners. . . . Sometimes, whites have refused to shake my hand or to have close contact. . . . However, these incidents should not be interpreted in terms of racial discrimination. Such curiosities in relation to foreigners are rather natural."[44] Kim's analysis of his own racial status in the South points to the inherent unreliability of the ethnographer as ethnographic subject; there is simply no alternative interpretation that can logically supplant the one that he chooses to deny—he is snubbed because of his race. What his testimony reveals is that one cannot enter an embedded system of social relations without developing elaborate mechanisms as a hedge against internalizing one's inferior status. The psychic violence that segregation enacts appears in the form of denial and rationalization. Both are readily apparent within the discourse of the willfully unknowing subaltern subject in ways that undermine any uncomplicated understanding of his status, even at the moment when he wants to render it straightforwardly.

In highlighting what lies in excess of the subject's apprehension of the social meaning of his own experience—even one who makes his living analyzing the social behaviors of others—I do not mean merely to substitute one presumably more authentic narrative for another, in this case, one in which the evidence of racial oppression counters the assertion of its attenuation. Rather, the pressures of representing incompletion produce a contestatory counter-narrative existing in dialectical tension with the narrative at hand. Here, the narrative situating Asian Americans as a vehicle for measuring and affirming racial progress generates its own excess at the moment of enunciation. At times, the duality of representation that creates both dissonance and the ever-presence of a counter-narrative is overtly acknowledged; contradicting points of view are portrayed side-by-side in competition and irresolution. Historian Judy Yung's representation of the Asian American experience in the South engages this strategy; in *Chinese Women of America*, the contradiction produced by the simple question, "How were Asians treated in the Deep South?" must be resolved by the reader-viewer who is confronted with two versions of the Asian southern belle: a cheerleader and a debutante.

While the parallel images might speak to the assimilationist success of the Chinese, the captions deliberately introduce dissonance between the image and the text. Whereas one caption attests to the fact that the girl from Arkansas "experienced no prejudice," the other caption cites its subject from Mississippi as saying, "We were made fun of all the time . . . [and had to] deal with those who could not totally understand us as Chinese."[45] Such a schizy division generates no comment in this pictorial history; rather, it merely asks the reader/viewer to process the contradiction as a result of individual experience—or, perhaps of the difference between Mississippi and Arkansas.

Yung's representation introduces an inherent duality in the ways one can read history by presenting the viewer-reader with the incommensurability between two women's experiences as well as between the verbal testimony and the image. Both photographs ask the viewer to infer a relationship between each girl's class position and femininity and her level of integration. While both are depicted in poses of heightened civic presence—the school and church as twin stages for the production of public femininity—according to no apparent logic, feminine sexuality deflects race-baiting for one but not the other. Yung's choice to represent the community in a disjunctive parallel partially undermines situating the photographs as evidence of Chinese American class attainment in the South via the communal rituals of womanhood. While the cheerleader confirms a salutary racial invisibility as a testament to achieving white normativity, the other provides evidence of the obverse. The photograph captures the latter subject side-by-side with her white female peers as if to imply that she is their equal, but her accompanying testimony betrays what the photograph makes obvious: she is different. Rather than attempt to reconcile the two experiences, Yung places them in dialectical tension.

The "Death" of Segregation?

To what extent does the duality of such a representation question the narrative of progressive modernity as it is affixed to this "rising" interstitial population? At one level, such contradictions succeed in questioning a broader narrative based on a pre- and post-1954 periodization, a before-and-after national snapshot that locates the end of segregation as the dividing line between racial ignorance and enlightenment. Because one difference between the study and the film *Mississippi Triangle* is its historical address, the filmmakers attribute Chinese status elevation not, like Loewen, to behind-the-scenes concessions to white oligarchy, but to the Civil Rights Movement. For example, one Chinese American public official—his position itself a testimony to change—testifies, "The Civil Rights Movement helped the Chinese to attain certain status among the white world, more or less, whereas we didn't have anything to gain in the black world because they didn't have nothing for us to step in to."[46] Nevertheless, the film perhaps unintentionally presents a more complicated and inherently ambiguous picture of post–Civil Rights race relations in the Delta and its mediation of a segregated past in ways that question a progressive chronology, which can often conflate the end of state-enforced segregation with the end of racism. Yet that historical cusp occludes a more fragile boundary between past and present, a fragility that is disturbed, as I have highlighted here, by discursive dissonance and contradiction. After establishing that the demise of Jim Crow created opportunity via education, the film cuts to a high school pep rally as the site of integration, as a symbol of the fruit of civil rights activism.

As if to support Loewen's comment in a new afterword to his study that the 1980 Greenville High School yearbook is an "integrationists' dream," the camera pans the bleachers of a Delta high school to give evidence of black and white fellowship in this "new" era of race relations. The cheerleading squad, the marching band, the pep rally performers, and the general assembly all display blacks and whites (and a few strategically placed Chinese Americans) mutually involved in constructing school spirit. The sequence carries the weight of the film's suggestion that public education was the white supremacists' last line of defense. Yet this sequence, designed to convey at least the surface-level success of desegregation, ends up witnessing something beyond the filmmakers' overt intent. Serendipitously, the crew witnesses a student pantomime that is itself highly suggestive when read in the context of Chinese crossover to "near-white" status.

After establishing shots of interracial unity, the film briefly depicts a performance being enacted at the rally: a mock funeral complete with coffin, distraught mourners dressed in black, and a minister of ceremonies. After calling for silence, the student playing the preacher ponderously intones over intermittent cheering, "We have gathered here, my children, on this very sorrowful occasion to pay our last respects to our dearly, *dearly* departed School Spirit of 1982." His discourse is rudely interrupted by the presumed corpse who, to the horror of the mourners and delight of those in the bleachers, leaps from the coffin. The "Spirit," a girl made up in ghostly white, scampers around the floor of the basketball court only to be chased down by the funeral-goers who, to the glee of the crowd, catch her, hoist her aloft, and triumphantly bear her back toward the coffin. The scene reverses melancholic mourning: the lost love object's restoration erupts, in Anne Cheng's terms, as pathological euphoria.[47] The scene confronts the viewer with a positive image of desegregation: boys and girls of all races together enacting the (very vocal) rituals of shared community. It intends to confirm the Civil Rights Movement's reach into the institutional state apparatus of the public school system. But, the sequence carries meaning beyond that intended by the students (school spirit is not dead) and by the film (segregation *is* dead).

But, what to make of this sequence in a film about the *Chinese American* transition from "colored" to honorary white, a sequence in which few Chinese Americans appear? Fittingly—or perhaps ironically—school spirit in the pageant is performed by an African American girl in what one could interpret as "whiteface." Intended merely to give her an otherworldly appearance as a ghost (significantly, not a corpse), the costume does not intend to invoke racial mimicry. Yet I would argue that her getup carries other resonance in a film *about* race relations and the attempts of a formerly "partly colored" community to elevate its status within the context of the historically saturated tradition of blackface minstrelsy in the South. In effect, the figure is a subtle reminder of the assimilative pressure to mimic whiteness as a condition of people of color's civic presence. Thought to be "dead" in this new era, this symbolic figure instead rises up to disturb the recently achieved interracial harmony. This ghost of the past cannot be fully contained and thus must be subject to capture: ironically, the film portrays African American students giving chase. The white paint cannot disguise the performer's blackness; whiteface becomes an offense to the interracial assembly. Yet there is inherent ambiguity in the film's witnessing of this meaning-saturated pageant: the sequence cuts off at the moment that the African American girl in whiteface is borne away amid the crowd's increasing hysteria. Is the Spirit of 1982 going to be restored to her grave to make way for the Spirit of 1983, for example, or does she symbolize a unity triumphantly resurrected and now displayed to former naysayers? In either case, the figure is positioned in the film ambiguously: as the crowd roars its approval, the students lay hands upon her either to restore her to her rightful death or to fete her as the embodiment of their solidarity, a solidarity then contingent on whiteface. The sequence at the high school ends moments later with a similar image: two male students, one black, the other white, are lifted above a crowd—presumably the football team—as a token of honor, their heroism on the field celebrated as a point of school pride and unity. The girl is made to fulfill a similar symbolic function, but—as with all women made to serve as symbolic boundary markers of community—she figures more ambivalently: is she a symbol of communal loathing (bury her) or the corporeal icon of their collectivity (parade her)?

Reading this visual pantomime as an instance of whiteface is certainly a subtle interpretation beyond the intent of the film. Yet the parallel does open up the space of farce and the performative. The newly acquired racial status of the Chinese in the Delta can likewise be read as merely "acting" white, a tomfoolery that deserves, like the School Spirit of 1982, to be buried as a retrograde artifact of the past. If touted as a sign of unity between "colored" and white, the performance reveals the uneven, incomplete transference of status, one that is so blotchy that the darker shades cannot help but show through. Designed to incite unity in a high school gymnasium, the students' staging of this mock funeral is certainly beside the point of the film's own self-conscious staging of race, but like the ghost itself, it pops out perhaps inopportunely to disrupt any uncomplicated or unironically celebratory portrayal of a post–Civil Rights landscape. The pep rally introduces the inherent ambiguity in the film's attempt to validate Loewen's findings on Chinese status shift by asking the viewer to consider what lies in excess of those findings, not only for the Chinese but for African Americans as well.

Comparative Race Relations and the Black-White Binary

In occupying a space of racial interstitiality, the Asian in the segregated South suggests a conceptual lens for reading comparative race relations. At one level, as the archive that I discuss here has shown, interstitial populations serve to unveil the mechanisms, political processes, and stakes behind the making of status. Cultural documents across disciplinary boundaries by Robert O'Brien, George Rummel III, Jonathan Daniels, James Loewen, Christine Choy et al., Ruthanne McCunn Lum, Judy Yung, Robert Seto Quan, and Choong Soon Kim explore the answer to the question, "How did the system of segregation accommodate the aberration of the neither-nor?" This archive reveals the ways in which both "colored" and "white" become enmeshed within the interplay of other oppositions that construct American norms, particularly those regarding class advancement: progressive vs. regressive; modern vs. feudal; prosperous vs. indigent. The context of Asian racial indeterminacy in this context highlights the emergence of subjects whose values and beliefs were either recognized as potentially worthy of incorporation—hence, "near whiteness"—or, conversely, unworthy.

In contributing to an empirical understanding of how segregation's "third space" was perceived and managed, such work represents a perhaps alternative southern archive. Yet, I would make clear that while resurrecting such an archive might contribute to a more multifaceted understanding of the South, my intent is the continued exploration of what Michael Kreyling has called one of the "old categories" of Southern Studies, that is, race in black and white.[48] But, I hope to contribute to the "new Southern studies" insofar as I situate southern regionalism here not as an exception to national processes, but as a site where the production of racial hierarchy is rendered in hyper-relief. In this sense, the South itself might be seen not, in the words of Houston Baker Jr. and Dana Nelson, as the "abjected regional Other" enabling American cohesion but, in effect, as a microcosm of the national.[49] Looking at Asians—or Latinos and American Indians—under segregation does not fundamentally challenge the South's historically embedded investment in a black-white binary, nor does it simply offer a pluralist corrective that prefigures the emergence of a more multicultural South. Rather, in the spirit of Baker's and Nelson's 1991 call for "a new Southern studies"—one echoed in Smith and Cohn's *Look Away! The U.S. South in New World Studies*—I would suggest that "aberrant" groups can be sites in which to explore the epistemological instability—or retrenchment—of Jim Crow itself, with particular relevance for the ways in which race in the United States continues to be read along a black-white continuum.[50]

As a model for Ethnic Studies, then, the concept of racial interstitiality emphasizes the tri-part, comparative nature of U.S. race relations. It highlights the antagonism (and coercion) underlying Toni Morrison's assertion that the Africanist presence underwrites immigrant acculturation. "Only when the lesson of racial estrangement [from African Americans] is learned" she writes, "is assimilation complete."[51] Yet for Asian immigrants formerly known as "colored," such assimilation is never complete; what I focus on here are the jarring moments that indicate its failure, what refuses to be buried. As I discuss, if one of the determinants of status is perceived to be "race by association," to what extent does the history of intimacy with African Americans suffer historical erasure, and to what extent does the individual's apprehension of his treatment as "partly colored" suffer erasure as well?

What becomes apparent in these temporal unearthings is the way in which class mobility in this southern context becomes articulated in racial terms; communal representations of interstitial populations reflect two options: backsliding into blackness or racial uplift. As the physical manifestation of the law's instability and the point of interpellation's excess, such populations and their histories nonetheless reflect an American racial epistemology applied both within the confines of the nation and within its imperialist endeavors. The racial "other" becomes knowable within the crucible between "not black" and "not white," within a society where, in Cherríe Moraga's words, "Black is divided from white and the rest of us are required to fall inside that great divide."[52] In reading Asian Americans through the lens of racial interstitiality—between black and white—I am reminded why they are such a significant cultural site: they are uneasily positioned in American culture as American but not quite; as middle class—almost; as minority but not one of "those" minorities; as like us but not like us.

What I highlight, then, is not merely the resurrection of an incidental southern archive, but its contribution to our understanding of how social status becomes articulated via racial discourse and, more particularly, via the space between racial abjection and normative invisibility. The Asian's uneasy relationship to power in this historical context is likewise reflected in the uneasy discourses that intend to convey it. Whether one of liminality, stasis, or indeterminacy, this gap, the space between black and white, is, in Judith Butler's words, "beset by ambivalence." For the "partly colored races," identifying with whiteness involves, to draw an analogy to Butler's analysis of gender, "identifying with a set of norms that are and are not realizable."[53] The space between the social enactment of an identity and its idealization reveals the structures that consolidate social power in its multiple manifestations.

Yet this ambivalence surfaces not only as an anxiety *about* status, but as an anxiety within discourse. As I have shown, the residues of a repressed or unacknowledged history—of intimacy, of discrimination, of collusion, of self-degradation—emerge within a field of representation surrounding the historical context of racial interstitiality, a context produced by the hierarchies of segregation. What surfaces only as a discursive haunting nevertheless interrupts the drive to create linear chronologies out of the messiness and untenability of middleman status.

Racial interstitiality, then, may be conceived as a site where identifications with power go unrecognized or remain incomplete. It is a site where social norms are themselves "insistently approximated." Within every narration of status transformation, there lies both an ambivalence and an incompletion that can unveil the stakes underlying its emergence. If there is a messiness to living in the interstices, it is revealed in the very discourses that seek to represent it.

Notes

I would like to thank Victor Bascara, Shilpa Dave, Grace Hong, Lisa Nakamura, and Michael Peterson for their insightful comments on an early draft of this work.

1. Cited in George Rummel III, "The Delta Chinese: An Exploratory Study in Assimilation" (MA Thesis, University of Mississippi, March 1966): 34.

2. Joan Nathan, "East Meets South at a Delta Table: Chinese-Americans Bring the Tastes of Their Ancestors Down Home," *New York Times*, June 4, 2003: D1.

3. Robert Seto Quan, *Lotus among the Magnolias: The Mississippi Chinese* (Jackson: University Press of Mississippi, 1982).

4. William E. B. DuBois, "The Souls of Black Folk," in *Three Negro Classics* (New York: Avon, 1965 [1903]), 239.

5. As Mamie Garvin Fields notes, whites did not go into town on Saturdays, reserving that day of the week for blacks to do their shopping: "They frowned on black presence in town on the weekdays because it connoted leisure time." Cited in Edward L. Ayers, *The Promise of a New South* (New York: Oxford University Press, 1992), 132.

6. Max Sylvius Handman, "Economic Reasons for the Coming of the Mexican Immigrant," *American Journal of Sociology* 35.4 (January 1930): 609–610.

7. Brewton Berry, *Almost White* (New York: Macmillan, 1963), 47.

8. James W. Loewen, *The Mississippi Chinese: Between Black and White* (Prospect Heights, Ill.: Waveland Press, 1988 [1971] second edition), 72, 194.

9. Ibid., 135.

10. Other ethnographies include Kit-Mui Leung Chan, "Assimilation of Chinese-Americans in the Mississippi Delta (MA Thesis, Mississippi State University, 1969); Pao Yun Liao, "A Case Study of a Chinese Immigrant Community" (MA Thesis, University of Chicago, 1951); Sieglinde Lim de Sanchez, "Crafting a Delta Chinese Community: Education and Acculturation in Twentieth-Century Southern Baptist Mission Schools," *History of Education Quarterly* 43.1 (Spring 2003): 74–90; Robert W. O'Brien, "Status of Chinese in the Mississippi Delta, *Social Forces* (March 1941): 386–390; Quan, *Lotus among the Magnolias*; Rummel, "The Delta Chinese"; Mary Jo Schneider and William M. Schneider, "A Structural Analysis of the Chinese Grocery Store in the Mississippi Delta," in *Visions and Revisions: Ethnohistoric Perspectives on Southern Cultures*, eds. George Sabo III and William M. Schneider (Athens: University of Georgia Press, 1987), 83–97; Shih-Shan Henry Tsai, "The Chinese in Arkansas," *Amerasia Journal* 8.1 (1981): 1–18; and Shih-Shan Henry Tsai, *The Chinese in Arkansas: Final Report* (Little Rock: University of Arkansas, 1981). For historical context surrounding this community, see Gunther Barth, *Bitter Strength: A History of the Chinese in the United States, 1850–1870* (Cambridge, Mass.: Harvard University Press, 1964); and Lucy M. Cohen, *Chinese in the Post–Civil War South: A People without a History* (Baton Rouge: Louisiana State University Press, 1984). For a personal

narrative regarding the Chinese community in Georgia, see John Jung, *Chopsticks in the Land of Cotton: Lives of Mississippi Delta Chinese Grocers* (yinandyang.wix.com: Yin and Yang Press, 2008), 22 (accessed March 12, 2013).

11. Edna Bonacich, "A Theory of Middleman Minorities," *American Sociological Review* 38 (October 1973): 582.

12. Avtar Brah, *Cartographies of Diaspora: Contesting Identities* (London: Routledge, 1996), 1.

13. My usage here deliberately invokes Richard Gray's *Southern Aberrations*, which highlights the ways in which southern self-fashioning proceeds with the self-consciousness of its own "otherness" to the North and the nation: the South "is placed on the boundary, posed as an (albeit preferable) aberration." Such regional theorizing acknowledges an overt debt, ironically, to Edward Said's *Orientalism* (London: Penguin, 1977). Richard Gray, *Southern Aberrations: Writers of the American South and the Problems of Regionalism* (Baton Rouge: Louisiana State University Press, 2000), 500.

14. Loewen, *Mississippi Chinese*, 79.

15. Gary Y. Okihiro, *Margins and Mainstreams: Asians in American History and Culture* (Seattle: University of Washington Press, 1994), 34.

16. Karen Blu, *The Lumbee Problem: The Making of an American Indian People* (Cambridge: Cambridge University Press, 1979); Neil Foley, *The White Scourge: Mexicans, Blacks, and Poor Whites in Texas Cotton Culture* (Berkeley: University of California Press, 1997); Clara Jean Kim, *Bitter Fruit: The Politics of Black-Korean Conflict in New York City* (New Haven, Conn.: Yale University Press, 2000).

17. Judith Butler, *Bodies that Matter: On the Discursive Limits of 'Sex'* (New York: Routledge, 1993), 126.

18. Toni Morrison, "On the Backs of Blacks," in *Arguing Immigration: Are New Immigrants a Wealth of Diversity or a Crushing Burden?*" ed. Nicolaus Mills (New York: Simon and Schuster, 1994), 98. See also her fictional restatement of such sentiments in *Sula*: "As a matter of fact, baiting [black people] was the one activity that the white Protestant residents concurred in. In part their place in this world was secured only when they echoed the old residents' attitude toward blacks." Toni Morrison, *Sula* (New York: Plume, 1973), 53.

19. Karen Brodkin, *How Jews Became White Folks and What That Says about Race in America* (New Brunswick, N.J.: Rutgers University Press, 1999); Noel Ignatiev, *How the Irish Became White* (New York: Routledge, 1996) and *Are Italians White?: How Race Is Made in America*, eds. Jennifer Guglielmo and Salvatore Salerno (New York: Routledge, 2003).

20. David Roediger, *The Wages of Whiteness: Race and the Making of the American Working Class* (London: Verso, 1991); Alexander Saxton, *The Rise and Fall of the White Republic: Class Politics and Mass Culture in Nineteenth-century America* (London: Verso, 1990); Ruth Frankenburg, *White Women, Race Matters: The Social Construction of Whiteness* (Minneapolis: University of Minnesota Press, 1993); Ian F. Haney Lopez, *White by Law: The Legal Construction of Race* (New York: New York University Press, 1996); Mike Hill, *After Whiteness: Unmaking an American Majority* (New York: New York University Press, 2004).

21. Robyn Wiegman, "Whiteness Studies and the Paradox of Particularity," *boundary 2* 26.3 (1999): 121–122.

22. Zora Neale Hurston, "How It Feels to Be Colored Me," in *I Love Myself When I Am Laughing*, ed. Alice Walker (New York: The Feminist Press, 1979), 154.

23. Chester Himes, *If He Hollers Let Him Go* (New Jersey: Chatham, 1973), 41.

24. David. R. Roediger, *Colored White: Transcending the Racial Past* (Berkeley: University of California Press, 2002), 130–131.

25. Jonathan Daniels, *A Southerner Discovers the South* (New York: Macmillan, 1938); *Mississippi Triangle*, dir. Christine Choy, Worth Long, Allan Siegel, 80 min., New York: Third World Newsreel, 1984, videocassette; Ruthanne McCunn Lum, *Chinese American Portraits: Personal Histories 1828–1988* (San Francisco: Chronicle Books, 1988); Choong Soon Kim, *An Asian Anthropologist in the South: Field Experiences with Blacks, Indians, and Whites* (Knoxville: University of Tennessee Press, 1977); Judy Yung, *Chinese Women of America: A Pictorial History*, ed. Crystal K. D. Huie (Seattle: University of Washington Press, 1986).

26. *Gong Lum v. Rice*, 275 U.S. 78 (1927).

27. Ibid.

28. *Plessy v. Ferguson*, 163 U.S. 537 (1896).

29. O'Brien, "Status of Chinese," 386.

30. Rummel, "Delta Chinese," 49.

31. *My America (. . . or Honk if You Love Buddha)*, dir. Rene Tajima-Peña, 87 min., New Jersey, 1997, videocassette. On the racial classification of the Chinese in the 1870, 1880, and 1900 census records, see Cohen, *Chinese in the Post–War Civil War South*, 167–170. Cohen notes that Chinese in Louisiana were either classified as white, black, or mulatto. Interestingly, the mixed-blood descendants of Chinese who immigrated from Cuba mistakenly believed that their forebears came from Mexico and were classified as Mexican, an identification that ironically allowed them to pass as white (Cohen, 170).

32. Daniels, *Southerner Discovers the South*, 194.

33. Ariela Gross, "Litigating Whiteness: Trials of Racial Determination in the Nineteenth-Century South," *Yale Law Journal* (October 1998): 111.

34. Mississippi Code Ann. 2361 (1930) 1158.

35. Cited in Eric Dittus, "Mississippi Triangle: An Interview with Christine Choy, Worth Long, and Allan Siegel," *Cineaste* 14.2 (1987): 40.

36. Toni Morrison, *The Bluest Eye* (New York: Simon and Schuster, 1970), 68.

37. Ruthanne McCunn Lum's *Chinese American Portraits* devotes a chapter to Arlee Hen, giving a full page to her portrait and using her family's history, as in the film, as an origin point for the Chinese community in Mississippi. While *Mississippi Triangle* impresses upon the viewer Hen's distance from the community, McCunn Lum characterizes that relationship as one of qualified integration (McCunn Lum, 82).

38. Adria Bernardi, "Heat in the Delta: Reactions to the Triangle," *Southern Exposure* (July/August 1984): 22. This reaction is confirmed by Ray Lou who worked as a consultant on the film. Personal communication, April 15, 1999.

39. Quan, *Lotus among the Magnolias*, 86.

40. Cited in ibid., 124.

41. Loewen, *Mississippi Chinese*, 96.

42. Choong Soon Kim, "Asian Adaptations in the American South," in *Cultural Diversity in the U.S. South: Anthropological Contributions to a Region in Transition*, eds. Carole E. Hill and Patricia D. Beaver (Athens: University of Georgia Press, 1998), 138.

43. Ibid.

44. Kim, *Asian Anthropologist in the South*, 122.

45. Yung, *Chinese Women of America*, 92.

46. Cited in Dittus, "Mississippi Triangle."

47. In Cheng's view, the over-the-top display of national belonging on the part of the marginalized is a veil for its lack. Anne Anlin Cheng, *The Melancholy of Race: Psychoanalysis, Assimilation, and Hidden Grief* (Oxford: Oxford University Press, 2001).

48. Michael Kreyling, "The South in Perspective," *Mississippi Quarterly* 54.3 (Summer 2001): 383–391.

49. Houston A. Baker Jr. and Dana D. Nelson, "Preface: Violence, the Body and 'The South,'" *American Literature* 73.2 (June 2001): 236.

50. I am aware of the contentiousness surrounding the homogenizing tendencies of positing a single southern regionalism; for my purposes, I choose to invoke "one South" along the lines suggested by W. J. Cash's *The Mind of the South*, which identifies "a fairly definite social pattern—a complex of established relationships and habits of thought, sentiments, prejudices, standards and values, and associations of ideas" that emerge across the region. W. J. Cash, *The Mind of the South* (Garden City, N.Y.: Doubleday, 1941), viii. On "new Southern Studies," see Baker and Nelson, "Preface," and the anthology *Look Away! The U.S. South in New World Studies*, eds. Jon Smith and Deborah Cohn (Durham, N.C.: Duke University Press, 2004).

51. Morrison, "On the Backs of Blacks," 98.

52. Cherríe Moraga, *Loving in the War Years*, expanded edition (Cambridge, Mass.: South End Press, 2000 [1983]), 183.

53. Butler, *Bodies That Matter*, 126.

CHAPTER 3

Racism without Recognition

Toward a Model of Asian American Racialization

Amy Brandzel and Jigna Desai

Far from the galvanizing figure of Vincent Chin sits another figure, that of Seung-Hui Cho. Vincent Chin was a Chinese American man beaten to death by two white men in what appeared to be a frenzy of anti-Japanese scapegoating and xenophobia in the economically depressed city of Detroit in 1982. The figure of Chin, the victim of racial violence, instigated Asian American politics, activism, and communities. Located in the urban North, the racialized violence and the subsequent lack of justice became flashpoints for mobilizing within Asian America via political claims based on civil rights, inclusion, and citizenship as Americans. In other words, Chin was recognized, marked, and claimed as an (Asian) American through claims of normative belonging to America—Asian American activists demanded justice based on Chin's rights as an American citizen. However, the failure to indict Chin's murderers in the civil rights trial following his death revealed the ways Asians in the United States receive only conditional and partial validation as Americans within the nation and state.

Twenty-five years later, Seung-Hui Cho shockingly emerged as a perpetrator of mass violence, but not clearly as an Asian American, in the South. Specifically, on April 16, 2007, Seung-Hui Cho killed thirty-two people on the Virginia Tech campus in Blacksburg, Virginia. The media soon dubbed the event the "deadliest shooting rampage in American history," and news coverage was inundated with uncovering the "madness at Virginia Tech."[1] What stood out beyond the numbers of murdered individuals in a "school shooting" was the shooter himself, a Korean American whose identity and location as "alien-other" marked him as always already suspicious, dangerous, and outside. We suggest here that it is important for Asian American Studies scholars to develop frames for understanding and engaging with Cho and other Asian American male figures associated with violence, such as Dharun Ravi and One Goh.

In our previous work on the Virginia Tech massacre,[2] we noted the important ways in which Seung-Hui Cho was simultaneously racially othered as an Asian immigrant alien and whitened as disenfranchised male youth. We suggested that this construction of Cho benefited and forwarded a few national narratives, most importantly, the dominant narrative of a wounded *white* heteromasculinity that has been victimized by feminism and multiculturalism. We suggested that this twofold reading of Cho, as wounded white male and Asian-other, was a particularly useful means of foreclosing another possible reading of him: as a disabled representative of politically, culturally, and economically disenfranchised people of color vengefully and violently expressing his dislocation from citizenship, rights, and belonging in the United States. We return here to Cho, to continue to think further about his complex racialization and disabilities and how they extend narratives of a postracial *South* and United States.

We want to think about how Cho, who unlike Chin, could not be recognized as wounded by and suffering from racial injury and, subsequently, did not engender an Asian American political response.[3] In other words, why didn't Cho mobilize and incite Asian American communities? How might Asian American communities need to develop more nuanced and complex analyses that engage responsibility for violence, disability, and racial discrimination?[4] How were Cho's actions dismissed as symptoms of an individual's mental illness or medicalized forms of racial inadequacies? We claim that Cho's simultaneous and multiple racializations, in part, cast Cho as an assimilated American (white) male school shooter in order to mitigate and resolve other contradictory racializations, namely as a disenfranchised and disabled[5] immigrant (alien-other). We argue that the school shooter racialization is used to signal assimilation and mitigate Cho's alien status, thereby providing "evidence" for the supposed success of inclusion and postraciality in the South and the nation. Furthermore, Cho fails to incite and mobilize Asian America not simply because he is a perpetrator of violence, rather than the target of violence, but because his violence and death have been understood primarily through paradigms of assimilation and normalization to white heteromasculine American racial formations (i.e., the "school shooter type"). In the subsequent years, Cho has become increasingly emblematic of the white shooter with mental illness. We also suggest that mental illness itself operates through racialized terms in which the pathology of a white school shooter is understood as symptom of a social ill while the mental illnesses of Cho and other men of color are attributed to their failures to adjust and integrate into white society.[6] Hence, these multiple racializations of Cho prevented alternative interpretations of the cause of the violence—such as anti-Asian racism or disenfranchisement—from emerging. We want to emphasize two significant points: first, it is important to keep in mind that while white heteromasculine injury was used to understand and racialize Cho, he did not benefit from white privilege; and second, in the years following the massacre, Cho has become a ubiquitous reference for (white) violent shooting crimes and mental illness, simultaneously minimizing his Asian American racialization in relation to mental illness while criminalizing mental illness as naturally violent.

Moreover, it appears to us that more *has* to be said on the ways in which the racial, gender, disability, and sexual politics of the representations of Virginia Tech reflect, impact, and transform Asian America and the American South. While we were able to think through the Virginia Tech shootings and their media representations soon after the event, we find ourselves needing to address the ways the shootings have been framed since then and expand our reflections. We continue to be struck by the discrepancies in analyses of media coverage whereby some scholars, such as ourselves, claimed that the media described Cho through both predictably and unpredictably race-based descriptions, while others suggested that the media was more restrained, "less racialized" in their productions. Importantly, we would argue that the scholarship on the Virginia Tech massacre and the various incongruencies on how Cho was and was not racialized in the media mirrors the challenges for Asian American studies to articulate Asian American racializations. In this essay, then, we use the Virginia Tech massacre as a vehicle to offer a model for how to productively locate and analyze the complex racializations of Asian Americans in the United States in general, and in the (supposedly postracial New) South in particular. We hope it will provide some possibilities for being able to discuss Asian American perpetrators of harm and violence that take into account responsibility for violence *and* injury by violence through a discussion of racism, nationalism, xenophobia, ableism, sexism, and homophobia.

Those invested in a color-blind discourse might certainly accuse us of going out of our way, to "see" (as in locate and conceptualize) racialization and othering in these events, experiences, and discourses. In other words, when we say that race is significant to understanding Cho, we demarcate and scrutinize whiteness and Asianness as racial formations. Therefore, we posit that when we are "looking" for racism or the deployment of racialization, we must precisely understand the ways in which racism can function through normativities—that is, unspoken, hegemonically produced norms. Whiteness studies and critical race scholars have written extensively about the ways in which whiteness has been historically as well as contemporaneously racialized as the deracialized norm, the unstated, natural state from which all "others" are racialized against. Hence, rather than see Cho as deracialized, we see him as racialized, in part, as normatively white.

Critical race scholarship has been essential for parsing the ways in which whiteness has become naturalized as the normative identity in the United States, especially through its reoccurring productions as a supposedly *non*racial formation. This scholarship and the work of whiteness studies scholars has been instrumental in understanding how whiteness has been produced as this normatively nonracialized racial formation through the ways in which other groups have been specifically named and described as racial formations. Historically, for example, racial definitions in law focused on outlining what made someone "Black," and very rarely defined who was "white." And in the current age of colorblindness, whiteness has only increasingly become a quintessential normativity—a norma-tivity being that which often remains, unstated and unspoken, yet understood all the same. And yet it strikes us that critical race studies, whiteness studies, and even Asian American studies has been too quick to presume that nonwhites are 1) racialized *discursively*, and 2) in such a way as to be recognizable as a *racialized* discourse.

When we consider the Virginia Tech shootings within the specific backdrop of the New South, we are able to consider how racializations of Asian Americans require and rely upon a particular form of normativity—a normativity of inar-ticulation and nonrecognition of the racialization of and racism against Asian Americans. The South may raise a particular challenge for this inarticulation, especially because of the hegemony and embeddedness of the Black/white binary. For example, one simple consequence of this binary is that anti-Black racism (including state and social violences such as Jim Crow and lynchings) is the hegemonic paradigm for understanding racism. Moreover, the narrative of the "New South" emphasizes simultaneously the South as a place with a distant his-tory of racial trauma and a contemporary transcendence of race within a new global economy (what we refer to here as postraciality). While there are certainly limits and detriments to seeing racism and racializations "too much," it is far too dangerous to see too little. As discourses of colorblindness and postraciality grow to dominate the national and Southern landscapes, it seems even more imperative to ponder how Asian Americans become erased, illegible, and dera-cialized in these discourses. This is to say that the inarticulations of racism and racializations are a critical cog in the wheel of colorblindness that continues to turn the U.S. nation-state into a "postracial" nation of white privilege and white normativity. Moreover, it is important to understand how such colorblindness may work to shape and limit Asian American politics at the cost of erasing the Asian immigrant or alien-other.

We would point out that racial formations in the South are often dominated by several dominant discourses: 1) race as a Black and white binary, 2) the South as the enclave of American Black/white racial trauma, and 3) the assertion of a wounded white masculinity. All of these discourses impact the ways in which Vir-ginia Tech and Cho were racialized within the context of the South; furthermore, we want to suggest that Cho's racialization alternatively as white and alien-other, as well as terrorist, had particular resonance in relation to these dominant nar-ratives about race. In this essay, we first overview some of the influential models for understanding racializations of Asian Americans and add to the arguments on behalf of understanding regionalism within Asian American studies. We then turn to the history of Virginia Tech, as well as the representations of the mas-sacre, in a call for scholars to work toward understanding the constant specters of racialized imaginaries that exist with and without tacit racialized discourses.

We argue against normalizing discourses, however galvanizing they may be, in order to understand how the figure of Cho can engender a nonnormative reading of race within Asian American Studies.

Beyond the Color Line: Asian American Racialization in the U.S. South

Scholars[7] have often asked where yellow and brown fall on the spectrum of race as Black and white in America. They have noted that in response to the call to go "beyond Black or white," that one of two approaches is generally deployed: either 1) racialization processes are examined in terms of only one racial category at a time, thereby losing sight of the ways in which race is relationally constructed in and through its many othered deployments, or 2) a triadic "racial hierarchy approach" is offered whereby whiteness holds the top position and blackness is abjectly resigned to the bottom, locating all "other nonwhites"[8] variously "in-between."[9] While the first approach is obviously unable to account for the ways in which race functions in and through other categories of race (not to mention how race is "intersectional" with productions of gender, sexuality, class, disability, and nation),[10] the second approach relies upon, while repositioning, the Black/white binary into a Black/white ladder in which Asian Americans cling to some unspecified and changing middle rungs. With assimilation and normalization, the Asian immigrant is thought to move from Black abjection asymptotically toward assimilation as an off-white ethnic American. Moreover, claims to citizenship or its lack by Asian Americans often deploy or are read through static and fixed understandings of Black and white. We suggest that Asian Americans have been unevenly defined in relation to Black and white racial formations in ways that reify the binary itself; rather than seeing Black and white as stable racial formations that are applied to Asian Americans, it may be productive to see how Black and white are constituted through Asian Americanness.

Other scholars have emphasized the ways in which Asian Americans have been implicated in the citizen/alien-other binary as deployed historically in U.S. legal mechanisms (such as immigration, citizenship, land ownership, and so on), as well as in U.S. public culture.[11] This large body of scholarship on the racialization of Asian Americans as the alien-within has provided a critical and implicit interrogation of the inadequacy of Black/white binary to account for Asian American racial formations historically or in the contemporary moment. Building on these insights, Claire Jean Kim, for example, offers an alternative account, suggesting that we might see Asian American racialization in terms of triangulation, whereby Asian American is one of three nodes (the other two being Black and white) in the national landscape of race. In this "field of racial positions," Kim argues that U.S. racial discourses have relationally "measured" and mapped Asian Americans in terms of whiteness and blackness; that is, Asian Americans have been ostracized due to their supposed unassimilatability and essentialized foreignness (as opposed to whites and African Americans), while embraced in terms of their abilities to be civilized and educated (like-whites and, therefore, non-Black), as in the "model minority" construct.[12] Yet we are left with a particularly large lacuna as to how the nationally deployed "citizenship" binary of citizen/Asian-other fluctuates and manifests within different spaces and places, and how it is intertwined with and illuminates the racial structure of blackness and whiteness. Methodologically, we may need to move away from some notion of fixed racializations (binary, interstitial, or triangulated) to locating analyses of racialization that are contingent and relational within their specific and shifting contexts.

In turning to the South and moving away from an "East of California" or even bicoastal paradigm, we ask how to read Asian American racial formations in the South as a significant lens, rather than addendum, for reading race in the nation. The paradigm of race as Black/white so dominates our narratives of the South, that other racial projects are either disappeared into or mapped onto the Black and white binary to gain legibility. One strategy of negotiating this has been to try to understand how yellow and brown appear within and undermine the Black/white binary. However, our approach is not so much to locate Asian American within and then dismantle the structure from within as it is to probe it from without. By attending to how Asian American racial formations continue to be inside—within the binary—and outside—transnational, alien, and unassimilated, *we demonstrate their fluidity and indeterminacy.*

We want to also add that shifts in Muslim-looking and South Asian racial formations have impacted panethnic Asian American racial formations since 9/11. That terrorism jumps to the minds and lips of many viewers upon learning about Virginia Tech's massacre suggests that it is now a salient component of our racialized national imaginary. Knowing that the perpetrator is of an unidentified ethnicity and Asian American indicates that an association with terror engenders all Asian American ethnicities suspect. This suggests that there is a certain absorbancy to Asian American racializations.

We turn here to the South not as an exceptional region within Asian America, but rather to make an argument that spacialization and localization within racial projects is significant. The essay, like the larger collection, implicitly and explicitly, argues for the centrality of region and place in the epistemological and methodological approaches to Asian American Studies. While Asian American Studies scholarship has long struggled for new paradigms that move us "East of California," we have, at best, assumed a bicoastal option that emphasizes California and the Northwest, or alternatively, the mid-Atlantic and Northeast. We have yet to reckon with how nuanced and careful considerations of region and place transform our frames and approaches within Asian American Studies.[13]

It is here that scholars such as Moon-ho Jung, James W. Loewen, and Leslie Bow have shown how Asian American racial formations in the South read as regional can illuminate our understandings of race in the United States. The narrative of the Black/white binary is often applied to the Chinese Americans in Mississippi during the twentieth century. In the early 1970s, James Loewen argued that Chinese communities in the Mississippi Delta were placed within the racial schema of "in-betweenness," whereby they maneuvered from "near-Black" to "near-white" in the span of a few decades. Loewen posits in his much-cited text that the Chinese American community shifted and claimed whiteness, distancing themselves from their status as "colored." In the historic case *Gong Lum v. Rice* (1927), the Supreme Court ruled that Christian Chinese Americans in Mississippi were "colored" when it came to the question of access to white segregated institutions of education. However, deploying a Black-white assimilationist model of race, Loewen's ethnography posits that Chinese Americans had "achieved" near-white status in Mississippi by the 1960s.[14] In the logic of Southern regional and racial exceptionalism, if Asians can become white in the South, they can become white anywhere. Leslie Bow (this volume) argues that it might be much more useful to see Asian Americans in the South in terms of "racial interstitiality," whereby the racial flexibility of Chinese Mississippians can be understood not as a simple and clear indicator of agency and power, but as a means to "focus on the space between normative structures of power . . . [and] its incompletion and irresolution."[15] In other words, in looking to how Asian American racial formations have been, in Bow's terms "*unevenly* oppressed" between Black and white, one can see how models positing that Asian Americans as approaching whiteness, achieving assimilation, and indicating integration are not only inadequate to understanding Asian American racial formations, but actively mask the failures of inclusion. Bow, in other words, interrogates the Asian American racializations along the Black-white binary to emphasize the inadequacy of a simple notion of agency within an inclusionary model. Similarly, but from another vantage point, we seek to explore how racializations operate to further models of assimilation, inclusion, and normalization at the cost of erasing and/or assimilating the alien-other.

The Black/white binary certainly offers a shorthand for how the United States ideologically communicates about race. This is especially true in how America understands the South, namely regarding it as the sole location of slavery, the Civil War, lynchings, and Jim Crow segregation in the popular imaginary. For these reasons, we find the critique of the Black/white binary via interstitiality (Bow) to be helpful. However, our critique of assimilation follows a different track as we seek to challenge normalization through racialization as American. When we suggest that Asian Americans are racialized as white, we do not mean to suggest that they have somehow achieved assimilation, citizenship, and belonging; instead, we seek to demonstrate the violence of white normativity—a racialization without privilege. We want to probe how the Black/white binary curtails our readings of race as it reflects the fact that we *lack an adequate language for Asian American racializations*, particularly those that are normatively and hegemonically entrenched into understandings of "others." We maintain that the racialization of Asian Americans as white and American is often read as nonracialization and implicitly works to normalize Asians as Americans. By pointing out how normalization and racializations operate, we show how the racial injury of the Asian immigrant or alien-other is put under erasure in the South.

In making Asian Americans legible primarily through the Black/white binary, the definition of what counts as racism becomes narrow and anti-Asian racism becomes erased. Hence, a narrative claiming the successful whitening and integration of Asian Americans in the modern South becomes a way to recuperate Asian Americans and the South in the service of greater narratives of race in the nation. The ways that Asian Americans have been understood (via Orientalism and racialization as alien-other and model minority) in the national landscape are significant to not only race in the South, but formulations of the South itself. Discourses on the South often frame it as an abject region, one against which the modern, liberal, and cosmopolitan North defines itself. One might ask what is served and gained by theorizing it as such. Narratives of this abjection function to mark the South as exceptional within the nation. Interestingly, while many scholars have written about the scapegoating of the U.S. South and the ways in which it has become a repository of American racial trauma and white supremacy, one scholar argues that this process is a form of "internal orientalism." Cultural geographer David R. Jansson has written extensively, in fact, on his expansion of Edward Said's concept of Orientalism in "spatial terms," whereby "internal orientalism is a discourse that involves the othering of a region within the state and the simultaneous production of an exacted national identity."[16] Jansson notes that internal orientalism is different from Said's Orientalism in that, because it is an Othering of a region that is included within the dominant norm (in this case, the U.S. nation-state), this Other (the South) has "some degree of access to national political, cultural, and economic institutions.[17] Internal orientalism mirrors Orientalism, however, in the ways that it names a fairly consistent discursive production of the South as the U.S. nation-state's Other, an essentially different, subordinate, and distinct region that has become a repository of national vices. Importantly, Jansson locates the active promotion and production of the "New South" as a particular effort to disrupt internal orientalism. By countering the "internal orientalist view" of the South as "backward, preindustrial, and premodern," the New South was modern, industrial, entrepreneurial, and, comparatively, tolerant.[18]

We cannot help but be interested in how, through this framing, U.S. orientalist discourse—as an othering device in which Asian/Americans are denoted as the essential other to the white-citizen subject, is erased from the South and the nation-state as a whole. Somehow, Jansson imagines an orientalism without "Orientals," a feat that, we would argue, is made possible only via his focus on the South. We are reminded that Said's objectives were not only to name Orientalism as a specifically racialized (as in anti-Oriental) discourse, but to also call out academics for their central roles in the production of the "Orient" as an object of study, the epitome of Other to the Western Self. This is not, however, an effort to disparage Jansson. Rather, this example of the erasure of Orientals from Orientalism is directly related to mechanisms that work to expunge Asian Americans from the South, Cho from Asian America, and alien-others from racial formations.

The Embodiment of Everything Virginia Tech Is Not, or at Least Not African American

As a whole, Asian Americans constitute approximately 5.5 percent of Virginia's population.[19] However, most Asian Americans live in a handful of Virginia's counties clustered in Northern Virginia and the greater Washington, D.C., area as well as in and around Virginia's larger cities and university cities, including Richmond, Charlottesville, and Blacksburg. Cho and his family migrated from South Korea to Maryland, settling in Centreville, Virginia (Fairfax County), which is known particularly for its large Korean American community. Within this northern Virginia (NOVA) community, there may have been a critical mass of Asian Americans (Chinese, Vietnamese, and Korean Americans) to create a more supportive and aware racial and ethnic environment. While his family was affiliated with and participated in a Korean church, reports indicate that Cho was bullied at school and teased in his Christian youth group.[20] Growing up in a city with a large Korean American community should not be seen as an indication that Cho was somehow protected from the experiences of racism, ableism, and xenophobia because these forms of discrimination and oppression exist even where the numerical presence of minorities may be relatively high. Nevertheless, it is very likely that the demographics of this affluent suburb of Washington provided Cho access to an Asian American, if not Korean American, community and more importantly to educational and mental health assistance that provided more appropriate support for him as a minor and as Asian American than he received as a student at Virginia Tech.

Subsequent to graduating from high school, Cho attended Virginia Tech from 2003 until his death in 2007. Ironically, his move to Virginia Tech in Blacksburg may have led to further isolation and alienation.[21] Although universities constitute themselves as sites of racial and global diversity, their institutionalization of difference often reifies established networks of power. In fact, while promoting themselves as purveyors of global knowledge and racial difference, white normativity and neoliberalism reinforce unequal economic distribution with few resources for international and minority students, especially ones that are vulnerable or in need of support. This lack of resources and oppressions exists within universities despite their best attempts to suggest otherwise. Moreover, as scholars have noted, college is often a time where ethnic identity and coethnic friendships are formed; while roommates and campus organizations attempted to befriend him, Cho ultimately remained isolated partly due to racism, ableism, and xenophobia at the university where adequate resources may not have been available in meeting his needs.

Within this context, we can observe that the last several decades have seen a transformation in universities' self-representations.[22] The impacts of multiculturalism, globalism, and cosmopolitanism are visible in how universities seek to present themselves *regardless of actual equitable transformations in access and experience*. As critical race scholars have observed repeatedly, universities now feel compelled to present themselves as inclusive and diverse in terms of race, ethnicity, and nation. David Roediger, in a recent essay,[23] analyzes several Midwestern universities' use of racial representations for such purposes. Roediger examines how pictures of African American alumni are displayed to suggest a long history of racial acceptance and tolerance while faked publicity materials promote the contemporary university as racially integrated and culturally diverse. Thus, American universities frequently strive to offer impressions of themselves as cosmopolitan, diverse, and worldly. This serves both as a means to indicate their nonracist cultures and communities, but also an attempt to appeal to broad global audiences. Universities market themselves as nonracist to assuage guilt of white students and draw students of color to their campuses. Simultaneously, universities portray themselves as nonprovincial and cosmopolitan institutions targeting international students as well. The neoliberal university is interested in projecting its inclusion of difference, both transnational and domestic.

The university's call for inclusion of "global difference" is an extension of the institution's power and claim to globality. The (American) university seeks to market its globality. As securing a location in global economy and culture became a mechanism for asserting national space simultaneously, universities began to market themselves to both white American and international audiences as global sites of cosmopolitanism. They seek to appeal to white Americans as purveyors of knowledge about the global. On the flip side, universities desire to make themselves desirable to international students seeking an education in the United States that is simultaneously nonprovincial and cosmopolitan American.

Before we turn to some of the media and scholarly representations of the Virginia Tech shootings, we think it is useful to take a quick turn to the institutional history of Virginia Tech in light of this understanding of universities, race, and cosmopolitanism. As much as this narrative would not offer too many surprises in regard to a slowly desegregated state university in the U.S. South, there are some interesting in/articulations in regard to Asian students that might provide a useful window for thinking through the later representations. There is an uneasiness with the appearance and emergence of Asian presences on the university campus. Interestingly, the historical narrative of Virginia Tech showcases the ability—and responsibility—of Asian American bodies to be the gauges of the university *and* the American South as a racialized space.

The narrative starts out simple enough and mirrors other land-grant institutions in the South; Virginia Polytechnic Institute and State University, popularly known as Virginia Tech, originated as the Virginia Agricultural and Mechanical College in 1872, a white, male-only institution, and is one of few public universities also to be a military college and house the Corps of Cadets. Importantly, one of the few history texts dedicated to providing the historical account of Virginia Tech focuses primarily on the incorporation of others as the central narrative of Virginia Tech's history.[24] But, as might be expected in historical accounts of integration in the South, two groups in particular stand out as the bodies in which inclusion is measured: white women and African American men.

There are ways in which Peter Wallenstein's text reveals a racialization process in the early-twentieth-century South that relies upon the deployment of a black/white binary, and the racial project that the binary serves. For example, one of the central socialization and educational aspects of Virginia Tech has been its military training; all students (i.e., white men) were expected to enroll and participate fully in the Corps of Cadets at Virginia Tech up until 1964 (at which time it became optional). White women were not allowed to be members until 1973, and the first African American man entered the Corps in the 1950s. As Wallenstein observes, in an interesting use of words, the Corps remained all white and male, "or at least non–African-American," well into the 1950s.[25] While Wallenstein does not elaborate on what (or who) might be included in the "*not* African American" group, his phrasing suggests there might be a racialized presence beyond white or Black, a presence that, nonetheless, cannot be fully captured in the language of race as nation.

Perhaps what appear as a few detours in his text reveal a much more interesting process of racialization at work. In various small sections throughout the book, Wallenstein focuses on the "global" presence in Blacksburg, Virginia, and Virginia Tech in particular. It is here that we see the ways in which a few international students, faculty, and speakers are deemed capable, not of bringing *the mark of racial diversity* to the South (that is, alas, the job of African Americans), but *the mark of the global and the cosmopolitan*. In one such section focused on "The Cosmopolitan Club," the author suggests the club was formed in 1947 "to reflect some North American students' interest in foreign cultures as well as a few international students' presence at Virginia Tech."[26] The author notes that the largest number of foreign students, such as Cato Lee and Yvonne Rohran Tung, was from China and Hong Kong. Cato Lee is described as one of the first non-U.S. students at the school, graduating in mechanical engineering in 1927. Lee's difference, however, is made both hypervisible and invisible in *The Bugle*, Virginia Tech's school yearbook; as Wallenstein notes, "After quoting a line from Rudyard Kipling, the Bugle said with reference to Lee that 'the gentleman of the East is not different from the gentlemen of the West.'"[27] And Yvonne Rohran Tung's difference is made unequivocal, as she is noted not only as a member of the club, but its "most exotic member" because she was "not male, not white, not military; not Virginian or even American."[28] In this way, defined through negation, Tung is positioned to "embod[y] everything that the early student population at Virginia Tech was not."[29] *Cosmopolitanism* here refers more specifically to its cultural manifestation, a global version of multiculturalism in which national borders are crossed by numerous cultures to create a diverse society within a specific nation. Hence, cosmopolitanism on a university campus does not render the university a space of moral or political cosmopolitanism, but rather serves to provide evidence of the emerging globality of the inclusive (American) university.[30]

To be the embodiment of "everything" not normative of the Virginia Tech's community—that is, to "go global" here, seems to suggest a few particular moves to the author, one of which is to continuously connote the lack of blackness. As he explains, "The membership of the Cosmo Club signaled a much more cosmopolitan student population—and the presence of nonwhite students on a 'white' campus in a Southern state. Tech was beginning to go global and multiracial. If it was no longer a white campus, it was still non–African-American."[31] But another interesting component of these descriptions is the ways in which Asians are consistently located as signs of cosmopolitanism, otherness, and foreignness in relation to whites and blacks. We want to suggest that these racializations offer us some insight into how Asian/Black/white are being mutually and relationally constituted. A cursory glance through Virginia Tech's historical narrative reminds us as much, such as Wallenstein's phrasing of "at least non–African American," which conjures up the Black/white binary while at the same time noting the binary's inescapable incompleteness. We see how the racism against African Americans works as a paradigm for measuring oppression and signaling Americanness in this framework. Rather than suggesting that different and related racializations may be at play in viewing Asian and Latino students, Wallenstein merely suggests them as different and therefore on a different axis. We are not seeking to collapse international and race, and yet to suggest them as unconnected follows the logic of race within a Black and white binary. We might also go even further here to point out the ways in which Asian bodies are culpable, if not downright responsible, for marking the national American South as a global space, at least temporarily.

Within the contemporary narrative of Virginia Tech, it is apparent that Cho was repeatedly made and read as not-Black. In evoking only the history of lynching, civil rights, and segregation in relation to Virginia Tech, antiblack racism was the only racial project made legible and visible in relation to the university and race. The presence of Cho and many of the students and faculty of color were evoked as a counterpoint to the history of segregation and racial violence. In this way, Cho's presence, while signaling a complex migration of Asians to universities, the South, and the greater United States, did not provoke a stronger analysis of anti-Asian racism and the failure of the project of inclusion on the colorblind campus.[32]

Race-ing Asian America in the Virginia Tech Shootings

To reiterate, the media portrayals of Seung-Hui Cho and the Virginia Tech shootings motivate us to intervene in the scholarship on racialization of Cho and Asian Americans in the South by suggesting that insufficient understandings of racial formation and region should not be read as an absence of racialization. In our analysis of the discourses surrounding Seung-Hui Cho, we were struck by the concurrent deployment of three seemingly divergent elements of racialization: 1) the ways in which Cho was deemed "white-like" in his supposed congruence with the "school shooter type," 2) the ways in which Cho was figured via the alien-other, and 3) the laboriously silenced option of Cho as aggrieved racialized other avenging his experiences of subordination and oppression. We would argue that the simultaneity of these racial productions serve as merely one more example of the ways in which our epistemologies, politics, and language fail to articulate the contradictory ways in which racialization functions and is manifest, historically as well as contemporaneously. We also want to suggest that Asian American communities themselves did not see Cho as a disabled and racially injured other who could be the subject of Asian American mobilizing. One could further argue that rather than suggesting a "schizophrenic" approach to race—the possibility of Cho being racialized as Asian, foreign, other, white, and terrorist[33]—indicates the ways in which multiple racializations are simultaneously interrelated and enmeshed; moreover, we see that the simultaneity of such complex and compound racial formations have begun to ironically foster ideas of a postracial and transnational America in which Asian racial injury and disability are ignored in the service of ensuring that white heteromasculinity is seen as wounded and in need of action, defense, and protection.

What explanations were provided for Cho's actions? It is interesting to see that discussions of Cho and mental illness rarely mention race beyond whiteness. We do not discount that mental illness, depression, and/or disability were critical to Cho's experiences and actions; in fact quite the opposite, we see them as integral to understanding the violence he perpetrated. However, we are surprised to see in many accounts an inability to consider race and disability.[34] Violence associated with racialized masculinity is read as a sign of woundedness or injury (in

relation to whiteness), criminality (in relation to Blackness), traditional patriarchal or nonmodern culture (in relation to Asianness), or terror (in relation to
brownness). For example, while Black men's historical racial injuries are duly
noted, greater emphasis is placed on their supposed contemporary propensity
for violence that is attributed to such factors as a culture of poverty, familial
deviance, and inherent criminality. Similar logic is used for other men of color
whose racial injury may be acknowledged but is largely dismissed or ignored
in order to emphasize their deviance. Asian American men are predominantly
associated with just a few forms of violence, namely patriarchal gendered violence and gang violence, in the American imaginary. However, this violence is
rarely attributed to experiences of race; instead, Asian American traditions and
cultures are seen as responsible for engendering familial/domestic and criminal
violence. Hence, racial injury and violence are rarely linked in narratives of Asian
American masculinity. White men's woundedness, however, is attributed to larger
social deficiencies wherein their injuries are read as pathologies of greater society,
rather than as deficiencies of the group. In other words, white men's violence is
read as a sign of social dysfunction and pathology rather than being an attribute
of white men. Consequently African American men and some other men of
color are seen as inherently violent and deviant, while white men's woundedness
instigates national mobilizations as we discuss below.

    To elaborate this understanding of white men's injury, in our earlier article,
"Race, Violence and Terror," we argued that the typecasting was cemented through
the Columbine High School massacre that took place on April 20, 1999, in the
quintessential American suburb of Littleton, Colorado. The perpetrators, Dylan
Klebold and Eric Harris, killed twelve students and one teacher, wounded twenty-
three others, and then killed themselves, thereby sparking a "series of debates
about the influence of violence in media, gun control (or the lack thereof), and
the tyranny of high school cliques."[35] The media was particularly invested in
examining Klebold and Harris's psyche, increasingly suggesting that they were
the victims of alienation at the hands of working mothers (i.e., feminists), high
school jocks, and uninterested girls. Critically, then, the prototype of the school
shooter was figured as not only victimized by cliquish high school cultures, but by
the distancing of white male privilege—the privilege easily accessed by the jocks,
and the privilege purchased through the sexual and domestic labor of women.[36]

    In this regard, what script of racialized masculinity and violence would Cho's
fluid racialization activate? Asian American men are thought to have inherently
wounded masculinities, not to suffer from racism and racial injury, and not to
have grievances, hence not be associated with or have cause for gun violence.[37]
Asian American masculinities are seen as invulnerable to injury and racism;
they do not suffer except from their own traditional or nonmodern "culture"—
hence, culture became a frequent explanation of cause for Cho's actions. Their
deviant masculinities foreclose them from being subjects of wounded violent

masculinities with "legitimate" causes and justifications for violence.[38] When Asian American men are imagined as perpetrators of violence, it is most often as improperly masculine hyperpatriarchal perpetrators of domestic and/or familial violence. We believe that Asian American male violence and patriarchy in the American imaginary is primarily associated with violence directed toward family as a form of patriarchal Asian tradition and culture. Asian American male violence is rarely perceived to be targeted toward nonfamilial units, while Black and white male violence are seen as directed toward larger publics and communities. As we have discussed elsewhere, in order to characterize Cho as violent as Asian American, sources took recourse to discussing his Koreanness (rather than his Asian Americanness) through references to "hyperviolent" Korean media, including films such as *Oldboy*.[39]

Primarily, Asian American men are seen as neither capable of injury nor capable of injuring others as alien-others; they must be assimilated as (near-white) American males to be read and rendered as such. Commenting on violence and Asian American masculinity, Sonjia Hyon writes that there are many reasons for the erasure of anti-Asian racism and its subsequent absence from national narratives about race, violence, and injury:

> 1) Historically, their racialization is confounded by perceptions of their proximity to whiteness—culturally and somatically—which has constructed them as impervious to "injury." 2) Related, their racial otherness or "blackness" is reproduced through assumptions around their foreignness, which constitutes them as always partially, if not wholly, alien to America. 3) Their "injury" has been mandated and instituted under the guise of the state through its laws and its apparatuses such as anti-immigration acts and internment.[40]

It is here that we insist that despite Cho's attempts to make visible his injuries as a disabled, hetromasculine Asian alien-other in the South, he was misrecognized by white America and unrecognized by and unexpected in Asian America.

We note here our divergence from other readings of Cho that offer less race-inflected interpretations of him and his actions. For example, Min Hyoung Song's astute analysis in "Communities of Remembrance: Reflections on the Virginia Tech Shootings and Race" suggests that Cho and the media coverage on Virginia Tech were resistant to racialization, partly due to the fact that the work of the media spectacle—especially in a form that has been so ridden with typecasting as school shootings—has a reasonably short lifespan in the popular memory of the American populace. But another reason that Song reads Cho as resistant to a specifically Asian American racialization is due to the predominance of the "school shooter type." In Song's analysis, Cho was moved more toward the "less racially inflected psychological profile of a school shooter,"[41] thereby allowing for a "comforting banality" that the "school-shooter profile overlooks the unique oddity of Cho's behavior."[42] However, as we elaborate below, we join scholars such as Michael Kimmel and Douglas Kellner in arguing that the profile of the school shooter is far from "less racially inflected," but is, in fact, racially coded as white. Moreover, we think much is at stake for Asian American Studies and politics in this and Cho's other racializations.

As previously mentioned, the racialization of Cho was not only generated through the citizen/alien binary, but also through the more recent production of the "school shooter type." It is interesting, then, to see how these two racializations of Cho rely on splitting the *mode* of his violence (in the form of a white or assimilated school shooter) from the *cause* of his violence (caught between cultures and inadequate access to adequate mental health care due to his Asianness). In this way, Cho is racialized as both near-white and alien-other. Masculinity scholar Michael Kimmel, for example, can at once acknowledge the possibility of Cho's experience of racialized other in one moment (see below), while in the next claiming that Cho's mode of violence was like other school shooters in that he "followed the time honored script of the American western. . . . American men don't get mad, they get even."[43] Kimmel, while whitening Cho, also normalizes him as American. However, in order to accomplish this, Kimmel remains silent in regard to what injustices cause Cho to seek to get even. In divorcing cause from his mode, the separation oddly ensured that the mode of violence garnered attention and whitened Cho, while at the same time deflected away from Cho's own possible motivations, disability, and racialization.

"Culture"—a cause or injury that does not require redress—rather than social, economic, and political disenfranchisement becomes the explanation for Asian American men's violence. More specifically, in looking to explain Cho's actions, the possibility and the failure of full assimilation as American were in tension, hence Asian "culture" was brought in as a mediating explanation. For example, media coverage narrated his family's migration as a life of struggle in Korea that was transformed into a suburban middle-class, mostly assimilated, life in America. In these media portrayals of Cho, there was a reoccurring thematic claiming that migration itself is a form of pathology as he was caught "in-between," an in-betweenness located via the binary of assimilated/immigrant or citizen/alien. In other words, Cho was figured as disabled by being torn "between" Korean/immigrant and (Korean) *American* cultures. Scholarship has followed suit. For example, sociologist Douglas Kellner notes in his book, *Guys and Guns Amok: Domestic Terrorism and School Shootings from the Oklahoma City Bombing to the Virginia Tech Massacre*, "Seung-Hui Cho's construction of violent masculinity and identity seemed to have taken place within the conflicting pressures of Korean patriarchy and U.S. media, gun, and popular culture. His Korean and American background apparently tore him between the strictures of a conservative Korean patriarchy and the pressures to succeed in American society."[44] Later in the text, Kellner observes that "Cho obviously had difficulties in mediating the space between the Korean and the American and could not produce a viable synthesis."[45]

Clearly the inadequate and failed product of model minority immigrant neoliberalism, generational assimilation, and nonmodern and traditional Asian family, Cho supposedly could not manage the pressure of achieving ethnic familial and cultural expectations or resist the lure of American violence. Media portrayals of Cho, especially in the beginning of the coverage, continuously questioned whether or not Cho "cracked" under the extreme pressure of model minority status—that is, from the pressure placed on young Asian Americans by their immigrant parents and not, presumably, by systemic racisms and processes of othering within the United States.[46] Other narratives also explained this "cracking" as caused by the inability of Korean culture [*sic*] to adequately deal with mental illness; media coverage repeatedly stated that a supposed stigma associated with mental and developmental disabilities in Korean culture prevented Cho (and his family) from seeking help or being identified as needing and then accessing help.[47]

Douglas Kellner argues throughout his text that the anger at the perceived loss of white male privilege is one of the most important thematics in looking at school shooters and other "domestic terrorists" in the United States, discussing at length that this is one of the organizing principles around the Columbine High School incident, the Unabomber, the Oklahoma City bombing, and, inadvertently, Virginia Tech.[48] Kellner dedicates one chapter in particular to explain the ways in which Klebold and Harris, Theodore Kaczynski, and Tim McVeigh exemplify the narrative of white male identity politics, with the narrative of Seung-Hui Cho simply appearing at the end of the chapter as some type of unacknowledged addendum. Sutured together through an emphasis on gendered modes of violence, we see how a certain form of incoherency allows for various racializations being amalgamated despite a dissonance between cause and effect; in this case, there is a refusal to link Cho's cause of violence to a dissatisfaction with a lack of (Asian American) privilege. Instead, the cause of violence circles back to the loss of white privilege in a postracial and postfeminist society. Rather than reflecting a disorganized analysis, we think this might epitomize the way in which Asian Americans can be subsumed under narratives of whiteness while simultaneously uneasily located as the Asian alien-other within the rhetoric of postracial South and America.

Cho fit easily into the "school shooter type"—perhaps too easily—as his Asian American racialized identity (racially castrated male) already placed him within the realm of the loner/nerd who is unable to access heteromasculinity. In as much as the media and scholarly debates have offered psychological profiles of Cho, suggesting that he was—like all school shooters—ostracized and taunted in school, readily influenced by violent media, and emasculated by all, something about Cho marked him as especially obvious and quintessentially typecast; Cho was figured as the typical school shooter *amplified*, in that he was like these other (white) school shooters, but even more alienated from heteromasculinity. In Kellner's analysis, the question of sexual identity—i.e., the potential for latent and, therefore, supposedly violent homosexuality (a particularly pernicious and ever-present heterosexist reading of male homosexuality)—is raised delicately when it comes to Klebold and Harris, while elaborated upon in regard to Cho. Kellner disregards the possibility of Klebold and Harris as "gay" due to the understanding that one of them had a girlfriend, while the rumored possibility of Cho's (homo)sexuality is given weight. After raising the question of whether or not Cho was "really" gay, Kellner notes that "at least in the Virginia Tech public sphere he pursued a straight male identity, even if this was not possible. . . . And when it was impossible for him to create a normative male sexual identity, he went amok constructing an ultraviolent masculine identity, with tragic results."[49] Again, we would point out the ways in which Cho is continuously racialized whereby his Asianness works as a normative frame of reference to effeminacy and the specter of homosexuality.

Hence, it is through gun violence that Cho achieves the elusive American masculinity that he is denied prior to the event. As Viet Thanh Nguyen poses "it is violence and its reenactment that serves as a key element of the shared experience between Asian Americans and other Americans; it is through violence that Asian Americans are first marked by others, as aliens, and then marked by themselves, as Americans.[50] Sonjia Hyon in her cogent discussion of *Better Luck Tomorrow*, further notes that "[t]he regeneration and renegotiation of an Asian American heteronormative patriarchal masculinity must execute the potential threat of being mistaken as an immigrant—foreign and feminine—by staging its violence intraracially."[51] While not intraracial, the violence enacted by Cho critically transforms his gendered and racialized social location, making him legible and visible through normativity.

In order for school shooters such as Klebold and Harris to be held up as American men with American wounds symptomatic of American injuries, they must be normalized citizen subjects who serve to warn us about the dangers of American society to its most vulnerable members—white heterosexual men. Interestingly, mental illness and disability are deflected as ways of understanding here. In this way, then, we would argue that the school shooter type is, in fact, racialized and gendered as the (supposedly disenfranchised) white heterosexual male who epitomizes the nation. In that Cho's deviance(s) via race, citizenship, masculinity, and disability expunged him from serving as a figure of the nation, his injuries, despite his attempts, were unrecognized.

Looking back from this vantage point, we want to point out how Cho has become the reference point for a new figure, namely the white mentally ill or autistic shooter, a reference point that has been used repeatedly in regard to James Holmes within the context of the Aurora, Colorado, shootings. Autism and, sometimes, schizophrenia are offered casually as informal and explanatory diagnoses of Cho's behavior and actions within a myriad of media sources that speculate about Cho's condition.[52] Whether or not Cho had autism is not only open to question, but also possibly misleading. What is more significant is the increasing association of autism with violence and danger that has had a recent resurgence as is evidenced by the comments made by MSNBC host Joe Scarborough who asserted that it was likely that James Holmes was "on the autism scale" [*sic*]. It is clear that Scarborough has Cho in mind as he criminalizes autism and creates the profile of the "autistic shooter."

> I looked at the Virginia Tech shooter. I look at this shooter. So many shooters are like this . . . are young males. In fact, before . . . you don't want to generalize, but as soon as I heard about this shooting, I knew who it was . . . a young, white male, probably from an affluent neighborhood, disconnected from society, it happens time and time again. . . . Most of it has to do with mental health. You have these . . . people that are somewhere, I believe, probably on the autism scale. I don't know if that's the case here, but it happens more often than not. . . . People that can walk around in society, they can function on college campuses, they can even excel on college campuses, but are socially disconnected. I have a son who has Asperger's who is loved by everybody in his family . . . for those that may not have a loving family and support group, who may be a little further along on the autism scale . . . and face . . . a terrible challenge day in and day out. Again, I don't know the specifics about this young man, but we see too many shooters bearing, in these types of tragedies, bearing these same characteristics mentally.[53]

From these statements, several observations can be made. First, Cho, not Holmes, is the paradigmatic white autistic shooter in Scarborough's frame. Scarborough does generalize, despite his protestations to the contrary, to formulate a profile based on a whitening of Cho that is then projected onto Holmes. Second, autism is being diagnosed after the event of violence so that autism is equated to the ability and desire to harm; that autism involves a lack of empathy, a propensity for violence, and a tendency toward "evil" has become a myth within popular and even academic discourses.[54] Third, this violence results from untreated autism due to the negligence of families. Scarborough implicitly poses autistic children and young adults as neurocitizens in need of recovery by the institution of the family through intense social, medical, and educational interventions; they must be "rescued" and rehabilitated in a form of biomedical neoliberalism—a convergence of biomedical and political discourses, in which it is the responsibility of the family to manipulate the neuroplasticity of the autistic citizen-child through its choices of intervention, regulation, and management. Unfit families (such as Cho's Korean American family who did not secure mental health care and services[55]), in contrast to Scarborough's loving and supportive family, unleash these broken white men unto society. This kind of coverage in relation to mental illness and autism is played out throughout the discussions of Cho who is depicted as having inadequate care due to his parents' lack of assimilation. In this case, the autistic shooter has become another disabled figure whose traumatic social injury—a lack of proper mental health is cathected back to the injury of white heteromasculinity.

Asian Americans and the Postracial South

Why is this relevant to the constructions of the South? One might answer that the South is the site where injured white heteromasculinities dwell in America. If Cho was racialized as white and alien-other, we want to ask what it means to locate Cho as a perpetrator of violence in the American South, which itself plays such a significant role in the American imaginary in regard to racial trauma, the memorializing and distancing of this racial trauma, and a corresponding narrative of white victimization. We have already discussed how Janssen frames the South as the Orient of the North. Here we turn to how other aspects of the South as a racialized region operates within the American imaginary. While the Columbine High School shootings were a frequent and significant reference point for Cho and Virginia Tech within media discourses, lynchings and Civil Rights were another set of common touchpoints in media discourses. Specifically, references to slavery, lynchings, segregation, and opposition to the Civil Rights movements were located in the distant past of the "Old South," thereby dislocating anti-Black racism as a contemporary systemic or structural form of oppression in the "New South." Having deflected these moments of racial trauma to the distant past, the figure of the white male was permitted to vacate the position of perpetrator of racial terror and the recipient of racial and gender privilege. This localization of Cho within the South facilitated the positioning of white men alongside others (people of color, women, transnational and cosmopolitan immigrants) as fellow victims, and this positioning of white males as oppressed victims, rather than as perpetrators, of racial trauma by an alien-other helped configure the South as postracial.

Media stories emphasized over and over the multicultural and global diversity of Virginia Tech and the presence of African American professors such as Nikki Giovanni on campus as signs of transformation.[56] In part, the media was adamant in pointing out how Cho's victims represented the transnational; as one *New York Times* headline aptly claimed, "Intersecting on a Fateful Day, Lives That Spanned the Country and the World."[57] As the article suggests, "with one devastating act, the 32 men and women from places as far apart as Romania, Peru, and Quebec were united in a horrifying fate, massacre by a student who was born in another land, a 23-year-old South Korean." A magazine article, which notes that the members of the Virginia Tech community "cheered" at hearing about Martin Luther King's assassination in 1968, is also quick to point out that victims of the Virginia Tech shootings represent the new, transnational Blacksburg: "This college town, where Black and white, male and female, Puerto Rican, Indian, Indonesian and

Egyptian, Christian, Muslim and Jew all died together—and mourned together—is a place that has changed profoundly over the years. A place that need not fear changes ahead."[58]

We want to suggest that the suppression of the narratives of (colonialism and) anti-Black racism and the valorization of cosmopolitanism has much to do with the current climate about race in a postracial and post-9/11 South and America. Namely, the ability to locate racism in the South is no longer desirable. Racism against African Americans needs to be narrated into a historical past. Furthermore, in order to recuperate the South and by extension those Hokies who are now us, it is necessary to scrub it clean of its taint of racism. In doing so, because of Cho's rupturing of so many racial national discourses, Virginia Tech and the South need be rewritten largely as part of the modern South—i.e., transnational and postracial America. Why, we ask, is there a necropolitical emphasis on the transnational? What function does this discourse serve in rendering Cho and Virginia Tech an American tragedy? It is here that we want to reiterate that the location of Virginia and the South matters. Histories of racism and colonialism are seen to be somehow corrected by the invocation of the postracial university campus located in the South. Specifically, the heightened visibility of African American women professors works to supplant a history of Black racial abjection with a narrative of a post–Civil Rights future for the South. In the account above, the historical "fact" that Martin Luther King's assassination was cheered is used also to suggest a present in which Black abjection cannot exist because the transnational is no longer foreign.

Correspondingly, if the South is postracial, then racial trauma is really distanced to the past and the legacy of white racial violence is absolved because the perpetrator is a nonnative alien-other within a postracial and cosmopolitan South. In this way, Asian Americans' status as nonwhites (or near-Blacks in the spectrum) allows for the South to be constituted as postracial. In suggesting that the presence of Asian Americans signals a lack of anti-Black racism, these discourses deploy Asian Americans' racial ambiguity in the service of white hegemony in the "postracial" South.

We suggest a specifically *postracial* and *transnational* South was furthered precisely in order to perpetuate American nationalism. The pedagogic and performative enunciations of *American* loss here enact a chain of associations in which our mourning for the dead is 1) a condemnation and exclusion of the incommensurable Cho, 2) a rendering of African Americans as docile and postracial patriots who are with "us," 3) a unification and domestication of the foreign and international into an inclusionary postracial South and transnational America, and 4) a reassertion that America remains the victim, rather than the perpetrator, of tragedy. In this way, the incidents at Virginia Tech illustrate so clearly how narratives of a postracial and transnational South further advance American nationalism and empire.

Cho and Asian America

Finally, we ask, how is it that Cho remained "unrecognized" by Asian America? To be more precise, we are less suggesting that Cho is unrecognized within Asian America, but that he did not incite Asian America. It is amply clear as Sylvia Shin Huey Chong posits in her article, "'Look, an Asian!' The Politics of Racial Interpellation in the Wake of the Virginia Tech Shootings," that one of the most formative ways in which Asian Americans might be racialized, particularly in regard to the Virginia Tech incident, is through Asian Americans' *anticipation* of racialization and othering. She points out, for example, that the media was put on notice by the Asian American Journalists Association that they would be on the lookout for prejudicial coverage.[59] In this sense, she offers the insightful suggestion that the expectation of a backlash against Asian Americans is a part of the process of race-making in the United States. Min Song too follows this trajectory when he suggests that Cho's foreignness was marked much more readily by Koreans and Korean Americans,[60] and that Asian Americans emphasized Cho's race more so than the mainstream press, especially toward the end of the coverage.[61]

While there certainly is an element of anticipation-as-racialization, we would also suggest that the ability to see or read for racialization reflects the knowledge that racial projects are produced through racialized imaginaries or, put differently, *the lurking presence of racialized apparitions.* Critical race scholars have been particularly attentive to the ways in which whiteness functions via the unspoken, and presumptive or normative, referent. Whiteness is marked, then, by what is not said much more so than via explicit representations. But we would be amiss if we did not consider the ways in which other forms of racialization are also produced by tacit norms, values, and expectations. The anticipation of Cho's racialization should be more directly understood as the expectation that old and new discourses on the monstrous globalization and militarization of Asian countries, the anxieties of a "majority-minority" American populace, the continuing migration by Asian "hordes," and, perhaps most importantly, the transformation of the Oriental despot of the past into the "extremist Muslim terrorist" of the post-9/11 present both directly and indirectly impact any and all conversations about Asian Americans in the United States.[62] While the citizen/alien binary has inflected understandings of Asian Americans in the past, we would argue Asian Americans—in fact, all identity groups in the United States—are read through and against the specters of terrorism and the virulent production of the "Muslim, Arab, and Middle Eastern looking" racial formation.[63] Moreover, precisely because of their illegibility and incoherency, Asian Americans may well be accustomed to "misrecognition" in relation to the norm.

The reason that Cho might appear to resist racialization is not that he was resistant; rather it was because discourses of terror and 9/11 had already predetermined the media coverage[64] on Virginia Tech. What was said in the beginning, for example, and what needed to be said later in the coverage reveal the ways in which terrorism and post 9/11 rhetoric fashioned the terms by which Cho would be evaluated. Douglas Kellner aptly describes Virginia Tech as "academia's 9/11," demonstrating the impossibility of reading Cho outside of 9/11 as a frame of reference. Moreover, soon after reports spread that the shooter was "Asian," the blogosphere speculated whether or not the shooter was "Paki" or a member of other racialized-as-terrorist groups and nationalities.[65] Once Cho was deemed Korean American (at first, some reports seemed incapable of noting the distinction between Korean and Korean American), the media fixated on locating his difference via narratives of the immigrant experience and the hardships of being raised by assiduous Asian parents. And later still, after Cho's manifesto of videos and pictures aired on NBC News and were reproduced throughout the Internet and print media, folks directly and indirectly compared them to the videos of "suicide bombers" and hyperviolent Asian films such as *Oldboy*.[66] Precisely because of these backpedalings, we want to suggest that Cho was racialized as terrorist by proximity and panethnicity.

How is it that Asian America worked to distance itself from Cho rather than mobilize around him? Clearly we do not want to suggest that Asian America could and should have "embraced" Cho. But what does it mean that it was difficult to recognize and acknowledge Cho as Asian American, to name these complex racializations, to raise a critique of American assimilation, to challenge the narrative and image of wounded white heteromasculinity again? How can we, by pointing out the inadequacies of understanding the simultaneous, complex, and compounding systemic forms of oppression and difference—disability, gender, sexuality, race, nation, and region—that shape Cho's location and condition, begin to forge an Asian American politics that does not abandon him? We neither seek to fetishize and legitimate violent masculinities, nor seek inclusion and justice based on their visibility. Asian America cannot mobilize around only those subjects who can be recognized through normalized frames of citizenship. In other words, we want to critique the project of inclusion and rights as inadequate for the basis of our Asian American politics as they are inadequate in addressing those who cannot be made legible and legitimate within these rubrics; thus we want to imagine a politics incited by the figure of Cho. Seung-Hui Cho was no Vincent Chin, but neither should he be forgotten within Asian America.

Notes

1. See, for example, Brian Friel and James Barnes, "For Democrats, a Loaded Issue," *National Journal* 39.16 (April 21, 2007): 75, and Richard Lowry, "Madness at Virginia Tech: Doing Nothing about the Kid behind the Sunglasses," *National Review* 59.8 (May 14, 2007): 27. It was even described as "the worst domestic massacre in U.S. history" by Liz

Halloran in "For a Moment, We Are All the Hokie Nation," *U.S. News and World Report* 142.15 (April 30, 2007): 12–14.

2. Amy L. Brandzel and Jigna Desai, "Race, Violence and Terror: The Cultural Defensibility of Heteromasculine Citizenship in the Virginia Tech Massacre and Don Imus Affair," *Journal of Asian American Studies* 11.1 (February 2008): 61–85. This essay includes a fuller discussion of the media coverage of Cho and Virginia Tech. As we do not want to replicate the analysis done there, we focus here instead on the ways that subsequent discussion (scholarship, more so than media) of Cho continues to erase race. Therefore, we do not seek to critique individual reflections by our colleagues but rather the broader arguments that seem to be repeated in the scholarship.

3. It may be that Cho's location in the South partially erased him from the map of Asian America, which is so strongly centered around California and the Northeast. Similar arguments for marginalization and erasure from Asian America and Asian American politics due to region can be made for Chai Vang, a Hmong American hunter who killed six deer hunters in Wisconsin. Vang's location in the Midwest (and as a Hmong American) has meant that he has not become a mobilizing figure at the national scale. This is not to argue that Vang and Cho are identical, as clearly Vang's racialization as a Hmong refugee is different from that of Cho. One could argue that Vang incited stronger Asian American politics in that Hmong and other Asian American communities stood in support and defense of Vang in ways that were not possible for Cho.

4. This question seems to be critical to understanding the complex case of Dharun Ravi in relation to his former roommate Tyler Clementi.

5. Here, the understanding of disability we want to employ is one that does not see the physical, psychological, and/or developmental impairment as the primary cause of the individual's disability. Instead, the social model of disability advocates that it is the normative understanding of bodies, ability, and functionality that creates systemic barriers, oppression, and exclusion. In this case, we suggest that it is not necessarily possible or desirable to tease apart Cho's race and mental health. Unfortunately, this provocative assertion is beyond the scope of this essay.

6. We make this argument that parallels recent discussion about the racialization of mental illness that is emerging within the history of psychiatry in works such as Jonathan Metzl, *The Protest Psychosis: How Schizophrenia Became a Black Disease*, Boston: Beacon Press, 2011. Popular media coverage is also discussing these issues: Jamilah King, "Young, Depressed, and of Color: Why Schools and Doctors Get It Wrong," *Colorlines*, http://colorlines.com/archives/2012/05/mental_health_diagnosis.html (accessed January 10, 2013). It is clear that Cho did get assistance with depression during his high school years, but services and care were irregular once he became an undergraduate student.

7. See Gary Okihiro, *Margins and Mainstreams*, Seattle: University of Washington Press, 1994, and Daniel Kim, *Writing Manhood in Black and Yellow*, Stanford: Stanford University Press, 2005, among others. Where brown may stand in relation to Black, white, and yellow is a separate but related question.

8. See, for example, Neil Gotanda, "Other Non-Whites in American Legal History: A Review of *Justice at War*," *Columbia Law Review* 85 (June 1985): 1186–1192.

9. Claire Jean Kim, "The Racial Triangulation of Asian Americans," *Politics and Society* 27.1 (1999): 105–138.

10. For more on intersectionality, see the work of women of color feminism, such as Kimberly Crenshaw, *Mapping the Margins: Intersectionality, Identity Politics, and the Violence against Women of Color*, Palo Alto, Calif.: Stanford University Press, 1992.

11. While this scholarship is particularly vast, we are especially informed by the work of Lisa Lowe, *Immigrant Acts: On Asian American Cultural Politics*, Durham, N.C.: Duke University Press, 1996.

12. Kim, "Racial Triangulation of Asian Americans," 107.

13. See Special Issue of *Journal of Asian American Studies* on the Midwest as an exception.

14. James W. Loewen, *The Mississippi Chinese: Between Black and White*, London: Oxford University Press, 1971.

15. Leslie Bow, *Partly Colored: Asian Americans and Racial Anomaly in the Segregated South*, New York: NYU Press, 2010, 11. See Leslie Bow, this volume.

16. David R. Jansson, "'A Geography of Racism': Internal Orientalism and the Construction of American National Identity in the Film *Mississippi Burning*," *National Identities* 7.3 (2005): 267. See also Jansson, "Internal Orientalism in America: W. J. Cash's *The Mind of the South* and the Spatial Construction of American National Identity," *Political Geography* 22 (2003): 293–316; Jansson, "American National Identity and the Progress of the New South" in *National Geographic Magazine. Geographical Review* 93.3 (2003): 350–369; Jansson, "The Haunting of the South: American Geopolitical Identity and the Burden of Southern History," *Geopolitics* 12.3 (2007): 1–26; and Jansson, "Racialization and 'Southern' Identities of Resistance: A Psychogeography of Internal Orientalism," U.S. *Annals of the Association of American Geographers* 100.1 (2010): 202–221.

17. Jansson, "Geography of Racism," 267.

18. Jansson, "American National Identity," 360, 353.

19. See the Census 2010 Profile for Virginia. http://www.census.gov/geo/www/guidest-loc/pdf/51_Virginia.pdf (accessed January 10, 2013).

20. Evan Thomas, "Making of a Massacre," *Newsweek Magazine*, April 29, 2007. http://www.thedailybeast.com/newsweek/2007/04/29/making-of-a-massacre.html (accessed August 7, 2012).

21. College is often a time of ethnic and racial identity development for many students of color who are able to cultivate coethnic friendships and communities that are often inaccessible or less accessible during primary and secondary education. A critical mass of students and ethnic community formation within the university facilitates the emergence of self and ethnic identity.

22. This does not necessarily lead to a redistribution of resources, appropriate support, or shift from white hegemonic cultural practices.

23. David Roediger, "What's Wrong with These Pictures? Race, Narratives of Admissions, and the Liberal Self-Representations of Historically White Colleges and Universities," *Washington University Journal of Law and Policy* 18.1 (2005): 203–222.

24. Peter Wallenstein, *Virginia Tech, Land-Grant University, 1872–1997: History of a School, a State, a Nation*, Blacksburg: Pocahontas Press, Inc., 1997.

25. Ibid., 266.

26. Ibid., 173.

27. Ibid., 174.

28. Ibid.

29. Ibid.

30. Much scholarship has been written about cosmopolitanism as an ethics and politics for the contemporary moment; see, for example, Kwame A. Appiah, *Cosmopolitanism: Ethics in a World of Strangers*, New York: W. W. Norton, 2006, and Pheng Cheah and Bruce Robbins, eds., *Cosmopolitics: Thinking and Feeling beyond the Nation*, Minneapolis: University of Minnesota Press, 1998.

31. Cheah and Robbins, *Cosmopolitics*, 175.

32. Finally, we want to suggest that while historically white universities may have changed their representations and demographics, conditions on campuses can range from negligent to hostile for students of color and international students.

33. While we briefly discuss the racialization of Cho as a terrorist, we do not have the space here to elaborate on this racial formation.

34. See Lucinda Roy's *No Right to Remain Silent: What We've Learned from the Tragedy of Virginia Tech*, New York: Three Rivers Press, 2009, and Peter Langman's *Why Kids Kill: Inside the Minds of School Shooters*, New York: Palgrave Macmillan, 2010. Margaret Price's *Mad at School: Rhetorics of Mental Disability and Academic Life*, Ann Arbor: University of Michigan Press, 2011, makes strides in providing a more thoughtful perspective on race and disability.

35. Brandzel and Desai, "Race, Violence and Terror," 67.

36. See Brandzel and Desai, "Race, Violence and Terror," for further elaboration.

37. The few examples that pepper the press usually focus on some kind of violent culturally "Asian" patriarchy or failed achievement of model minority status; in other words, stories emphasize the figure of the violent husband-father abusing women and children or the failure of Asian graduate students to garner academic achievement.

38. For a more detailed discussion of racialized masculinity, see Brandzel and Desai "Race, Violence and Terror."

39. Ibid.

40. Sonjia Hyon, "Anxieties of the Fictive: Asian American Politics of Visibility," Minneapolis: University of Minnesota, unpublished dissertation, 2011.

41. Min Hyoung Song, "Communities of Remembrance: Reflections on the Virginia Tech Shootings and Race," *Journal of Asian American Studies* 11.1 (February 2008): 9.

42. Ibid., 12.

43. Michael Kimmel, "Profiling School Shooters and Shooters' Schools: The Cultural Contexts of Aggrieved Entitlement and Restorative Masculinity." In *There Is a Gunman on Campus: Tragedy and Terror at Virginia Tech*, Ben Agger and Timothy W. Luke, eds., Lanham, Md.: Rowman and Littlefield Publishers, Inc., 2008), 73.

44. Douglas Kellner, *Guys and Guns Amok: Domestic Terrorism and School Shootings from the Oklahoma City Bombing to the Virginia Tech Massacre*, Boulder: Paradigm Publishers, 2008, 132.

45. Ibid.

46. See, for example, Nancy Gibbs, "Darkness Falls" (cover story), *Time* 169.18 (April 19, 2007): 36–53, http://www.time.com/time/magazine/article/0.9171.1612715–1.00.html (accessed March 20, 2013), and Nancy Shute and Avery Comarow, "What Went Wrong?" *U.S. News and World Report* 142.15 (April 22, 2007): 42–46, http://health.usnews.com/usnews/health/articles/070422/30mental.htm (accessed March 20, 2013).

47. See Shute and Comarow, "What Went Wrong?," for example.

48. Kellner, *Guys and Guns Amok*.

49. Ibid., 133.

50. Viet Thanh Nguyen, *Race and Resistance: Literature and Politics in Asian America* (New York: Oxford UP, 2002), 88.

51. Hyon, "Anxieties of the Fictive," 155.

52. There has been much speculation and guesswork about Cho and autism with some reports suggesting that he was diagnosed as a young child in Korea. For example, see Dave

Cullen's "Talk to the Chos," *New York Times*, April 27, 2007, http://www.nytimes.com/
2007/04/27/opinion/27cullen.html?_r=2&oref=slogin (accessed July 30, 2012), and "Virginia Tech Gunman Had Problems as a Child," April 19, 2007, http://www.kwtx.com/home/
headlines/7101526.html (accessed July 30, 2012). Richard Roy Grinker suggests that it is
unlikely that Cho would have been diagnosed with autism prior to migration as reactive
attention disorder (RAD) is more commonly diagnosed in Korea. http://autismbulletin
.blogspot.com/2007/04/unconfirmed-diagnosis-in-virginia-tech.html (accessed August
14, 2012).

53. "Joe Scarborough: James Holmes Suspected Aurora Shooter May Have Been 'On the
Autism Scale.'" http://www.huffingtonpost.com/2012/07/23/joe-scarborough-james-holmes
-autism_n_1694599.html (accessed July 23, 2012).

54. Simon Baron-Cohen, *The Science of Evil: On Empathy and the Origins of Cruelty*,
London: Basic Books, 2011.

55. As we mentioned earlier, Koreanness is made equivalent to nonmodern and that
which stigmatizes mental illness. "Culture" becomes an explanation in anthropologist
Richard Roy Grinker's writing about Cho and autism as well. While discussing whether or
not it is likely that Cho received a diagnosis of autism, Grinker continues. "It is unlikely he
would have been diagnosed in Korea. In the United States it is also unlikely, if only because
Korean Americans are on the whole very reluctant to seek mental health care (since it is just
so stigmatizing). Doctors I've interviewed (including Korean American doctors) tell me
that by the time someone gets to a mental health professional that person may be acutely
mentally ill." Utilizing the anthropological concept of stigma, Grinker implicitly offers
"culture" as a totalizing explanation for why "Korean Americans stigmatize mental health
care." Furthermore, Grinker insinuates that "neglect by culture" within Asian America,
rather than autism, may be a causal factor. As Korean American psychologist Richard
Lee notes, there are many factors—including a lack of mental health literacy, utilization
of native treatments, lack of health insurance, and a paucity of culturally competent pro-
viders—rather than stigma, that impact or may explain the underutilization of mental
health services by Korean Americans (personal correspondence).

56. See Gibbs, "Darkness Falls," and Shute and Comarow, "What Went Wrong?"; see
also Alton Maddox Jr., "Racism and the Virginia Tech Massacre," *New York Amsterdam
News*, April 26, 2007: 12.

57. Pam Belluck, "Intersecting on a Fateful Day, Lives That Spanned the Country and
the World," *New York Times*, April 18, 2007.

58. David Von Drehle, "Finding Their Way Back to Life," *Time* 169.19 (May 7, 2007):
44–45.

59. Sylvia Shin Huey Chong, "'Look, an Asian!' The Politics of Racial Interpellation in
the Wake of the Virginia Tech Shootings," *Journal of Asian American Studies* 11.1 (February
2008): 27.

60. Song, "Communities of Remembrance," 6.

61. Ibid., 10.

62. For more on this astute connection between the Oriental despot of the past and the
Muslim terrorist of the present, see Amit Rai, "Of Monsters," *Cultural Studies* 18.4 (July
2004): 538–570.

63. Clearly, the increasing violence against Sikh Americans, including the massacre at
the Oak Creek, Wisconsin, gurdwara in August 2012 is another indication of the expansion of this racialization. How the Muslim-looking racial formation is impacting Asian

American racializations is the subject of Desai's "Cinema of Insecurity: Asian American Racial Formations in Post-9/11 Media" (unpublished).

64. In both events, the spectacle of the media was significant in establishing a wounded and victimized nation. This is not to suggest that the coverage was identical; in fact, we might argue quite the opposite. The media spectacles around both events worked through different means to produce histories of white American trauma.

65. Andrew Lam, "Let It Be Some Other 'Asian,'" originally posted to *New American Media* on April 17, 2007, and reprinted in *The Nation* and elsewhere. http://news.newamerica media.org/news/view_article.html?article_id=e3b9c4941f9d849f9358ddb3dbbbe5a3 (accessed June 29, 2009).

66. See, for example, Halloran, "For a Moment," 12–14.

PART II

Community Formation and Profiles

CHAPTER 4

Segregation, Exclusion, and the Chinese Communities in Georgia, 1880s-1940

Daniel Bronstein

Introduction

Between 1875 and 1943, the U.S. Congress passed several laws designed to curtail Chinese entry into the United States. Unregulated Chinese migration was deemed a threat to the employment opportunities of European American workers and the machinations of white labor groups who did not want employers to use Chinese "coolie" laborers. European American intellectuals and citizens supported restrictive legislation because they viewed Chinese as racially inferior and did not want them to settle permanently in the United States. To accomplish this aim, the statutes barred Chinese from becoming U.S. citizens so they could not vote in general elections and remained prone to deportation as illegal aliens.

While the federal law sought elimination of Chinese labor migration into the United States, it permitted entry to Chinese who belonged to certain class categories: 1) merchants, 2) travelers, 3) government officials, 4) students, 5) teachers, 6) U.S. citizens, and 7) laborers possessing certificates of residence. Unlike "laborers," who were viewed by Caucasians as taking away employment from white workers and lowering working wages, "merchants" were not seen as a threat to the American labor movement because they promoted trade between China and the United States. The definition of *merchant* remained flexible for decades and included small shop owners who did not have international ties with China. Immigration inspectors eventually admitted wives and young children of merchants and U.S. citizens with increasing frequency after 1910.

This essay examines the impact of the Exclusion laws on the Chinese communities in Atlanta, Augusta, and Savannah, Georgia. Chinese residents wishing to visit China had to undergo lengthy interrogations from immigration officials in the cities where they resided and when returning through immigration ports. Those engaged in the grocery business endured investigations of their business establishments by immigration officials who decided whether or not to grant them the merchant status. The merchant category benefited the economically successful grocers in Augusta and a few in Savannah who used it to reunify their families in the United States. The majority of the laundrymen in the three cities did not bring their families over. Most Chinese immigrants operated grocery stores in Augusta and Savannah after 1920 so their communities became more family-oriented and increased in size. Atlanta's community continued to decline in size until the 1940s because it consisted primarily of aging laundry and restaurant owners who lived without their family in residence.

The essay also probes into how the emerging Jim Crow system dealt with the Chinese since they were neither black nor white. Unlike the federal acts explicitly targeting Chinese, the white-controlled state government of Georgia sought to uphold and refine its Jim Crow statutes, enforcing de jure segregation against its larger African American population but not its smaller Chinese population, which were not seen as white and not necessarily as black. Nonetheless, Georgia's state legislature was concerned with the Chinese presence. Miscegenation was the primary anxiety of state legislators because some Chinese men married white women before the 1920s. The state eventually included Chinese and Asians as part of a harsher miscegenation law passed in 1927, which remained on the books until 1967. Another apprehension for the state government was whether children of Chinese descent could attend white schools. The legislature considered revoking funds to white public schools enrolling children with Asian ancestry in 1931, but testimony from Chinese parents and sympathetic whites convinced legislators to abandon the idea.

Asian immigrants and their descendants did not easily conform to the black-white dyad that defined southern race relations and, in the minds of older southern whites, could never quite conform to their understandings of "whiteness."[1] They did not have the African ancestry that defined them as being "colored" in the biracial world of Jim Crow. Even without the stigma of having black skin, the "yellow" complexion of Asians marked them for potential harassment and discrimination from southern whites. Chinese residents in Georgia were occasionally victims of press-reported violence and probably heard racial slurs and verbal assaults that did not make it into print. Yet, the state of Georgia issued driver's licenses to Chinese with a "W" and did not force Chinese to sit in the "colored" sections of railroad cars or movie theaters. In time, Chinese Americans came to realize "their place" as somewhere in-between people with European and African ancestry.[2]

Chinese Exclusion Legislation and Chinese and the Three Cities

Chinese immigrant communities living in Atlanta, Augusta, and Savannah between 1882 and 1943 lived in a harsh environment of federally sanctioned anti-Chinese discrimination. Passage of the first Chinese Exclusion Act in 1882 and its revisions and renewals in 1888, 1892, 1902, and 1904 strictly regulated the movement of all Chinese who wished to travel back and forth between the United States and China. These laws explicitly banned for the first time the entry of laborers, who were deemed by U.S. politicians, labor organizations, and ordinary people to be taking away employment opportunities from white male workers.[3] Chinese laborers who had resided in the United States prior to 1882 could reenter the United States if they possessed the appropriate paperwork required by the federal government to reenter. The definition of laborer included several unskilled and semiskilled occupations, but it came to be associated largely with Chinese immigrants in the laundry and restaurant businesses.

Racial politics influenced the passage and extension of the Chinese Exclusion laws. West Coast politicians had led successful opposition to Radical Republican efforts in the 1870s to strike down the clause granting U.S. citizenship to people only of European and African heritages because they did not want Chinese immigrants to become American citizens with the right to vote and bring over family.[4] White Southern politicians, while not having many Chinese in their states, did not want the introduction of a "third race" in their states while they were in the process of establishing a postbellum segregationist order against recently freed African Americans.[5] The conflating of "yellow" with "black" fueled the growing national movement to exclude the Chinese. Its passage in 1882 helped assure that most U.S. citizens would be of either European or African heritages until the revised Immigration Act of 1965 abolished the biased national origins system.

U.S. politicians, businessmen, and traders, however, did not want complete stoppage of Chinese immigration. The U.S. Congress created a "legally domiciled merchant" category, which allowed Chinese residents to travel to China and return to the United States more freely. Chinese immigrants engaged in the mercantile business in the United States were seen as fostering trade ties between the two nations and not as threatening to American workers and labor organizations.

The first Chinese Exclusion Act (1882) forbade the entry of Chinese laborers into the United States and required all Chinese male laborers departing from U.S. ports to be issued special reentry permits. Each voyager had to have his name, age, occupation, last place of residence, and a general personal description entered into registry books.[6] One Augusta "laborer," Lee Ping, departed for China from San Francisco in 1883 and was the first resident in the three cities to be recorded in the San Francisco ledgers. San Francisco remained the primary port of departure and arrival for Chinese immigrants throughout the United States because of its strategic position to help facilitate trade with Asia and the connections that the Chinese immigrant community in that city maintained with their homeland. Also residents of Augusta, Chong Loo Too, Wai Kum, and Chung Too gave their occupations as "book keepers" and were associated with grocery stores in the city, but they lacked enough business interest in the firms to be considered merchants.[7] Three Atlanta laundry operators and one "porter," probably a servant, also departed through San Francisco during the 1880s.[8] No Chinese in this ledger series (1882–1888) gave their last place of residence as Savannah. These men were entitled to reenter if they possessed the certificate issued to them when they departed and the description entered into the ledger of the applicant matched. The Scott Act (1888) severely curtailed labor migration from China by reaffirming the previous ban on laborers and invalidating all documentation that the federal government had previously issued to Chinese laborers for their reentry. This amendment stranded many laborers in China, probably including the immigrants mentioned above, if they had tried to reenter the United States.[9]

There were many roadblocks in the way of entry and reentry of Chinese using the exempted categories. The U.S. collector of customs at the port of San Francisco required after 1893 that all Chinese traveling as merchants provide sworn statements about their firms, which included the names of all partners and the estimated value of each partner's worth in the business. Although this was a decision by a local zealous official bent on discouraging all Chinese movement through his port, the decision had a national impact because so many Chinese used San Francisco as a point of departure and entry to the United States.[10] Three Augusta Chinese grocers underwent this revised process that same year when they departed on the steamer *New York* bound for China. All of these men were partners—along with one other person who was not accompanying them on the trip.[11]

The federal government renewed the Chinese Exclusion Act, also known as the Geary Act for the California Congressman who wrote it, in 1892 for another ten years. The revised law sought to clearly define the difference between the categories of merchant versus laborer along with expanding the powers of immigration officials in monitoring Chinese immigration. The laborer category was expanded to include peddlers and sellers of dried seafood in the late 1880s. Furthermore, a new "laundryman as laborer" clause was added: "This department has decided that laundrymen are laborers within the meaning of this act, and that the fact that a laundryman has accumulated capital and has become an employer of laborers in that same business does not change his status as a laborer."[12] The law would not grant wealthy Chinese laundry operators the same privileges of bringing over family like successful merchants. This reclassification impacted all three communities for decades, as well as Chinese immigrants throughout the United States.

Finally, the Geary Act included a provision that all Chinese laborers residing in the United States had to register with the federal government and carry a certificate of residence (known in Cantonese as "chock gee") at all times.[13] Unlike the first two acts, the Geary Act brought federal intrusion on the lives of all Chinese laborers in the United States, regardless of whether they had any intention of returning to China. The registration process went slower than the government anticipated and the time allocated nationally for required Chinese laborers to comply with the order was extended through 1894.[14] Registration for most of the Chinese in Georgia began in February 1894 when the Collector's Office of Internal Revenue of Georgia, which was based in Atlanta, sent letters to local officials throughout the state asking for the number and names of Chinese immigrants living in their jurisdictions. Since most of the Chinese in the state were laundry operators, an occupation defined by the government as not eligible for exemption, they would have to register or risk arrest and deportation.[15]

Over thirty officials, including those from Augusta, Savannah, and Atlanta, responded with the requested information and with more than half writing that their towns contained no Chinese. Thirteen towns reported that they had at least one Chinese resident. Their presence in these areas can be explained by the need for Chinese launderers by the local white population, even in more rural areas such as Dalton and Cartersville, Georgia. According to the *Augusta Chronicle*, the deputy collector of the state's Internal Revenue Office, John A. Cobb, visited Macon, Savannah, and Augusta so that each of its Chinese residents could fill out the necessary paperwork.[16] White witnesses were also required to corroborate the applicant's information for it to be accepted.

Augusta was a unique case in this process because, unlike the laundrymen communities in Savannah and Atlanta, merchants made up the majority of the Chinese immigrants in the city and were therefore exempt from registering. Most, however, chose to undergo the process anyway and have the certificates as protection from possible deportation. Cobb's visit fascinated the *Augusta Chronicle*, which wrote a long article about the steps involved in registration, including what information was on each certificate, the dimensions of the photographs to be attached, and even the names of most of the men who received them. It was almost a who's who of Augusta's Chinese immigrant community. One month later, the newspaper reported correctly that the city had the largest Chinese population in the state.[17] The "chock gee" remained an important means of federal identification of Chinese immigrants for decades, even when photographs and some of the information became outdated. The question "where were you at the time of the Geary Act?" continued to be asked of these aging men who pulled out documentation revealing much younger faces that were forever scarred by the legacy of the Geary Act.

Throughout the early years of the twentieth century, immigration officials enforced the lines of who was excluded with increasing rigor.[18] The majority of the Chinese immigrants, who managed to accumulate enough savings while working in Georgia, visited China, often leaving through San Francisco. Others decided to enter and reenter through Seattle, Washington; Portal, North Dakota (not a seaport); and other American seaports. To do any sort of travel outside the United States, however, Chinese immigrants were required—if they ever wanted to return—to fill out special documentation before their departure. Different forms had to be completed depending on the person's occupation or citizenship. Most Chinese from Georgia used the following papers: 1) "merchants, students, and teachers"; 2) "laborers"; and 3) "alleged American citizen[s] of the Chinese race."[19]

For the most part, investigations of the mercantile statuses of Augusta's grocery store operators usually resulted in the issuance of a return permit. At least fourteen reentry permits have been found for grocers who traveled to China via San Francisco between 1904 and 1941. An official from the immigration district office in Savannah usually came by rail and prepared the papers of the applicant. He inspected the residence and business, interrogated the prospective traveler and at least two *white* witnesses, and included reports detailing the value of the business and the physical dimensions of the store. Grocers generally gave their testimony in English—a skill also required to sell goods to their non-Chinese customers—while being interrogated in Augusta, which illustrated that some of them had acquired English while living there and in other American cities and towns.[20] Responding to the answers in English struck a positive chord with immigration officials who usually considered it as evidence that the person had been in the United States for a long time and should be issued the return permit. It appears that only one case has been found in which an immigration official decided to deny an applicant a merchant reentry permit. It occurred in Savannah in 1932 when Chinese and white witness testimony failed to convince the onsite immigration official of the applicant's mercantile status.[21]

Few laundrymen residing in Georgia's three largest cities applied for return applications. Chinese in the laundry business were considered "laborers" and therefore not exempt from the Chinese Exclusion Acts. Exceptions for travel to China were made only for those Chinese laborers who had lived in the United States before passage of the initial Chinese Exclusion Act in 1882 and who had also registered for a certificate of residence as a laborer in 1892. These men filled out the "legally domiciled laborer" form and had to, by federal law, deposit one thousand dollars in an American bank or have a person or persons financially indebted to the applicant for the same amount. This monetary requirement coupled with the expensive steamship ticket certainly discouraged many laundrymen from making the trip back home. Witnesses, usually bank representatives, also had to corroborate the statements of these would-be travelers and show written proof of the deposit amount before the applicant would be granted a return permit. It was more feasible for laundrymen to send remittances to family or save money to retire in China than to try to visit their homeland and then return to the United States.[22] Only five Chinese laundrymen went through the process required for legal laborer reentry.

The Chinese Exclusion laws complicated the lives of Chinese immigrants residing in the United States and their families in China. Chinese immigrants could gain admission only if they belonged to the federally recognized exempted categories and submitted to ruthless investigations by immigration officials to prove their status and family relationships. This practice discouraged many from traveling home who feared that the government would not let them return to the United States. One has no way of knowing how many Chinese in Atlanta, Augusta, and Savannah were deterred from voyaging for this reason.

Others could not save enough funds for a visit. Savannah's Chinese residents, who were mostly laundrymen between 1882 and 1943, either did not accrue enough money for a visit to China, returned to China without filing for a return permit, or did not give their last place of residence as Savannah when passing through immigration ports. Atlanta's predominately Chinese laundrymen population confronted the same problems as laundrymen in Savannah. Some Chinese grocers in Augusta were marginally successful enough in their businesses to afford a year away from their store and travel as merchants.

Family Reunification during the Exclusion Period

Chinese immigrants wishing to have family join them in the United States had to overcome a series of legal obstacles designed to discourage the reunification of Chinese families in the United States. The attempted exclusion of Chinese women from the United States began seven years before the passage of the Chinese Exclusion Act (1882) when Congress had passed the Page Act (1875) forbidding the importation of women for purposes of prostitution. Chinese women were the primary targets of the new law because of the popular stereotype of the time that all Chinese women in the United States were prostitutes.[23] A "guilty until proven innocent" attitude among immigration officials forced Chinese women to have to convince inspectors that they were not going to engage in prostitution and that they were the wives or daughters of Chinese immigrants already in the country. This law drastically reduced the number of women who were able to enter the United States. The Chinese Exclusion Act (1882), however, permitted the legal admission of wives and young children as dependents of merchants or as dependents of U.S. citizens. A U.S.-born Chinese American population emerged as a result of legal and illegal immigration of these two categories.

Chinese immigrants residing in Atlanta, Augusta, and Savannah were similarly affected by American immigration laws in their efforts to bring family over from China. Furthermore, because Chinese immigrants followed different occupational patterns in each city, they were also treated differently. Successful grocers in Augusta, who were considered merchants, used this category to reunify with loved ones back home and to expand their families in the United States. Chinese laundry operators in Atlanta and Savannah, however, faced many obstacles. As laborers, they were not legally able to have family join them. This limitation, combined with a meager income, meant that families rarely emerged among laundrymen. And, among those who were not able to retire in China, most died without family or with male relatives or friends. In Georgia, some laundry operators were able to persuade immigration officials of their U.S. citizenship although they had been born in China, which entitled them to bring over family members and sometimes friends and strangers as "paper sons."

Chinese merchants in Savannah and Augusta started sending for their sons and wives to join them following *United States v. Mrs. Gue Lim* (1900), in which the U.S. Supreme Court ruled that legally domiciled merchants were entitled to bring over family members from China.[24] Savannah's two Asian specialty dealers used their merchant status to bring over several dependents. Huie On, whose father owned the Kee Chung Company, joined his father in Savannah in 1908.[25] The two sons of Jung Kai Hen Shung, who owned Fat Shung Company, arrived in 1912.[26] Few other Chinese merchant male dependents passed through San Francisco with Savannah as their place of residence. Several families that eventually settled in Savannah also spent time in Augusta or another state.

In Augusta, Chinese grocers used their status as merchants to bring over at least 12 sons between 1903 and 1943. All entered through San Francisco. Exact statistics are not available for Seattle, but merchant sons also came through this port as well. A few of these sons were not permitted to enter the United States because they were over twenty-one years of age at the time they applied for admission and, therefore, were not considered to be dependents.[27] Woo Man Foo and Woo Piu, sons of Woo Lung and Woo Leong Tong, were denied entry because governmental physicians deemed them to be over twenty-one.[28]

An even greater change for the Chinese immigrant community in Augusta occurred with the arrival of wives and a few daughters. These women appeared at a time when more and more female dependents used these exemptions to be admitted. From 1910 to 1924, Chinese females enjoyed higher admission rates than Chinese males in the United States.[29] This success was mirrored in Augusta.

Between 1903 and 1943, seven merchant wives passed through San Francisco to join husbands living in Augusta or husbands who had once lived in Augusta. A smaller number entered through Seattle. Jam Nin Shee and her husband Wong Wing passed through Angel Island in early 1916. Wong was released in three days and Jam Nin in twelve days.[30] They arrived in Augusta later that year. Some women had to spend more time on Angel Island before they were granted entry. Ching Shee came over unaccompanied by her husband Wong Woey Too in 1921 and spent about three weeks on Angel Island before her admission.[31] The couple had married in 1902, a year before Wong immigrated to the United States via San Francisco where he lived until 1918. The entry of these women and others enabled a U.S.-born Chinese population to appear by the 1920s.

There is also evidence showing that at least two Chinese Americans in Augusta masqueraded as grocers to bring over their wives and children. Lau Kwok Fui first came to the United States in 1921, using the paper identity "Ben Jung," and he worked in various laundries in the South. Lau entered as a "paper son" or a person who assumed the identity of someone else so he could legally enter the United States. Usually, the Chinese applicant claimed to be the son of a U.S. citizen. As a Chinese-born laundryman, he could not bring over a wife from China based on American immigration law. Six years after his entry, while making a living as a laundry worker in Augusta, he claimed to be a grocer. Officials believed him, and he visited China and returned to Georgia with his wife.[32] Posing as a merchant was also a commonly used practice to bring family over from China.

The only known case of a Chinese immigrant using his merchant status to reunify his family was Thomas Young. Young was a Chinese herbalist in Atlanta from 1914 until 1932. His wife, Yee Shee, came through Seattle in 1923 and they had a family of two sons and a daughter.[33] Another daughter, Apple, died as an infant and is buried in the old Chinese section of Greenwood Cemetery.[34] The Young family had their residence/store in an affluent neighborhood of the city where they could cater to the white middle-class population and the city's small Chinese community.[35]

Chinese immigrants living in Atlanta, the majority of which were laundrymen, did not have family with them. It was a combination of necessity and restrictive immigration laws that hindered family reunification for these immigrants. Exclusion laws barred laborers, including laundrymen by 1892, from bringing in family.[36] Furthermore, families living in China sought to maximize the remittances sent back by relatives in the United States and realized that, having a wife and young children join their father would drain the flow of these funds.

Evidence has come to light, however, of Chinese immigrants in Atlanta using the "native born" category for bringing over sons and "paper sons" from China. During the Chinese Exclusion Era, many Chinese came to the United States as "paper sons" using a "slot system," which was developed in which Chinese, who were either born or asserted to be born in the United States, said to federal authorities upon reentry that they had given birth to a child, usually a son. This slot was then given to a male relative (perhaps a cousin) and, even more often, to a stranger whose family had bought the slot. The procedure involved the applicant assuming the identity of the "paper son" and learning as much as possible about that family to induce immigration inspectors that he was indeed the child of that person and therefore a U.S. citizen.[37]

U.S. vs. Wong Kim Ark (1898) laid the foundation for an increasing number of Chinese claiming that they had a right to reenter the United States after visiting China because they had been born on American soil and were, therefore, citizens. Federal law prevented those born in China from becoming American citizens. Furthermore, the case also set the precedent for the transmission of American citizenship from parents to children born in China.[38] The 1906 San Francisco earthquake and fire destroyed the birth records of the city so even more Chinese living in the United States and China could claim they were born in San

Francisco's Chinatown. The Wong Supreme Court ruling and the destruction of San Francisco's records helped more Chinese enter the United States, claim U.S. citizenship, and bring over paper sons.

The usage of the paper son slot system is evident with Atlanta laundry operator Yee Min's travels to and from China. Yee, who visited China twice, asserted that he had been born in San Francisco in 1883. On his first visit, he sailed out of Vancouver, Canada, to marry Huey Shee and allegedly conceived two sons. His second visit was made while he lived in Atlanta; he returned through San Francisco in 1914 reportedly after the birth of a third son.[39] Two "paper sons" were successful in 1922 and 1935 in entering the United States, but a third one failed the interrogation and was deported in 1923. None of them went to Atlanta to become laundrymen. Instead, one went to work as a delivery boy in Philadelphia. It is not known what happened to the other after his admission through New York City. The first "paper son" lived for decades as a "Yee" until he confessed his true lineage and name in the mid-1960s.[40] His confession was part of a larger Confession Program instigated by the federal government to weed out Chinese communist sympathizers in the 1950s and 1960s. Chinese who agreed to divulge that they had illegally entered would be permitted to stay if they did not have ties with the Chinese communist government or had professed communist sympathies.[41]

One Atlanta laundry operator also entered the United States under the paper name of "Jew Shiu Dun." In 1936, he claimed to be the son of an American citizen who owned a restaurant in Dallas, Texas. Instead of going to Texas to be with his "father," he went into the laundry business with the help of his biological cousins, who lived in Georgia.[42] Other Atlanta laundry operators undoubtedly used this process as a means of entry as well, but precise figures are difficult to compile because false entries are impossible to detect in the immigration files without subsequent confessions in the 1950s and 1960s. Laundry operators in Augusta also used the "slot system." One laundryman, who was either born or claimed to be born in San Francisco, visited China four times. After each trip, he declared the births of more children and was eventually documented as having seven sons and one daughter. Four male dependents came to the United States, two in 1909 and two in 1913, using the "son of native" status. One of the dependents later used his U.S. citizenship to bring over a blood or paper relative during the late 1920s as a "son of a son of a native."[43]

Some laundry operators and even grocers used their American citizenship to bring over female dependents, usually wives. American citizenship status had its advantages over the merchant category for several reasons. It did not require the retention of a mercantile business at the time of the application for the reentry permit or when sponsoring China-born family members. Furthermore, merchants invariably needed two white witnesses to support their claims, but this was not consistently required for U.S.-born Chinese Americans. Finally, it was a status difficult for immigration officials to verify because of the lack of white witnesses to births in San Francisco's Chinatown. Furthermore, the destruction of immigration files in the 1906 San Francisco earthquake also meant that inspectors had no way to verify whether someone had immigrated to the United States prior to that year unless he had records maintained elsewhere.[44]

Harry (Duer) Wong, the proprietor of a laundry in Atlanta, apparently used his native-born status to bring over a wife and son from China. The 1930 census listed his birthplace as "California" and his wife and son as being born in "China."[45] Based on U.S. immigration laws of that time, he could not have brought over dependents using his occupational status and therefore used his citizenship to bring family over. Immigration officials would have had to have verified his "native born" status and probably did so sometime in the late 1920s. Sadly, no immigration materials have been found to show what status he actually used to get her into the United States.

Although most of Augusta's China-born residents used the merchant category for entry, a few grocers opted to bring over wives and sons using their American citizenship. Chinese American males continued to find wives in China because of the skewed male-to-female sex ratio in Chinese American communities. Out-marriage was discouraged within Chinese communities because of cultural pride. European Americans feared "racial pollution" and amended antimiscegenation statutes in several states to include people of Asian descent, as well as exerting social pressure to keep Asians from marrying "whites." The 1924 Immigration Act suspended the admittance of spouses of U.S. citizens for six years but did not greatly impact Augusta's Chinese community since most grocers were born in China and used their merchant status to bring over family. It is unknown how this law impacted the laundry and restaurant operators in the three cities. None attempted to bring family over after the passage of this law, perhaps because they had resigned themselves to the fact that it would be impossible to do so. Other reasons—such as lack of monies—also could have contributed. In 1930, the Immigration Act (1924) was amended to allow Americans of Chinese descent to bring over Chinese-born wives if they had married prior to 1924.[46]

Chinese immigrant grocers in Augusta continued to send for family during the 1930s until the Japanese attack on Pearl Harbor on December 7, 1941, which shut down almost all immigration to the United States across the Pacific Ocean. Sons of Chow Sang and Lam Chi (C. H. Lam) joined their fathers in 1932 and 1941 respectively. Chow entered the United States through New Orleans, using a merchant's certificate issued to him by the Nicaraguan government while he lived in Bluefields, Nicaragua.[47] Lam, a scholar-educator originally from the Sun Wei District in Guangdong Province, settled in Augusta in 1937 after living in San Francisco since 1922. He had come to the United States for education and later became a principal of a Chinese school in San Francisco for nine years prior to settling in Augusta.[48] Like most Chinese Americans in Augusta at that time, he opened a grocery store in a black neighborhood.[49] Chinese laundry and restaurant operators in all three cities continued the pattern of not sending for their wives and children in China.

Sixty-one years of exclusion deterred many Chinese immigrants in the United States from having wives and young children join them. The laws explicitly banned laborers, who were the largest number of Chinese immigrants in the United States, and their dependents. With the expansion of the laborer categories in the 1890s to include laundry operators and restaurant owners, even more Chinese immigrants were unable to bring over their families. Two categories were exempt from the law—the dependents of merchants and of U.S. citizens. Family members, however, had to substantiate these claims through rigorous interrogations by hostile immigration officials. Those that survived this process were ultimately able to reunite with their fathers and husbands.

Chinese Immigrants and Jim Crow Georgia

The failure of Georgia's state legislature and other local and county governing bodies in the years prior to World War II to pass many anti-Chinese laws is also significant. As Chinese immigrants moved into the postbellum South during the 1870s and 1880s, they entered a society already seriously shaken by the abolition of slavery and the introduction of racial equality by the federal government. Efforts to redefine the relationship between the white and black populations were still "in play" during this period and, in some places, into the 1890s. The hope of establishing a "New South" based on racial integration gave way to a rigidly segregated biracial order in which whites sought to deny public voice to African Americans and assure white domination of all political, economic, and social structures in the region. Whites in Georgia and other states protected this new racial order by passing state statutes in all Southern states, known popularly as "Jim Crow laws," to reinforce these desires and attitudes. And, when the law was not enough, white mobs turned to lynchings in order to control African Americans through fear and intimidation.

The biracial order of Jim Crow quickly took hold in postwar Southern states, although faster in some states than others. For the most part, it was a piecemeal process that completely restricted African American economic, social, and political mobility in the South. Georgia passed statutes against interracial marriage in 1865, African American male suffrage in 1871 and 1877, school integration in 1872 and 1877, and integrated railroad cars in 1890 and 1899.[50] Besides the enactment of restrictive legislation and housing segregation, African Americans were often victims of organized and spontaneous violence carried out to keep them in their increasingly subordinate status. The number of reported lynchings of African Americans remained high during these decades.[51] African Americans protested these discriminatory practices through the courts and boycotts. One of the more well-known events in Georgia was the boycott of Savannah trolleys by the African

American community in 1907.[52] Those of mixed ancestry and of wealth within the African American community were not exempted from discriminatory treatment in this new southern racial hierarchy.[53]

Chinese immigrants did not fit the popular and scientific understanding of whiteness in the South, which could have protected them from possible race-based persecution. Because they were of Asian descent (often associated with the color "yellow"), Chinese immigrants were potential targets for discrimination in the emerging Jim Crow system. However, unlike western states with their blatantly anti-Asian legislation and violence, the Jim Crow South did not have a monolithic response for dealing with Chinese immigrants, and it was unclear to many where to place Chinese immigrants within the black-white paradigm. Racial stereotypes formulated on the West Coast by white settlers, including some southerners, threatened to conflate yellow and black, but Chinese immigrants in the South were relatively few and were not necessarily seen as a threat.[54] State, county, and city governments in Georgia had little need for passing laws directly aimed at regulating the activities of Chinese residents.

The two areas in which the Chinese presence in Georgia caused controversy was whether they could attend white schools and marry women of European ancestry. Furthermore, surviving documentation reveals few incidents of violence perpetrated against Chinese in Atlanta, Augusta, and Savannah stemming from local white fears of a "yellow peril," or a supposed Chinese invasion. Some of this can be attributed to the collective behavior of most Chinese in these three cities. Like other immigrants, they socialized among themselves, remained at their place of business most of the time, and went only to venues where they knew they were welcomed guests. Even with these precautions, Chinese Americans who came to the South were cognizant of their precarious position in the emerging black-white divide.

Violence against the Chinese Americans in Georgia is more difficult to discern in surviving records from the period. Chinese laundry operators in Atlanta and Savannah did not appear to be targets of rising racial animosity; no evidence has been found that the forty or so Chinese laundries and their workers were damaged or injured during the 1906 Atlanta Race Riot.[55] Since most of the Chinese laundries were in white areas, it is unlikely that they would have been purposely targeted. This does not mean, however, that Chinese Americans were not victims of more subtle forms of discrimination such as verbal insults and racial slurs. These incidents would not show up in newspapers or in court records.

Anti-Chinese feelings, however, were felt in Augusta and in a neighboring town during the 1880s. The best-known case of "sinophobia" in the state occurred in Waynesboro, Georgia, a town near Augusta. The victims of the crime were all men who had lived in Augusta prior to moving to Waynesboro. Known popularly as the "Loo Chong Case," it was named for William Loo Chong, who had gained wealth in Augusta as a grocer and tea dealer with his brothers or cousins. His marriage to Denise Fulcher in Augusta, however, provoked controversy in 1882. Georgia's antimiscegenation law did not contain any explicit language saying whether a man of Chinese descent was legally entitled to marry a white woman. After this marriage, Loo Chong and his partners had hoped to open a grocery store in Waynesboro with the help of Loo Chong's in-laws, who were local farmers. The store was set to begin operations when some of the town's residents threatened them with physical violence and told them to leave town. White antipathy in this case stemmed from fears about the possibility that more Chinese-white marriages (along with anxieties surrounding possible economic competition) would result if there were no regulation to prevent them—including threats of violence.[56]

The Loo Chong episode prompted Richmond County representative M. V. Calvin and his supporters to revise Georgia's 1865 antimiscegenation statute, which already banned black-white marriages. Calvin submitted a bill to the state legislature in 1884 "forbid[ding] marriages between persons of Mongolian descent and persons of the white race."[57] The consideration of changing the law was a sign of the times with states, such as California and Mississippi, adding clauses to their antimiscegenation statutes forbidding clerks from issuing marriage licenses to Chinese-white couples.[58] Georgia's bill, however, did not pass the state house of representatives and was never introduced in the state senate.[59] Perhaps, with the exception of Augusta, the Chinese presence was so small that other county representatives did not see a need to revise the law.[60]

An even more serious issue for Augusta's Chinese occurred in 1885 and 1886 when the white merchants sought local governmental intervention against Chinese-operated grocery stores. White merchants petitioned the Augusta City Council to not issue business licenses to Chinese merchants. The Council rejected this petition in December 1885.[61] A few months later, the white merchants sent a second petition to the Council, which received a great deal of attention in the local newspaper. The newspaper involved itself closely with the issue and reported the grievances from both sides. In particular, white merchants claimed that they could not compete successfully with Chinese because they had families to support and homes to care for while Chinese immigrants lived frugally in the back of their stores. The white grocers were not aware of or ignored the fact that Chinese immigrants sent money to China to support their families. Moreover, they also accused the Chinese of cheating the "ignorant class[es]," most likely African Americans and poor whites, to whom they sold. The paper printed a Chinese response by Lee Ting, a Chinese visitor to the area, who also summed the size of the Chinese population in the city and refuted local fears that the city would soon be inundated by large numbers of Chinese. "We have sixteen grocery stores here and two laundries, twenty-one in grocery business and four in the laundry and six visitors, so our whole number is thirty-one. If any more to come that is more than we know."[62]

Fears of impending violence reached a peak a few days later when Chinese immigrants locked themselves in their homes and refused to come out. The mayor persuaded them to reopen and reaffirmed the Council's original ruling.[63] Anti-Chinese violence flared up in several states and the events in Augusta have to be situated in this national context.[64] The council's ruling, however, went against the tide of the times and enabled the Chinese to continue in the grocery business. Furthermore, had the decision been to the contrary, the majority of the Chinese would have lost their status as "merchants" and the privileges that came with this designation. These years appear to be the nadir of tolerance toward the Chinese presence in Augusta.

After the merchant protest, Augusta's city government did not consider the issue of regulating Chinese occupational choices. It remained true to its original ruling even when the Chinese presence in the grocery business continued to get bigger through the 1950s. One possible explanation for this enduring silence was the Chinese choice to live in black neighborhoods.

Unlike Augusta, most Chinese in Atlanta and Savannah were hand-laundry operators, an occupation that competed with African American laundresses, and later in the twentieth century with the power laundries. The heyday for the Chinese-operated hand laundries in Atlanta and Savannah was during the first two decades of the twentieth century, reaching its apex in Savannah around 1900 with thirty-one laundries, in Atlanta around 1914 with forty-two laundries.[65] At least one negative article appeared in an Atlanta labor newspaper about the local Chinese laundries circa 1910.[66] However, no opposition movement ever exerted enough pressure on the city governments in Atlanta and Savannah to impose restrictions on Chinese in the laundry business.

No state or city laws were ever passed for regulating the location of Chinese restaurant owners. Less than a handful did business in white neighborhoods in Atlanta, Augusta, and Savannah combined. More Chinese restaurants in Augusta were located in black sections like the grocery stores so as to attract black patrons.

The 1920s marked the first time since the 1880s that the state government of Georgia involved itself in regulating the actions of its Asian immigrant population when it sought to update its racial classification system. It was a decade of heightened nativism throughout the United States and expansion of white supremacy organizations, which not only intimidated African Americans but also immigrants. Eugenics also influenced the U.S. Congress to pass the Immigration Act (1924), a bill regulating immigration in such a way to keep out all Asians and most southern and eastern European immigrants who were deemed undesirable.[67] This legislation contributed to the notion of Chinese, Japanese, Filipinos, and other Asians in the United States and in Asia as being "foreign and unassimilable to the nation" and became identified as part of a legal racial category called "Asiatic."[68]

That same year, eugenicists influenced the passage of a rigid miscegenation law in Virginia that was to be emulated in Georgia.[69] House Representative James Davis of Dekalb County introduced in July 1925 a bill "to define who are persons of color and who are white persons and to prohibit the intermarriage of such persons." This legislation became signed into law in August 1927 stating that: "The term 'white person' shall include only persons of the white or Caucasian race, who have no ascertainable trace of either Negro, African, West Indian, Asiatic Indian, Mongolian, Japanese, or Chinese blood in their veins. No person shall be deemed a white person any one of whose ancestors has duly registered with the State Bureau of Vital Statistics as a colored person or person of color. . . . After passage of this Act it shall be unlawful for a white person to marry any save a white person."[70] Unlike the failed 1884 bill, this legislation was not introduced in the wake of an anti-Chinese event or statewide fear of a new impending "yellow peril." The *Augusta Chronicle*, covering the city with the largest Asian population in the state, devoted one line to the bill, "To prevent intermarriage between races."[71] The Savannah and Atlanta papers printed similar accounts without commentary. The widening of the definition of a nonwhite person in Georgia occurred within a larger national debate over the definition of "white" versus "nonwhite."[72] The denial of citizenship to Japanese immigrant Takao Ozawa in 1922 and the divesting of citizenship from South Asian immigrant Bhagat Singh Thind in 1923 were the two most exemplary U.S. Supreme Court cases of the period demonstrating how these debates spilled over to the federal government.[73]

Four years later, the state legislature of Georgia considered barring children of Chinese ancestry from attending white public schools on the grounds that they were not "white" and therefore would have to enroll in "colored" schools.[74] This debate was based on the 1877 ban against school integration and was given federal sanction in the *Plessey vs. Ferguson* (1896) ruling that upheld "separate but equal" as constitutional. The arrival of Chinese American children of school age presented a possible test to the law. Before the mid-1920s, the local education officials in Savannah ruled that the few Chinese American children in Savannah could not attend white schools.[75] Atlanta and Augusta, however, did not have such a restriction. In July 1931, the Richmond County delegation introduced a bill to the house to cut off funds to white public schools that had Chinese American students.[76] The legislation also stated that the presence of children of Asian descent in white schools violated Georgia's constitution.[77] Chinese American parents took action by going to Atlanta to induce legislators to vote against the bill. Legislators and school officials investigated the situation and concluded by the end of the month that the bill should be rejected.[78] This decision contrasted with Mississippi's segregation law regarding Chinese American children, which was upheld in the state supreme court in the case *Gong Lum v. Rice* in 1924–1925 and then the U.S. Supreme Court in 1927.[79] Georgia's different decision prevented a possible exodus of Chinese American families from Augusta and other cities.

This ruling was also the last time the state legislature took up the issue of regulating where people of Chinese ancestry stood in the Jim Crow system.

Population statistics from the 1920s through the 1960s also show that local government officials were confused as to how to classify the Chinese in Georgia's bipolar racial system. State death certificates required for all who died in the state after 1919 varied in their racial classifications. Examination of thirty-five of these certificates between 1919 and 1927 and selected ones from 1934 to 1960, reveal several designations including abbreviations or full spellings of "Chinese," "Yellow," "White," and "Mongolian."[80] The different classifications can be illustrated with the death certificates for Chin Sing, Jung Wing, and Jung Chong Gue, all of whom died in Chatham County during the 1920s. Chin Sing's certificate stated his race was "yellow," which had become the standard abstract racial designation used for East Asians and their descendants living in the United States. On Jung Wing's certificate, however, the registrar wrote "W" for white instead of "yellow" or "y." A few days later, someone changed his racial designation to "yellow or Mongolian" on an insert page. Jung Chong Gue's certificate was not changed and remained a "W."[81] Chinese who died in Fulton and Richmond Counties also had different racial designations on these documents. Governmental officials did not know precisely how to classify them. However, perhaps most importantly, they were never categorized as black and therefore avoided most—although not all—of the adverse effects of segregation.

Chinese immigrants in Atlanta, Augusta, and Savannah lived within the cracks of de jure segregation constructed for whites and blacks. Their uncertain position forced them to avoid the stigma of being considered black while recognizing that they also could be victims of discrimination because they were Chinese, as the Loo Chong case demonstrates. Most Chinese socialized within their small communities and ventured only to places where they knew they would be welcomed. The local behavior of Chinese immigrants also persuaded governmental bodies within the state not to pass anti-Chinese laws. State and local Jim Crow laws in Georgia remained obsessed with regulating contact between European Americans and African Americans and did not see Chinese immigrants and their children as a threat to the bipolar racial order.

Conclusion

This essay looks at the effect of federal and state laws on Chinese immigrants residing in Atlanta, Augusta, and Savannah. Federal Chinese Exclusion laws established a highly selective exemption system designed to prevent most Chinese from entering and reentering the United States. The law explicitly barred the first-time entry of laborers but allowed Chinese to come over as merchants, students, government officials, teachers, and U.S.-born citizens. Chinese in Georgia were similarly affected when they wished to travel in and out of the United States.

Occupational patterns established in the 1880s in these three cities influenced the type of exemptions they used. Since most Chinese in Augusta were in the grocery business, they were allowed to travel under the exempted merchant category and their wives and children as merchant dependents. Augusta's Chinese community grew in size and became one of the largest Chinese communities in the South before 1965. Chinese in Savannah and Atlanta generally worked as laundry operators, an occupation not exempted; they could not legally bring over dependents because of their occupation. Atlanta's Chinese population experienced continual decline until the end of the Second World War and Savannah's stabilized with the migration of some Chinese families from Augusta to Savannah who ran grocery and convenience stores. The few laundrymen with the financial wherewithal to support a family in Atlanta and Savannah claimed to be U.S. citizens, a status that allowed them to send for wives and children as dependents of American citizens. A few laundry operators who had established their claims to U.S. citizenship with immigration officials, however, sponsored dependents who were not immediate family or nonblood relatives, but instead were "paper sons."

The Georgia state legislature and local governments rarely passed or considered specific legislation restricting Chinese Americans, because their population was small and unobtrusive. Chinese residents worked in occupations shunned by local whites, socialized among themselves, and had their store-residences in neighborhoods that were either black or bordered on black areas. A few Chinese marriages to white women in the 1880s and the attendance of Chinese children in white schools in the 1920s prompted the state to revise its Jim Crow laws to include Chinese Americans. Both failed for different reasons. State representatives outside of Richmond County did not amend the existing antimiscegenation law in 1884 to include them, because few or no Chinese lived outside of that county at the time. A ban against allowing Chinese American children in white schools in 1931 was considered because of the state's policy of separating white and "colored" children. Testimony from Chinese parents convinced the legislature not to pass the ban. The only piece of legislation with anti-Chinese language passed as part of a revised 1927 antimiscegenation law defining the state's definition of "white" versus "nonwhite." State legislators most likely wanted the statute updated to reflect current racial theories predicated on the superiority of "whites" and the need to tighten the law so all other inferior "races" could be lumped together in a "nonwhite" designation. Georgia's de jure segregation remained a biracial system with the Chinese having very little legal acknowledgment of their racial status.

Notes

1. "Whiteness" studies has become a popular field of inquiry with works such as Noel Ignatiev, *How the Irish Became White* (New York: Routledge, 1995); Matthew Frye Jacobson, *Whiteness of a Different Color: European Immigrants and the Alchemy of Race*

(Cambridge, Mass.: Harvard University Press, 1998); Matthew Pratt Guterl, *The Color of Race in America, 1900–1940* (Cambridge, Mass.: Harvard University Press, 2001); David R. Roediger, *Working toward Whiteness: How America's Immigrants Became White: The Strange Journey from Ellis Island to the Suburbs* (New York: Basic Books, 2005).

2. For the most recent treatment of the anomaly of the Asian presence in the South during the Jim Crow era, see Leslie Bow's *Partly Colored: Asian Americans and Racial Anomaly in the Segregated South* (New York: New York University Press, 2010). This study does not seek to add to the recent literature arguing that the Jim Crow South was actually more diverse than previously thought. Bow is interested in complicating what "we think we know about discrimination during an era that rendered it in black and white terms" (20). Although this work uses the Mississippi Chinese, the Chinese and Japanese in Georgia also complicated the definition of "white" and "colored" in that state.

3. Scholars continue to debate the origins of the anti-Chinese movement and how it influenced the passage of the Chinese Exclusion Act. The literature is vast and cannot all be cited. See Gary Okihiro's bibliographic essay "The Anti-Chinese Movement," in *The Columbia Guide to Asian American History* (New York: Columbia University Press, 2001), 75–99, for an excellent treatment of the different interpretations.

4. Najia Aarim-Heriot, *Chinese Immigrants, African Americans, and Racial Anxiety in the United States, 1848–82* (Urbana: University of Illinois Press, 2003), 152–153.

5. Southern planters considered bringing in Chinese immigrants to work as laborers in the late 1860s and early 1870s. Chinese "coolie" labor became noticeable only in a few states such as Louisiana, Arkansas, and Mississippi. For an in-depth look at this period, see Moon-Ho Jung, *Coolies and Cane: Race, Labor, and Sugar in the Age of Emancipation* (Baltimore, Md.: Johns Hopkins University Press, 2006), 7–8.

6. Immigration and Nationality Laws, M2033, roll 2, pp. 230, 231, 236; Hyung-chan Kim, *Asian Americans and Congress: A Documentary History* (Westport, Conn.: Greenwood Press, 1996), 123–128.

7. *Augusta Directory*, 1881–1888; Registers of Chinese Laborers Returning to the United States through the Port of the Port of San Francisco, 1882–1888 (National Archives Microfilm Publication M1413, roll 2, 9, 10).

8. *Atlanta Directory*, 1881–1888; Registers of Chinese Laborers Returning to the United States through the Port of the Port of San Francisco, M1414, roll 11 and 13.

9. Immigration and Nationality Laws, M2033, roll 2, pp. 230, 231, 236. Kim, *Asian Americans and Congress*, 137.

10. Erika Lee, *At America's Gates: Chinese Immigration during the Exclusion Era, 1882–1943* (Chapel Hill: University of North Carolina Press, 2003), 52–53.

11. *Partnership Lists of Chinese Firms in San Francisco, California, and Nationwide, 1893–1907; and Index of Chinese Departing from San Francisco, California, 1912–1943* (National Archives Microfilm Publication A3362, roll 2); Box 93, Folder 13561/20 Ching Yick; Box 94 Folder 13561/88; Kwong Cham; Box 94, Folder 13561/94 Lay Chong, Chinese Partnership Case Files, 1882–1944, RG 85, NA-SF. These were the only Chinese in the three cities to have these affidavits issued.

12. Records of the Immigration and Naturalization Service, Series A, Subject Correspondence Files, Pt. 1: Asian Immigration and Exclusion, 1898–1941, reel 1, page 42.

13. Emma Woo Louie, *Chinese American Names: Tradition and Change* (Jefferson, N.C.: McFarland and Company, Inc., 1998), 108–109; Immigration and Nationality Laws, M2033, roll 2, pp. 242, 243, 244, 245. It is not known how "chock gee" appears in Chinese characters.

14. Segregated Chinese Files in Washington, D.C., Record Group 85, National Archives and Records Administration I, Washington, D.C. (NARA 1), entry 138; Kim, *Asian Americans and Congress*, 100–101, 138–139.

15. Ibid., entry 137, box 33.

16. "Chinese Photographed," *Augusta Chronicle*, February 21, 1894. The cities of Macon and Columbus did have some Chinese laundry operators, but never at any time before 1965 did they have a sizable Chinese population comparable to Augusta, Savannah, or Atlanta.

17. Ibid. "Augusta Leads," *Augusta Chronicle*, March 29, 1894. This article reported around 250 Chinese in the state, with Augusta and Atlanta leading in numbers.

18. Records of the Immigration and Naturalization Service, Series A, Subject Correspondence Files, Pt. 1: Asian Immigration and Exclusion, 1898–1941, reel 1, page 42. For more information about the Bureau of Immigration and Naturalization and its predecessors and successor bodies, see Peggy S. Christoff, *Tracking the "Yellow Peril": The INS and the Chinese Immigrants in the Midwest* (Rockport, Me.: Picton Press, 2001), xi–xvi.

19. Daily Record of Applications for Return Certificates (Merchants), 1903–1912, unnumbered microfilm, NA-SF. This indexes the 9190 series of case file.

20. Interrogation transcripts of Wong Kit, December 8, 1921, Box 2185, Folder 24835/2-1 Wong Kit, RG 85, NA-SF; Interrogation transcripts of Joe Gum, September 23, 1941, Box 148, Folder 12017/15785 Joe Gum, RG 85, NA-SF.

21. Atlanta District Director of Immigration Joseph H. Wallis, Atlanta to Commissioner-General of Immigration, Washington, D.C., June 22, 1932, Box 502, Folder 12017/44718 Woo Hay, RG 85, NA-SF.

22. Paul Siu, *The Chinese Laundryman: A Study in Social Isolation*, edited by John Kuo Wei Tchen (New York: New York University Press, 1987), 129–132.

23. George A. Peffer, *If They Don't Bring Their Women Here: Chinese Female Immigration before Exclusion* (Urbana: University of Illinois Press, 1999), 73–86; Sucheng Chan, "The Exclusion of Chinese Women, 1870–1943," in *Chinese America: History and Perspectives, 1995*, 78–79, 111–117.

24. Madeleine Y. Hsu, *Dreaming of Gold, Dreaming of Home: Transnationalism and Migration Between the United States and China, 1882–1943* (Stanford, Calif.: Stanford University Press, 2000), 95; Chan, "Exclusion of Chinese Women," 96–97.

25. Lists of Chinese Applying for Admission to the United States through the Port of San Francisco, 1903–1947 (National Archives Microfilm Publication M1476, roll 3).

26. Box 210, Folder 29982 Jung Shu Lum, RG 85, NA-WA.

27. Lee, *At America's Gates*, 209.

28. Commissioner of Immigration, Seattle, Washington to Inspector in Charge, Tampa, Fla., September 12, 1910, Box 138, Folder RS 26135 Woo Lung, RG 85, Chinese Exclusion, NA-WA; Box 923, Folder 14390/19-9 Woo Leong Tong, RG 85 Chinese Exclusion, NA-SF.

29. Lee, *At America's Gates*, 207; Erika Lee, "Defying Exclusion: Chinese Immigrants and Their Strategies during the Exclusion Era," in *Chinese American Transnationalism* (Philadelphia: Temple University Press, 2006), 10–12; Adam McKeown, *Chinese Migrant Networks and Cultural Change: Peru, Chicago, Hawaii, 1900–1936* (Chicago: The University of Chicago Press, 2001), 30–32.

30. "Action Sheet, Arrival," January 1916, Jam Nin, Box 156, Folder 12017/16820 Jam Nin, RG 85, Chinese Exclusion, NA-SF.

31. For more about Angel Island, see Erika Lee and Judy Yung, *Angel Island: Immigrant Gateway to America* (New York: Oxford University Press, 2010).

32. John Jung, *Southern Fried Rice: Life in a Chinese Laundry in the Deep South* (yinand yang.wix.com: Yin and Yang Press, 2005), 22 (accessed March 12, 2013).

33. *1930 Federal Population Census Schedule*; Fulton County Georgia: *Atlanta*; Roll: *362*; Page: *12B*; Enumeration District: *97*; Image: *1037.0*. http://www.ancestry.com (accessed February 22, 2013).

34. *Standard Certificate of Death for Apple Young, Fulton 9279* (April 24, 1926), *Death Certificates, RG 26-5-95, Georgia Archives.*

35. Interrogation transcripts of Yee Shee, March 17, 1928, Box 69, Folder 32/3009 Hong Foong, RG 85, NA-WA; *Atlanta Directory*, 1913–1929. Unlike the chop suey houses, which served cuisine adapted for non-Chinese palates, Chinese herbalists did not alter their practices to compete with other non-Chinese medical methods. Haiming Liu, *The Transnational History of a Chinese Family: Immigrant Letters, Family Businesses, and Reverse Migration* (New Brunswick, N.J.: Rutgers University Press, 2005), 3–4.

36. Records of the Immigration and Naturalization Service, Series A, Subject Correspondence Files, Pt. 1: Asian Immigration and Exclusion, 1898–1941, reel 1, page 42.

37. Estelle Lau, *Paper Families: Identity, Immigration Administration, and Chinese Exclusion* (Durham, N.C.: Duke University Press, 2006), 36–41; Mae M. Ngai, *Impossible Subjects: Illegal Aliens and the Making of Modern America* (Princeton, N.J.: Princeton University Press, 2005), 204–206.

38. Hyung-chan Kim, *A Legal History of Asian Americans, 1790–1990* (Westport, Conn.: Greenwood Press, 1994), 92–95; Lee, *At America's Gates*, 101–105.

39. "Exempt Class Landed Direct from Steamer" sheet and "Application and Receipt for Certificate of Identity" paper, April 3, 1914, and April 6, 1914, Box 787, Folder 1334/3-3 Yee Min, RG 85 Chinese Exclusion, NA-SF.

40. May 19, 1966, Box 657, Folder 7030/7497 Yee Hing Root, RG 85, NA-WA.

41. Lau, *Paper Families*, 115–116; Ngai, *Impossible Subjects*, 218–224.

42. "Application and Receipt for Certificate of Identity," October 22, 1914, and October 30, 1936, Box 3476, Folder 36330/8-5 Jew Shiu Dun, RG 85 Chinese Exclusion Files, NA-SF; Jung, *Southern Fried Rice*, 141–142.

43. "X," RG 85, Chinese Exclusion, NA-SF. Information has been omitted because of privacy issues.

44. Lee, *At America's Gates*, 202.

45. 1930 Federal Population Census Schedule; Fulton County, Georgia; Atlanta Ward Roll 361; Page 15A; Enumeration District 53; Image 320.0.

46. Hsu, *Dreaming of Gold, Dreaming of Home*, 96; Judy Yung, *Unbound Feet: A Social History of Chinese Women in San Francisco* (Berkeley: University of California Press, 1995), 168–169. It seems that the Immigrant Act of 1917 also did not affect the three Chinese communities. Immigration files used in this study do not mention it.

47. Interrogation transcripts of Chow Sang, January 15, 1932; Box 846, Folder 7031/291 K. J. Chow, Chinese Exclusion, NA-WA. It is not known why Chow Sang went to Bluefields, Nicaragua. Sang's immigration file from the New Orleans district where he first immigrated to the United States has not survived.

48. "New Year's Day: Chinese Trade a Rat for an Ax," *Augusta Chronicle*, February 15, 1961.

49. Interrogation transcripts of Lam Chi Hang, January 28, 1941; Box 26, Folder 41478/4-7 Lam Yuen Jock, Chinese Exclusion, NA-SF.

50. William Cohen, *At Freedom's Edge: Black Mobility and the Southern White Quest for Racial Control, 1861–1915* (Baton Rouge: Louisiana University Press, 1991), 204–222; Oscar

Joiner, gen. ed., James C. Bonner, H. S. Shearouse, T. E. Smith, *A History of Public Education in Georgia, 1734–1976* (Columbia, S.C.: R. L. Bryan Co., 1979); Peter Wallenstein, *Tell the Court I Love My Wife: Race, Marriage, and the Law* (New York: Palgrave MacMillan, 2002), 96–98; Charles F. Robinson II, *Dangerous Liaisons: Sex and Love in the Segregated South* (Fayetteville: University of Arkansas Press, 2003), 35–37.

51. Linda McMurry Edwards, *To Keep the Waters Troubled: The Life of Ida B. Wells* (New York: Oxford University Press, 1998).

52. Walter E. Campbell, "Profit, Pride, and Protest: Utility Competition and the Generation of Jim Crow Street Cars in Savannah, 1905–1907," in *African Americans and the Emergence of Segregation, 1865–1900* (New York: Garland Publishing, 1994), 197–231.

53. Anderson Kent Leslie, "No Middle Ground: Elite African Americans and the Coming of Jim Crow," in *Paternalism in a Southern City: Race, Religion, and Gender in Augusta, Georgia*, edited by Edward Cashin and Glenn T. Eskew (Athens: University of Georgia Press, 2001), 110–111, 130–131.

54. Robert G. Lee, *Orientals: Asian Americans in Popular Culture* (Philadelphia: Temple University Press, 2000), 42–43; Aarim-Heriot, *Chinese Immigrants*, 9–13, 47–48.

55. Literature about the 1906 Riot is vast and includes among the more recent works, Barbara Tagger, "The Atlanta Race Riot and the Black Community" (MA thesis, Emory University, 1978); Gregory L. Mixon, "The Atlanta Riot of 1906" (PhD dissertation, University of Cincinnati, 1989); Mixon, *The Atlanta Riot: Race, Class, and Violence in a New South City* (Gainesville: University Press of Florida, 2005).

56. Bess Beatty, "The Loo Chong Case in Waynesboro: A Case of Sinophobia in Georgia," *Georgia Historical Quarterly* 67, no. 1 (Spring 1983): 35–48.

57. *House Bill No. 330, November 26, 1884, Bills and Resolutions, Georgia State Legislature,* RG 37-1-1, Box 83, Georgia Archives; *Journal of the House of Representatives of the State of Georgia* (Atlanta: Jas. P. Harrison and Co., November 5, 1884), 313. Illegible writing on the original bill seems to indicate that it was withdrawn before a vote was taken.

58. Megumi Osumi, "Asians and California's Anti-Miscegenation Laws," in *Asian and Pacific American Experiences: Women's Perspectives*, edited by Nobuya Tsuchida (Minneapolis: Asian/Pacific American Learning Resources Center, University of Minnesota, 1982), 6–7; Hrishi Karthikeyan and Gabriel J. Chin, "Preserving Racial Identity: Population Patterns and the Application of Anti-Miscegenation Statutes to Asian Americans, 1910–1950," *Asian Law Journal* 9 (2002): 1–39, 14–19.

59. Catherine Brown and Thomas Ganschow, "The Augusta, Georgia, Chinese: 1865–1980," in *Georgia's East Asian Connection, 1733–1983*," edited by Jonathan Goldstein (Carrolton: West Georgia College, 1983), 30–31.

60. U.S. Bureau of the Census, Tenth Census of the United States (1880), Federal Population Census Schedules, Richmond County, RG 29.

61. "December Meeting—The Chinaman Must Stay," *Augusta Chronicle*, December 8, 1885.

62. "The Chinese Question," *Augusta Chronicle*, March 12, 1886.

63. "The Chinese Excited," *Augusta Chronicle*, March 16, 1886.

64. Roger Daniels, ed., *Anti-Chinese Violence in North America* (New York: Arno Press, 1978); Arif Dirlik and Malcolm Yeung, eds., *Chinese in the American Frontier* (Lanham, Md.: Rowman and Littlefield, 2001).

65. *Savannah Directory*, 1900–1920; *Atlanta Directory*, 1900–1920.

66. Tera W. Hunter, *To 'Joy My Freedom: Southern Black Women's Lives and Laborers after the Civil War* (Cambridge, Mass.: Harvard University Press, 1997), 26–27, 56–57.

67. Matthew Frye Jacobson, *Barbarian Virtues: The United States Encounters Foreign Peoples at Home and Abroad, 1876–1917* (New York: Hill and Wang, 2000), 190–201.

68. Mae M. Ngai, "The Architecture of Race in American Immigration Law: A Reexamination of the Immigration Act of 1924," *Journal of American History* 86, no. 1 (June 1999): 4. She writes that the law constructed a white American race with a growing shared whiteness among European immigrants. People from Asia, in contrast, became identified as part of a legal racial category called "Asiatic."

69. Peggy Pascoe, "Miscegenation Law, Court Cases, and Ideologies of Race in the Twentieth Century," *Journal of American History* 83, no. 1 (June 1996): 59; Pascoe, *What Comes Naturally: Miscegenation Law and the Making of Race in America* (New York: Oxford University Press, 2009), 140–145.

70. *House Bill No. 460, July 13, 1925, Bills and Resolutions, Georgia State Legislature, RG 37-1-1, Box 247, Georgia Archives; Georgia House Journal* (Atlanta: Longino and Porter, 1925), 1199. The bill can be seen online at Georgia Legislative Documents, 157. http://galfe2.gsu.edu/cgi-bin/homepage.cgi (accessed February 19, 2008). The vote on the bill was unanimous with 117 ayes and 0 nays.

71. "To Prevent Intermarriage between Races," *Augusta Chronicle,* August 21, 1927.

72. Guterl, *The Color of Race in America,* 5–13.

73. Jacobson, *Whiteness of a Different Color,* 234–236.

74. Eileen Law and Sally Ken, "A Study of the Chinese Community," *Richmond County History* 5, no. 2 (Summer 1973): 35.

75. George B. Pruden Jr., "History of the Chinese in Savannah, Georgia," in Goldstein, ed., *Georgia's East Asian Connection, 1733–1983,* 17.

76. "Measure Provides Board to Replace Four Commissions," *Augusta Chronicle,* July 3, 1931. The bill also targeted schools that had children of Japanese descent.

77. "Primary Grades Called Important," *Augusta Chronicle,* July 11, 1931; "Harmony Urged on Education Board," *Augusta Chronicle,* July 12, 1931.

78. Law and Ken, "A Study of the Chinese Community," 34–35.

79. James Loewen, *The Mississippi Chinese: Between Black and White* (Cambridge: Cambridge University Press, 1971, reprint, Prospect Heights, Ill.: Waveland, 1988), 66–68; John Thornell, "Struggle for Identity in the Most Southern Place on Earth," in *Chinese America History and Perspectives* (San Francisco: Chinese Historical Society of America, 2003), 67–68; Sieglinde Lim de Sanchez, "Crafting a Delta Chinese Community: Education and Acculturation in Twentieth Century Mission Schools," *History of Education Quarterly* 43, no. 1 (Spring 2003): 78–81. Chinese American families in Mississippi had to move to other states so that their offspring could go to white schools or to privately educate them with help from sympathetic white churches.

80. Many of the certificates in possession of the Georgia Department of Archives and History up to 1927 and selected ones in the possession of the Georgia Vital Records Office have been used in this analysis. Certificates from 1919 and 1927 are indexed and can be viewed online at the Georgia Department of Archives and History website. More death certificates up to 1936 have since been released to the State Archives but are either not indexed or have not been put online. The Georgia Vital Records Office in Atlanta still has custody of certificates from 1937 through the present. Copies are available only with payment of an exorbitant fee. http://content.sos.state.ga.us/cdm4/gadeaths.php (accessed February 23, 2013).

81. *Standard Certificate of Death for Chin Sing, Chatham County No. 14149-B* (1920 May 8), *Death Certificates, RG 26-5-95, Georgia Archives; Standard Certificate of Death for Jung*

Wing, Chatham County No. 31337-D (December 29, 1922), *RG 26-5-95, Georgia Archives*; *Standard Certificate of Death for Jung Chong Gue, Chatham County No. 737-E* (1923 January 6), *RG 26-5-95, Georgia Archives*.

Works Cited

ARCHIVAL SOURCES

Georgia Department of Archives and History (GDAH)
Bills and Resolutions of the Georgia House of Representatives, 1838–2000
Georgia Death Certificates, 1919–1932
National Archives and Records Administration, Northeast Region, New York (NARA-NY)
Record Group 85 (RG 85), *Chinese Exclusion Case Files, 1880–1960*
National Archives and Records Administration, Pacific Northwest Region, Seattle (NARA-WA)
Record Group 85 (RG 85), *Chinese Exclusion Case Files, 1895–1943*
National Archives and Records Administration, Pacific Region, San Bruno (NARA-SF).
Record Group 85 (RG 85), *Chinese Exclusion Case, 1884–1944* (Textual)
———, *Chinese Partnership Case Files, 1894–1944* (Textual)
———, *Daily Records of Applications [by Chinese Laborers] for Return Certificates, 1903–1912* (Microfilm)
———, *Daily Records of Applications [by Chinese Merchants, Students, and Teachers for Return Certificates], 1903–1912* (Microfilm)
———, *Lists of Chinese Applying for Admission to the United States through the Port of San Francisco, 1903–1947* (Microfilm)
———, *Partnership Lists of Chinese Firms in San Francisco, California, and Nationwide, 1893–1907; and Index of Chinese Departing from San Francisco, California, 1912–1943* (Microfilm)
———, *Records of Natives [United States–born Chinese Americans] Departing, 1909–1913* (Microfilm)
———, *Registers of Chinese Laborers Returning to the United States through the Port of San Francisco, 1882–1888* (Microfilm)
———, *Return Certificate Application Case Files of Chinese Departing, 1912–1944* (Textual)

CHAPTER 5

Moving out of the Margins and into the Mainstream

The Demographics of Asian Americans in the New South

Arthur Sakamoto, ChangHwan Kim, and Isao Takei

With a focus on the South, this study investigates current demographic characteristics of Asian Americans. Statistical data are analyzed in regard to population
sizes, geographic distribution, multiracial and ethnic diversity, socioeconomic characteristics, migration, and other basic demographic variables. Among the many
results, the high rate of demographic growth of Asian Americans in the South is
notable. More Asian Americans now reside in Texas than in Hawaii, and in Atlanta
than in San Francisco. Although Asian Americans are generally more likely than
whites to migrate, Asian Americans in the South are the most likely to be recent
migrants. In contrast to the racial differentials in other regions, Asian Americans
in the South have clearly higher levels of education and hourly wages than whites
in the South. When compared to Asian Americans in other regions, Asian Americans in the South have higher levels of education, hourly wages, and employment
in professional and technical occupations. After adjusting for regional differentials
in the cost of living, Asian Americans in the South have higher levels of earnings,
household income, and per capita household income than Asian Americans do
in other regions. Overall, we interpret these results as suggesting the beginning of
a new stage of Asian American population distribution that is characterized by
improved socioeconomic opportunities that are facilitating a movement away from
the geographic margins of the nation such as Hawaii and California. In this current
era of Asian Americans in the twenty-first century, the New South is leading the
way toward a more open labor market that is better at restraining the primordial
racial conflicts over job competition, which often characterized relations between
whites and Asian Americans during the nineteenth and twentieth centuries. Perhaps the more important challenge facing Asian Americans in the twenty-first
century is ameliorating the consequences of rising levels of class inequalities that
to some extent cut across racial and ethnic categories but may be somewhat more
pronounced in the Asian American population.

* * *

"The South shall rise again" was the motto for recovery in the aftermath of the Civil War, which brought huge devastation to the Confederate States. The leaders of the Confederate States could not have envisioned, however, that in the societal transformation that has become the New South of the twenty-first century, the Asian American population is rising as well in a new era of greater multiracial diversity. For most of the history of the South, Asian Americans were absent from the public consciousness of the majority population, and were seen to represent at most an obscure group of sojourners that one might only rarely encounter. To be sure, the stories of pioneering individual and small bands of Asian Americans continue to be uncovered in Southern history (Rhoads 1977; Cohen 1984; Walls 1987; Loewen 1988; Tang 2007). Nonetheless, only since the start of the twenty-first century have Asian Americans begun to represent a significant demographic component of the Southern population. In this new era of multiracial diversity, many Asian Americans are flocking to the New South in order to take advantage of its improved socioeconomic opportunities that in the past would have been reserved primarily for whites.

In the following we provide a demographic portrait of Asian Americans using the most currently available statistics. Our focus is on Asian Americans in the South, but for comparative purposes the demographics of Asian Americans elsewhere are also considered. The statistical data that are presented in the tables may serve as reference material for the study of Asian Americans in the South as well as for the nation as a whole.

Demographic Data Sources and Definitions

Our study uses two different data sources. The first is the U.S. Census of 2000. Specifically, we use a random sample from the records of that decennial Census as provided by the 5% *Public-Use Microdata Sample*, which the U.S. Census Bureau makes available to researchers. The second source of data that we study is the American Community Survey, which has been conducted annually in recent years by the U.S. Census Bureau. Because this latter source is based on a random sample rather than a census (i.e., a complete tallying of the total population), we combine the 2005 and 2006 data for the American Community Survey in order to increase the precision of our estimates by utilizing a larger total sample size. Nonetheless, we caution that our reported results for 2005/2006 are statistical estimates that are subject to errors of various sorts.

The data from the U.S. Census of 2000 as well as the American Community Survey utilize the same classification system of five major racial categories. For both of these data sources, the race question on the questionnaire is the same and it asks individuals to self-identity their race based on the categories printed in the questionnaire. If they wish, individuals are permitted to identify with more than one of the categories. The five standard racial categories used include 1) white, 2) black or African

American, 3) Asian or Asian American, 4) Native American or Alaskan Native, and 5) Native Hawaiian or other Pacific Islander. In addition, both the U.S. Census of 2000 and the American Community Survey include a sixth residual category that is labeled "Some other race" with which respondents may choose to identify.

Although this U.S. Census classification system considers Asian American to be a standard racial category in statistical tabulations and official designations, the questionnaire does not actually refer to that term per se. Instead, the six largest Asian ethnic groups are specifically enumerated on the questionnaire including Asian Indian, Chinese, Filipino, Japanese, Korean, and Vietnamese. "Other Asian" is then listed on the questionnaire and a blank space is provided for persons who are instructed to "Print race" in that space.

In the racial classification used by the U.S. Census Bureau in 1980 and 1990, Native Hawaiians and Pacific Islanders were categorized as belonging to the same group as Asian Americans. Older statistical data and reports therefore often make reference to "Asian and Pacific Islander" Americans or "API's." The reclassification of Native Hawaiians and Pacific Islanders into a separate category in the U.S. Census of 2000 represents, however, current practice in the federal statistical system. In our investigation below, we follow this current practice and exclude Native Hawaiians and Pacific Islanders from the Asian American category. Nevertheless, we note that because Native Hawaiians and Pacific Islanders are an exceedingly small group (even as compared to Asian Americans) almost all of our substantive generalizations and conclusions would remain essentially the same had we used the older API classification.

In order to describe the multiracial dimension of the Asian American population, our analysis refers to two different generic components. "Asian American-S" refers to single-race Asian Americans and includes those who identify with only some Asian ethnic group (i.e., persons who identify with an Asian ethnic group only and not also with any of the other racial categories defined by the U.S. Census Bureau, such as white or black). On the other hand, "Asian American-M" refers to multirace Asian Americans and includes those who identify with some Asian ethnic group as well as with at least one other racial category. When combined, single-race Asian Americans and multirace Asian Americans constitute the total "Asian American-SM" population (i.e., persons who in some way identify as Asian American).

Regarding geography, the U.S. Census Bureau defines four standard regions including the West, Midwest, Northeast, and South. The latter is defined to include Texas, Oklahoma, Louisiana, Arkansas, Alabama, Kentucky, Tennessee, Mississippi, Delaware, Maryland, the District of Columbia, Florida, Georgia, North Carolina, South Carolina, West Virginia, Virginia. Although other slightly different regional definitions are available, we use this U.S. Census Bureau classification, which is the most popular and defines the South as lying below the Ohio River and ranging from Texas to Delaware.[1] Because our focus is on the South, most of our reported regional statistics collapse together the West, Midwest, and Northeast, which we refer to as "other regions" below.

Demographic Growth and Geographic Distribution

The total population size of a person's demographic group is one of the broadest contextual aspects of social interaction. We can estimate total population figures for 2005/2006 using the information on sampling weights provided in the American Community Survey. Table 5.1 shows the population size of Asian Americans by region for 2000 and 2005/2006.

Table 5.1 indicates that the total population of the United States increased from 288.4 million in 2000 to 293.9 million in 2005/2006. Across this time period, the total population of Asian American-S increased from 10.3 million to 12.9 million. Although Table 5.1 shows that the total population of Asian American-M declined from 1.7 million to 1.5 million, this reduction probably derives from some methodological differences between the U.S. Census of 2000 and the American Community Survey.[2] What is likely to be somewhat more reliable is the overall increase in the total population of Asian American-SM from 12.0 million in 2000 to 14.4 million in 2005/2006. As shown in Table 5.1, this increase represents a percentage growth of the Asian American-SM population from 4.2% in 2000 to 4.9% of the total American population in 2005/2006.

Regarding regional variations, the West has been well known as the area in which traditionally most Asian Americans live. This pattern has been changing over the past couple of decades, however, as the growth rate of the Asian American population in other regions has exceeded that of the West (Sakamoto and Ha 2003). In 2000, as shown in Table 5.1, the West had one-half of the total Asian American-SM population (i.e., 6.0 million of 12.0 million). A turning point was reached in 2005/2006 when less than one-half of the total Asian American-SM population resided in the West (i.e., 7.0 million of 14.4 million or 49%). More Asian Americans now live in the Midwest, Northeast, and South than in the West. Our interpretation of this trend is that Asian Americans are either leaving the West or are not immigrating there because its population congestion has raised its cost of living and reduced the availability of socioeconomic opportunities in comparison to other places including especially the South.

Other results in Table 5.1 indicate that the South has recently overtaken the Northeast as the region with the second largest population of Asian Americans. In 2000, more Asian Americans lived in the Northeast than in the South. The higher growth rate of Asian Americans in the South, however, has resulted in a larger population of Asian American-SM in that region than in the Northeast by 2005/2006. These foregoing regional trends seem generally consistent with the prediction of Sakamoto and Ha (2003, 181) that the population of Asian Americans in the South will exceed that in California by 2040.

What remains distinctive about Asian Americans in the South is that they continue to be proportionately small and below the national average in relative terms. As noted above, the Asian American-SM population represents 4.9% of the total U.S. population in 2005/2006. Although the Asian American-SM population in the

Table 5.1. Population Size of Asian Americans by Category, Year, and Region

	Total		South		Northeast		Midwest		West	
	2000	2005/2006	2000	2005/2006	2000	2005/2006	2000	2005/2006	2000	2005/2006
Total Population	288,398,819	293,898,652	100,238,521	106,798,468	53,596,978	53,829,259	64,369,231	65,174,179	63,217,176	68,096,747
Asian American-S	10,330,546	12,945,216	1,924,134	2,571,440	2,106,361	2,697,758	1,176,601	1,522,463	5,123,450	6,153,556
% of total population	3.67%	4.41%	1.92%	2.41%	3.93%	5.01%	1.83%	2.34%	8.10%	9.04%
Asian American-M	1,684,249	1,486,721	357,859	322,541	246,974	161,832	195,949	172,081	883,467	830,268
% of total population	.60%	.51%	.36%	.30%	.46%	.30%	.30%	.26%	1.40%	1.22%
% of total Asian Am	14.02%	10.30%	15.68%	11.15%	10.49%	5.66%	14.28%	10.16%	14.71%	11.89%
Asian American-SM	**12,014,795**	**14,431,937**	**2,281,993**	**2,893,981**	**2,353,335**	**2,859,589**	**1,372,550**	**1,694,544**	**6,006,917**	**6,983,824**
% of total population	4.17%	4.92%	2.28%	2.71%	4.39%	5.31%	2.13%	2.60%	9.50%	10.26%

Note: Asian American-S refers to single-racial persons; Asian American-M refers to biracial and triracial persons. The total population of Asian Americans is denoted as Asian American-SM, which refers to the combination of Asian American-S and Asian American-M. See text for further information.

South is numerically large in absolute terms, this demographic group nonetheless constitutes only 2.7% of the total population of the South in 2005/2006 because that region is by far the most populous in the nation (i.e., 106.8 million in 2005/2006, as shown in Table 5.1). That is, many Asian Americans live in the South but they still constitute a smaller fraction of the total Southern population than the proportionate representation of Asian Americans in the Northeast or the West.

Although the Asian American-SM population is only 2.7% of the total population of the South in 2005/2006, one should bear in mind that this figure is a statistical average for a very broad area. To a certain degree, Asian Americans in the South are often clustered in specific cities and are numerous enough within that particular locale to develop their own ethnic communities. As shown in the bottom panel of Table 5.2, several metropolitan areas in the South have Asian American populations that exceed the national average of 4.9% including Washington, D.C. (9.2%), Houston (6.2%), Dallas (5.6%) and Austin (5.2%). Furthermore, these and several other metropolitan areas in the South have large populations of Asian Americans in absolute terms, as is also shown in Table 5.2. For example, with an Asian American-SM population size of over 214,000 in 2005/2006 (see Table 5.2), Atlanta now has more Asian Americans than Honolulu or San Francisco (because the latter two metropolitan areas have Asian American-SM populations below 200,000).

The top panel of Table 5.2 shows statistics for the ten states with the largest Asian American-SM populations. As is well known, California stands out as having by far the largest number of Asian Americans including 4.2 million in 2000 and increasing to 4.9 million in 2005/2006. Outside of Hawaii, California also has the highest proportion of Asian Americans. As shown in Table 5.2, 14.5% of Californians were Asian American-SM in 2005/2006.

The state with the second largest Asian American-SM population is New York. It is the only state other than California where the Asian American-SM population exceeds the 1 million mark as shown in Table 5.2. In relative terms, the percentage of New York residents who are Asian American-SM is well above the national average, but does not reach double digits as is the case with California.

As indicated in Table 5.2, the state with the third largest Asian American-SM population in 2000 is Hawaii. Hawaii remains highly distinctive as the only state where the majority of residents are Asian American (i.e., 64.8% in 2000). However, in contrast to Southern states, Hawaii has a comparatively low rate of population growth due to its limited geographic size combined with an economy that has become highly specialized around tourist industries, which are not known for substantial economic expansion. By 2005/2006, Texas had surpassed Hawaii as the state with the third largest Asian American-SM population (i.e., about 821,000 in Texas versus approximately 805,000 in Hawaii in 2005/2006) even though the percentage of Texas residents who are Asian American-SM (i.e., 3.7%) is below the national average.[3]

Other than Texas, two more Southern states are listed in Table 5.2 as being in the top ten. These include Florida and Virginia. Although Florida has the smallest Asian American-SM population in percentage terms among the ten states shown

Table 5.2. States with the Ten Largest Asian American Populations and Metropolitan Areas with the Ten Largest Asian American Populations in the South by Year

	2000			2005/2006		
	Total Pop	Asian American-SM	% Total Population	Total Pop	Asian American-SM	% Total Population
States with the Ten Largest Asian American Populations in the U.S.						
California	33,884,660	4,190,527	12.37%	33,439,850	4,861,124	14.54%
New York	18,976,061	1,161,179	6.12%	18,290,654	1,349,776	7.38%
Hawaii	1,211,717	784,863	64.77%	1,258,528	804,567	63.93%
Texas	20,848,171	649,660	3.12%	22,451,035	820,958	3.66%
New Jersey	8,416,753	525,532	6.24%	8,280,124	669,299	8.08%
Illinois	12,417,190	472,682	3.81%	12,345,047	569,131	4.61%
Washington	5,894,780	402,860	6.83%	6,018,397	498,367	8.28%
Florida	15,986,890	343,888	2.15%	17,496,972	442,001	2.53%
Virginia	7,080,588	302,776	4.28%	7,277,609	397,261	5.46%
Massachusetts	6,353,449	265,442	4.18%	6,151,947	322,753	5.25%
Metropolitan Areas with the Ten Largest Asian American Populations in the South						
Washington, DC/MD/VA	4,733,359	368,637	7.79%	5,131,741	471,580	9.19%
Houston-Brazoria, TX	4,173,800	240,040	5.75%	4,762,165	296,317	6.22%
Dallas–Fort Worth, TX	3,377,635	157,169	4.65%	3,830,674	215,350	5.62%
Atlanta, GA	3,987,990	147,867	3.71%	4,649,537	214,074	4.60%
Baltimore, MD	2,513,661	80,442	3.20%	2,571,960	107,128	4.17%
Fort Worth–Arlington, TX	1,666,241	59,620	3.58%	1,889,325	78,317	4.15%
Tampa–St. Petersburg, FL	2,386,781	56,810	2.38%	2,642,833	78,141	2.96%
Norfolk, Newport, VA	1,553,838	53,518	3.44%	1,587,106	61,581	3.88%
Orlando, FL	1,652,742	52,714	3.19%	1,946,299	76,204	3.92%
Austin, TX	1,167,216	49,866	4.27%	1,358,311	70,486	5.19%

Note: Dallas–Fort Worth, TX and Fort Worth–Arlington, TX are classified as separate metropolitan areas.

in Table 5.2, Florida has a large geographic size with a high rate of population growth. The increase in the absolute size of the Asian American-SM population in Florida may rival that of Washington by the time of the next decennial census.

Multiracial and Ethnic Diversity within the Asian American Category

Table 5.3 shows the population figures for the multirace groups as well as the specific ethnicities within the Asian American category for the nation as a whole. Absolute population sizes are shown for 2000 as well as for 2005/2006. The percentage figures shown in Table 5.3 are relative to the total Asian American-SM population. They thus indicate the percentage that the particular ethnicity or multirace group constitutes of the total Asian American-SM population for the given year.

The top panel of Table 5.3 lists the figures for Asian American-S while the bottom panel lists them for Asian American-M. Of the total Asian American-SM population in 2000, 86% are Asian American-S and 14% are Asian American-M. Thus, the majority of Asian Americans are single-race rather than multirace.

Because most Asian Americans are foreign-born (i.e., 64% in 2000, as shown in Table 5.6, later in this essay), their ethnic identity is usually closely associated with their place of birth which is typically described with a single term. In contrast to foreign-born Asian Americans, however, native-born Asian Americans (i.e., those born in the United States) are known to have high rates of racial intermarriage. Qian and Lichter (2007, 79) report that a majority of native-born Asian Americans are intermarried (over two-thirds in the case of women) while intermarriage is 21% for foreign-born Asian American men and 33% for foreign-born Asian American women. As the population of native-born Asian Americans increases and as they age into adulthood, get married, and have children, then some increase in the Asian American-M population may perhaps be evident in the future.

Although we refer to Asian American-M as multiracial, the vast majority of this group identifies as biracial rather than triracial. Table 5.3 indicates a total Asian American-M population of 1.7 million of which only about 250,000 identified as triracial in 2000. This finding implies that biracial Asian Americans are approximately 85% of the total Asian American-M population while triracial Asian Americans are 15%.

Given the small size of the Asian American-M population relative to the Asian American-S population, and given the equally small size of the triracial Asian American group relative to the biracial Asian American group in the Asian American-M population, whether triracial Asian Americans will expand as an identifiable demographic group in the future remains questionable. Biracial Asian Americans may to some degree be recognizing the ethnicities of their racially intermarried parents, but whether the offspring of biracial Asian Americans will adopt triracial identities in appreciable numbers remains to be seen. As is evident in Table 5.3, most biracial Asian Americans are Asian Americans who also identify

Table 5.3. Population Sizes of Ethnic Subgroups of Asian Americans

	2000		2005/2006	
	Size AA-SM	% among	Size AA-SM	% among
Asian American-S				
Chinese	2,436,581	20.28%	2,993,414	20.74%
Japanese	793,575	6.60%	835,867	5.79%
Filipino	1,869,880	15.56%	2,308,679	16.00%
Asian Indian	1,645,329	13.69%	2,379,932	16.49%
Korean	1,075,707	8.95%	1,300,905	9.01%
Vietnamese	1,108,329	9.22%	1,446,385	10.02%
Cambodian	178,316	1.48%	218,044	1.51%
Hmong	173,841	1.45%	198,131	1.37%
Laotian	169,941	1.41%	196,582	1.36%
Thai	109,985	.92%	150,488	1.04%
Bangladeshi	39,766	.33%	53,341	.37%
Indonesian	38,137	.32%	62,151	.43%
Malaysian	10,198	.08%	12,632	.09%
Pakistani	163,906	1.36%	198,020	1.37%
Sri Lankan	17,837	.15%	32,098	.22%
Other Asian Single-Ethnicity	285,793	2.38%	331,539	2.30%
Multiple-ethnic Asian	213,425	1.78%	227,011	1.57%
Asian American-S Sub-Total	10,330,546	85.98%	12,945,216	89.70%
Asian American-M				
White and Chinese	103,747	.86%	143,252	.99%
White and Japanese	175,315	1.46%	197,292	1.37%
White and Filipino	216,072	1.80%	260,863	1.81%
White and Asian Indian	55,093	.46%	72,574	.50%
White and Korean	85,330	.71%	100,207	.69%
White and Vietnamese	35,368	.29%	43,802	.30%
White and Other Asian	192,224	1.60%	140,319	.97%
Black and Chinese	12,179	.10%	12,401	.09%
Black and Japanese	13,191	.11%	10,301	.07%
Black and Filipino	26,225	.22%	32,684	.23%
Black and Asian Indian	18,364	.15%	18,369	.13%
Black and Korean	11,363	.09%	12,879	.09%
Black and Other Asian	25,436	.21%	19,298	.13%
Native Am and Asian	51,328	.43%	26,591	.18%
Pacific Islander and Asian	136,461	1.14%	101,453	.70%
Other Biracial Asian	276,223	2.30%	95,625	.66%
Triracial Asian	250,330	2.08%	198,815	1.38%
Asian American-M Sub-Total	1,684,249	14.02%	1,486,721	10.30%
Asian American-SM Total	*12,014,795*	*100.00%*	*14,431,937*	*100.00%*

as white as the latter is the largest racial group that supplies by far the greatest number of potential marriage partners. Indeed, continued intermarriage with whites may even reduce the propensity of some offspring (e.g., those with only one Asian American grandparent) to identify as Asian American at all. The latter process may be occurring to some degree among Japanese Americans whose single-race population size has actually been shrinking in recent decades.

In regard to specific ethnic groups in the Asian American-S category in 2000, the Chinese numbered 2.4 million and represented 20.3% of all Asian American-SM, as shown in Table 5.3. The second largest group is Filipino with a population size of 1.9 million in 2000 (i.e., 15.6% of all Asian American-SM), while the third largest group is Asian Indian with a population size of 1.6 million (i.e., 13.7% of all Asian American-SM). All of the remaining single-race ethnic groups have percentages of less than 10% in 2000, including (in order of their relative population sizes) Vietnamese, Korean, Japanese, Other Single-Ethnic Asians (e.g., Bhutanese, Mongolians, Nepali, etc.), Multiple-ethnic Asians (e.g., Chinese and Japanese; Chinese and Asian Indian), Cambodian, Hmong, Laotian, Pakistani, Thai, Bangladeshi, Indonesian, Sri Lankan, and Malaysian.

In terms of 2005/2006 national population estimates shown in Table 5.3, all of the Asian American-S ethnic groups increased in absolute numbers relative to 2000. In particular, the population of Asian Indians is growing appreciably and they have now overtaken Filipinos as the second largest ethnic group. Although the 2005/2006 national population estimates indicate some decline in the size of the Asian American-M population, as mentioned earlier this pattern may be partly a methodological artifact (largely deriving from the lower count of persons in the Other Biracial Asian category, as discussed in note 2).

Table 5.4 shows the population figures broken down by region for the multiracial components as well as the specific ethnic groups in 2000 and 2005/2006. Due to space constraints, the regions are simplified into the dichotomous classification of South versus non-South. While the differences are not dramatic, the South is distinctive in having a larger percentage of Asian Indians. In fact, Asian Indians are the largest ethnic group in the South (i.e., 18.9% in 2000 and 22.1% in 2005/2006) while the Chinese are the second largest (15.1% in 2000 and 15.4% in 2005/2006) in contrast to elsewhere in the nation where the Chinese are clearly the largest group (22.1% in 2005/2006). Relative to other regions, Table 5.4 also shows that the South has fewer Filipinos and Japanese but a lot more Vietnamese. The proportion of the total Asian American-SM population than is multiracial is also slightly larger in the South which may derive in part from the comparatively low percentage of Southern residents who are Asian American as well as perhaps the greater preponderance of military personnel and military-related intermarriages (Tang 2007, 7–11).

Table 5.5 shows the percentage frequency distribution of Asian American ethnic groups for nine metropolitan areas in the South with large concentrations of Asian Americans based on the 2005/2006 data. (For the total population sizes of Asian Americans in these metropolitan areas, refer to Table 5.2.) In order to

Table 5.4. Population Sizes of Ethnic Subgroups of Asian Americans by Region

	South				Other Regions			
	2000		2005/2006		2000		2005/2006	
	Size	% among AA-SM	Size	% among AA-SM	Size	% among AA-SM	Size	% among AA-SM
Asian American-S								
Chinese	344,626	15.10%	445,901	15.41%	2,091,955	21.49%	2,547,513	22.08%
Japanese	76,718	3.36%	92,515	3.20%	716,857	7.37%	743,353	6.44%
Filipino	246,556	10.80%	334,944	11.57%	1,623,324	16.68%	1,973,735	17.11%
Asian Indian	430,570	18.87%	640,763	22.14%	1,214,759	12.48%	1,739,170	15.07%
Korean	220,103	9.65%	276,392	9.55%	855,604	8.79%	1,024,513	8.88%
Vietnamese	334,563	14.66%	430,925	14.89%	773,766	7.95%	1,015,460	8.80%
Cambodian	24,889	1.09%	41,027	1.42%	153,427	1.58%	177,017	1.53%
Hmong	12,605	.55%	17,292	.60%	161,236	1.66%	180,839	1.57%
Laotian	38,527	1.69%	48,402	1.67%	131,414	1.35%	148,180	1.28%
Thai	30,400	1.33%	44,270	1.53%	79,585	.82%	106,218	.92%
Bangladeshi	10,250	.45%	14,364	.50%	29,516	.30%	38,977	.34%
Indonesian	7,200	.32%	11,707	.40%	30,937	.32%	50,444	.44%
Malaysian	2,705	.12%	3,674	.13%	7,493	.08%	8,958	.08%
Pakistani	55,094	2.41%	64,564	2.23%	108,812	1.12%	133,457	1.16%
Sri Lankan	5,534	.24%	8,144	.28%	12,303	.13%	23,955	.21%
Other Asian Single-Ethnic	51,352	2.25%	66,124	2.28%	234,441	2.41%	265,415	2.30%
Multiple-ethnic Asian	32,442	1.42%	30,436	1.05%	180,983	1.86%	196,575	1.70%
Asian Am-S Sub-Total	1,924,134	84.32%	2,571,440	88.85%	8,406,412	86.37%	10,373,776	89.91%

Table 5.4. (cont.)

	South				Other Regions			
	2000 Size	% among AA-SM	2005/2006 Size	% among AA-SM	2000 Size	% among AA-SM	2005/2006 Size	% among AA-SM
Asian American-M								
White and Chinese	19,674	.86%	24,786	.86%	84,073	.86%	118,466	1.03%
White and Japanese	28,158	1.23%	35,680	1.23%	147,157	1.51%	161,612	1.40%
White and Filipino	44,665	1.96%	59,087	2.04%	171,407	1.76%	201,776	1.75%
White and Asian Indian	17,900	.78%	21,548	.74%	37,193	.38%	51,026	.44%
White and Korean	23,361	1.02%	29,861	1.03%	61,969	.64%	70,346	.61%
White and Vietnamese	11,573	.51%	13,910	.48%	23,795	.24%	29,892	.26%
White and Other Asian	49,372	2.16%	34,529	1.19%	142,852	.88%	105,790	.64%
Black and Chinese	4,696	.21%	4,222	.15%	7,483	.08%	8,180	.07%
Black and Japanese	3,430	.15%	2,181	.08%	9,761	.10%	8,120	.07%
Black and Filipino	7,832	.34%	9,734	.34%	18,393	.19%	22,950	.20%
Black and Asian Indian	6,144	.27%	8,389	.29%	12,220	.13%	9,980	.09%
Black and Korean	4,172	.18%	6,240	.22%	7,191	.07%	6,640	.06%
Black and Other Asian	8,573	.38%	8,122	.28%	16,863	.09%	11,176	.06%
Native Am and Asian	10,246	.45%	6,435	.22%	41,082	.42%	20,156	.17%
Pacific Islander and Asian	15,197	.67%	6,241	.22%	121,264	1.25%	95,212	.83%
Other Biracial Asian	58,072	2.54%	20,061	.69%	218,151	2.24%	75,564	.65%
Triracial Asian	44,794	1.96%	31,518	1.09%	205,536	2.11%	167,297	1.45%
Asian Am-M Sub-Total	357,859	15.68%	322,541	11.15%	1,326,390	13.63%	1,164,181	10.09%
Asian American-SM Total	2,281,993	100.00%	2,893,981	100.00%	9,732,802	100.00%	11,537,957	100.00%

Table 5.5. Ethnic Composition of Asian Americans in Selected Metropolitan Areas of the South, 2005/2006

	Atlanta	Austin	Baltimore	Dallas–Fort Worth	Houston	Norfolk/Newport	Orlando	Tampa	Washington
Asian American-S									
Chinese	13.7%	18.8%	19.2%	14.3%	19.9%	6.0%	15.7%	9.6%	18.7%
Japanese	2.5%	4.0%	2.4%	1.9%	1.5%	5.0%	3.0%	1.9%	2.9%
Filipino	3.6%	9.3%	10.6%	6.5%	10.3%	41.3%	14.2%	14.5%	10.5%
Asian Indian	28.9%	19.8%	22.7%	25.2%	23.4%	6.3%	28.5%	21.9%	22.6%
Korean	16.3%	11.9%	18.7%	9.9%	3.1%	7.4%	4.4%	6.2%	14.7%
Vietnamese	15.0%	15.4%	4.6%	20.9%	24.9%	5.9%	14.9%	19.2%	11.6%
Cambodian	2.4%	0.7%	0.2%	2.1%	1.4%	0.8%	0.3%	2.5%	1.1%
Hmong	1.1%	0.0%	0.0%	0.1%	0.2%	0.0%	0.0%	1.8%	0.0%
Laotian	2.1%	0.0%	0.3%	3.4%	0.5%	0.0%	1.1%	1.9%	0.7%
Thai	0.6%	0.8%	1.1%	1.6%	0.7%	2.7%	1.4%	2.0%	2.0%
Bangladeshi	0.9%	0.3%	0.1%	0.8%	0.2%	0.0%	0.6%	0.0%	0.8%
Indonesian	0.6%	0.5%	0.4%	0.3%	0.5%	0.0%	0.1%	0.5%	0.5%
Malaysian	0.2%	0.4%	0.0%	0.2%	0.2%	0.1%	0.0%	0.1%	0.1%
Pakistani	1.5%	3.8%	3.2%	2.5%	5.1%	0.0%	2.1%	0.4%	2.5%
Sri Lankan	0.1%	0.6%	0.1%	0.2%	0.4%	0.3%	0.3%	0.3%	0.5%
Other Asian Single-Ethnic	2.3%	1.9%	2.6%	1.9%	1.5%	2.4%	1.7%	1.9%	2.2%
Multiple-ethnic Asian	1.1%	0.8%	1.1%	1.0%	1.1%	1.2%	1.1%	0.9%	1.3%
(Total)	93.0%	89.0%	87.4%	92.8%	94.9%	79.4%	89.4%	85.4%	92.6%
Asian American-M									
White Biracial Asian	4.4%	8.0%	8.8%	5.3%	3.4%	12.9%	6.8%	9.6%	5.2%
Black Biracial Asian	1.4%	0.3%	2.3%	0.5%	0.6%	3.2%	2.0%	2.1%	0.8%
Other Asian-M	1.2%	2.6%	1.4%	1.3%	1.0%	4.5%	1.8%	2.8%	1.4%
(Total)	7.0%	11.0%	12.6%	7.2%	5.1%	20.6%	10.6%	14.6%	7.4%

conserve space, we have collapsed the Asian American-M groups into White Biracial Asian, Black Biracial Asian, and Other Asian American-M (i.e., all others in the Asian American-M category).

Being the largest group in the South, Asian Indians reside in appreciable percentages in each of these cities with the one exception of Norfolk-Newport, Virginia. The latter metropolitan area is highly specialized around U.S. Naval activities and related military installations. The other significant industry in Norfolk-Newport is cargo shipping. Asian Indians are not employed in substantial numbers in these industries. In fact, in general, few Asian American groups are. The Asian American population in Norfolk-Newport is very heavily concentrated with Filipinos, including a substantial fraction of their biracial offspring (most of whom are included in the White Biracial Asian category shown in Table 5.5). Many Filipinos in the Norfolk-Newport area have had some connections with the U.S. military due to the legacy of substantial U.S. military bases that operated in the Philippines until the early 1990s (Kitano and Daniels 2001).

The Vietnamese are another major group in the South, and Table 5.5 shows that they are more concentrated in Houston and Dallas–Fort Worth, Texas. Although many Vietnamese immigrants originally came to the Gulf Coast area to work in fishing and shrimp industries, the Vietnamese in more recent years have moved in significant numbers to nearby big cities. The Vietnamese have become highly competitive in small business enterprises there such as nail salons (Ha 2007). Their offspring appear to have furthermore overcome obstacles to become a highly educated group (Sakamoto and Woo 2007), which also facilitates more urban employment. In particular, second- and 1.5-generation Vietnamese have high rates of employment in the medical and health fields, which are well developed in Houston and Dallas–Fort Worth.[4]

The Chinese are the second largest Asian American group in the South and their presence is fairly evenly evident in most of the metropolitan areas shown in Table 5.5. The only exceptions include Norfolk-Newport (which, as noted above, has an economy based on military industries and shipping) and to some extent, Tampa, Florida. The economy of Tampa is based on regional service, finance, insurance, and real estate industries, which do not employ the bulk of the Chinese in Florida. By contrast, an above-average percentage of Chinese lives in nearby Orlando, Florida, which has a substantial high-tech sector, including many engineering firms and a significant medical industry.

Other Basic Demographic Characteristics

Table 5.6 shows descriptive statistics regarding basic demographic characteristics by year. While whites and Asian Americans do not significantly differ in terms of the proportion female, Asian Americans are a younger population with a much smaller proportion of elderly persons. This latter characteristic reflects the large immigration streams that occurred only after 1965.

Table 5.6. Basic Demographic Statistics by Year

	White		Asian American-SM	
	2000	2005/2006	2000	2005/2006
Female (%)	51.1	50.9	50.0	51.6
Age Groups (%)				
0–15	22.6	21.7	26.9	25.7
16–24	8.6	8.7	11.2	9.7
25–44	29.4	26.7	35.2	34.2
45–64	24.3	28.0	19.7	22.2
65+	15.1	14.9	7.1	8.3
Education (%, Age 25+)				
Less than high school	14.6	11.1	19.3	14.1
High school graduates	30.0	30.5	16.7	17.8
Some college	28.5	38.5	21.6	20.1
Bachelor degree	17.2	18.9	25.8	28.8
Graduate degree	9.8	11.1	16.6	19.1
Mean years of schooling (Age 25+)	13.4	13.7	13.6	14.1
(Standard Deviation)	(2.9)	(2.8)	(4.4)	(4.0)
Marital Status (%, Age 15+)				
Married	57.8	55.4	58.3	58.9
Separated/Divorced/Widowed	18.8	19.4	10.2	10.7
Never Married	23.4	25.2	31.5	30.5
Asian American Spouse (%)[a]	1.1	1.2	87.4	86.4
Foreign-born (%)	4.2	4.6	63.9	62.5
Years in the U.S. (Among Foreign-born)	25.2	25.4	14.3	16.5
Other Than English at Home (%, Age 5+)	6.0	5.9	72.6	70.5

[a] Among persons classified as married household heads.

Table 5.6 shows that Asian Americans have higher levels of educational attainment, as is well known. Our results further suggest, however, that the gap between whites and Asian Americans may be increasing. The mean years of schooling completed by whites increased by .3 years between 2000 and 2005/2006 (i.e., from 13.4 to 13.7) while the mean years of schooling completed by Asian Americans increased by .5 years between 2000 and 2005/2006 (i.e., from 13.6 to 14.1).

At the same time, however, educational attainment among Asian Americans is more varied or unequally distributed. This feature of the distribution is indicated by the higher standard deviation of years of schooling for Asian Americans in 2005/2006 (i.e., 4.0) compared to whites (i.e., 2.8). In terms of educational categories, Table 5.6 similarly shows that, compared to whites, Asian Americans are more likely to have never completed a high school degree. To some extent, this bifurcation of the educational distribution for Asian Americans may reflect immigration patterns associated with family reunification policies that admit elderly parents who were educated in Asia decades ago.

Other results in Table 5.6 indicate that Asian Americans are more likely to be currently married as well as to be never married. The latter is common for persons who are younger and more highly educated, which is more characteristic of Asian Americans than whites. The greater proportion that is currently married may stem from a lower divorce rate among Asian Americans, which is reflected in their much smaller percentage in the separated/divorced/widowed category.

Table 5.6 further shows that the majority of Asian Americans are foreign-born (i.e., 64% in 2000 as noted earlier). Among the foreign-born, their average length of time residing in the United States was 14.3 years in 2000. A majority of Asian Americans speak a language other than English at home, and a majority is married to another Asian American.

Table 5.7 shows these demographic statistics broken down by region. Asian Americans in the South are slightly more likely to be foreign-born than Asian Americans in other regions (i.e., 67% versus 61%, respectively). Asian Americans in the South are also slightly more likely than Asian Americans elsewhere to be

Table 5.7. Basic Demographic Statistics by Region, 2005/2006

	South		Other Regions	
	White	Asn Am	White	Asn Am
Female (%)	51.0	51.6	50.9	51.6
Age Groups (%)				
0–15	21.5	26.8	21.7	25.4
16–24	8.6	9.4	8.8	9.7
25–44	26.8	36.2	26.7	33.7
45–64	27.8	21.4	28.1	22.4
65+	15.3	6.2	14.7	8.8
Education (%, Age 25+)				
Less than high school	13.5	13.3	9.8	14.3
High school graduates	30.6	17.3	30.5	17.9
Some college	27.8	18.6	28.9	20.5
Bachelor degree	18.0	28.2	19.3	28.9
Graduate degree	10.2	22.6	11.5	18.4
Mean years of schooling	13.5	14.4	13.8	14.0
(Standard Deviation)	(2.9)	(3.9)	(2.7)	(4.0)
Marital Status (%, Age 15+)				
Married	57.0	61.7	54.5	58.2
Separated/Divorced/Widowed	20.4	10.0	18.8	10.8
Never Married	22.6	28.4	26.6	31
Asian American Spouse (%)[a]	.9	84.7	1.5	86.9
Foreign-born (%)	3.5	67.1	5.1	61.4
Years in the U.S. (Among Foreign-born)	25.0	15.8	25.6	16.7
Other Than English at Home (%, Age 5+)	4.2	73.0	6.7	69.9

[a] Among persons classified as married household heads.

married, to speak a language other than English at home, to have a graduate degree, and to be in the age range of 25 to 44. This demographic profile suggests that the South has a higher proportion of what Kim and Sakamoto (2010) referred to as the 1.25-generation: immigrants from Asia who came to the United States to obtain a college or graduate degree and then stayed in the country to work.

Labor Force and Related Socioeconomic Characteristics of Workers

Table 5.8 shows statistics relating to the labor force and socioeconomic characteristics of workers by year. Relative to whites, Asian Americans have slightly higher rates of unemployment and poverty. Because these disadvantages are more prevalent among immigrants, and because such a large percentage of Asian Americans are foreign-born, their slightly higher rates of unemployment and poverty are undoubtedly partly related to their immigrant characteristics. In contrast to whites, however, the poverty rate for Asian Americans actually declined from 2000 to 2005/2006 perhaps reflecting a smaller percentage of

Table 5.8. Labor Force and Socioeconomic Characteristics of Workers by Year

	White		Asian American-SM	
	2000	2005/2006	2000	2005/2006
Unemployed (%, Age 16+)	4.31	5.27	5.47	5.61
Self Employed among Employed (%, Employed)	10.6	11.6	9.2	10.2
Below Poverty Line (%)	10.2	10.4	14.3	12.2
Annual Earnings ($)[a]	39,675	41,205	39,995	43,719
Annual Earnings-COLA ($)[a]	39,150	40,703	38,016	41,936
Hourly Wage ($)[b]	31.1	33.4	31.9	35.3
Hourly Wage-COLA ($)[b]	30.7	33.0	30.6	34.1
Inequality				
St.Dev. of log-Annual Earnings	1.21	1.32	1.21	1.28
St.Dev. of log-Annual Earnings-COLA	1.21	1.32	1.21	1.28
St.Dev. of log-Hourly Wage	.96	1.02	1.02	1.04
St.Dev. of log-Hourly Wage-COLA	.96	1.02	1.02	1.04
Occupation (%, Employed)				
Manager	13.9	14.3	12.6	14.0
Professional, Technician	20.2	21.0	27.2	29.3
Other White Collar	42.0	42.4	41.5	41.3
Blue Collar	23.0	21.5	18.0	14.8
Agriculture/Fishing/Forestry	.6	.6	.4	.3
Military	.2	.3	.2	.3

[a] Among workers with positive earnings. Adjusted to 2005 constant dollars using CPI-U.
[b] Among wage workers with positive income. Adjusted to 2005 constant dollars using CPI-U.

lesser educated Asian Americans who recently immigrated to the United States as well as the entering of more highly educated native-born Asian Americans into the labor force.

Table 5.8 also shows that, compared to whites, Asian Americans are much more likely to have a professional or technical job and are less likely to have a blue-collar job. Regarding labor force remuneration, Table 5.8 further indicates that mean annual earnings and mean hourly wages in 2005/2006 are higher for Asian Americans than for whites. On average, Asian Americans are earning more money than whites. This conclusion remains evident for 2005/2006 after adjusting earnings and wages for regional differentials in the cost of living using a classification of the states into nine regions (Berry, Fording, and Hanson 2000). Using that methodology, "COLA" in the tables refers to income figures that are regionally cost-of-living adjusted. The higher earnings and wages of Asian Americans in 2005/2006 after adjusting for regional cost-of-living differentials represent a change from the results for 2000, which indicate that Asian Americans had lower earnings and wages after making that adjustment.

Higher earnings, wages, and occupational attainment as well as slightly higher rates of poverty and unemployment for Asian Americans relative to whites in 2005/2006 are not contradictory. Instead, these trends suggest greater socioeconomic diversity of Asian Americans relative to whites. Greater socioeconomic diversity—which may also be referred to as a higher level of inequality among Asian Americans—is reflected in the slightly larger standard deviation of log-hourly wage for Asian Americans in 2005/2006 (relative to whites), as shown in Table 5.8. This larger standard deviation is equally evident whether or not wages are adjusted for regional differences in the cost of living.[5]

The standard deviation of log-earnings as shown in Table 5.8 is not, however, larger for Asian Americans. The distribution of annual earnings can differ significantly from hourly wages because workers often vary in the number of hours worked during the year. The lower standard deviation of log-earnings for Asian Americans derives from a greater homogeneity of Asian American workers at some part of the distribution (perhaps a greater clustering as middle-class earners rather than as working-class earners at least in comparison to whites). In sum, the distributions of earnings and wages for Asian Americans are somewhat different from whites due to slightly different patterns of bifurcation, which should be the subject of more detailed analysis in future research.

Table 5.9 shows statistics relating to the labor force and socioeconomic characteristics of workers by their region of residence in 2005/2006. Regarding unemployment and poverty, the South is rather distinctive from the other regions in that it has the lowest racial gap. That is, the rates of unemployment and poverty among Asian Americans in the South are only barely higher than for whites in the South. By contrast, the racial gap in unemployment and especially poverty are larger in the other regions.

Table 5.9. Labor Force and Socioeconomic Characteristics of Workers by Region, 2005/2006

| | South | | Other Regions | |
	White	Asn Am	White	Asn Am
Unemployed (%, Age 16+)	5.1	5.2	5.4	5.7
Self Employed among Employed (%, Employed)	11.8	11.4	11.5	9.9
Below Poverty Line (%)	11.4	11.6	9.9	12.4
Annual Earnings ($)[a]	39,972	41,871	41,827	44,200
Annual Earnings-COLA ($)[a]	43,529	45,528	39,279	41,002
Hourly Wage ($)[b]	31.6	38.7	34.4	34.5
Hourly Wage-COLA ($)[b]	34.4	42.0	32.3	32.0
Inequality				
St.Dev. of log-Annual Earnings	1.31	1.28	1.32	1.28
St.Dev. of log-Annual Earnings-COLA	1.31	1.28	1.32	1.28
St.Dev. of log-Hourly Wage	1.03	1.09	1.01	1.03
St.Dev. of log-Hourly Wage-COLA	1.03	1.08	1.01	1.03
Occupation (%, Employed)				
Manager	14.2	13.7	14.3	14.1
Professional, Technician	20.5	31.4	21.2	28.8
Other White Collar	42.2	40.3	42.4	41.6
Blue Collar	22.1	13.9	21.2	15.0
Agriculture/Fishing/Forestry	.5	.2	.6	.3
Military	.5	.6	.2	.2

[a] Among workers with positive earnings. Adjusted to 2005 constant dollars using CPI-U.

[b] Among wage workers with positive income. Adjusted to 2005 constant dollars using CPI-U.

Furthermore, Asian Americans in the South have the highest mean hourly wage. Asian Americans in the South earn on average $38.70 per hour as compared to $34.50 for Asian Americans in other regions. This regional difference is substantially increased after adjusting for differentials in the cost of living. In terms of COLA figures as shown in Table 5.9, Asian Americans in the South earn $42.00 per hour compared to just $32.00 per hour for Asian Americans elsewhere. In short, Asian Americans in the South are being paid more per hour especially after factoring in the lower cost of living in the South.

Table 5.9 reveals other favorable socioeconomic circumstances of Asian Americans in the South. First, Asian Americans in the South earn more per hour than whites in any region (including the South) whether or not adjusted for cost-of-living differentials. By contrast, Asian Americans in other regions have a slightly lower wage than whites in other regions after adjusting for cost-of-living differentials. Second, Southern Asian Americans are more likely to have a professional or technical occupation than Asian Americans in other regions. Third, after adjusting for cost-of-living differentials, the average earnings of Asian Americans in the

South exceed that for Asian Americans elsewhere and for whites in any region. Fourth, Asian Americans in the South have a lower poverty rate than Asian Americans in other regions.

Household Socioeconomic Characteristics

The statistics discussed above are based on the individual as the unit of analysis. By contrast, the statistics shown in Table 5.10 use the household as the unit of analysis. Individuals pool their incomes to a significant degree at the level of the household, which is also the unit at which most economic consumption takes place.

Table 5.10 shows that mean household income for whites in 2005/2006 was $69,662 whereas for Asian Americans it was $83,628. After adjusting for regional differentials in the cost of living, mean household income for whites in 2005/2006 was $68,854 whereas for Asian Americans it was still much higher at $80,327. Table 5.10 furthermore indicates, however, that on a per capita basis (i.e., adjusting for the number of persons in the household), mean household income is only slightly greater for Asian Americans than for whites ($35,430 versus $35,116, respectively). After adjusting for regional variation in the cost of living, then mean per capita household income is actually slightly lower for Asian Americans than for whites ($34,027 versus $34,705, respectively).

The income-to-needs ratio refers to household income divided by the official poverty line where the latter varies depending upon the size and type of the household (as stipulated by the U.S. Census Bureau). The income-to-needs ratio is slightly more complicated than a per capita adjustment because the number of adults and the number of children are taken into account in the determination of the poverty line (i.e., the denominator of the income-to-needs ratio). Table 5.10 shows that the mean income-to-needs ratio is slightly higher for Asian Americans

Table 5.10. Socioeconomic Characteristics of Households by Year

	White		Asian American[a]	
	2000	2005/2006	2000	2005/2006
Household Income ($)[b]	69,433	69,662	80,912	83,628
Household Income-COLA ($)[b]	68,562	68,854	77,659	80,327
Standard Deviation of log-HH Income[b]	.94	.97	1.01	1.02
Standard Deviation of log-HH Income-COLA[b]	.93	.97	1.01	1.02
Household Income per Person ($)[b]	34,714	35,116	33,314	35,430
Household Income per Person-COLA ($)[b]	34,270	34,705	31,985	34,027
Income-to-needs ratio[b]	3.43	3.36	3.44	3.48

[a] Either household head or spouse is Asian American.

[b] Among households with positive income. Adjusted to 2005 constant dollars using CPI-U.

Table 5.11. Socioeconomic Characteristics of Households by Region, 2005/2006

	South		Other Regions	
	White	Asian[a] American	White	Asian[a] American
Household Income ($)[a]	66,489	79,237	71,330	84,800
Household Income-COLA ($)[b]	72,377	86,109	67,001	78,783
Standard Deviation of log-HH Income[a]	.98	1.00	.97	1.02
Standard Deviation of log-HH Income-COLA[a]	.98	1.00	.96	1.02
Household Income per Person ($)[b]	33,535	33,539	35,946	35,935
Household Income per Person-COLA ($)[b]	36,486	36,435	33,769	33,384
Income-to-needs ratio[b]	3.28	3.45	3.40	3.48

[a] Either household head or spouse is Asian American.
[b] Among households with positive income. Adjusted to 2005 constant dollars by using CPI-U.

than for whites, especially in 2005/2006. This result implies that, on average, the Asian American population is economically further away from living in poverty than is the white population.[6] This result is not contradictory with our earlier finding of a higher poverty rate among Asian Americans. Rather, the Asian American distribution of household income is more bifurcated than among whites.

Another way to consider the bifurcation issue is to refer to the standard deviation of log-household income, which is shown in Table 5.10. The figures indicate that the standard deviation of log-household income is higher for Asian Americans than for whites. This conclusion is evident whether or not the COLA is applied. These findings imply that, at the household level, Asian American income inequality is slightly greater. This conclusion is consistent with our other results showing that, compared to whites, Asian Americans have both a higher poverty rate as well as a slightly higher mean income-to-needs ratio.

Table 5.11 provides the household statistics broken down by region for 2005/2006. In terms of household income among Asian Americans, it is on average lower in the South than elsewhere. However, Table 5.11 shows that after adjusting for regional differentials in the cost of living, average household income among Asian Americans is actually substantially higher in the South (i.e., $86,109) compared to other regions (i.e., $78,783). In addition, per capita household income among Asian Americans is higher in the South after adjusting for cost-of-living differentials. Indeed, per capita household income–COLA for Asian Americans in the South is not only greater than that for Asian Americans in other regions, but it is also greater than for whites in other regions. Table 5.11 further reveals that the income-to-needs ratio for Asian Americans in the South exceeds that for whites in the South somewhat more than is the case for the other regions. This latter finding in part reflects the greater regional concentration of poverty in the South among whites than is the case for Asian Americans.

Table 5.12. Demographic and Socioeconomic Characteristics for Ethnic Subgroups of Asian Americans, 2005/2006

	Mean Years of Schooling [Age 25+] (Year)	Asian American Spouse [HH Head] (%)	Foreign Born (%)	Other Than English at Home [Age 5+] (%)	Poverty Rate (%)	HH Income per Person -COLA ($)
Asian American-S						
Chinese	14.2	91.5	70.6	83.1	13.6	35,196
Japanese	14.5	75.4	42.2	45.5	10.5	39,954
Filipino	14.3	82.4	69.2	66.6	6.5	32,304
Asian Indian	15.4	93.9	75.0	79.0	9.1	40,345
Korean	14.6	90.0	77.4	80.4	15.2	31,356
Vietnamese	12.3	94.6	68.2	86.5	15.4	26,390
Cambodian	10.2	93.3	62.6	85.2	21.7	17,887
Hmong	8.8	99.3	45.2	94.0	29.7	11,470
Laotian	10.3	94.9	62.8	89.3	15.9	18,082
Thai	13.6	69.8	78.8	76.7	16.6	31,705
Bangladeshi	14.2	99.6	76.6	91.0	24.4	21,722
Indonesian	14.6	78.1	77.8	77.4	15.7	27,527
Malaysian	15.2	66.3	87.1	79.3	13.9	34,939
Pakistani	14.3	91.4	72.1	85.2	15.3	27,348
Sri Lankan	15.3	89.7	83.6	76.2	12.2	31,382
Other Asian Single-Ethnic	13.5	68.3	37.0	44.8	17.8	31,112
Multiple-ethnic Asian	13.7	78.9	38.7	52.0	11.2	31,373
(Total)	14.1	88.9	67.9	75.7	12.3	33,788
Asian American-M						
White and Chinese	14.9	32.9	11.8	19.3	9.6	38,715
White and Japanese	14.4	28.4	14.0	15.2	9.4	37,392
White and Filipino	14.0	23.0	12.7	11.3	8.6	32,644
White and Asian Indian	14.1	52.0	20.0	23.4	12.0	33,420
White and Korean	14.2	21.7	19.8	14.3	12.4	34,380
White and Vietnamese	13.6	43.2	19.3	25.8	11.1	30,657
White and Other Asian	14.0	48.8	19.8	25.3	10.9	35,315
Black and Chinese	14.2	25.1	31.3	12.3	11.3	34,066
Black and Japanese	14.5	7.8	18.6	22.1	17.8	38,666
Black and Filipino	13.7	25.2	12.6	11.3	13.3	27,789
Black and Asian Indian	13.4	58.4	40.0	20.6	19.4	31,523
Black and Korean	13.8	51.0	18.5	17.6	23.6	28,343
Black and Other Asian	13.4	40.2	22.5	25.1	24.3	24,181
Native Am and Asian	13.6	58.4	31.3	26.7	13.4	28,920
Pacific Islander and Asian	13.3	56.7	10.6	15.3	13.4	28,493
Other Biracial Asian	13.7	63.8	30.5	47.7	10.9	28,374
Triracial Asian	13.9	44.6	6.0	10.6	15.5	28,694
(Total)	14.0	40.5	15.6	18.6	11.7	32,693

Demographic and Socioeconomic
Characteristics of Asian Ethnic Groups

Table 5.12 shows demographic and socioeconomic statistics for Asian ethnic groups whose population sizes were discussed earlier in regard to Tables 5.3 and 5.4. In terms of the single-race groups (listed as Asian American-S in Table 5.12), the extremes for mean years of schooling completed ranges from a low of 8.8 for the Hmong to a high of 15.4 for Asian Indians (among persons aged 25 or more). Other groups that are above the single-race average of 14.1 include the Chinese, Japanese, Filipinos, Koreans, Bangladeshis, Indonesians, Malaysians, Pakistanis, and Sri Lankans. Groups other than the Hmong that are below that average include the Vietnamese, Cambodians, Laotians, Thai, Other Asians, and Multiple-ethnic Asians.

The Vietnamese, Cambodian, Hmong, and Laotian stand out particularly since their means for years of schooling are lower than for whites (which is 13.4 as shown in Table 5.6) whereas Thai, Other Asians, and Multiple-ethnic Asians are still slightly above whites. Table 5.12 further shows that the Hmong have the highest poverty rate (i.e., 29.7%) among Asian Americans, and indeed, that poverty rate is even higher than for African Americans in 2005. Poverty is also high among Cambodians (i.e., 21.7%) whose rate is approximately the same as Hispanics in 2005. The poverty rates for Vietnamese and Laotians are 15.4% and 15.9%, respectively, which are higher than the poverty rate for whites (i.e., 10.4% in Table 5.8). Nonetheless, it should be noted that the poverty rates for the Vietnamese and Laotians have been declining significantly over time because their rates in the early 1980s exceeded African Americans, while in the early 1990s their poverty rates were similar to Hispanics. Currently the poverty rates of Vietnamese and Laotians are clearly below the poverty rate of Hispanics although still higher than whites.

Among the single-race Asian American groups that have above-average educational attainment, most of their poverty rates are above whites but below Hispanics. The exceptions are the Filipinos and Asian Indians whose poverty rates (i.e., 6.5% and 9.1% as shown in Table 5.12) are actually lower than for whites, while the poverty rate for Japanese (i.e., 10.5%) is very similar to whites. The other notable case is the Bangladeshis, who have a high poverty rate that is greater than Hispanics for some unknown reason.

Other results in Table 5.12 confirm that most single-race Asian American groups consist of mostly foreign-born persons. The well-known exception is the Japanese who are mostly native-born. What is less well known, however, is that the Hmong have joined the Japanese as the other specific Asian American ethnic group that is mostly native-born. As shown in Table 5.12, only 45.2% of Hmong are foreign-born. But in contrast to the Japanese, the high rate of American nativity among the Hmong—a group of relatively recent immigrants who came to the United States during the aftermath of the Vietnam War—undoubtedly reflects their high fertility in this country.

Table 5.12 further indicates that Other Asians and Multiple-ethnic Asians consist of mostly native-born persons. In the case of Multiple-ethnic Asians, many of them may have parents who married since the 1980s when intermarriages between Asian Americans of different ethnicities began to increase (Lee and Fernandez 1998). In the case of Other Asians in this single-race category, however, the high rate of American nativity seems surprising because groups such as the Bhutanese, Mongolians, Nepali, and so forth are largely post-1965 immigrants who are likely to be highly selective of more educated persons with educational, occupational, or governmental sources for their visas; they also are quite unlikely to have high levels of fertility comparable to the Hmong. Our speculation is that the majority of persons listed as Other Asians in the single-race category are actually persons who wrote down on the form "Asian American," which is a term that the questionnaire does not explicitly use. "Asian American" is clearly a U.S. conceptualization and would be consistent with the finding that only 37% of Other Asians are foreign-born, as shown in Table 5.12.

Regarding the Asian American-M category in Table 5.12, a somewhat disparate set of groups is included under this rubric. Biracial Black Asians tend to have poverty rates that are above their respective single-race Asian ethnic group but below the poverty rate for single-race African Americans. Poverty rates among biracial White Asians seem to vary around the poverty rate for single-race whites ranging from a low of 8.6% for White Filipinos to a high of 12.4% for White Koreans, as shown in Table 5.12. The latter poverty rate is perhaps not outstandingly high, however, because the poverty for Asian Americans as a whole was 12.2% in 2005/2006 as is shown in Table 5.8.

The demographic and socioeconomic statistics by ethnic group and region are shown in Table 5.13. In order to conserve space, the Asian American-M groups have been collapsed into three subgroups including biracial White Asians, biracial Black Asians, and all others in the Asian American-M category. Table 5.13 presents a large amount of data, so readers with specific interests may refer to it according to their particular research concerns.

In terms of the highlights, we point out only a few of the more notable patterns in Table 5.13. In general, with a few exceptions, each of the single-race Asian American groups tends to be slightly more highly educated in the South than in other regions and to be slightly less likely to be living in poverty as well. For example, while we have already noted the relatively high poverty rates among the Vietnamese, Cambodian, Hmong and Laotian, Table 5.13 indicates the poverty rates for these groups are slightly lower in the South than in other regions. The mean years of schooling among Cambodians in the South is 10.9 while it is 9.9 for Cambodians in other regions. The mean years of schooling among Hmong in the South is 10.6 while it is 8.6 for Hmong in other regions. As for other groups, the mean years of schooling is 15.3 for Chinese in the South but only 13.9 for Chinese in other regions. Not

Table 5.13. Demographic and Socioeconomic Characteristics for Ethnic Subgroups of Asian Americans by Region, 2005/2006

	Mean Years of Schooling [Age 25+] (Year)	Asian American Spouse [HH Head] (%)	Foreign Born (%)	Other Than English at Home [Age 5+] (%)	Poverty Rate (%)	HH Income per Person -COLA ($)
South						
Asian American-S						
Chinese	15.3	89.2	75.0	82.4	11.7	39,498
Japanese	14.5	60.5	71.1	66.0	12.6	44,018
Filipino	14.5	72.8	73.7	66.4	7.1	37,209
Asian Indian	15.6	94.1	75.6	78.8	8.9	43,362
Korean	14.3	88.3	78.5	80.3	13.9	33,424
Vietnamese	12.2	95.0	68.1	87.0	12.9	27,986
Cambodian	10.9	89.2	66.9	85.9	14.0	21,892
Hmong	10.6	100.0	41.3	90.4	24.9	12,218
Laotian	10.6	95.8	65.5	91.6	10.4	22,217
Thai	13.1	58.2	78.8	73.4	17.4	31,200
Bangladeshi	15.0	98.5	73.5	83.9	22.3	26,523
Indonesian	15.0	79.3	78.4	72.4	19.8	27,163
Malaysian	15.8	66.9	82.2	70.7	9.6	38,801
Pakistani	14.5	93.8	73.0	86.6	15.8	28,304
Sri Lankan	15.4	96.4	85.4	77.0	12.3	39,491
Other Asian Single-Ethnicity	13.7	64.5	49.3	54.6	18.9	35,977
Multiple-ethnic Asian	13.7	84.7	51.8	67.4	12.8	31,578
(Total)	14.4	87.9	72.7	78.6	11.5	36,735
Asian American-M						
White Biracial Asian	14.2	30.4	21.4	20.3	9.9	35,289
Black Biracial Asian	13.6	31.9	25.5	15.9	19.7	29,809
Other Asian-M	14.2	53.0	29.3	32.2	14.4	29,559
(Total)	14.1	36.0	23.4	22.2	12.0	33,288
Other Regions						
Asian American-S						
Chinese	13.9	91.9	69.8	83.2	13.9	34,415
Japanese	14.4	77.0	38.7	43.0	10.1	39,514
Filipino	14.2	84.1	68.5	66.7	06.3	31,438
Asian Indian	15.3	93.8	74.8	79.1	09.1	39,193
Korean	14.6	90.5	77.2	80.4	15.4	30,841
Vietnamese	12.3	94.4	68.3	86.3	16.3	25,691
Cambodian	9.9	94.4	61.7	85.0	23.4	16,974
Hmong	8.6	99.3	45.7	94.3	30.1	11,401
Laotian	10.2	94.5	62.0	88.6	17.6	16,547
Thai	13.8	74.9	78.8	78.0	16.2	31,912
Bangladeshi	13.8	100.0	77.8	93.6	25.1	19,505
Indonesian	14.5	77.8	77.7	78.5	14.7	27,613
Malaysian	14.9	66.1	89.2	82.6	15.5	33,443
Pakistani	14.2	90.2	71.8	84.6	14.9	26,904
Sri Lankan	15.2	87.6	83.0	75.9	12.2	28,663
Other Asian Single-Ethnicity	13.4	69.2	34.0	42.4	17.4	29,992
Multiple-ethnic Asian	13.6	77.8	36.7	49.5	10.9	31,336
(Total)	14.0	89.1	66.8	75.0	12.4	33,057
Asian American-M						
White Biracial Asian	14.3	34.3	13.7	16.3	10.1	35,107
Black Biracial Asian	13.9	39.2	21.0	18.3	16.8	31,079
Other Asian-M	13.6	55.1	11.6	20.0	13.8	28,385
(Total)	14.0	42.0	13.5	17.6	11.6	32,498

surprisingly, we noted above in regard to Table 5.9 that Asian Americans in the South have a lower poverty rate than Asian Americans elsewhere.

Table 5.13 also shows that Japanese in the South are quite likely to be foreign-born in stark contrast to Japanese elsewhere. This result appears to be symptomatic of the more general tendency of Asian Americans in the South to be slightly more likely to be foreign-born than Asian Americans in other regions at least for most of the groups listed in Table 5.13. However, no clear pattern emerges across these groups regarding intermarriage. For some groups it is higher in the South while for others it is lower.

Table 5.14 shows additional socioeconomic statistics by region for the largest fifteen Asian ethnic groups. As was noted earlier in regard to Table 5.9, Asian Americans in the South have a considerably higher hourly wage than Asian Americans in other regions after adjusting for regional cost-of-living differentials. Asian Indians, for example, have a mean hourly wage-COLA of $48.10 in the South while it is $34.80 in other regions. The largest regional differential is among Pakistanis among whom the mean hourly wage-COLA is $64.80 in the South and $28.30 elsewhere. Table 5.14 further indicates that Asian Indians and Pakistanis in the South are more likely than those elsewhere to be employed in managerial, professional, and technical occupations and less likely to be employed in blue-collar occupations.

In general, Table 5.14 also shows that for most groups self-employed tends to be greater in the South. At the same time, however, inequality in the South is also greater at least as measured by the standard deviation of the log-hourly wage. The group that is often inconsistent with these trends is the Japanese who have lower self-employment and a lower mean hourly wage-COLA in the South than Japanese in other regions.

Migration Statistics

In terms of migration, Asian Americans are more mobile than whites as is evident in Table 5.15. Whereas 62.8% of whites in 2005/2006 resided in the same state in which they were born, only 27.9% of Asian Americans did so. Among whites in 2005/2006, Table 5.15 indicates that 76.9% resided in the same region that they were born in whereas only 32.1% of Asian Americans did so.

To some degree, these foregoing migration differentials based on place of birth reflect the high proportion of Asian Americans who were born overseas (as was noted above in regard to Table 5.6). However, Asian Americans are still more mobile than whites in terms of recent migration statistics that do not directly depend on place of birth. Table 5.15 shows that, in 2000, 89.9% of whites lived in the same state for the last five years whereas only 74.6% of Asian Americans did so. Similarly, 97.1% of whites lived in the same state during the last one-year

Table 5.14. Socioeconomic Statistics by Region for Ethnic Subgroups of Asian Americans-S, 2005/2006

	Self Employed (%)	Hourly Wage -COLA[b] ($)	St.Dev. Log Hourly Wage[b]	Manage (%)	Prof/ Technician (%)	Other White Collar (%)	Blue Collar (%)
					Occupation[a]		
South							
Chinese	12.0	54.8	1.10	17.2	42.6	33.2	6.6
Japanese	9.8	36.4	1.00	17.2	33.0	39.5	9.0
Filipino	5.3	31.2	.99	11.0	33.2	43.3	11.2
Asian Indian	11.7	48.1	1.10	16.7	43.8	32.0	7.2
Korean	20.9	58.3	1.19	15.4	25.0	46.1	12.4
Vietnamese	13.0	26.2	1.01	8.0	17.1	46.7	26.8
Cambodian	8.1	29.7	1.21	8.4	10.8	39.9	38.7
Hmong	4.0	19.1	1.01	6.3	6.6	37.0	46.2
Laotian	7.0	22.3	.77	4.7	7.0	33.9	54.0
Thai	8.6	28.5	1.16	10.8	15.7	56.1	16.9
Bangladeshi	9.7	23.3	1.28	14.2	32.3	46.6	6.8
Indonesian	15.1	22.4	.90	17.0	22.7	51.3	7.4
Malaysian	9.0	46.4	.98	21.0	42.7	20.3	15.9
Pakistani	14.7	64.8	1.16	14.3	27.9	46.3	11.3
Sri Lankan	3.1	33.4	1.21	18.4	48.0	28.1	4.5
Other Regions							
Chinese	10.6	34.2	1.07	17.1	32.1	38.6	11.8
Japanese	11.6	41.7	.98	20.0	28.9	40.4	10.1
Filipino	4.9	32.4	.96	11.3	26.6	47.1	14.1
Asian Indian	10.5	34.8	1.05	16.3	42.2	30.6	10.6
Korean	19.4	34.1	1.08	16.0	26.9	44.7	11.9
Vietnamese	10.4	25.0	.98	9.1	19.5	43.1	27.7
Cambodian	7.2	20.5	.95	6.7	12.6	45.0	34.7
Hmong	3.5	22.8	1.04	5.6	13.5	44.7	35.1
Laotian	5.3	18.4	.97	6.1	9.9	39.7	43.5
Thai	12.4	25.0	.97	13.7	21.2	50.2	14.5
Bangladeshi	10.2	18.1	.97	8.6	21.5	50.9	18.7
Indonesian	9.2	24.6	.84	14.7	20.2	50.4	14.4
Malaysian	3.1	25.1	.85	8.4	41.9	38.3	11.2
Pakistani	13.3	28.3	1.01	12.4	26.8	42.3	17.9
Sri Lankan	7.3	30.0	1.07	13.4	39.5	35.7	11.0

[a] Among workers employed.

[b] Among wage workers with positive income.

Table 5.15. Migration Statistics by Year

	White		Asian American-SM	
	2000	2005/06	2000	2005/06
Born in the same state of residence (%)	63.2	62.8	24.9	27.9
Born in the same region of residence (%)[a]	76.9	76.9	32.0	32.1
Lived in the same state for last 5 years (%)[b]	89.9	-	74.6	-
Lived in the same state for last 1 year (%)[c]	-	97.1	-	94.4

[a] Based on 4-region classification.

[b] Age 5+.

[c] Age 1+.

period whereas the corresponding figure for Asian Americans was lower (i.e., 94.4% as shown in Table 5.15).

The migration statistics by region of current residence in 2005/2006 are shown in Table 5.16. All of the statistics indicate that Asian Americans are more mobile than whites. However, Asian Americans in the South are also more mobile than Asian Americans in other regions. Whereas 19.2% of Asian Americans in the South were born in the same state as their current residence, the corresponding figure for Asian Americans in other regions is 30.1%. Table 5.16 further shows that 23.5% of Asian Americans in the South were born in the South while 34.2% of Asian Americans elsewhere were born in the same region as their current residence. Thus, Asian Americans in the South are more likely to be new to their current region or to be originally from some region other than their region of current residence. The greater mobility of Asian Americans in the South is also evident in their lower percentage that lived in the same state as their current residence during the last one-year period (i.e., 92.1% versus 95.1% for Asian Americans in other regions).

Table 5.17 shows the origins of persons who migrated to the South but resided there in 2005/2006. Among Asian Americans who were born outside of the South but resided there in 2005/2006, Table 5.17 indicates that the vast majority (i.e., 87.7%) were born overseas while the corresponding figure for whites is only 13.0%. Other places of birth among Southern Asian Americans who were born outside the South include the West (i.e., 5.5%), the Northeast (i.e., 3.9%) and the Midwest (i.e., 2.9%). Broken down by state, 3.1% were born in California while 1.9% were born in New York.

Table 5.17 also provides information about migration in terms of prior place of residence among those who moved to the South during the past year. Among Asian Americans, 52.2% resided overseas. This figure is substantially less than 87.7% mentioned above in regard to migration based on place of birth. In other words, a substantial portion of Asian Americans who reside in the South but who were born overseas first resided in another region in the United States before moving to the South.

Table 5.16. Migration Statistics by Region, 2005/2006

	South		Other Regions	
	White	Asn Am	White	Asn Am
Born in the same state of residence (%)	57.0	19.2	65.9	30.1
Born in the same region of residence (%)[a]	72.9	23.5	79.0	34.2
Lived in the same state for last 1 year (%)[b]	96.5	92.1	97.4	95.1

[a] Based on 4-region classification.
[b] Age 1+.

Table 5.17. Origin of Migrants into the South, 2005/2006

	White	Asian American
Birthplace of those who were born outside the South but currently reside in the South (%)		
Northeast	36.2	3.9
Midwest	37.2	2.9
West	13.6	5.5
Foreign Countries	13.0	87.7
(Total)	(100.0)	(100.0)
[Population Size]	[36,484,351]	[4,428,720]
Selected Birth States		
California	6.5	3.1
Hawaii	0.4	1.1
New York	13.8	1.9
Previous place of residence among those who migrated to the South during the past year (%)		
Northeast	27.0	16.8
Midwest	30.3	12.5
West	23.8	18.5
Foreign Countries	18.8	52.2
(Total)	(100.0)	(100.0)
[Population Size]	[2,586,237]	[350,785]
Selected Resident States 1 Year Ago		
California	8.9	10.9
Hawaii	0.9	2.2
Illinois	4.4	3.1
Ohio	7.5	2.8
New York	9.1	6.5
New Jersey	3.8	4.2

Among Asian American migrants in the South (including both the foreign-born and the native-born), the particular regions of prior residence one year ago include the West (i.e., 18.5%), the Northeast (i.e., 16.8%) and the Midwest (12.5%). Broken down by state of residence one year ago, 10.9% of migrant Southern Asian Americans are from California, 6.5% are from New York, and 4.2% are from New Jersey. Other sending states with smaller though still significant percentages include Illinois, Ohio, and Hawaii, as shown in Table 5.17.

Discussion and Conclusions

This study has investigated current demographic characteristics of Asian Americans. Statistical data were considered in terms of population sizes, geographic distribution, multiracial and ethnic diversity, socioeconomic characteristics, migration, and other basic demographic variables. In general, Asian Americans as an overall group are characterized by a high degree of ethnic diversity and a lower degree of multiracial diversity. Compared to whites, Asian Americans are more likely to be highly educated, more likely to be younger, more likely to have a professional or technical occupation, and less likely to be divorced or separated (both nationally as well as in the South). The majority of Asian Americans are foreign-born and speak some language other than English at home.

Reflecting post-1965 patterns of immigration, Asian Americans have been slowly increasing their proportionate representation in the total U.S. population. Asian Americans currently number about 14.4 million persons, which constitutes approximately 4.9% of the total population or about one out of twenty Americans. Concurrent with the increasing size of the Asian American population is the trend toward a greater presence of Asian Americans in all geographic areas of the nation. Although the majority of Asian Americans were concentrated in the West prior to the twenty-first century, most Asian Americans now live in the South, Midwest, or Northeast.

The high rate of demographic growth of Asian Americans in the South is particularly notable. More Asian Americans now reside in Texas than in Hawaii, and in Atlanta than in San Francisco. Although Asian Americans are generally more likely than whites to migrate, Asian Americans in the South are the most likely to be recent migrants. Due to the large demographic and geographic sizes of the South, Asian Americans in the South still remain a small proportion of the total Southern population. Nonetheless, Asian Americans in the South have reached a substantial population size in absolute terms, and more Asian Americans currently reside in the South than in any other region outside of the West. The South is now dotted with many Asian American individuals and neighborhoods that have often become members of established Asian American communities in particular locales.

These high levels of Asian American demographic growth and migration to the New South are facilitated by a less discriminatory labor market than was characteristic of the pre–Civil Rights era (Sakamoto and Xie 2006). Many Asian Americans are flocking to the New South to take advantage of its improved socioeconomic opportunities. Whereas the better-paying and more desirable jobs were reserved for whites in the Old South, Asian Americans in the New South no longer appear to be automatically excluded from the top of the "racial hierarchy." Compared to whites in the South, Asian Americans in the South actually have higher levels of education, hourly wages, annual earnings, professional occupational status, and income-to-needs ratios. As relative newcomers with a small proportionate population size in the South, Asian Americans undoubtedly have yet to compete with white elites in terms of substantial political power, large landholdings, or major capitalist fortunes, but Asian Americans in the broader society of the South as a whole by and large appear to enjoy socioeconomic circumstances that are at least as favorable as those of most whites, on average.

In earlier decades most Asian Americans resided in the West, including especially California and Hawaii. Family, ethnic, and other social ties to those areas had been adequate to foster the continued concentration of Asian Americans in the West. With the population of California reaching nearly 34 million at the start of the twenty-first century, however, push factors have become more prominent. California is now so crowded that it has some of the worst traffic congestion in the nation along with exorbitant housing prices, water and electricity shortages, ecological repercussions involving air pollution and wild fires, huge budget shortfalls, higher energy costs, and various metropolitan maladies such as violent crime, juvenile gangs, and a rising number of inadequately funded school systems. While no state is entirely free of all of these problems, the extraordinary level of population concentration in California undoubtedly exacerbates them. Perhaps not surprisingly, among Asian Americans who had moved to the South during the past year, nearly 11% were coming from California.

The socioeconomic opportunities of the Southern labor market become all the more attractive in light of the overcrowding of many places in the West. This issue is related to our statistical results when we adjusted the income figures for regional differentials in the cost of living. After doing so, Asian Americans in the South have by far the highest mean hourly wage compared to Asian Americans in other regions as well as to whites in any region. After factoring in the lower cost of living, Southern Asian Americans have higher average levels of earnings, household income, and per capita household income than Asian Americans elsewhere.

Asian Americans as a group have been characterized as being more family oriented in the sense of being more likely to marry after completing schooling, less likely to become divorced, more likely to focus on the educational and related childrearing activities of their children, and more likely to form three-generational families (Min 1995; Sun 1998; Kamo 2000; Xie and Goyette 2004). Some evidence accordingly suggests that, despite being younger on average, Asian Americans have higher levels of home equity than whites (Krivo and Kaufman 2004), in part due to the preference for larger homes. In this Asian American subcultural context that places a premium on family functioning, the lower housing costs of the South (as compared to the West and Northeast) are a noteworthy attraction.

In closing, we reiterate that the Old South was characterized by a strict racial hierarchy in which the dominant power and socioeconomic advantages of whites were unrivaled and Asian Americans were severely disadvantaged (Tang 2007). By contrast, we interpret our foregoing demographic results as suggesting the beginning of a new stage of Asian American population distribution, which is characterized by improved socioeconomic opportunities that are facilitating a movement away from the geographic margins of the nation such as Hawaii and California. In this current era of Asian Americans in the twenty-first century, the New South is leading the way toward a more open labor market that is better at restraining the primordial racial conflicts over job competition that often characterized relations between whites and Asian Americans during the nineteenth and twentieth centuries. Asian Americans are thus entering into the social and geographic mainstreams of American society by often successfully competing for many desirable job opportunities, which are frequently located in the New South.

Perhaps the greater challenge for Asian Americans in the twenty-first century is dealing with the consequences of rising levels of class inequalities. So far, Asian Americans have fared better than other minority groups because Asian Americans tend to have higher levels of education, which is becoming more important in the contemporary labor market. Nonetheless, this latter generalization is based on statistical averages. Our other results also indicate that Asian Americans tend to be characterized by a high level of socioeconomic variation and class inequalities that are sometimes even greater than for whites. The greater dispersion of socioeconomic circumstances among Asian Americans is most obviously evident in their higher unemployment and poverty rates than whites. Overcoming the social problems exacerbated by rising class inequalities is likely to be one of the most important challenges facing America in the twenty-first century and especially perhaps for Asian Americans. As stated by Sakamoto and Xie (2006, 75), "It can be argued that increases in class inequality in the American labor market pose a serious threat to the fabric of our society. . . . Such class inequalities need to be recognized, addressed, and ameliorated even if they are not rooted primarily in racial discrimination per se."

Notes

We thank the editors and anonymous reviewers for helpful comments in this research. All opinions expressed herein are the sole responsibility of the authors.

1. Later we also make use of a more refined nine-category regional classification but only to adjust income figures for geographic differences in the cost of living. For a detailed map of the Asian American population distribution, refer to http://www.census.gov/prod/2002pubs/c2kbr01–16.pdf (accessed January 12, 2013).

2. Most of the decline in the Asian American-M population is associated with biracial Asians who also identify with the miscellaneous "Some other race" category. In the printing of the U.S. Census of 2000 questionnaire "Some other race" is visually obvious and almost inviting. By contrast, in the American Community Survey questionnaire, "Some other race" is visually difficult to find and seems to be "in the fine print." Because "Some other race" is not a widely recognized or well-defined concept, the visual difference in the printing of the questionnaires might affect the number of people who realized that they could identify with that category. Note that a substantial portion of biracial Asian Americans who identify with "Some other race" may include persons who view themselves

as being partly Mexican and who consider Mexican to be its own racial group (Choi, Sakamoto, and Powers 2008).

3. The population of Asian Americans in Hawaii still remains slightly larger than in Texas if Pacific Islanders are included together with Asian Americans, because Hawaii has a significant number of Pacific Islanders whereas that group in Texas is very small.

4. The population figures for Vietnamese in Austin, Dallas–Forth Worth, and Houston are likely to include a relatively small proportion of Vietnamese evacuees from New Orleans and neighboring areas following Hurricane Katrina in 2005. Many of these Texas evacuees appear to have since returned to their homes in Louisiana (Ha 2007, 287).

5. The standard deviations are calculated after taking the logarithm of earnings or wages. The standard deviation of the logged values is a common statistical measure of inequality. This measure is standardized so that the level of inequality in earnings can be compared to the level of inequality in wages even though these two variables have very different average values.

6. We do not adjust for regional differences in the cost of living when computing the income-to-needs ratio because by convention, the U.S. Census Bureau poverty lines are constant throughout the nation.

References

Berry, William D., Richard C. Fording, and Russell L. Hanson. 2000. "An Annual Cost of Living Index for the American States, 1960–1995." *Journal of Politics* 62:550–567.

Choi, Kate H., Arthur Sakamoto, and Daniel A. Powers. 2008. "Who Is Hispanic? Hispanic Identity among African Americans, Asian Americans, Others, and Whites." *Sociological Inquiry* 78:335–337.

Cohen, Lucy M. 1984. *Chinese in the Post–Civil War South*. Baton Rouge: Louisiana State University Press.

Ha, Thao. 2007. "The Vietnamese Texans," in *Asian Texans: Our Histories and Our Lives*, edited by Irwin A. Tang. Austin, Tex.: The It Works.

Kamo, Yoshinori. 2000. "Racial and Ethnic Differences in Extended Family Households." *Sociological Perspectives* 43:211–229.

Kim, ChangHwan, and Arthur Sakamoto. 2010. "Have Asian American Men Achieved Labor Market Parity with White Men?" *American Sociological Review* 75:934–957.

Kitano, Harry H. L., and Roger Daniels. 2001. *Asian Americans: Emerging Minorities*. New York: Pearson.

Krivo, Lauren J., and Robert L. Kaufman. 2004. "Housing and Wealth Inequality: Racial-Ethnic Differences in Home Equity in the United States." *Demography* 41:585–605.

Lee, Sharon M., and Marilyn Fernandez. 1998. "Trends in Asian American Racial/Ethnic Intermarriage: A Comparison of 1980 and 1990 Census Data." *Sociological Perspectives* 4:323–342.

Loewen, James W. 1988. *The Mississippi Chinese: Between Black and White*. 2nd ed. Prospect Heights, Ill: Waveland Press.

Min, Pyong Gap. 1995. "An Overview of Asian Americans," in *Asian Americans: Contemporary Trends and Issues*, edited by P. G. Min. Thousand Oaks, Calif.: Sage, 10–57.

Qian, Zhenchao, and Daniel T. Lichter. 2007. "Social Boundaries and Marital Assimilation: Interpreting Trends in Racial and Ethnic Intermarriage." *American Sociological Review* 72:68–94.

Rhoads, Edward J. H. 1977. "The Chinese in Texas." *Southwestern Historical Quarterly* 81:1–36.

Sakamoto, Arthur, and Thao Ha. 2003. "A Brief Profile of the Demographic Growth of Asian Americans in the South," in *Asian American Nation: Demographic and Cultural Change 2000 and Beyond*, edited by Eric Lai. San Francisco: Asian Week, 175–181.

Sakamoto, Arthur, and Hyeyoung Woo. 2007. "The Socioeconomic Attainments of Second-Generation Cambodian, Hmong, Laotian, and Vietnamese Americans." *Sociological Inquiry* 77:44–75.

Sakamoto, Arthur, and Yu Xie. 2006. "The Socioeconomic Attainments of Asian Americans," in *Asian Americans: Contemporary Trends and Issues*, 2nd ed., edited by P. G. Min. Thousand Oaks, Calif.: Sage, 54–77.

Sun, Yongmin. 1998. "The Academic Success of East-Asian-American Students: An Investment Model." *Social Science Research* 27:432–456.

Tang, Irwin A. 2007. "Historical Overview," in *Asian Texans: Our Histories and Our Lives*, edited by Irwin A. Tang. Austin, Tex.: The It Works, 1–23.

Walls, Thomas K. 1987. *The Japanese Texans*. San Antonio: Institute of Texan Cultures.

Xie, Yu, and Kimberly Goyette. 2004. *A Demographic Portrait of Asian Americans*. New York: Russell Sage.

CHAPTER 6

Natives of a Ghost Country

The Vietnamese in Houston and Their Construction of a Postwar Community

Roy Vu

The post–World War II economic and population boom of the Sunbelt states, particularly Texas, transformed Southern cities such as Houston into an attractive economic and geographical center for migrants, immigrants, and refugees to resettle. With ties to the oil refining industry, Houston experienced a dramatic economic growth period as oil production and prices soared during the 1970s. The city emerged as one of the fast-growing "New South" cities during the mid-1970s. This time period coincided with the Communist takeover of Sai Gon and the subsequent influx of approximately 130,000 Vietnamese refugees who migrated to the United States and other countries for fear of Communist persecution. With Houston's high job growth, relatively low cost of living, increase in affordable housing, and potential higher income, thousands of Vietnamese refugees made a secondary migration and forged a community[1] in a city once labeled, "the 'golden buckle' of the Sunbelt."[2]

Bui Tien Khoi's decision to relocate his family to Houston is the story of thousands of other Vietnamese refugees who relocated to Houston. After the closing of Fort Chaffee, Arkansas, one of four makeshift Vietnamese refugee camps in 1975, Bui Tien Khoi moved to Houston. On his decision Bui remarked, "The weather is very warm here, and when I read about Houston at the time there was only two percent unemployment. . . . The society was beautiful, too; the income, the schools and from 1965 to 1975 there had been no deficit. . . . That's a prosperous city. I'd like to live there."[3]

By 2010, Houston's Vietnamese population alone reached to 34,838, the third-largest Vietnamese community in the United States.[4] In the Houston–Sugar Land–Baytown, Texas, metropolitan area, or the Greater Houston metropolitan area (GHMA),[5] including the heavily Asian-populated Fort Bend County, the Vietnamese population alone jumped to 103,525, which represented more than 26 percent of the area's Asian American population.[6]

Upon establishing the community, the Vietnamese in the GHMA made an effort to reestablish their homeland in the United States and create a community. This essay addresses the efforts of the Vietnamese in Houston and vicinity,[7] to challenge racial marginalization by seeking ways to establish and sustain a community. Furthermore, Vietnamese Houstonians construct an identity via community formation strategies such as utilizing transhistorical[8] Southern Vietnamese nationalism and creating spatiality. Such strategies would help bind and stitch the community together, albeit the community would transform itself with tremendous fluidity over the years.

Critical factors in the process of community formation include 1) organizing to challenge the racialization of Vietnamese Americans from whites and marginalized minorities, 2) redeeming transhistorical Southern Vietnamese[9] nationalism by galvanizing political capital[10] through strident, anticommunist activism *and* changing anticommunist tactics, and 3) creating spatiality[11] or "making space" that engendered feelings of belonging through the establishment of smaller social communities, major shifts in central business districts (CBDs), and the establishment of religious, linguistic, and social service institutions.

The Vietnamese American community in Houston is different from other Vietnamese ethnic enclaves across the United States in one very significant way. The Vietnamese in Houston and vicinity reside in several major residential areas as well as smaller, defined social communities throughout the city; there is no single center. For example, the Vietnamese populace in New Orleans has Versailles Village in the Ninth Ward, while the Vietnamese community in Boston has Fields Corner in Dorchester, a suburb south of Boston. The Vietnamese community in the GHMA is a multinodal community with large concentrations of Vietnamese residents living in northeast, southwest, and southeast Houston. Furthermore, it is a multinodal community because several smaller, defined social communities exist in the Alief and Park Place neighborhoods. Correspondingly, Vietnamese business districts in the Greater Houston metropolitan area shifted from downtown adjacent to Old Chinatown, to the Midtown commercial sector along the Milam corridor, and finally, to Bellaire Boulevard in southwest Houston.

The Racialization of the Vietnamese

The Vietnamese as the Marginalized "Other"

Not all Americans welcomed Vietnamese refugees into the country during the mid-1970s.[12] In Houston, some local groups and politicians worried openly about the economic impact of these new refugees on jobs, welfare, and government services; some deployed racist tropes of contagion and cited the refugees bringing in tropical diseases.[13] After the influx of Vietnamese refugees after 1978, a nationwide Harris Poll found that 62 to 72 percent of the respondents believed that there were numerous problems resettling the Vietnamese refugees right after the war, and thus it would be a mistake to allow more to settle in the United States.[14] The differences in customs and appearance, combined with the Vietnamese emphasis on industriousness and lack of observance of local mores and laws such as overharvesting of shrimp, also caused tensions in housing and employment.[15]

Many Vietnamese refugees, who resettled along the southeast Texas Gulf Coast[16] near Houston, once made a living by fishing in their native coastal waters. Therefore, they could make an easier economic transition from fishing to shrimping along the coastal towns of Brazoria, Chambers, and Galveston counties. According to one study, by 1983, the number of Vietnamese-owned fishing and shrimping boats totaled about 280 vessels (11.2 percent) out of a total fishing fleet of 2500 in Texas. Approximately thirty-five miles southeast of Houston, in nearby Seabrook and Kemah, about sixty Vietnamese-owned boats were moored in the Texas Gulf waters.[17]

The successes of the Vietnamese community did not go unnoticed. Conflicts arose as Texan shrimpers accused the Vietnamese fishermen along Texas's Gulf Coast of overharvesting shrimp.[18] The Vietnamese shrimpers were surprised that their hard work would incur resentment and anger among many native Texans. Native Texans along the Gulf Coast exhibited a sense of entitlement that stemmed from the fact that many were not only born and raised in the area, but also inherited the same occupations and were accustomed to their fishing and shrimping lifestyle. Therefore, the Vietnamese "latecomers" were perceived as an invading force, who disrupted their work space and home community.

The most intense conflicts took place in the Harris–Galveston County area. Conflicts escalated from verbal threats to violence in August of 1979, when a fight erupted between a local white crabber, Billy Joe Aplin, who had a reputation for harassing Vietnamese shrimpers, and Sau Van Nguyen.[19] Aplin threatened Sau's life and cut him with a knife. Sau returned to the dock, with a gun, to confront Aplin. Aplin hit Sau and in retaliation, Sau shot and killed Aplin.[20] Sau was acquitted of murder and accomplice charges on November 2, 1979.[21]

The violence against Vietnamese shrimpers continued in January 1981 when arsonists destroyed a Vietnamese American shrimp boat in Seabrook, Texas. Two months later, another fire destroyed one Vietnamese American–owned boat and damaged a second. At a rally in the Galveston County city of Santa Fe in February 1981, the Ku Klux Klan burned a shrimp boat replica in effigy and instructed listeners on how such fires should be set.

The 1981 Klan demonstration incident proved to be the tipping point for the Vietnamese community and led to the first post–Viet Nam War Asian American coalition effort to combat racism in the Greater Houston metropolitan area. The rally was organized by Glenda Kay Joe, a well-known community activist of Irish and Chinese descent, in Houston's Asian American community.[22] When the

violence between the KKK and Vietnamese refugees erupted, she got involved
and supported the Vietnamese fishermen and shrimpers, who were harassed
and threatened by Klan members, by fighting on their behalf and educating the
Vietnamese on their rights.

Glenda Joe and Michael Chou, her longtime friend, sent one-page letters in
Vietnamese and English to the families of the shrimpers and fishermen, telling
them what to expect and not to let the KKK provoke them to violence. Joe and
Chou became liaisons between local law enforcement agencies and the communities. They formed the Council of Asian American Organizations (CAAO),
which was credited with defusing white antagonism against the Vietnamese
refugees.[23] This organization's historic political maneuver was monumental in
aiding the Vietnamese not only to stem the tide of Klan violence, but it ultimately
led to the Klan leaving the area. In 1982, with the assistance of Asian American
community leaders, Vietnamese American shrimpers and fishermen filed a collective injunction against the KKK to stop it from harassing and threatening the
refugees with their weapons. The Vietnamese refugees also built political agency
by forming the Vietnamese Fishermen's Association and filed a permanent injunction against the Klan members and their affiliates. On June 9, 1982, in the
case of *Vietnamese Fishermen's Association v. The Knights of the Ku Klux Klan*
(KKK), the U.S. District Court Houston Division ruled that Klan members were
permanently enjoined from engaging in unlawful acts such as placing an armed
person or persons within the personal view of the Vietnamese fishermen and
using intimidation tactics against the refugees.[24] As a result, the ruling legally
protected the right of Vietnamese fishermen and shrimpers to continue to fish
along the Texas Gulf Coast.

Regardless of the harassment from a racist, violent organization like the KKK
and in spite of being targeted by white Texan fishermen whose anti-Vietnamese
sentiments derived from fear of economic competition and loss from a hard-
working refugee group that out-competed them, the Vietnamese fishermen and
their families emerged from this conflict largely unscathed. The Vietnamese
became more unified, coalescing into a tight-knit fishing and shrimping community when external forces threatened to remove them from the area and
destroy their livelihood. With assistance from Asian American activists such
as Glenda Joe, the Vietnamese learned the importance of working together and
pooling their political capital to resolve a racial conflict. Glenda Joe's actions
provide evidence of panethnic Asian American solidarity, the first such movement in the Greater Houston metropolitan area since the end of the Viet Nam
War and the arrival of Vietnamese refugees. For Vietnamese Americans, gaining
political capital would be substantial in the formation of their own community.
By taking the necessary legal steps, the Vietnamese fishermen and shrimpers
created political agency in the early 1980s as a strategy to safeguard and protect
their own fishing community.

Contested Space: From Allen Parkway Village to Sunnyside

Since the postwar influx of Vietnamese arrivals in Houston in 1975–1976, the relationship between Vietnamese Americans and other marginalized minorities has been racially tense over the years. For marginalized minorities such as African and Vietnamese Americans, establishing and contesting spatiality in both residential and business areas would lead to heightened violence and cultural misperceptions. African American residents of Allen Parkway Village, Acres Home, and Sunnyside neighborhoods have felt threatened economically and socially by the influx of Vietnamese refugees. Their social communities have been transformed with the presence of Vietnamese refugees as early as 1976. With assistance from the Housing Authority of the City of Houston (HACH), the first concentration of Vietnamese refugees resettling in Houston began as early as 1976 in one-thousand-unit Allen Parkway Village, located in Midtown, just south of the downtown area.[25] Robert Bullard claims, "Beginning in 1976 there appears to have been a 'replacement' policy on the part of the HACH for Allen Parkway Village, that is, Indochinese [Southeast Asian refugees, including mostly Vietnamese] rather than blacks would be selected for placement in the development."[26] In 1976, an estimated 5 percent of all habitable units of Allen Parkway Village were occupied by Southeast Asian refugees, but by 1984, that number had increased to approximately 58.1 percent.[27] While the replacement of black residents in Allen Parkway Village provided affordable albeit deteriorating public housing for the influx of Southeast Asian refugees, thus creating Houston's first Vietnamese residential community, such action by the HACH eradicated the black community of the historic Fourth Ward.[28] It remains unclear where African American residents resettled.

As for the Vietnamese newcomers, the opportunity provided an affordable housing alternative, and for Catholics, a residential space within walking distance to the Holy Rosary Catholic Church where a Vietnamese priest performed religious services.[29] Allen Parkway Village became a social center for the Vietnamese residents because they could live relatively comfortably with their Vietnamese neighbors and converse in their native language. Furthermore, Vietnamese residents cultivated an economic niche by turning empty lots into large, green gardens to grow herbs and vegetables not only for themselves, but to sell to their fellow Vietnamese and earn a supplemental income. By 1985 however, due to worsened conditions and outside real estate pressures to demolish the deteriorating government housing project as the area became gentrified, Vietnamese residents began to leave Allen Parkway Village.[30] Throughout the rest of the 1980s, gentrification and eviction conflicts increased between HACH and the remaining Vietnamese and African American residents.[31] Ironically, by the mid-1980s, Vietnamese refugees who resided in the Allen Parkway Village public housing project became victims of HACH much like their fellow African American tenants were when the Vietnamese first relocated here in 1976.

Another form of contested spatiality deals with commercial space occupied and owned by a recently arrived minority group, Vietnamese Americans, who provide a variety of services in a setting where the majority clientele has been historically marginalized, African Americans. Throughout the 1990s, rising tensions boiled over between Vietnamese American storeowners and African American customers. Many Vietnamese American shopkeepers owned businesses located in predominantly black neighborhoods and ran into problems with African American patrons. Several Vietnamese American clerks perceived their black customers as disruptive and untrustworthy, watching them cautiously. On the other hand, many African Americans complained about the rudeness and cold reception they received upon entering the stores. This lack of communication created tension that resulted in violent and deadly confrontations between Vietnamese clerks and black shoppers.[32]

Yet throughout the struggle, leaders of both communities made efforts to reconcile and compromise in hopes of forging a healthy relationship and dialogue between the two minorities. Such actions of cooperation were out of necessity due to the aftermath of the violence that resulted on several occasions when Vietnamese American clerks shot and fatally wounded African American customers. For instance, on July 24, 1992, the shooting death of an African American male sparked a boycott of a far southwest Houston service station.[33] Eric DeLeon Hicks, 22, was killed by a store clerk at Chevron Food Store, 6600 W. Fuqua, over a shoplifting incident. Nguyen Hung, eighteen, was originally charged with murder, and bond was denied. In response, within days of the fatal shooting, demonstrators started marching outside the store, encouraging residents to boycott.[34] In a *Houston Chronicle* interview, Nguyen stated that he fired the gun only after Hicks damaged the family's store with a golf club, struck him on the head and threatened his father and younger brother.[35] Claiming that he was not even aiming at Hicks when he fired the fatal shot, Nguyen apologized to the Hicks family.[36] Nguyen was eventually no-billed and exonerated by a third grand jury.[37]

Reacting to Hicks's death, the Council of Asian American Organizations prepared a guide for Asian American merchants on how to deal with their customers.[38] The death of Hicks served as part of a larger robbery prevention campaign.[39] The guides were available in Vietnamese, Chinese, Korean, and Cambodian; they explained the disadvantages of using deadly force, the concepts of customer relations in the United States, and the importance of supporting community activities.[40] The guide was picked up by local Asian American media outlets, the National Association for the Advancement of Colored People (NAACP), and the Acres Home Community, as well as the *Houston Chronicle, Los Angeles Times*, and *Wall Street Journal*.[41]

In 1994, approximately twenty-five African and Asian Americans gathered in northwest Houston in search of a peaceful solution to the conflict between Asian merchants and predominantly black neighborhoods.[42] "Peace in the City," one specific program started by Glenda Joe and the Rev. Ralph West, minister at Brookhollow Baptist Church, resulted in this group participating in a Lunar New Year/Black History Month program at Sharpstown High School, which was hosted by Sharpstown High's Asian and African American student organizations.[43]

Even after such programs aimed at conflict resolution and community building, there were still violent incidences in these areas. In 1998, the director of the U.S. Justice Department agency for ethnic and racial conflicts called the Sunnyside coalition's promising practices and its program potential models for other programs nationwide and presented the Sunnyside Asian/African American Task Force with a citation.[44] With the involvement among local Vietnamese and African American leaders, church organizations, civic groups, Houston City Council members and law enforcement agencies, race relations have improved between the two communities.

However, despite its diverse population, the city of Houston remains a fairly segregated urban area. With a low population density, Houston's metropolitan area is largely composed of "decentralized villages," where people of similar socio-economic and ethnic backgrounds live in relative isolation.[45] With racial groups living in isolated neighborhoods from each other, Houston remains largely a segregated population with numerous pockets of ethnic communities separated from one another. Such de facto segregation leads to higher cases of cultural conflicts. Isolated ethnic groups also allow cultural misperceptions to develop, inciting negative racial attitudes toward one another and, therefore, less favorable perceptions of intergroup relations.

Grappling with the Model Minority Myth

In some cases, so-called "positive" stereotypes are employed to divide marginalized populations. Perhaps the most deliberate of such stereotypes would be the mythologizing of the Asian ethnic group as a model minority. Such a typecast, of course, introduces a plethora of problems for Asian Americans. Many scholars such as Roger Daniels, Stacey J. Lee, and the late Ronald Takaki have written works dispelling the model minority myth and how unjustly such a label stigmatizes Asian Americans as proof that the "rags-to-riches" immigrant narrative is the norm and that marginalized minorities such as African Americans and Latinos have no one else to blame but themselves for their downtrodden socioeconomic standing.[46] In reality, such scholars have proven that the model minority tag not only glosses over the racialization of Vietnamese Americans and ignores the acts of direct and indirect racial violence against them, but it shuns the many Vietnamese and other Southeast Asian refugees who live in abject poverty.

As for the Vietnamese in Houston and vicinity, they are generally facing more difficult challenges than other Asian ethnic groups. From his 2002 survey, Stephen Klineberg reports, "Fewer than 38 percent of the Vietnamese have college or professional degrees, compared to 58 percent of all Asians in the Houston area and to a striking 78 percent of the Filipinos although South Asians and Chinese are more likely than Filipinos to have post-graduate degrees."[47] In terms of job occupation, the Vietnamese are more likely than other Asian respondents to be working in semiskilled production work or as unskilled laborers, and they are less likely to be in professional or managerial positions. Six out of ten reported personal earnings of less than $25,000; this was true of fewer than 40 percent in the other communities.[48] About 28 percent of the Vietnamese have low-skilled production or laboring jobs, as did 30 percent of their fathers.[49] In contrast, only 13 percent of all the Asian respondents were in low-paid production or day-labor jobs.[50] Furthermore, the Vietnamese refugee population in Houston may also be less likely to receive the help they need, in a language they can understand, from a city that continues to believe that all Asians fit the "model minority" image.[51]

Klineberg's statistics refute the stereotype of the financially successful and overachieving model minority status, which is unfairly tagged on Vietnamese Americans, by discovering that Houston's overseas Vietnamese do not fare economically as well as other Asian American ethnic groups nor the average Houstonian. He argues, "In terms of income and occupation, the Vietnamese in Houston are doing somewhat better than most Blacks and Hispanics, but they are faring much worse than most other Asians."[52]

The residential Vietnamese American communities in GMHA are segregated based on socioeconomic class, year of arrival, educational status, and English competency. There are also smaller communities, which are more like isolated Vietnamese villages throughout the greater metropolitan area. They are segregated not only from the rest of Houston's population, but are invisible from other Vietnamese Americans as well. For the Vietnamese in the GHMA, since the existence of their community they rely on redeeming Southern Vietnamese nationalism, a transhistorical anticommunist narrative from the Cold War that would help them negate, to a certain degree, their racialization as a perpetual foreigner as well as a model minority.

Redeeming Transhistorical
Southern Vietnamese Nationalism

The Third Red Scare

One essential example of formulating spatiality via political agency is how Vietnamese in the GHMA made efforts to revive and redeem transhistorical Southern Vietnamese nationalism and galvanize political capital from the community. By using political rhetoric and action to denounce communism in hopes of one day returning to a democratic Viet Nam, Vietnamese Houstonians rely on transhistorical Southern Vietnamese nationalism to create space that defines their community—erecting monuments honoring their veterans, hoisting Southern

Vietnamese flags that are ubiquitous along Bellaire Boulevard in southwest Houston, and naming their varied businesses after the moniker "Sai Gon," the former capital of their ill-fated country of the Republic of Viet Nam.

In the aftermath of the Viet Nam War and resettlement in a country that was still reeling, the Vietnamese had to maintain an anticommunist narrative in the postwar years in order to construct their own space and community and to stem the rising nativism from Americans, many of whom were either struggling to make sense of the war or dealing with the economic recession of the late 1970s, or both. In other words, the Viet Nam War for many Americans was a diplomatic defeat and psychological blow. The combination of the aforementioned factors, along with the rising xenophobic attitude toward Vietnamese and other Southeast Asian refugees who arrived en masse, led to violence against and racialization of the refugees. To fend themselves from possible racist motives from other Americans and to create and galvanize their own community, the Vietnamese relied heavily on the anticommunist narrative.

After resettling in the GHMA in 1975–1976, early anticommunist politics became an alluring force that aided Vietnamese refugees in community formation, which unified thousands of people to work for the eradication of the Vietnamese Communists and make their subsequent return home to a democratic Viet Nam. However, pooling political capital via transhistorical Southern Vietnamese nationalism has been a divisive and costly strategy that inflicted great harm on the community. The anticommunist politics tempered over time as Vietnamese Americans modified their political strategies to emphasize less on *homeland politics* in Viet Nam and accentuate the *politics at home* to address the serious problems afflicting the community's spatiality. Yet, the fundamental shift in political strategies did not occur until after the demise of a national Vietnamese anticommunist organization.

Founded on June 30, 1981, by former South Vietnamese military officers in California, the National United Front for the Liberation of Viet Nam (*Mat Tran Quoc Gia Thong Nhat Gia Phong Viet Nam*) or simply the Front, offered refugees a plan to retake their homeland.[53] The scheme to raise a guerrilla army in the countries bordering Viet Nam sounded far-fetched, but was nonetheless enticing. Strong anticommunist sentiment gained momentum in the late 1970s and early 1980s as the Front garnered popular support not just in California, but also in Houston. The group had considerable financial backing and the donors believed they were aiding a good cause—to assist the Front's guerrilla war in Southeast Asia and throttle the Vietnamese Communists.

Front members in Houston wrote a resolution expressing their opinions of the Communist government in 1981. They demanded that "the Communist government in Viet-Nam return or at least account for all Americans missing in action in Indochina, that the communists release the hundreds of thousands of former members of the Vietnamese Armed Forces and Government still in reeducation camps, that the Vietnamese communists stop exporting slave labor to the Soviet Union, and that they abandon their aggression against Cambodia and Laos."[54] The resolution was formally adopted and ratified at the organization's meeting. The resolution's authors also called upon "the entire world to bring the maximum weight of public opinion to bear on Hanoi to alleviate the suffering of the Vietnamese people, so that they would not feel forced to flee the country on perilous journeys across the seas in search of freedom and a better life and thus impose an unreasonable burden on neighboring countries of Southeast Asia and on the rest of the world which has to resettle the refugees."[55] For local Vietnamese, condemning communism became a temporary useful political tool not only to unify the community, but also to convey a shared sense of loss and anger toward the Vietnamese Communist government that has taken away their homeland and persecuted their Southern Vietnamese brethren after the war.

At another meeting, American and Southern Vietnamese veterans of the war gathered to commemorate the Republic of Viet Nam Armed Forces Day.[56] Remembering and honoring their homeland of Southern Viet Nam, while collaborating with the U.S. government, a hegemonic ally during the Viet Nam War, to denounce the human rights violations committed by the Communist regime were powerful political strategies that furthered community formation.

However, one Vietnamese journalist dared to challenge the Front's political motives and funding activities, and thus he questioned the community's political agency of anticommunist politics. Phong Dam Nguyen left Sai Gon in 1975 and started a newspaper in Houston called *Tu Do*, meaning "freedom."[57] Nguyen exposed fraudulent refugee aid programs. Although he was a fierce anticommunist, Nguyen dedicated his final issues of *Tu Do* to a series accusing the Front's leaders of fraud. Nguyen's paper received anonymous phone threats, fellow journalists pleaded with him to back off, and Nguyen even started carrying a gun. On the early morning of August 25, 1982, he was murdered on the doorstep of his house in southeast Houston.[58] The crime remains unsolved. Vietnamese American community leaders and the Houston Police Department (HPD) suspected that his assassination was the direct result of the articles he published about the Front. The HPD report pointed to the anticommunist organization as the main suspect. The FBI eventually indicted leaders of the Front for money laundering, extortion, bribery, and misappropriation of funds when members used generous donations from the Vietnamese community to run their own restaurant chain and produce adult films. Along with these scandals and the death of the group's leader, Admiral Minh Co Hoang (whose failed attempt to raise an anticommunist guerrilla army in Southeast Asia ended with his death), disenchantment with the Front led to its decline by the early 1990s.

Forging a Post-Anticommunist Narrative?

The dissipation of the Front paved the way for Vietnamese to seek alternative political strategies by the start of the community's third decade. For Dai Huynh, she admits that every time she attends meetings in the Vietnamese community, the focus is on "what can the United States government do to boycott Viet Nam."[59] Nonetheless, she is determined to assist the Vietnamese elderly in Houston and concentrate on "what can we do to make the government here to help the Vietnamese here."[60] Dai Huynh demonstrates a common attitude among the 1.5 and second generations of Vietnamese Americans as they concentrate on reallocating their political capital to shift the community's attention toward politics at home and away from overseas homeland politics. More Vietnamese Americans are bucking the old political trends and establishing new ones such as embracing the need to become more involved in the U.S. political system, establishing transnational linkages with Viet Nam, and reconstructing their community and spatiality through new anticommunist political strategies. Such a political transition allows the Vietnamese to address their social and economic problems mentioned earlier; problems that may be shrouded by the model minority myth.

Political Participation and Hubert Vo's Historic Victory

Although anticommunist politics cannot be separated from the Vietnamese American political framework, Vietnamese Houstonians do participate in mainstream domestic politics by getting involved in presidential elections, running for public office, pushing for voter registration drives and participating in national political parties. Vietnamese Americans have commonly been perceived as Republican voters since the community's staunch anticommunist views, support of the U.S. Cold War policy against communism, and conservative family values dictate their party affiliation.

Among Vietnamese Houstonians, a generational split is apparent with the first generation, those who were born and raised in Viet Nam, favoring the Republican Party. By comparison, the 1.5 and second generations, those who were raised or were born in the United States, are more receptive in supporting the Democratic Party. However, this does not mean that a majority of younger Vietnamese Houstonians are supporting the Democrats, but rather that they are more amenable toward alternative political parties. Community activist and former VNCH Vice President, Binh Q. Nguyen reaffirmed the growing generational divide in terms of party affiliations for Vietnamese Americans: "[M]y parents' generation prefers Republicans because their experience with Republicans is that they're anticommunist."[61] However, Nguyen also asserted, "But young people are more often Democrats because it's more real in their daily lives."[62] Nguyen and many other Vietnamese Houstonians are aware that the older generation will remain loyal to the Republican Party and its conservative economic and social values that fit with their anticommunist narrative and concerns about family values. Whereas younger Vietnamese Houstonians tend to be more tolerable and willing to be affiliated with the Democratic Party since Democrats in recent years have been perceived as the party that focuses on social concerns such as public education, health care, and social security—domestic issues that the 1.5 and second generations want to address more than fighting communism abroad.

Furthermore, community-based organizations (CBOs)[63] such as My (Michael) Cao Nguyen's VN Teamwork have taken greater interest in voter registration drives and educating other Vietnamese about how to participate in the American electoral process. More Vietnamese seek public offices and even win them, such as Democrat Hubert Vo who ran for the Texas State Legislature seat 149 and defeated the Republican incumbent Talmadge Heflin in their hotly contested 2004 election.[64] Yet, such momentous political gains are revolutionary not because more Vietnamese are becoming registered voters or that Hubert Vo is the first Vietnamese American to serve on the Texas State Legislature.[65] Rather, such historic occasions mark a dramatic transition from the overseas homeland politics of defeating communism to politics at home where more Vietnamese stress greater involvement in the American electoral process to further formulate their community and space.

Hubert Vo's narrow victory signifies the transformation of the demographic makeup of not only District 149 in Alief, but also the city of Houston as well. The city's metropolitan area continues to show a demographic trend where Latinos and Asian Americans are dramatically increasing in numbers. Also, Vo's victory reflects a more common attitude among Vietnamese Houstonians of whom many are determined to resolve socioeconomic problems, close the generational gap, and turn their backs on anticommunist politics to create a less segmented community. An increasing number of Vietnamese Houstonians are more receptive toward sending financial remittances to Viet Nam, returning to their native land, and even acknowledging U.S. cooperation with Viet Nam as inevitable progress for the two nations to heal the old wounds of war.

This monumental shift in the political narrative does not necessarily weaken the Vietnamese anticommunist fervor in the GHMA, but rather the populace's flexible response demonstrates how the Vietnamese can change and adapt to the current political landscape to help their community and maintain their spatiality despite their racialization by Americans and the eventual political and social divides caused by extreme anticommunist politics. A transition to a kinder, gentler, and nonviolent form of Vietnamese anticommunism remains a work in progress.

Constructing Space Via Community Institutions

Building Social Communities

As soon as they resettled in Houston and vicinity in 1975, Vietnamese exiles started developing smaller, defined social communities, which have become an integral part of the larger Vietnamese community in Houston. These smaller communities are not just enclosed by physical boundaries of major roads and highways but are created and defined by Vietnamese residents themselves. As mentioned earlier, the first, defined Vietnamese residential community took place in Allen Parkway Village in 1976. However, by the mid-1980s, the first wave of Vietnamese refugees began to move out of Allen Parkway Village as gentrification and eviction conflicts heightened between the Housing Authority of the City of Houston (HACH) and the remaining Vietnamese and African American tenants.[66]

Yet, with the influx of second and third waves of Vietnamese refugees throughout the 1980s, many Vietnamese newcomers sought affordable condominiums and low-rent apartment complexes to live; developed their own political infrastructure; and established mutual aid networking to seek financial assistance, jobs, and ESL and computer skills courses. In these smaller communities, Vietnamese residents actively re-create their own "little Vietnamese world" to construct religious institutions, hold English language and computer courses to assist fellow refugees, and maintain a familiar political infrastructure by selecting a president or a "village chief" to head the residents. Residents of each village community refer to their complex as a village and the president of the condominium association the Village Chief.[67] They contribute to the formation of Vietnamese spatiality by retaining what remains of their cultural authenticity (after refuge and resettlement) of their social enclaves, and thus ensure that there will always be a need for religious, linguistic, and social service institutions while redeeming transhistorical Southern Vietnamese nationalism to build and sustain the community.

By the early 1990s, the Vietnamese established their own social communities in run-down apartment complexes and condos known as "villages"[68] in southeast Houston near Hobby Airport and in southwest Houston in the Alief and Bellaire neighborhoods. Thus, their condominium status and governing structure differentiate them from other apartment complexes in Houston where Vietnamese have settled.[69] Today there are approximately four thousand Vietnamese residents who live in the villages, but they struggle to preserve the infrastructure of their buildings and improve sanitation and safety standards that are in dire need of expensive and extensive repairs.[70]

Despite their squalid housing conditions, many residents remark that they continue to live in the Park Place villages in southeast Houston for several reasons—the relative security of their villages, the ability to trust their neighbors, inexpensive housing, and utilization of Vietnamese as their primary language. Impoverished living conditions have not dissuaded them from building Catholic chapels, erecting Buddhist statues, operating ESL and computer classes, or raising the Republic of Viet Nam flags at the main entrance. For instance, in front of the Thai Xuan Village on Broadway Street, a large Southern Vietnamese flag flaps alongside the U.S. and Texas flags. Using community formation strategies of building religious, language, and social service institutions and performing a transhistorical act of redeeming Southern Vietnamese nationalism, the villagers maintain a degree of cultural authenticity by constructing their own unique community, which, in turn, helps rejuvenate the spatiality of the larger Vietnamese community in Houston.

Development of a Multinodal Business Community

In terms of mutual aid networking, many Vietnamese Americans who decided to venture into the discount nail salon industry became successful entrepreneurs. Thao Ha explains that Vietnamese American women and men who started their nail salons were able to help friends and family members by giving them advice on the business, showing them techniques, and giving them their first jobs as nail salon technicians.[71] Once they started as nail technicians, they could save enough money to open their own shops.

Such strategies helped Vietnamese entrepreneurs survive, succeed, and sustain their business community. Within five years after the fall of Sai Gon, Vietnamese business districts began to take shape.[72] The Vietnamese businesses quickly developed, reviving not only old business districts of lower rent that preceded their arrival but also expanding other once-decrepit economic sectors. Thus, the discount nail salon industry became a viable economic niche for Vietnamese entrepreneurs, and nail salon–related businesses remain integral to the community's commercial spatiality.

The first Vietnamese business district was known as "Vinatown" which was established in downtown, nearby Old Chinatown and what is now the George R. Brown Convention Center. However, by the mid-1980s, Vietnamese entrepreneurs began relocating their businesses down the street and farther west along Milam Street.[73] By decade's end, a new "Little Sai Gon" along the Milam corridor became the key cultural center for Vietnamese Americans to shop, eat, browse, and socialize.[74] Local Vietnamese American leaders under the direction of My Cao Nguyen,[75] President of the Vietnamese Community of Houston and Vicinity (VNCH) from 1998–2002, the community's official liaison group, even passed a resolution to post Vietnamese street signs along Milam Street.[76] Though recent gentrification since the late 1990s has occurred along the corridor, Vietnamese Americans have used Milam Street between McGowen and Holman streets, the area officially designated as "Little Sai Gon" in May 2004, as the Vietnamese social, cultural, and commercial hub for numerous years. However, by the late 1990s, Bellaire Boulevard in southwest Houston became the largest Vietnamese business district.

The Bellaire Boulevard area comprises numerous Vietnamese restaurants, groceries, private medical offices, legal services, churches, temples, realtors, and community centers. Largely thanks to the influx of Southeast Asian refugees and immigrants to Houston in the post–Viet Nam War years, Bellaire Boulevard has become the largest Asian business district in the South.[77] Bellaire Boulevard, once a barren and run-down area, started its revitalization in 1983 when Hong Kong native T. D. Wong developed a shopping center called Diho Plaza. The Asian business district area began as a center for Taiwanese businesses, but Vietnamese entrepreneurs have driven much of the recent growth in the 1990s and 2000s.[78]

Arguably, the main social gathering place for Vietnamese Houstonians is the sizeable Hong Kong City Mall (#4). Completed in 1999, the Hong Kong City Mall was developed by Vietnamese immigrant Hai Du Duong. Constructed along Bellaire Boulevard, the mall is the largest shopping complex on the strip, with four hundred thousand square feet of Asian-owned clothing shops, video stores, *pho* (Vietnamese noodles) restaurants and cafes. Because of its location, size, and recognition as the "heart" of Houston's Vietnamese community, in late August and September of 2005, the mall served as a rallying point for Vietnamese Katrina evacuees from New Orleans seeking immediate relief and shelter (see Maps 6.1 and 6.2).[79]

These prominent and flourishing business enclaves continue to solidify the Vietnamese community. For more than 30 years, the Vietnamese business districts, starting with "Vinatown" to "Little Sai Gon" and to Bellaire Boulevard,

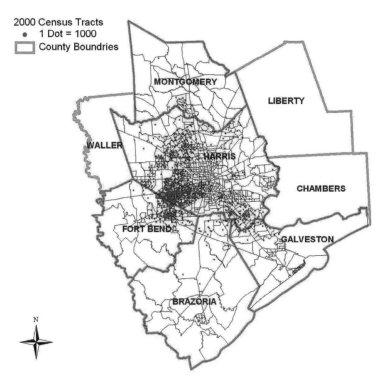

Map 6.1.   2000 Census Tracts of the Asian American Population. This census map illustrates where Asian American residents are concentrated by using dots to pinpoint neighborhoods with a high number of Asian Americans. Source: United States Census 2000. U.S. Census Bureau, U.S. Department of Commerce, 2000.

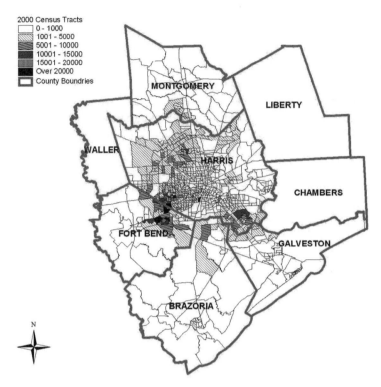

Map 6.2.   Change in Population from 1990 and 2000 by Super Neighborhoods, Non-Hispanic Asian Population. According to this census map, the super neighborhoods with the fastest growing Asian American population are located in the Southeast along Interstate 45 and Beltway 8, the Southwest between the 610 loop and Beltway 8 along Highway 59, the West along Interstate 10, and the Northwest along Highway 249 and Beltway 8. Source: United States Census 2000. U.S. Census Bureau, U.S. Department of Commerce, 2000.

the unofficial "Little Sai Gon," have helped Vietnamese Houstonians establish, strengthen, and expand their community.

By 2005, the official "Little Sai Gon" along the Milam corridor continued to decline as a major Vietnamese business district, whereas along Bellaire Boulevard in southwest Houston Vietnamese-owned businesses are thriving, and thus, locals refer this area as the real "Little Sai Gon." Bellaire Boulevard has become the true "center" of the Vietnamese community. Yet, "center" is being loosely applied here because the urban sprawl and boundary of Houston provides the concurrent existence of multiple nodes of center. The fact that no formal zoning codes exist in Houston allows the city to have multinodal centers and thus, the history of the Vietnamese community runs parallel with the city's development by having two concurrent business centers: three distinct residential areas with a heavy concentration of Vietnamese residents, and several smaller, defined social communities. As a result of this fluid, spatial environment, Vietnamese commercial districts relocated from one part of the city to another, dramatically shifting the entrepreneurial and social centers of the Vietnamese community itself.

This multinodal business community is a public space where Vietnamese Houstonians congregate, shop, socialize, network, organize, hold cultural events and political demonstrations, and reconstruct a sense of "homeland" in their new home since the existence of Houston's Vietnamese community in 1975. This reconstruction of the homeland includes the public and private displays of the Southern Vietnamese flag, the Vietnamese street signs, and the emphasis on maintaining Vietnamese language schools for future generations.

The Significance of Religious, Linguistic, and Social Service Institutions

Religious, linguistic, and social service institutions provide critical support for the Vietnamese American communities. Religious institutions have a dual role as a place of worship and community center for Vietnamese Americans. Linguistic institutions ensure that the Vietnamese language will be spoken and preserved for future generations. Social service institutions reach out and communicate to the Vietnamese populace and discover what their needs are. Vietnamese Americans use such institutions as strategies to construct spatiality and strengthen and expand their community. Once resettled in Houston, the Vietnamese worked and interacted with voluntary agencies and religious institutions to adjust to the city's economy and social environment. Local Vietnamese also formed their own nonprofit organizations or mutual aid networks to further coalesce their community.

Since the Vietnamese exiles first made a secondary migration from U.S. resettlement centers to places such as Houston and vicinity, religious institutions have played a crucial role in the formation of their community. Religious institutions provide Vietnamese Houstonians with opportunities to worship, as well as access to social services. During the mid-1970s, the Associated Catholic Charities of the Diocese of Galveston-Houston responded to the tremendous influx of Southeast Asian refugees by creating its Refugee Resettlement Program.[80] The program aided refugees in achieving economic self-sufficiency by finding employment for them soon after their arrival. The program offered housing assistance and until the early 1990s, the Vietnamese and other Southeast Asians were the majority group to receive housing assistance.[81] By 2005, in the Galveston-Houston Diocese, the Vietnamese Catholic population was estimated at just over 33,000,[82] with four parishes: *Giao Xu Duc Me La Vang* (Our Lady of Lavang), *Giao Xu Duc Me Lo Duc* (Our Lady of Lourdes), *Giao Xu Cac Thanh Tu Dao Viet Nam* (Vietnamese Martyrs Catholic Church), and *Giao Xu Duc Kito Ngoi Loi Nhap The* (Christ the Incarnate Word Parish).[83]

Moreover, they make up a considerable percentage of parishioners in five other Catholic parishes, including Holy Rosary Catholic Church and Sacred Heart Catholic Church, which hold weekly masses in Vietnamese.[84]

Vietnamese Buddhists along with Catholics fled from Viet Nam after the fall of Sai Gon, and many of them would also resettle in Houston and vicinity. According to Klineberg's 2005 survey, most Vietnamese respondents declared "they were Buddhists whereas the majority of the first-wave Vietnamese were Catholics or Protestants."[85] Within the first three decades, several dozen Buddhist temples have been constructed in the Houston metropolitan area.[86] Some Vietnamese Buddhist temples include housing for the monks, a worship area, a school for younger students training to become monks, a dining area, and numerous elaborate statues of Buddha among other settings.[87] Thus, Buddhist temples, not unlike Catholic churches, serve multiple purposes: a place of worship, an educational center for youths, and a space where Vietnamese congregate, socialize, and celebrate cultural and religious events.

Religious institutions have become vital building blocks in constructing community for Vietnamese Houstonians. For example, at each of the four Vietnamese Catholic parishes, both catechism classes and Vietnamese language (*Viet Ngu*) lessons are taught. Parishes are also sites for cultural festivities and celebrations of Vietnamese holidays such as the Lunar New Year (*Tet*) or Mid-Autumn Festival. At Buddhist temples, Vietnamese worshippers celebrate Vietnamese holidays and congregate and socialize in community dining halls. In Catholic parishes and Buddhist temples, efforts are made to engage the 1.5 and second generations in order to preserve their language and culture. Vietnamese American youth groups are formed so that they can attend camps or retreats and bond with others as they learn more about their Vietnamese heritage and not just their faith. Consequently, Catholic parishes and Buddhist temples become integral spaces for the Vietnamese to formulate community and strengthen their spatiality. Increasingly, Vietnamese youth from the 1.5 and second generations are enrolling in Vietnamese as a Second Language (VSL) courses at churches and temples and participating in youth activities.

Community institutions such as language schools also have a significant role in constructing Vietnamese spatiality. Early voluntary agencies meet the immediate needs of Vietnamese refugees, and both old and new social service institutions are attempting to meet the current challenges of the community in recent years. Starting in the mid-1990s, along with ESL classes for the first generation, several linguistic, social service, and religious institutions offer VSL courses to help the 1.5 and second generations improve their Vietnamese language skills and overcome communication barriers with their Vietnamese-born parent generation. Language barriers causing breakdowns in social communication can create or exacerbate family problems when discussing daily matters, such as spending enough time on homework and dating, and demonstrating respect for elders.[88] The Vietnamese Culture and Science Association (VCSA) or *Van Hoa Khoa Hoc Viet Nam* (VHKHVN) has programs that aim to help 1.5- and second-generation adults relearn how to read, write, and speak Vietnamese.[89] Many 1.5- and second-generation Vietnamese Americans are currently more exposed to English as compared to Vietnamese. As a result, many Vietnamese-speaking parents have a hard time communicating with their English-speaking children, resulting in a generational language barrier.

Both Vietnamese and mainstream organizations are assisting with language retention for 1.5- and second-generation community members. At temples, churches, and offices, teachers, laypeople, and volunteers have taught *Viet Ngu* courses to children, adolescents, and young adults. Furthermore, Vietnamese language courses are offered at Houston Community College and the University of Houston. Such *Viet Ngu* and VSL classrooms allow younger Vietnamese Houstonians an opportunity to improve their communication with Vietnamese-speaking parents and adults, retain their Vietnamese identity, and help formulate spatiality by removing the language barrier across multiple generations. By closing the distance in the language gap across generations, Vietnamese Houstonians enhance their spatiality to communicate more effectively while preserving the Vietnamese language for generations to come.

Another social service organization that serves as an outreach to the local Vietnamese population about health care issues is the Vietnamese-American Community Health Network, Inc. (VACHNET), which has held several health fairs.[90] Such health fairs are rotated throughout the Houston city area, usually in low-income neighborhoods and Vietnamese villages to provide free, basic medical care and advice to those who cannot afford or access it. Vietnamese health care professionals donate their time to the health fairs. The attendance has ranged from three hundred to one thousand people, 85 to 90 percent of whom were of Vietnamese descent.[91]

Strong religious, linguistic, and social service institutions provide Vietnamese Americans the necessary tools to continue their creation and development of a postwar community and carve out a "space" of their own. No longer just exiles, Vietnamese Americans in the GHMA have embraced strategies such as developing nonprofit organizations, building mutual aid networks, holding both ESL and VSL courses, and using church space and temple grounds to hold community events that will have a significant impact on future generations.

Conclusion

Vietnamese Houstonians have responded and continue to respond to their migration, racialization, and marginalization in several ways. To challenge the stigma of Orientalism[92] during the Cold War, as a marginalized Asian American minority, they seek ways to bond together, organize, and build racial solidarity with other

Asian American groups to challenge the racial violence from the Ku Klux Klan. History has proven that Vietnamese American leaders have stepped in to work with other racial minorities to improve relations and curb racism in and against both communities. Although some embrace the model minority tag as a socially acceptable or even beneficial label, others reject the stereotype, viewing it as part of the existing structural racism that conveniently neglects the fact that Vietnamese Americans work extremely hard to barely scrape by and make ends meet.

To challenge the racialization of Vietnamese Americans as perpetual foreigners or as a model minority, they turn to redeeming transhistorical Southern Vietnamese nationalism not only as a socially acceptable post–Cold War narrative within the framework of U.S. foreign policy, but also as an *ongoing* Cold War narrative for the Vietnamese themselves, many of whom are still "fighting" the war until the day of liberation for Viet Nam from Communist rule.

Simultaneously, more Vietnamese Americans seek new ways to reconstruct the Southern Vietnamese homeland by enhancing their spatiality in Houston and vicinity; for those still fighting the Cold War, their struggle against communism in hopes of returning home remains an integral part of their space-making here. At first, redeeming transhistorical Southern Vietnamese nationalism became a fix-all solution—an acceptable response to the displacement of exiles, a method to address racism within America, and a political agency to build a community and galvanize political capital in the struggle against worldwide communism. Yet, over time, transhistorical Southern Vietnamese nationalism sharply divided the community, leaving the Vietnamese in Houston and vicinity bereft of participation in the American political process and forcing them to revise and occasionally challenge their anticommunist political narrative. Henceforth, they essentially needed to change their political strategy by tempering anticommunist political violence and intimidation in order to preserve the community's spatiality.

Still, Vietnamese Houstonians continue to proudly wave and hoist the Southern Vietnamese flag in private and public spaces to demonstrate their longing for a deceased nation as if it were to return to life one day. Here lies the conundrum of a transhistorical sentiment being carried forth across the maddening seas of war, refuge, and resettlement; a sentiment that remains a burden and a ray of hope for natives of a ghost country. Since Southern Viet Nam ceases to exist, except in the hearts and souls of the Vietnamese diaspora, Vietnamese Houstonians nevertheless relentlessly forge a new Southern homeland to stake not only their own survival and success in America, but to also remember their old homeland.

As for creating spatiality, social communities and commercial districts shift and relocate due to gentrification, and thus concurrently create multinodal social centers. Religious, linguistic, and social service institutions act as space-making institutions that allow the Vietnamese to actively maintain and transform their community and alter their objectives to adroitly respond to current socioeconomic problems and generational concerns within their community.

Vietnamese Houstonians have constructed spatiality by developing an emerging and vibrant postwar community in the GHMA through challenging racisms; reformulating transhistorical nationalism and political participation; creating small, well-defined social communities; shifting their central business districts; and establishing religious, linguistic, and social service institutions. Vietnamese Houstonians have created an exceptional, multinodal community that remains in flux, responding to the constant changes and challenges that they have faced and endured.

Notes

1. For the purpose of this essay, a *community* is defined as a group of people who share common values and historical experiences. In this case, community formation is made possible by Vietnamese Houstonians who hold similar traditional values as well as migration and resettlement experiences. A community may also include, but is not limited to, geographic boundaries. Therefore, a smaller social community may exist within a larger community. For example, the Thai Xuan Vietnamese Village near Hobby Airport exists as a separate, standing social community which shares some attributes of the whole Vietnamese community in Houston.

2. Robert D. Bullard, *Invisible Houston: The Black Experience in Boom and Bust* (College Station: Texas A&M University Press, 1987), 7.

3. Barbara Boughton, "Refugee's Poems Praise New Home," *Houston Post*, April 18, 1980.

4. U.S. Census Bureau, 2010 Census. Within Houston's Asian population, the Vietnamese population alone ranks first ahead of the Asian Indians (26,289) and the Chinese, excluding Taiwanese (25,246). The Asian alone population in Houston numbered at 126,378, accounting for 6 percent of the city's population.

5. The Greater Houston metropolitan area comprises eight adjacent counties: Harris, Galveston, Fort Bend, Liberty, Brazoria, Montgomery, Chambers, and Waller.

6. U.S. Census Bureau, 2006–2010 American Community Survey 5-Year Estimates, 2010.

7. *Houston and vicinity* is in reference to the Greater Houston metropolitan area. Much of Houston is located within Harris County, but the city's boundary also stretches into other counties, including Ft. Bend County.

8. *Transhistorical* is in reference to the Vietnamese diasporic community's post–Viet Nam War struggle to retain and redeem Southern Vietnamese nationalism despite the fact that the created state of the Republic of Viet Nam ceased to exist in 1975. Therefore, I prefer to use transhistorical over transnationalism as the more appropriate term. *Transnationalism* indicates meaningful linkages between communities from two different, *existing* nations. *Transhistorical* reflects a meaningful and relevant connection of an idea—in this case Southern Vietnamese nationalism—across time. For the Vietnamese diaspora, Southern Vietnamese nationalism is perceived as a real and tangible idea that remains an integral part of how they live and construct their spatiality (or even platiality; please see endnote on Karin Aguilar-San Juan's *Little Saigons: Staying Vietnamese in America* (Minneapolis: University of Minnesota Press, 2009) for more information) even though the Republic of Viet Nam no longer exists.

9. South Viet Nam is sometimes referred to as Southern Viet Nam. For an example, see Robert Buzzanco, *Masters of War: Military Dissent and Politics in the Vietnam Era* (Cambridge: Cambridge University Press, 1997). His reference to South Viet Nam as Southern Viet Nam is to provide a clearer purpose behind the establishment of South Viet Nam as a created state mandated by the Geneva Accords and not the will of the Southern Vietnamese populace. Thus, Southern Viet Nam was separated from the rest of Viet Nam, and based from that perspective, there was no such thing as a separate North and South Viet Nam but rather a single country and population that was divided by the geopolitics of the Cold War between the United States and Soviet Union.

10. In this setting, political capital relates to the ability and availability of not only using a community's resources but of expanding such resources to further a political agenda or cause. For the Vietnamese Americans in Houston and vicinity, staunch anticommunist community leaders, elected or self-appointed, call for their constituents to pool their resources and unite for a greater cause—in this case, the continuing struggle against Vietnamese communism.

11. For now, the author will use the more widely accepted concept of spatiality or "making space." For an excellent read on the Vietnamese American community and its ethnic space, please see Linda Tran Vo, "Constructing a Vietnamese American Community: Economic and Political Transformation in Little Saigon, Orange County," *Amerasia Journal* Vol. 34, No. 3 (2008). However, some scholars would argue that platiality provides a better analysis of a diaspora's efforts in community-building. In Karen Aguilar San-Juan's work, she demonstrates the importance of platiality for the Vietnamese communities in Boston, Massachusetts, and Orange County, California. *Platiality* emphasizes the act of making place rather than simply inhabiting space. Platiality is a place that has *meaning* to someone or a group of people; more so than space that can be limited to a place that is void of value before platiality or place-making occurs. Platiality differs from spatiality. Space may have dimensions, but place-making is the use of such dimensions to give the space a value. Aguilar San-Juan states, "To 'platialize' community or race is to acknowledge and understand the significance of place, placefulness, and platiality in the production of communities and racial formations." See Aguilar-San Juan, *Little Saigons*, xxvi.

12. Fred R. Von der Mehden, *The Ethnic Groups of Houston* (Houston: Rice University Studies, 1984), 88.

13. Ibid., 98.

14. Ibid.

15. Ibid.

16. The Southeast Texas Gulf Coast in proximity to Houston would include the shores of Brazoria, Galveston, and Chambers counties.

17. Ibid.

18. Communication and Language Line, Inc., *Non-Traditional Crime in America: A Handbook for Law Enforcement Officers*. Robert Walsh Collection, Box 1, Folder 19. (Irvine, Calif.: UC Irvine Libraries Special Collections and Archives, April 1989), 12.

19. Irwin A. Tang, ed., *Asian Texans: Our Histories and Our Lives* (Austin, Tex.: The It Works, 2007), 269.

20. Ibid.

21. Ibid., 270.

22. Von der Mehden, *The Ethnic Groups of Houston*, 83.

23. Ms. Glenda Joe, interview by author, Houston, June 6, 2007.

24. 543 F. Supp. 198. *Vietnamese Fishermen's Association et al., Plaintiffs, v. The Knights of the Ku Klux Klan et al., Defendants.* Civ. A. No. H-81-895. United States District Court, S.D. Texas, Houston Division. June 3, 1982. Final Judgment June 9, 1982. The author procured this source from the Tomorrow Vietnamese Forum (TVF) website (www.tvf.com, accessed March 11, 2013) created by Dr. Long Le, assistant clinical professor and director of International Initiatives for Global Studies, C. T. Bauer College of Business, University of Houston. However, the website is no longer available.

25. Bullard, *Invisible Houston*, 45.

26. Ibid.

27. Ibid., 45–46.

28. Ibid., 46.

29. Carol Rust, "The Longest Street," *Houston Chronicle*, April 19, 1992.

30. Laura Rodriguez, "They Want Us to Get Out of Here," *Houston Chronicle*, October 18, 1985.

31. Wayne King, "Houston's Housing Authority Accused of Racial Steering," *New York Times*, March 19, 1985.

32. This is similar to the case of deteriorating relations between Korean store clerks and African American customers that reached its nadir during the 1992 Los Angeles riots following the acquittal of four police officers in the beating of Rodney King Jr. Throughout the riots, Korean-owned businesses were targeted, looted, and destroyed by rioters.

33. Norma Martin, "Dead Man's Mother Shuns Station Boycott," *Houston Chronicle*, August 5, 1992.

34. Ibid.

35. Patti Muck, "Ex-clerk Cleared in Store Death/Shooting of Alleged Shoplifter Sparked Community Outrage from Blacks," *Houston Chronicle*, February 9, 1993.

36. Norma Martin, "Dead Man's Mother Shuns Station Boycott."

37. Patti Muck, "Eternity of Guilt: Memories Haunt Teenager Cleared in Store Shooting," *Houston Chronicle*, February 14, 1993.

38. Norma Martin, "Dead Man's Mother Shuns Station Boycott."

39. Ms. Glenda Joe, interview by author, Houston, June 8, 2007.

40. Rad Sallee, "Asian Group Tries to Ease Racial Strife," *Houston Chronicle*, September 5, 1992. Houston, Metropolitan Research Center, H-Ethnic groups-Asian. Houston, Tex.

41. Ms. Glenda Joe, interview by author, Houston, June 8, 2007.

42. David Elison, "Black History Month/ TWO CULTURES, ONE GOAL/Project Targets Concerns of Asians, African-Americans," *Houston Chronicle*, February 7, 1994.

43. Ibid.

44. Ibid.

45. Stephen L. Klineberg, *Houston's Economic and Demographic Transformations: Findings from the Expanded 2002 Survey of Houston's Ethnic Communities* (Houston: Rice University Publications, 2002), 22.

46. For more on the model minority myth, see Roger Daniels's *Coming to America: A History of Immigration and Ethnicity in American Life*, 2nd ed. (New York: Perennial, 2002), Stacey J. Lee's *Unraveling the Model Minority Stereotype: Listening to Asian American Youth* (New York: Teachers College Press, 1996), and Ronald Takaki's *Strangers from a Different Shore: A History of Asian Americans*, 2nd ed. (New York: Little, Brown and Company, 1998).

47. Klineberg, *Houston's Economic and Demographic Transformations*, 33. Dr. Klineberg released his latest survey on Houston's ethnic communities in 2012.

48. Ibid.

49. Ibid.

50. Stephen L. Klineberg, *Public Perceptions in Remarkable Times: Tracking Change through 24 Years of Houston Surveys* (Houston: Rice University Publications, 2005), 26.

51. Ibid.

52. Stephen L. Klineberg, *Houston's Ethnic Communities: Updated and Expanded to Include the First Ever Survey of the Asian Communities* (Houston: Rice University Publications, 1996), 14.

53. Claudia Kolker, "Casualties of War," *Houston Press*, February 9–15, 1995.

54. Viet Mai Ha, "Letter addressed to the President of the United States of America," Associations and Organizations of Former Members of the Republic of Viet Nam Armed Forces, James Ridgeway Files (uncataloged) (Irvine, Calif.: UC Irvine Libraries Southeast Asian Archives, December 15, 1981).

55. Ibid.

56. Ibid.

57. Jo Ann Zuniga, "Group Calls Editor's Slaying Here Political: Vietnamese Journalist Murdered in '82," *Houston Chronicle*, December 5, 1994.

58. Ibid.

59. Ms. Dai Huynh, interview by author, *Houston Chronicle*, Houston, December 2003.

60. Ibid.

61. Josh Harkinson, "Taking Aim: Marching with an Evolving Minority Electorate, a Vietnamese Immigrant May Just Whip the GOP's Old Guard," *Houston Press*, October 21, 2004.

62. Ibid.

63. A CBO is a grassroots organization where members can build a unique, close relationship and interaction based on common interests, beliefs, and living conditions.

64. Harkinson, "Taking Aim."

65. Ibid.

66. King, "Houston's Housing Authority Accused of Racial Steering."

67. Dr. Jane Peranteau, interview by author, Houston, March 5, 2004.

68. Vietnamese residents referred to their condominiums as "villages" because they have organized a social system where a village chief is appointed to run the daily activities of the condominium and is responsible for the safety and well-being of the residents. The residents are accustomed to such a social system back in Viet Nam and have brought forth this structure to organize and maintain a social order. Furthermore, to preserve their Vietnamese identity and independence, each village is designated with a Vietnamese name, usually a city from Vietnam or a Catholic saint's name. These villages include St. Joseph Village, Saigon Village, Thai Xuan Village, Hue Village, St. Mary Village, Da Lat Village, and Thanh Tam Village. Living in poverty are the Vietnamese residents of five of the larger villages located in the Park Place neighborhood of southeast Houston. They live in condominiums in which the occupants own each apartment, paying off monthly mortgages. These Vietnamese villages were founded by Father Chinh Chan Trinh of St. Christopher's Catholic Church, who first brought Vietnamese refugees into the southeast Houston area by purchasing and refurbishing these village complexes for Vietnamese newcomers to occupy such affordable housing.

69. Ibid.

70. Jane Peranteau et al., *2004 Community Health Report: Houston's Alief and Park Place Super Neighborhood* (Houston: 2004 St. Luke's Episcopal Health Charities, 2004), 52.

71. Ibid., 10.

72. Ibid.

73. Deborah Jensen, "Houston's Indo-Chinatown: The First Generation," *Cite Magazine* (Winter 1987).

74. Ibid.

75. According to Vietnamese tradition, the person's last or family name is stated first, followed by the middle name, and finally the first name. The author has chosen to state Vietnamese names in accordance with American standards to avoid confusion unless such names are quoted under Vietnamese formality.

76. Every two years, the Vietnamese Community of Houston and Its Vicinity (now Vicinities) (VNCH) would hold an election for new officers. Despite little financial resources and lack of a complete mandate, VNCH is recognized as the unofficial, definitive political voice of the local Vietnamese community. For more information on VNCH, please visit the organization's website, www.vietnamesecommunityofhouston.net (accessed March 11, 2013).

77. Jonathan Bowles and Tara Colton, *A World of Opportunity* (New York: Center for an Urban Future, 2007), 53.

78. J. Peranteau et al., *2004 Community Health Report*, 52.

79. Ibid.

80. *Refugee Resettlement Services*, Associated Catholic Charities, Houston, Tex., 2000.

81. Ibid.

82. The Archdiocese of Galveston-Houston. http://www.archgh.org/Our-Programs/Ethnic-Ministries/Vietnamese (accessed January 21, 2013).

83. Richard Vara, "Area Asian Catholics to Come Together in Celebration," *Houston Chronicle*, August 21, 1999.

84. Ibid.

85. Klineberg, *Public Perceptions in Remarkable Times*, 25.

86. Molly Glentzer, "Roadside Warrior: Along I-45, a Quiet Temple to a Fierce Buddha," *Houston Chronicle*, January 18, 2001.

87. Ibid.

88. Ms. Thanh Trinh, interview by author, Houston, October 11, 2003.

89. Ibid.

90. Son Hoang, interview by author, Houston, October 25, 2003. He served as vice president (2002–2004) of the Vietnamese-American Community Health Network, Inc. He currently works for the Center for Research on Minority Health at the University of Texas M. D. Andersen Cancer Center.

91. Ibid.

92. For more on the complexities of Orientalism as well as Cold War Orientalism, please see Edward Said, *Orientalism* (New York: Vintage Books, 1979) and Christina Klein, *Cold War Orientalism: Asia in the Middlebrow Imagination, 1945–1961* (Berkeley: University of California Press, 2003).

CHAPTER 7

Standing Up and Speaking Out

Hindu Americans and Christian Normativity in Metro Atlanta

Khyati Y. Joshi

Introduction

Chick-fil-A is one of the most popular fast food establishments in the Atlanta metropolitan area, the chain founded by a devout Christian named S. Truitt Cathy. Chick-fil-A offers a free sandwich on Mondays to any patron who brings in a church bulletin,[1] and the entire chain, from coast to coast, closes every Sunday. The chain explains these policies in expressly religious terms, citing "the company's Corporate Purpose: To glorify God by being a faithful steward to all that is entrusted to us. To have a positive influence on all who come in contact with Chick-fil-A."[2] The company accurately says its religious orientation is "as much a part of the Chick-fil-A brand as the original Chick-fil-A® Chicken Sandwich."[3] Chick-fil-A restaurants are ubiquitous in the metropolitan area (Metro Atlanta).[4]

Almost as ubiquitous as Chick-fil-A are the South's "megachurches," large church buildings—sometimes sprawling complexes—serving Evangelical Protestant congregations that often number in the thousands. Megachurches, many displaying large crosses or tall steeples, are common at the intersections of Metro Atlanta's large boulevards, where their marquee boards display Christian scripture and other theological messages for all who drive by. (Megachurches also have "mega" parking lots, and some of Metro Atlanta's worst traffic congestion occurs not during the workday rush hour but on Wednesday nights, the traditional night for church-sponsored Bible study, and Sunday mornings and evenings when church services are held.)

The omnipresence of the megachurch, and the Chick-fil-A policy of accepting "*church* bulletins" as free-sandwich coupons, are only two minor everyday examples of the normative presence of Christianity in Metro Atlanta that the Indian American Hindu community and others encounter. The idea of Christianity's *normative* power refers to the ways in which a dominant group, in this case Christians, successfully disseminates social realities and social visions—comprised of ideas and images that are viewed as inherently positive—in a manner that results in their being accepted as "normal," universal, and common sensical.[5] Once this occurs, these norms are applied to convey advantage and approval upon those associated with the dominant group and, as a necessary result, disadvantage and disapproval upon those outside the dominant group. Thus, Christianity, and, in particular, Protestantism, combined with whiteness, is constructed as the normal against which the "other" is compared to the other's disadvantage. In the U.S. Christian normativity intersects with White normativity, so it is this intersectionality that is exhibited at all levels of society: individual, social, and institutional. For this essay, the focus is on how Christian normativity, which is at times subtle, permits and maintains patterns of oppression by neglect, omission, erasure, and distortion.[6]

These patterns are the backdrop against which Indian American lives are lived in Metro Atlanta, and the context in which Indian Americans have built ethnoreligious communities, established weekend religious schools for children, and preserved rituals and traditions in temples and in homes. They are also the milieu with which those communities may have complex relationships involving both isolation and contact, cooperation and conflict. This essay presents an examination of one particular eruption of Indian American Hindu self-advocacy in the context of Metro Atlanta's White- and Christian-normative society. I identify and discuss the constellation of factors that have played a role in the transformation of the Hindu community from one that is insular, with the common immigrant priority of cultural and religious reproduction, to one that is attempting to speak for Hinduism as a Georgian and American religion. In order to fully understand this evolution, a brief history of the Indian American Hindu community is provided along with analysis of the social context in which it develops.

This essay demonstrates how, as the community begins to engage with our religiously pluralistic democracy, it is staking a claim to public space and pursuing cultural and political struggles against misrepresentation. The stories told and phenomena observed in this essay illustrate the contemporary politics of pluralism. For Indian Americans, the politics of pluralism has three facets. First, the process of becoming American entails articulating a religious identity. The United States has been identified as the most religious country on the planet. This identification reflects the social dominance of Christianity in society, and its impact on all parts of life. It also reflects the idea that placing oneself or one's community on the societal map entails articulating a religious identity (or, less often, a rejection thereof).[7] Second, immigration is a "theologizing experience."[8] The departure from a homeland and the establishment of a home, family, and community in a new place often evokes in the migrant the ideas of purpose, destiny, and refuge that are the essential dimensions of most faith traditions. For example, many of those who were responsible for religious community-building have expressed that they were not very religious before leaving India.[9] The third facet of the politics of pluralism for Indian Americans involves the interplay of race and religion. Racial as well as religious minorities, Indian Americans are often unable or unwilling to see themselves as having a racial identity in the U.S. context. Immigrant groups often don't understand how they are racialized in the United States, and often choose not to stress that identity. The myriad reasons for this are beyond the scope of this essay. However, one of the results is that the Indian Americans' status as a religious minority becomes salient. The reader will observe, in the narrative and analysis below, the manifestation and interplace of these three facets of the politics of pluralism in the United States.

Christian Normativity, Privilege, and Hegemony

As a non-White and disproportionately non-Christian population, Indian Americans are "double minorities" in the United States, including Metro Atlanta. While religious discrimination against this community is recognized, what is more difficult to "see" is the normative nature of Christianity at levels of society. Some elements of Christian privilege are perceived as secularism or even "civil religion."[10] For example, the assertion that contemporary seasonal celebrations and decorations have nothing to do with religion *per se*—arguing, for example, that the Easter Bunny, Santa Claus, Christmas trees, garlands, wreaths, the colors red and green, and songs like "Here Comes Peter Cottontail," or "Rudolph the Red Nosed Reindeer" do not represent Christianity. Advocates contend that these are "seasonal" activities and, as such, are part of "American culture." While these images and activities often exclude specific reference to the associated Christian holidays, they have *clearly* religious meanings, symbolisms, positionalities, and antecedents, and upon critical analysis, claims that they are merely secular fail.[11] The effect of the so-called "secularization of religion," fortifies and strengthens Christian privilege by perpetuating Christian hegemony in such a way as to avoid detection or circumvent violating the codified doctrine of separation of religion and government. Christian dominance, therefore, is maintained by its relative invisibility, and with this invisibility, privilege is neither analyzed nor scrutinized, neither interrogated nor confronted. Dominance is perceived as unremarkable or "normal," and when anyone poses a challenge to those in the dominant position they are branded as "subversive"—or even "sacrilegious."[12]

Christianity's privilege as the cultural norm functions at all levels of society to convey upon Christians certain advantages, and concurrently to place non-Christians in the United States in a position of relative disadvantage wherein they are likely to face discrimination. The presence of a Christian norm is echoed in the attitude and words of Georgia's then-Governor Sonny Perdue. Asked by the editors of *Khabar*, a South Asian American monthly magazine, about his support for displaying the Ten Commandments on government property, and asked how he would feel about the displaying of verses from the *Bhagwad Gita* or the Holy *Quran* or from other religions, Perdue responded, "Well, I think the Ten Commandments transcends *[sic]* its mere religious or historical significance. It's also principle-centered in that way. I think if we incorporate those principles on which this country was founded, there would be opportunities for display of other historical documents significant to other populations in the United States. The Ten Commandments form that Judeo-Christian effort that led to the founding of America by the pilgrims on the idea of religious freedom. That has a stronger historical significance from my perspective."[13] When asked specifically whether the presence of the Ten Commandments on government property would be an imposition of Christianity (and therefore unconstitutional), he said "I don't think it's trying to impose Christianity. That would be wrong. That's the reason I began my statement saying that the Ten Commandments is *[sic]* a principle-centered basis that guides our moral lives. I don't view it strictly as a spiritual document that you have to adhere to, to be accepted in this country. That's the distinction I make."[14] There are two different things going on here. First, the Christian norm can be seen in the governor's assertion that the Ten Commandments "transcend[] its mere religious or historical significance."[15] His view that the "Ten Commandments is a principle-centered basis that guides our moral lives" further shows the normative nature of Christianity in his thinking. When something is the norm, its universality is stressed and it is seen to benefit everyone, or even impact everyone. In reality, other religious groups may respect the Ten Commandments but will not look to them (as opposed to some other source) for the transcendent principles Perdue says they represent. By making such statements, the Governor is manifesting the Christian privilege he enjoys: the ability to assume that his own belief system is "universal," or ought to be rendered universal without question or critique. He shows that he sees his own religion as uniquely universal and a reference point for all, and concludes therefore that providing government support for the promulgation of Christian teachings is nondiscriminatory. Second, Perdue is making these remarks as the Governor of Georgia. As a leader who claims the Christian faith, in a Christian-majority jurisdiction where Christianity functions as a powerful cultural norm, he is positioned to exert his political power in favor of Christianity by causing government to endorse Christianity and the Bible over other faiths and holy scriptures. (Such endorsement by government violates the Establishment Clause of the First Amendment to the U.S. Constitution.)

While Evangelical Protestantism is the hegemonic religion in the South; it is Christianity as a whole that defines Southern society at levels from institutional to the individual on-the-street interaction.[16] The mythologized "Southern exceptionalism" is a product of the social influence of evangelical Christianity in the context of geographic isolation, economic marginalization, and an historic sense of grievance toward and oppression at the hands of "the North" (and, by extension, a contempt for outsiders). However, it is important to realize that while Evangelical Protestantism may be the strain of Christianity most prevalent in the South, Christian normativity applies to all Christians. Analyzing society through the lens of Christian normativity and privilege invokes a sociological argument, not a theological one.[17] And while Christianity has provided hope for rural poor, "Biblical" justifications were used for slavery and later for segregation, and the organizing venue for the social and political life of the White majority and, separately, the Black minority. Historically, Christianity was also used to deny citizenship to Syrians and South Asians and used to deny social acceptance of the Jewish population.[18] In the United States, Christian normativity intersects with Whiteness. It is these two forces in tandem that have constructed U.S. society.[19]

Even much scholarship of the South carries biblical overtones. In his commentary on the writings of Kenneth Sanchagrin, for example, Charles Reagan Wilson commented, "The South has been born again and risen—created and recreated—so many times."[20] The very metaphor itself invokes the New Testament images of death and resurrection, and the evangelical Protestant emphasis on spiritual rebirth.[21] Thus, both in how the South thinks of itself and even in how others write of it, Biblical references abound. Coupled with the easy assumption of Christianity's unique righteousness—that is, with Christian privilege—it becomes an easy step from Christianity's historic role in justifying minority disadvantage and disenfranchisement to Christianity functioning as an element of an insider/outsider dynamic that can disadvantage Indian Hindus and others like them. It is this social context, embedded with many Christian forces, which influences the development of Hinduism. This is a product of living in a "pluralistic democracy" that in fact has an unofficial state religion—protestant Christianity.

Racial and Religious "Others"

Changes in U.S. immigration policy have wrought tremendous demographic, social and cultural changes in the South as in the rest of the United States. These changes have created a new context for religious life in the South, which is reflected in the changing physical, social, and symbolic landscapes of the region. Metro Atlanta's visible religious landscape, long dominated by megachurches, has begun to change with the arrival of "new" groups beginning in the early 1960s.

Religion and religious experiences cannot be addressed in a vacuum, but rather in the specific context of ethnicity and race in the southeastern United States. In particular, no discussion of the religious identity of people in the South, particularly people of color like Indian Americans, is complete without addressing the ways in which racial and religious identities intersect in the popular mind. This is true, first and foremost, because racial difference is the visible element of the Indian Americans' status as an "other" in Southern society; a Southerner who neither knew nor cared about an Indian American's faith would nevertheless immediately identify her as different from himself because of race.[22] At the same time, Indian Americans have been largely invisible in Southern society until recently, both because the community remains small in comparison to the total population of the area and because concepts of race remain largely defined by the dyadic paradigm of Black and White. Being neither Black nor White has slowed the process by which Indian Americans come to be located on the Southern racial map.

A discussion of race is also essential to understanding religious experiences because we live in a society where religion is *racialized*. The racialization of religion occurs when, through an association between real or imagined phenotypical characteristics and an assumption about religious identity, race becomes a proxy for a presumed belief system. The social effect of the racialization of religion is that the physical features associated with a group and attached to race in popular discourse become associated with a particular religion or religions.[23] More simply put, the fact of an individual's race creates an assumption as to her religious identity. In this process, a racial meaning is extended to a previously unclassified group, thus racializing the group. The racialization of religion exacerbates the "othering" of a religious group, compounding ideas of differentness in a way that disadvantages the non-White non-Christian. Racialization thus abets the unconstitutional elevation of Christianity to a position of privilege in American society and has frequently worked in tandem with the white supremacist beliefs in segments of the population.[24]

When it comes to the racialization of religion, regional identity also presents a unique backdrop within the context of American religious history. The South holds a place in the American imagination specifically as it relates to religion. The mythos of a deeply religious South shape a particular American narrative of poverty and exile; of faith tested in a hostile wilderness; and of finding divine blessing implied by material success (and, by contrast, Biblical permission to view Blacks as a spiritual burden). Many now-prominent Southern churches (e.g., the Church of Christ) developed during a period of social schism from the North, which came to a head in the Civil War but had economic and social as well as philosophical and spiritual dimensions throughout the nineteenth century and into the twentieth.

While religion's social importance in Southern culture is a part of the stories told in this essay, I am not making the case for "southern exceptionalism." The South is no more or less of an exception than any other region in the United States. Each region has its own character, norms, and mores. For example, while the South has more churches per capita than other regions of the United States, that fact alone does not necessarily indicate greater religiosity or imply the absence of socially influential religious movements elsewhere. While there have been efforts to supplant evolution with "intelligent design" in Georgia public school curricula, for example, similar efforts have been seen in Pennsylvania and other states outside the South. Likewise, "blue laws" that restrict commerce on Sundays are not unique to the South; they still have a strong presence in reputedly progressive northern states like New Jersey and Massachusetts.

Throughout U.S. history and across the nation, religious institutions and movements have interacted symbiotically with the social phenomenon of color hierarchy and with institutionalized discrimination such as the slave trade and Jim Crow legislation. White racism and White Christianity, particularly Protestant Christianity, are foundational elements of American society and culture, and each has served the other since the Colonial era. Given the parallels between Christian theological concepts of exclusivity and the "in group/out group" dynamic of racial discrimination, this interrelation is perhaps not surprising.

Its transcendent philosophy notwithstanding, a religion and its institutions reflect the society in which they exist. As institutions with social power, White churches in the United States buttressed the institution of slavery, utilizing the Bible's endorsements and justification of slavery to explain the plight of African Americans and non-Whites during the Jim Crow era. In contemporary times, Christian individuals and groups have invoked the Bible to fuel discrimination against Buddhists, Catholics, Jews, Hindus, Muslims, Sikhs and others. While churches, both Black and White, were a major venue for progressive social activism during the Civil Rights era, many other White churches participated in opposing the Civil Rights Movement. African American evangelical religious traditions have been present for nearly as long as White Christianity, and Native American religious cultures are indigenous to the region. Yet it is conjunction of Whiteness and Christianity that defines the historic and contemporary cultural norm of the South.

The Indian American Hindu Experience in Metro Atlanta

The story of Hinduism in America stretches back more than a century, but has undergone rapid and dramatic change with the influx of Indian immigrants made possible by the Immigration Reform Act of 1965. The U.S. Hindu population in the United States has grown dramatically over the past four decades, as a result of constant immigration and of the development of a second and now third generation. As the population grows and changes, we see the dynamic development of an American Hinduism.[25]

The Metro Atlanta region is one of the fastest growing areas in the United States, and immigrants fuel much of this growth.[26] Although this essay focuses specifically on Hindu communities, statistics on the overall Indian American population must inform the analysis and discussion because the U.S. Census does not collect data on religious groups.[27] The Pew report *Asian Americans: A Mosaic of Faiths* identifies Hindus as constituting .08 percent of the U.S. population. Although the majority of Hindus are Indian American, not all Indian Americans are Hindus. Still, Hindus are by far the largest Indian American religious group.

Nationally, the Indian American population has quadrupled since 1980 and currently is at least 2.7 million, making Indian Americans the third-largest Asian ethnic group nationally, behind Chinese and Filipinos.[28] The South[29] is the region with the second-largest Indian American population. Indians are now the largest Asian ethnic group in Metro Atlanta, rising from second largest in 1990. More than a quarter of Asians in Atlanta are Indian. The Indian American population quadrupled in size from 1990 to 2000, growing by a million people, or 25 percent, since the 2000 Census.[30] Few religious communities in Georgia are growing as quickly as are Hindus. Atlanta has seen in recent decades the arrival and dramatic growth of communities of Hindus as well as of Jains, Sikhs, and Muslims from South Asia. Indian American Hindus can be found throughout Metro Atlanta and have established thriving enclaves in Decatur and parts of Gwinnet and Cobb Counties. The Atlanta–Sandy Spring–Marietta portion of Metro Atlanta is the ninth most populous metropolitan area in the United States.[31]

In the late 1950s and 1960s, Indian students arriving to study at Georgia Institute of Technology ("Georgia Tech") began meeting in apartments for social gatherings and religious worship, among other reasons.[32] Most of the students were male; later, their wives joined them or they returned to India to marry and then, if they could, returned to the United States with their wives. Immigrants with families began arriving after the passage of the 1965 immigration reforms. These young families gathered in private homes for events that combined worship and social activities, including the replication of cultural elements such as cuisine, language, and attire. Finding themselves with few coreligionists, Hindus who would not likely have worshipped together in India due to regional and caste distinctions nevertheless gathered in the United States to perform rituals and celebrated religious holidays together. In some cases, the result was new forms of Hinduism created from the gestalt of their separate "original" traditions.

The earliest research on immigrant Hindus in the United States observed that most Hindus arriving in the United States became more religious after immigrating.[33] As immigrants to a country where Hinduism was unfamiliar and rare, they had to think for the first time about the meaning of their religion and religious identity, something they had previously been able to take for granted as members of the Hindu majority in India. It was the combination of their minority status and religion's utility as a reason for gathering socially with others who share their beliefs (and thus often their ethnic background) that made religion salient. As a result, for many of these Indian Hindu immigrants, their religious identity assumed prominence among other social identities. As these young families began to have and raise children, Hinduism and its practice also became a primary vehicle for the retention and transmission of ethnic culture to the second generation.[34]

In addition to gathering in individual homes, some Atlanta-area Hindu immigrants began to participate in religious functions at a preexisting ISKCON ("Hare Krishna") temple on Ponce de Leon Avenue. While the Hare Krishnas were not ethnically Indian, they were coreligionists and their facility provided a venue for worship. Families would go to temple for *aarti* and major holidays like New Year, Janmasthami, and Diwali.

The second step in community formation came about when the Indian Hindu community began to establish their own temples in the Metro Atlanta area. As the community continued to grow—reaching a population of 7,500 by about 1980— the Indian immigrants spent a great deal of time and energy building religious and cultural institutions. Whatever degree of attention these immigrants might have paid to their religion while in India, the fact that the religion functioned as an impetus for community formation in the United States caused religion to become a very strong and prominent identity for the first generation.

Houses of worship became focal points of the community. The first temple established in Metro Atlanta by the Hindu community was in the suburban Atlanta community of Smyrna. The Indian American Cultural Association (IACA) established a Hindu temple within an existing building—in fact, a former church—in 1986. The conversion of a preexisting house of worship to use by another faith is not uncommon; among other things, it avoids the rudimentary but unfamiliar local processes such as zoning, the required variances already having been earned by the departing faith community. As the Indian American Hindu community's collective financial resources increased, the Hindu Temple of Atlanta was established as the first freestanding temple built from the ground up as such—and thus displaying the architectural motif of a Hindu temple (in this case, in the South Indian style). Its groundbreaking took place in 1986, and in December of 1993 the first *murtis* were installed and religious functions began.

By the end of the 1980s, a critical mass of certain sects and linguistic communities had come into being. As Raymond Williams observed, this is the point in the development of an immigrant community when segmentation may occur. And indeed, in 2005 the Swaminarayan religious group began constructing a temple in Lilburn, a town in Gwinnett County. The Swaminarayans, an example of transnational Hinduism, are a Vaishnavite group originating in India's Gujarat state; their success in the United States has been buoyed by the large proportion of Gujaratis in the U.S. Indian population. The Swaminarayans have now built more than fifty temples across the United States and Canada.[35]

John Fenton correctly predicted, based on his study of the Indian American community in Atlanta, Georgia, in the late 1980s, that religion was likely to become even more important to the community over the decades that followed. Hindu temples serve ethnoreligious communities not only as religious centers, but also as a social nexus for Indian communities. The IACA facility in Smyrna, for example, contains not only a Hindu temple but also an auditorium space where secular national holidays, like Indian Independence Day in August, are celebrated, and other cultural events, such as the annual Miss India Georgia pageant, manifested.

Although temples are open during the work week in the evening with some local devotees attending, at most temples the largest numbers of people can be found during the weekend due to work and school schedules. This is also an interesting glimpse of an effect Christian normativity can have even on non-Christian groups. Southern culture carries certain expectations about church attendance.[36] This sentiment appears to have rubbed off on the new immigrants, including Hindu communities that are navigating the cultural expectations of the Southern milieu. There is no Hindu traditional or scriptural reason to engage in religious activity on Sunday. Rather, going to the Hindu temple on Sundays is not just the most practical reaction to a work week designed to accommodate the Christian day of rest. In addition, by replicating the Sunday ritual of their Christian neighbors, this practice responds to the expectations of Southern culture. (No word yet on whether the Hindu temples provide bulletins to devotees, or whether Chick-fil-A accepts them as chicken sandwich coupons.)

One of the religion's major functions for the first generation was to transmit ethnic culture and religious traditions, and religion is present in the everyday lives of second-generation American Hindus in a myriad of ways. However, it is not the Hindu American second generation that comprises the "young blood" in Hindu temple communities. Alongside the American-born and -raised second generation—now in their twenties and thirties—the immigration of tech professionals, particularly the "H-1B" visa-holding high-tech workers in the 1990s, continues. It is the continuously arriving immigrants, rather than the second generation, who are pouring into temples today and benefiting from the structures built by their predecessors.

Hindu Communities, Christian Hegemony, and the Politics of Representation

Much of the academic literature on Hindu communities in the United States focuses on immigration and adaptation,[37] community formation,[38] and temple building.[39] While adaptation and community formation are essential elements of the community's experience to date, the Indian American Hindu community in

Atlanta has come of age. It is interacting in new and different ways with the rest of the Atlanta community. A series of factors led to the evolution of the Hindu community from one that engages primarily in interaction with itself through activities that preserve rituals, traditions, and culture to one that speaks up for itself in the public square.

In 2003, a group of Indian American Hindus in Metro Atlanta joined with Hindus in other states to protest the scholarship of Paul Courtright, a professor in the Department of Religion at Emory University. Calling itself the "Concerned Citizens," the Atlanta group took issue with Courtright's depiction and analysis of the Hindu deity Ganesh in his book *Ganesa: Lord of Obstacles, Lord of Beginnings* (1985, Oxford University Press). Among other frames of reference in his examination of stories and practices, Courtright applied a Freudian psychological analysis to the story of Ganesh. (The central Ganesh story involves the boy god who was killed by his father Shiva while guarding his mother Parvathi as she bathed, and who was revived by Shiva at Parvathi's insistence.) In September 2002, a column on a popular Indian American website, *Sulekha.com*, accused Courtright of "besmirching Lord Ganesa in a book that pyschoanalyzed the Hindu god and legends surrounding him."[40] The Concerned Citizens objected to the aspects of Courtright's analysis that sexualized the holy stories, among other things. "Professor Courtright's work and his irresponsible scholarship and misleading representation concerning Hinduism has become a matter of much concern and distress to Indian American communities across the nation."[41]

The Concerned Citizens in Metro Atlanta were part of a multinodal campaign. Following the *Sulekha.com* publication, the Hindu Students' Council at the University of Louisiana-Lafayette created an online petition. Members of the Concerned Citizens group signed, disseminated, and supported the petition vociferously. The petition called for the following: "1) The author and the publisher(s) to give an unequivocal apology to Hindus, 2) The author [to] expunge . . . offensive passages and revise the book with clarifications and corrections, 3) Publisher(s) to immediately withdraw the book from circulation and the author to stop use of the book in academics."[42] The petition was signed by approximately 4,500 people before it was taken down at the urging of many involved with the campaign because some users began posting threats of physical violence against Professor Courtright. The campaign spread beyond the United States, with European academics involved (including scholars of both Indian and European origin) and with the Indian nationalist, right-wing group Shiv Sena writing a letter to President George W. Bush to demand that the book be withdrawn from circulation and that Professor Courtright apologize to Hindus worldwide.[43]

Members of the Hindu American community from Atlanta and beyond wrote editorials and letters to newspapers such as the weekly *India Abroad* and in various online blogs and discussion forums. Scholars, both Hindu and non-Hindu, also took part in the dialogue. Professor Courtright, in an interview with *India Abroad*, responded to the question "What might readers have found offensive?" this way: "Since when I wrote the book I did not (and do not now) believe my interpretation of Ganesha is offensive, I would like to learn from those who have felt offended what exactly caused the offense. I have yet to receive guidance on this issue. I welcome criticism based minimally on a reading of the book."[44]

In October 2003, the Concerned Citizens sent a letter to the President of Emory University, demanding that Professor Courtright resign or be fired, and requested to meet with the President to present their concerns in person.[45] In April 2004, the requested meeting finally took place; at the meeting, the Concerned Citizens presented Emory University with a briefing book outlining their concerns. The Concerned Citizens presented Emory with presentations and papers from authors in and beyond Atlanta; along with a list of "Action Items for the Department of Religion/South Asian Studies." The group's top priority was an examination of the curriculum on Hinduism and India and of the faculty that taught Hinduism. In terms of curriculum, the Concerned Citizens said, "The Department should take a serious look at the political biases and prejudices that guide the selection of textual and audiovisual material, sensational films, recommended for reading and viewing in Hinduism studies. Balance, fairness, and accuracy demand that when controversial material is introduced in classrooms that instructors go the extra length to provide their students the oppositional view. For this to happen, we recommend that the department start a dialogue with the Hindu community on the political and prejudicial nature of some of this material."[46] There were several other action items such as program/activities and use of the Emory facility, preventing the spread of further bias about Hinduism, and dissemination of information to press and intercultural communications training for faculty and administrators. Of particular importance to the Concerned Citizens, however, was the ethnoreligious identity of faculty teaching Hinduism. The Concerned Citizens insisted: "Emory University must make a good faith effort to find practicing Hindus and scholars in Hinduism and/or Sanskrit to teach Hinduism."[47]

Why did Courtright's academic book, which was not even used in undergraduate Hinduism courses, become the target of the Hindu community? And why did it take until 2003 for reaction to Professor Courtright's book, published in 1985, to develop and for the Concerned Citizens to form and present their demands to Emory? The formation of the group, and the proliferation of Hindu voices critiquing Courtright and other scholars, represents a Hindu eruption/interruption in the religious landscape of the Christian South—one that was not "ripe" in the 1980s, even had Courtright's work come to the community's attention at that time.

This "Courtright Situation" is a perfect case study that both illustrates the product that develops within the politics of pluralism and the social context of

Christian dominance. Without debating the merits of the Concerned Citizens'
position or the issue of academic freedom (both beyond the scope of this essay),
one can still note the Concerned Citizens' challenge to Christian hegemony in
two spaces as groundbreaking at the time. First, by questioning and challenging
a scholar who, like many scholars of Hinduism and Hindu studies, is White,
male, and Christian, the Concerned Citizens (and the larger campaign) pointed
out and challenged a perceived bias exhibited in the scholarship of non-Hindus.
Second, the Concerned Citizens insisted on being heard and seen by Emory
University, an institution of higher learning with a firm Methodist background
in the White Christian South. A minority religious community, often exoticized
and marginalized, challenged a university that was perceived as supporting the
White, Christian male who had insulted Hindus.

For a community just finding its voice, targeting a particular book or a particular scholar represented an achievable goal. Even if Courtright's work was
something apart from the community's daily experiences of Christian hegemony,
the idea of challenging the presence of megachurches in the metro area was
obviously impractical. (Indeed, how would one even do so?) The idea of talking
back to neighbors or colleagues who engaged in the daily insult of Christian
proselytization was just as unrealistic, in light of the social practicality of how that
could affect individual Hindus' place in mainstream professional or social circles.
The vigorousness and widespread popularity of the anti-Courtright campaign
also resulted from the fact that his disputed work was about Ganesh, a popular
deity whose worship has a major role in the traditions and practices of Hindus
from multiple regional and linguistic groups. It is this constellation of forces
that resulted in Professor Courtright's book becoming the rallying cry for the
Concerned Citizens in Atlanta, the HSC in Louisiana, and Hindu communities
and individuals elsewhere in the United States and overseas.

The Courtright matter was a manifestation of various forces that aligned and
came to a head for this Hindu community in the South: 1) frustration with misrepresentations of Hinduism in academic and popular discourse; 2) the growing
presence of Indian American Hindu college students, including the Concerned
Citizens' own children; 3) the formation and growth of the Hindu American
community resulting from accelerating immigration; 4) technology as a tool for
information-gathering and organizing; and 5) transnational Hinduism.

1. *Frustration with misrepresentations of Hinduism in academic and popular
   discourse*
   By the early 1990s, frustration at the perceived misrepresentation of Hinduism
   in academic scholarship, the media, and popular culture had become a subject
   of discussion in the Metro Atlanta Hindu community. Opinion leaders in the
   community began discussing the need to promote accurate and respectful

mainstream representations of Hinduism. For example, Dr. K. K. Vijay, one of the founders of the IACA, who moved to Atlanta in 1961 to join the faculty of the Chemistry Department at Morehouse College, spoke often in the 1980s and 1990s about the need for "a P.R. [public relations] offensive" in defense of Hinduism.[48]

This frustration was not unique to Metro Atlanta; many Hindu American communities have described frustration at what they perceive to be misrepresentations of Hinduism. For example, some common depictions of Hinduism challenged the symbolic representation of Hinduism—its use of vivid images and figures (*murtis*). These images and *murtis* are an important part of Hindu religious practice. The concept of *darshan*—of seeing god and being seen by god—is one of the central parts of the faith and is accomplished by many worshippers through interacting with physical images and *murtis*. However, such practices are often characterized as "idolatry" in Christian-dominated American popular culture and, through the application of Christian normativity, used to imply that Hinduism is illegitimate or bizarre.[49] In 1984, the blockbuster film *Indiana Jones and the Temple of Doom* introduced Americans to the idea that Hindus engage in human sacrifice and eat live snakes and "monkey brains." More recently, Hinduism has been cheapened by its commodification from "Henna tattoos" and Gap's "Om" perfume. Another misrepresentation of Hinduism, perpetuated even by those who may see themselves as friendly to Hinduism, is its characterization as a "New Age" religion, when in fact it is one of the world's most ancient religions.[50]

Dr. Vijay, who became one of the lead organizers of Concerned Citizens, gave voice to a common view in the community that mainstream journalists' and entertainers' failure to "get it right" when talking about Hinduism was harmful to the Hindu community. Frustration and dismay over negative depictions of Hinduism had been simmering in the community for many years and, as the other factors below came into play, ultimately boiled over through the Concerned Citizens initiative.

2. *Growing population of Indian American Hindu students*
The Hinduism that Indian American students encounter through their academic study of the subject is often at odds with the Hinduism that second-generation Hindus grew up with.[51] That the Concerned Citizens chose an academic target reflected their concern about how Hinduism was being taught to their children. By the early 1990s, the children of the first wave of post-1965 immigrants were in college. By the late 1990s, Indian Americans in the student body reached a critical mass at Emory University and institutions like it across the region and the nation. Their parents had used nascent temple communities to begin to convey Hinduism to the second generation; when they arrived at

college, many decided to pursue elective coursework on Hinduism. When they did so, these second-generation Indian Americans found the Hinduism taught in their college courses often to be very different than the Hinduism they had been taught in their ethnoreligious communities.[52] In particular, many found academic Hinduism unfamiliar to them, relative to the practices and teachings of their homes and communities, and they felt alienated from the coursework as a result. Across the dinner table on weekends, or on the telephone, community members—the second generation's parents—heard this frustration and began to look into the Hinduism being taught on college campuses. Although Courtright's book was a graduate-level academic text, and would not likely have been encountered in elective undergraduate coursework, its subject matter and Freudian deconstruction of popular Hindu stories struck at the nexus between the immigrant generation's frustration at Hinduism's misrepresentation and concern for their own children's religious education.

The idea of academic courses on religion being offensive or problematic to those of the religion taking the class is not unique to Hindus. For many, religious, academic course work about one's faith doesn't always jive with how they lived that faith growing up.

"Research assignment[s] provide occasions for students to tackle individual problems intrinsic to their lives as Hindus in America."[53] Hinduism's adherents are for the most part ethnically Indian or of Indian origin, yet most scholars of Hinduism are not. Rather, most scholars of Hinduism in the United States are White, many are male, and virtually all come from Christian or Jewish backgrounds. Perhaps inevitably, the racial and religious difference between the student and the teacher—the first an Indian American Hindu, the second very likely to be a White non-Hindu—can interact with the cognitive dissonance experienced by the student and become a facet of how and why academic Hinduism came to be seen as inadequate, inaccurate, and even offensive.

The controversy concerning Professor Courtright's book highlighted the issue of who has the authority to teach and write about, and by extension to speak for, Hinduism in America. This question has become a point of tension in many Hindu communities. When we think about who speaks for Hinduism in America, whether in the academic sphere or elsewhere, the cleavages between followers versus nonfollowers of the faith, and by people of Indian origin as against non-Indians become highly salient because of the inherent biases different groups bring to the table. Members of the Concerned Citizens and others in the diasporic community who were observing American academic approaches to Hinduism wanted such Western scholars to be introspective about their work and engage in efforts "to reduce prejudices against Hinduism."[54] Thus, an implicit element of the Concerned Citizens' challenge of Prof. Courtright related not merely to what he had written about Ganesh but also to the fact that he was a White *non-Hindu* scholar analyzing the religion. (This fact may be, among other things, ironic, because the academic study of Hinduism is virtually unheard of in India, and few Indian American immigrants are encouraging their children to pursue careers in academia.)

3. *Community formation resulting from increased immigration*
Indian American population growth in Metro Atlanta has been accelerating since the 1970s and saw a particular increase between 1990 and 2000. In the 1970s and 1980s, Hindus in Atlanta had engaged in the early stages of community building, as described earlier in this essay. With the continuing influx of immigrants, the breadth and depth of the community increased. As these new immigrants cycled into leadership positions in early temples and cultural organizations, the founders of those groups could now focus on engaging more in the civic community—having more of an external focus instead of focusing only on the construction and needs of the ethnoreligious community itself. Because many of them had achieved a degree of professional success, in addition to laying the groundwork and building the foundations of their communities, these individuals were positioned to be major players in the wider competition of ideas in Metro Atlanta.

As they increased their engagement at the civic level, Hindu communities understood that in order to have their voices heard and their concerns responded to, they must be visible to the broader Atlanta community. Achieving visibility meant undertaking activities that bring the Hindu community into contact with members of the area's other communities—particularly politicians, the media, and other opinion leaders. Hindu communities across the metropolitan area began to seek opportunities to become civically engaged. As early as the 1980s, and to an increasing degree thereafter, many cultural and religious organizations began inviting local, county, and state officials to their temples to attend worship services or speak on issues of public concern. Local governmental officials are responding, recognizing in the community a potential source of votes and political donations and an important facet of the local economic scene. In recent years, Diwali in particular has developed a "following" among government officials, and may be developing a position (warranted or not) as the major public holiday on the Hindu calendar.

By 2000, with temples firmly established and many of their own children in or recently graduated from college, the immigrant generation that made up Concerned Citizens' leadership constituted a large and growing group concerned about the politics of representation and ready to find its voice in the public square of religion and education.

4. *Technology and online activism*
The Concerned Citizens in Atlanta were one part of a coordinated effort to question Western academic approaches to the study of Hinduism and to stand

up against misrepresentation and perceived defamation. The symbiotic relationship between the Concerned Citizens and the Louisiana-based international internet campaign—the latter providing key language and the idea of
global attention and influence, and the former providing "boots on the ground"
whose children and neighbors' children were at Emory at the time—is an example of transnational Hindu cyber-activism. Many of the vociferous bloggers
on *Sulekha.com* and other websites are involved in the tech industry and were
part of the increase in the Indian population of the United States in the late
1990s. Indeed, Rajiv Malhotra, a New Jersey resident who "lit the match" by
first turning the Courtright issue into an internet campaign, made his money
in the tech industry.

Online organizing allowed the HSC petition to be created in Louisiana and
garner national and international attention and "signatures," and for a group
of people, prepared with notes and presentations from all over, to meet with
Emory's president. The internet proved to be a valuable tool for making contact
with strangers (both conationals and foreigners), to discuss and debate the issues. It was because of the internet that questions about Professor Courtright's
scholarship raised by a person in New Jersey resulted in a student group in
Louisiana creating a petition that came to be used by the Concerned Citizens in
Atlanta. The internet has become an organizing tool that allows long-distance
allies to influence events around the world because it is ubiquitous, nearly free,
and so well suited for establishing serendipitous ties with distant strangers. By
permitting new voices to enter the debate, it reduces the influence of gatekeep-
ers. Any individual can engage in journalistic or fact-checking endeavors.

5. *Transnational Hinduism*

Many involved with the Concerned Citizens, the internet campaign, and the
Hindu communities in Metro Atlanta are part of the Indian diaspora in the
United States. They are part of the "Global Indian Middle Class," which is
characterized by a growing transnational interaction between India and the
United States and influenced by the group's upward mobility in pluralistic host
lands and the transformative function of a high-technology culture.[55] Advances
in technology are a critical component of creating transnational communities
and present a different take on Benedict Anderson's idea of "Long Distance
Nationalism." Technology has gone beyond maintaining a connection to the
homeland to fostering virtual communities where geography is no barrier to
communication among people with shared interests and backgrounds. Hindu
communities in Metro Atlanta and elsewhere are part of Hindu transnational
communities in the Indian diaspora. The people, rituals, and structures simultaneously transcend borders while being rooted in particular places.[56]

At the same time, there is much more to transnationalism than technology, and the role of transnationalism in the development of Hindu American

assertiveness seen in groups like the Concerned Citizens is about more than internet petitions and blogs. Transnationalism also refers to a connection—real or imagined, accomplished through travel, communication, and consumption of cultural artifacts from film to food—between the diaspora and the country of origin.[57] This connection becomes a part of the individual and community identity of Hindus in the Indian diaspora. In this age of economic globalization and instant communication, it is far more accurate to assume, methodologically speaking, that social, cultural, and religious connections cross national borders.

The transnational paradigm allows researchers to understand more fully the ways Indian Hindus living in the United States are intimately connected to communities and families in India and elsewhere. While many of the scholars who have recently turned to transnationalism as a useful paradigm do not directly focus their attention on Hinduism in North America, much of the latest work on American Hinduism is informed by theories of transnationalism. In arguing for this new model in understanding the lives of migrants, Peggy Levitt explains: "[M]any immigrants don't trade in their home country membership card for an American one but belong to several communities at once. They become part of the United States and stay part of their ancestral homes at the same time. They challenge the taken-for-granted dichotomy between either/ or, United States or homeland, and assimilation versus multiculturalism by showing it is possible to be several things simultaneously, and in fact required in a global world."[58]

In the United States today there are many forms of Transnational Hinduism present in the Metro Atlanta area. Just a few examples show the diversity and influence of the phenomenon: The Swaminarayans/BAPS temples perpetuate a particular regional (Gujarati) language and flavor of Hinduism, and the Vendanta Society connects participants to a body of Hindu philosophy (Vedas) with global sources; ISKCON is an ethnically diverse global movement with its roots in Hinduism. Not just organizations, but also unnamed associations of families or friends, are part of the transnational Hindu phenomenon. At the same time, many if not most Hindu temples in the United States are independent and not associated with the aforementioned groups or any other.

As we continue this conversation, a scholarly bias needs to be acknowledged and debunked. Among nonreligious studies scholars, and particularly those in Asian American Studies and Ethnic and Racial Studies who don't research and write on religion, any discussion of Transnational Hinduism or American Hindu self-assertion is seen as the presence of *Hindutva*. *Hindutva* is the Hindu nationalist movement that gained momentum in 1998, when the BJP political won control of the Indian government for the first time. Hindutva is seen by some scholars as the manifestation of self-assertive Hindu identity, and is treated as necessarily associated with or inseparable from the politically conservative (and, some would argue, anti-Muslim) outlook of the BJP.

On the contrary, there is just one aspect of the story told in this essay that involves *Hindutva* ties: the online petition, sponsored by the Hindu Students Council, which is an arm of the VHP organization that is affiliated with the BJP in India. The leaders of Concerned Citizens did not identify themselves with Hindutva, and—despite the disproportionate attention paid to it by some scholars[59]—Hindutva is just one articulation of Hinduism, transnational or otherwise.

Conclusion and Implications

The story of Hinduism's acceptance into the social and cultural mainstream is part of a larger story of how the United States and its residents are coming to terms with modern pluralism. In light of most American Hindus' dual status as racial and religious minorities, the South provides a particularly instructive window on this process. It is arguably the part of this country where the cultural influence of the U.S.' dominant religion, Christianity (and, in particular, evangelical Protestantism) is strongest, and it is a place where the historic role of race and racism still resounds in contemporary social culture.

The Concerned Citizens and their encounter with the academy are an example of American Hindus engaged in what Prema Kurien calls the "politics of recognition" in multiculturalism.[60] The politics of recognition springs from the migrant's experience of marginality, in which religion is important and, to some degree, integration with the mainstream culture is a goal. It is also a manifestation of what this author has called the "politics of pluralism"—the process by which religious identity, and the minority religion's interaction with the Christian norm that defines the American milieu, are part of the story of immigrant religious groups' response to and ultimately engagement with that milieu. As the development and growth of religious organizations helped Hindus develop a sense of their own potency in Metro Atlanta and elsewhere, the community has gone from a phase when merely being acknowledged felt like a victory (for example, being happy just to have a festival noted in the popular media, however brief or hackneyed or inaccurate the mention) to a phase of feeling, and ultimately expressing, anger and disappointment at inaccurate and disrespectful depictions of Hinduism. This trend can be expected to continue and grow as the community continues to expand and mature, and as new targets arise from the inevitable misunderstandings between the South's Hindu and mainstream communities.

The controversy concerning Professor Courtright's book not only illustrated the growing activism of Hindu Americans but also highlighted the issue of who speaks for Hinduism in America. The question of who has the authority to write about Hinduism has become a point of tension in many Hindu communities. As noted, Professor Courtright's status as a White *non-Hindu* scholar was an element of the Concerned Citizens story.

These social and scholarly schisms can be expected to develop and evolve in the years to come. It remains to be seen, for example, whether there will develop a divergence of analysis between those scholars who are themselves Hindu and those who are not, or whether some other cleavage will take the fore. The academic themes and divisions that develop must be understood also in the context of a particular discipline, each of which comes with its own inherent biases. For example, a sociologist might be trained in India, where there is no academic emphasis on the study of Hinduism, or in the United States, where there is traditional bias against religion in disciplines outside of religious studies.[61] Each such academic experience, combined with the scholar's own ethnic and religious identity, may influence not only the scholar's approach (and biases), but also how her/his work is perceived by those who observe and consume it.

The activities of Concerned Citizens are an example of the development of new phenomena within the Atlanta Hindu community—in this case, the phenomenon of community activism. Other phenomena, such as the reproduction and transmission of religion and culture from India in America, have continued and developed in their own way. But this new strand of community activism, which has emerged since 2002, represents a maturation of the community and, most importantly, a conscious decision to engage with the wider milieu on its own terms.

The Courtright controversy galvanized not only the Hindu communities in Metro Atlanta, but also Hindu communities elsewhere in the United States and abroad. In this respect, the Concerned Citizens' experience was also an illustration of how American Hindu communities are linked to each other and to Indian and diasporic Hindu communities across the transnational world. It has been observed that transnational connections and experience influence the development of individual religious identities.[62] Likewise, we may now observe how the ability to communicate across distances—with the help of modern technology—can result in far-flung communities sharing ideas, expressing support for each other, and thereby exerting influence on each other and on the causes and communities relevant to each. It will be interesting to see how the Metro Atlanta Hindu community continues to fight for representations that it views as accurate. It will also be interesting in the coming years to see how Hindu communities across the United States, functioning in a global framework, impact and are impacted by coreligionists in India and in other Hindu Diasporic communities.

Notes

I would like to thank the two anonymous reviewers, as well as my colleagues Jigna Desai, Jane Iwamura, and John Bartlett for their helpful feedback on this essay.

1. This does not appear to be part of "official" company policy as it is nowhere expressed on the company website. However, franchises across the United States advertise this idea

on their respective websites and Facebook pages. Sometimes the coupons advertise the following promotion: buy-one-get-one-free coupons for a Chick-fil-A sandwich.

2. Chick-fil-A Corporation, 2010. http://www.chick-fil-a.com/Pressroom/Fact-Sheets #?release=sunday_2011. Accessed May 1, 2011.

3. Chick-fil-A Corporation, 2010. http://www.truettcathy.com/pdfs/ClosedonSunday.pdf. Accessed May 1, 2011.

4. The term *Metro Atlanta* is ill-defined and constantly changing as suburban sprawl spreads Atlanta's bedroom communities further into rural Georgia. Here, Metro Atlanta encompasses the city proper and the suburban communities inside and outside the Interstate 285 beltway whose economics, media coverage, and social orientation are shaped by their proximity to the City of Atlanta.

5. Bell, "Theoretical Foundations for Social Justice Education."

6. Blumenfeld, "Christian Privilege, the Public Schools"; Schlosser, "Christian Privilege: Breaking a Sacred Taboo"; Clark, "Unburning the Cross."

7. Eck, *A New Religious America.*

8. Smith, "Religion and Ethnicity in America," 1175.

9. Min, *Preserving Ethnicity through Religion in America*; Fenton, *Transplanting Religious Traditions.*

10. Bellah, "Civil Religion in America."

11. Blumenfeld, "Christian Privilege, the Public Schools"; Feldman, *Please Don't Wish Me a Merry Christmas.*

12. Adams and Joshi, "Religious Oppression," and Clark, "Unburning the Cross"; Howard, *We Can't Teach What We Don't Know.*

13. Parekh, "A Faith Driven Governor in a Secular Society."

14. Ibid.

15. It is interesting that the Governor makes this particular grammatical error—treating "the Ten Commandments" as singular. I think what's really going on in his mind is that he's talking about the Bible. Insert "Bible" in place of "Ten Commandments" and Perdue's position is essentially a Christian defense of government establishmentarianism.

16. Wilson, *Southern Missions.*

17. Progressive Christian denominations, perhaps the UU Church, or even the Episcopalians all exhibit Christian normativity. Evangelical Christianity is not the only group that is empowered because of the presence of a Christian norm or Christian privilege.

18. Gualtieri, "Becoming 'White'"; Ngai, *Impossible Subjects*; Rogoff, "Is the Jew White?"

19. See M. Emerson and C. Smith, *Divided by Faith: Evangelical Religion and the Problem of Race in America* (New York: Oxford University Press, 2000) for a discussion of Christianity and the "race problem" in contemporary society.

20. Wilson, *Southern Missions*, 8.

21. Bruce Murray, *Tracking Religious Membership in the United States*, 2002, FACSNET. http://www.facsnet.org/issues/faith/sanchagrin.php Accessed October 1, 2004.

22. Notwithstanding the fact that some religious markers—such as the *hijab* (Muslim headscarf), *dastaar* (Sikh turban), or religious jewelry such as a crucifix—are indeed visible, race is the single element of difference that is always and immediately visible and apparent to the otherwise-uninformed observer.

23. Joshi, "The Racialization of Religion in the United States"; Emerson and Smith, *Divided by Faith.*

24. Ibid.

25. Kurien, *A Place at the Multicultural Table.*

26. Robert Bernstein, "50 Fastest-Growing Metro Areas Concentrated in West and South," *U.S. Census Bureau News* (2007). http://www.census.gov/Press-Release/www/releases/archives/population/009865.html. Accessed March 10, 2013.

27. The law expressly permits the Census Bureau to collect data on religious affiliation, but the Bureau declines to do so on the basis of a law that prohibits "mandatory" questions about religion. See 26 U.S.C. s 1202. http://www.census.gov/prod/www/religion.htm. Accessed March 10, 2013.

28. United States Bureau of the Census.

29. *The South* refers to the states identified as such in the U.S. Census Bureau: Texas, Oklahoma, Louisiana, Arkansas, Alabama, Kentucky, Tennessee, Mississippi, Delaware, Maryland, the District of Columbia, Florida, Georgia, North Carolina, South Carolina, West Virginia, Virginia.

30. Narasaki and Kwoh, *Community of Contrast.*

31. Mackun and Wilson, *Population and Distribution Change: 2000–2010.*

32. "A Trip down Memory Lane," *Khabar Magazine*, December 2002. http://www.khabar.com/jsp/article.jsp?sessionid=dIBZglfeH0Q3eeIXrnjTecIE0RI&tempid=827040139111 7634369&_articleid=72. Accessed April 2011.

33. Narayanan, "Creating the South Indian 'Hindu' Experience in the United States"; Williams, *Religions of Immigrants from India and Pakistan.*

34. Fenton, *Transplanting Religious Traditions.*

35. Williams, *An Introduction to Swaminarayan Hinduism.* http://www.swaminarayan.org/globalnetwork/america/index.htm. Accessed March 10, 2013.

36. Lippy, "From Angels to Zen."

37. Fenton, *Transplanting Religious Traditions*; Min, *Preserving Ethnicity through Religion in America*; Sharma, "Hindu Leaders in North America?"

38. Jacob and Thakur, "Jyothi Hindu Temple"; Kurien, *A Place at the Multicultural Table.*

39. Bhardwaj and Rao, "The Temple as a Symbol of Hindu Identity in America?"; Dempsey, *The Goddess Lives in Upstate New York*; Ramey, "Temples and Beyond"; Waghorne, "The Hindu Gods in a Split-Level World."

40. Kumar, "'I Am Distressed that Anyone Found My Discussion of Ganesha Offensive.'"

41. Banerjee, "An American Community Gets Awakened."

42. Ramaswamy, De Nicolás, and Banerjee, *Invading the Sacred*, 468.

43. When the book's Indian publisher, Motilal Banarsidas, agreed to stop publishing Professor Courtright's book and apologized to readers, this was seen as a victory by many involved in the campaign.

44. Kumar, "'I Am Distressed that Anyone Found My Discussion of Ganesha Offensive,'" A25.

45. See also Rao, "A Hindu God Must Indeed Be Heathen"; Rao, "Ganesha, Shivaji and Power Play."

46. Banerjee, "An American Community Gets Awakened," 272.

47. Ibid., 272–273.

48. Dr. K. K. Vijay, interview by author, July 2009.

49. Shah, "Ganges Nourishes a Diverse Culture," 1A.

50. Don Lattin, "The Mystical Journey to Find God," *St. Petersburg Times*, December 30, 1989.

51. Fenton, "Academic Study of Religions and Asian Indian–American College Students"; Joshi, *New Roots in America's Sacred Ground*; Kurien, *A Place at the Multicultural Table.*

52. Ibid.

53. Fenton, "Academic Study of Religions and Asian Indian–American College Students," 272.

54. Banerjee, "An American Community Gets Awakened," 270.

55. Radhakrishnan, "Examining the 'Global' Indian Middle Class."

56. Mallapragada, "Home, Homeland, Homepage"; Levitt, *The Transnational Villagers.*

57. Bose, "Home and Away"; Schiller, Basch, and Blanc, *Towards a Transnational Perspective on Migration;* Bhattacharya, "The Indian Diaspora in Transnational Context."

58. Levitt, *The Transnational Villagers*, 2.

59. See Mathew and Prashad, "The Protean Forms of Yankee Hindutva"; Bhatt and Mukta, "Hindutva in the West"; and Reddy, *Religious Identity and Political Destiny.*

60. Kurien, *A Place at the Multicultural Table.*

61. As second-generation Hindu Americans earn advanced degrees in religious studies and the social sciences and develop research agendas focused on American Hindu communities, it will also be interesting to see how their work will impact scholarship.

62. Joshi, *New Roots in America's Sacred Ground*; Purkayastha, *Negotiating Ethnicity.*

Bibliography

Adams, Maurianne, and Khyati Joshi. "Religious Oppression." *Readings for Diversity and Social Justice.* Eds. Adams, Maurianne et al., 2nd ed. New York: Routledge, 2010. 227–33.

Banerjee, Aditi. "An American Community Gets Awakened." *Invading the Sacred: An Analysis of Hinduism Studies in America.* Eds. Ramaswamy, Krishnan, Antonio T. De Nicolás, and Aditi Banerjee. New Delhi: Rupa and Co., 2007. 262–79.

Bell, Lee Ann. "Theoretical Foundations for Social Justice Education." *Teaching for Diversity and Social Justice: A Sourcebook.* Eds. Adams, M., L. A. Bell, and P. Griffin. New York: Routledge, 2007.

Bellah, R. N. "Civil Religion in America." *Daedalus, Journal of the Academy of Arts and Sciences* 96.1 (1967): 1–21.

Bernstein, Robert. "50 Fastest-Growing Metro Areas Concentrated in West and South." *U.S. Census Bureau News (2007).* http://www.census.gov/Press-Release/www/releases/archives/population/009865.html. Accessed January 21, 2013.

Bhardwaj, S. M., and Madhusudana N. Rao. "The Temple as a Symbol of Hindu Identity in America?" *Journal of Cultural Geography* 17 (1998).

Bhatt, Chetan, and Parita Mukta. "Hindutva in the West: Mapping the Antinomies of Diaspora Nationalism." *Ethnic and Racial Studies* 23.3 (2000): 407–41.

Bhattacharya, Gauri. "The Indian Diaspora in Transnational Context: Social Relations and Cultural Identities of Immigrants to New York City." *Journal of Intercultural Studies* 29.1 (2008): 65–80.

Blumenfeld, W. J. "Christian Privilege, the Public Schools, and the Promotion of 'Secular' and Not-So 'Secular' Mainline Christianity." *Equity and Excellence in Education* 39.3 (2006): 195–210.

Bose, Pablo Shiladitya. "Home and Away: Diasporas, Developments and Displacements in a Globalising World." *Journal of Intercultural Studies* 29.1 (2008): 111–31.

Clark, Christine. "Unburning the Cross—Lifting the Veil on Christian Privilege and White Supremacy in the United States and Abroad: Building Multicultural Understanding of Religion, Spirituality, Faith and Secularity in Educational and Workplace Settings." *Religion in Multicultural Education.* Eds. Hoosain, Rumjahn, and Farideh Salili. Greenwich, Conn.: Information Age Publishing, 2006.

Dempsey, Corrinne G. *The Goddess Lives in Upstate New York: Breaking Convention and Making Home at a North American Hindu Temple.* New York: Oxford University Press, 2006.

Eck, Diana. *A New Religious America: How a Christian Country Has Now Become the World's Most Religiously Diverse Nation.* San Francisco: Harper Collins, 2001.

Emerson, M., and C. Smith. *Divided by Faith: Evangelical Religion and the Problem of Race in America.* New York: Oxford University Press, 2000.

Feldman, Stephen M. *Please Don't Wish Me a Merry Christmas: A Critical History of the Separation of Church and State. Critical America.* New York: New York University Press, 1997.

Fenton, John Y. "Academic Study of Religions and Asian Indian–American College Students." *A Sacred Thread: Modern Transmissions of Hindu Traditions in India and Abroad.* Ed. Williams, Raymond Bradbury. Chambersburg, Pa.: ANIMA Publications, 1992. 258–77.

———. *Transplanting Religious Traditions: Asian Indians in America.* New York: Praegar, 1988.

Gualtieri, Sarah. "Becoming 'White': Race, Religion and the Foundations of Syrian/Lebanese Ethnicity." *Journal of American Ethnic History* 20.4 (2001): 29–58.

Howard, Gary R. *We Can't Teach What We Don't Know: White Teachers, Multiracial Schools.* Multicultural Education Series. 2nd ed. New York: Teachers College Press, 2006.

Jacob, Simon, and Pallavi Thakur. "Jyothi Hindu Temple: One Religion, Many Practices." *Religion and the New Immigrants: Continuities and Adaptations in Immigrant Communities.* Eds. Ebaugh, Helen Rose, and Janet Saltzman Chafetz. Walnut Creek: Altamira Press, 2000.

Joshi, K. Y. "The Racialization of Religion in the United States." *Investigating Christian Privilege and Religious Oppression in the United States.* Eds. Blumenfeld, Warren, K. Y. Joshi, and Ellen Fairchild. Amsterdam: Sense Publisher, 2008. 37–56.

Joshi, Khyati Y. *New Roots in America's Sacred Ground: Religion, Race, and Ethnicity in Indian America.* New Brunswick, N.J.: Rutgers University Press, 2006.

Kumar, NandaTanmaya. "'I Am Distressed that Anyone Found My Discussion of Ganesha Offensive.'" *India Abroad* 2003, XXXIV ed.: A25.

Kurien, Prema. *A Place at the Multicultural Table: The Development of an American Hinduism.* New Brunswick, N.J.: Rutgers University Press, 2007.

Lattin, Don. "The Mystical Journey to Find God." *St. Petersburg Times,* December 30, 1989, City Edition ed., sec. Religion: 5E.

Levitt, Peggy. *The Transnational Villagers.* Berkeley: University of California Press, 2001.

Lippy, Charles. "From Angels to Zen: Religion and Culture in The Contemporary South." *Religion in the Contemporary South: Changes, Continuities, and Contexts.* Eds. Norman, Corrie E., and Don S. Armentrout. Knoxville: University of Tennessee Press, 2005. 123–38.

Mackun, Paul, and Steven Wilson. *Population and Distribution Change: 2000–2010.* Washington, D.C.: U.S. Census Bureau, 2011.

Mallapragada, Madhavi. "Home, Homeland, Homepage: Belonging and the Indian-American Web." *New Media Society* (2006).

Mathew, Biju, and Vijay Prashad. "The Protean Forms of Yankee Hindutva." *Ethnic and Racial Studies* 23 (2000): 516–34.

Min, Pyong Gap. *Preserving Ethnicity through Religion in America: Korean Protestants and Indian Hindus across Generations.* New York: New York University Press, 2010.

Murray, Bruce. "Tracking Religious Membership in the United States." 2002. FACSNET. October 1, 2004. http://www.facsnet.org/issues/faith/sanchagrin.php. Accessed January 21, 2013.

Narasaki, Karen, and Stewart Kwoh. *Community of Contrast: Asian Americans and Pacific Islanders in the United States.* Washington, D.C.: Asian American Justice Center/Asian Pacific American Legal Center, 2008.

Narayanan, Vasudha. "Creating the South Indian 'Hindu' Experience in the United States." *A Sacred Thread: Modern Transmissions of Hindu Traditions in India and Abroad.* Ed. Williams, Raymond Bradbury. Chambersburg, Pa.: ANIMA Publications, 1992. 147–76.

Ngai, Mae M. *Impossible Subjects: Illegal Aliens and the Making of Modern America. Politics and Society in Twentieth-Century America.* Princeton, N.J.: Princeton University Press, 2004.

Parekh, Parthiv N. "A Faith Driven Governor in a Secular Society." *Khabhar Magazine* (2004). January 20, 2009. http://www.khabar.com/magazine/editorial/a_faith_driven _governor_in_a_secular_society.aspx. Accessed March 6, 2013.

Pew Research Center's Forum on Religion & Public Life. 2012. *Asian Americans: A Mosaic of Faiths.* Washington, D.C.: Pew Research Center's Forum on Religion & Public Life.

Purkayastha, Bandana. *Negotiating Ethnicity: Second-Generation South Asian Americans Traverse a Transnational World.* New Brunswick, N.J.: Rutgers University Press, 2005.

Radhakrishnan, Smitha. "Examining the 'Global' Indian Middle Class: Gender and Culture in the Silicon Valley/Bangalore Circuit." *Journal of Intercultural Studies* 29.1 (2008): 7–20.

Ramaswamy, Krishnan, Antonio T. De Nicolás, and Aditi Banerjee. *Invading the Sacred: An Analysis of Hinduism Studies in America.* New Delhi: Rupa and Co., 2007.

Ramey, Steven W. "Temples and Beyond: Varieties of Hindu Experiences in the South." *Religion in the Contemporary South.* Eds. Norman, Corrie E., and Don S. Armentrout. Knoxville: University of Tennessee, 2005. 207–24.

Rao, Ramesh. "A Hindu God Must Indeed Be Heathen." *India Abroad* 2003, XXXIV ed.: A24.

Rao, R. Ramesh. "Ganesha, Shivaji and Power Play." *India Abroad* 2004, XXXIV ed.: A22.

Reddy, Deepa. *Religious Identity and Political Destiny: 'Hindutva' in the Culture of Ethnicism.* Lanham, Md.: Rowman and Littlefield, 2006.

Rogoff, Leonard. "Is the Jew White? The Racial Place of the Southern Jew." *American Jewish History* 85.3 (1997): 195–230.

Schiller, Nina Glick, Linda G. Basch, and Cristina Szanton Blanc. *Towards a Transnational Perspective on Migration: Race, Class, Ethnicity, and Nationalism Reconsidered.* Annals of the New York Academy of Sciences, V. 645. New York: New York Academy of Sciences, 1992.

Schlosser, L. Z. "Christian Privilege: Breaking a Sacred Taboo." *Journal of Multicultural Counseling and Development* 31 (January 2003): 44–51.

Shah, Reena. "Ganges Nourishes a Diverse Culture: India's Holiest, Dirtiest River Is a Font of Tradition." *St. Petersburg Times,* 1989, City Edition ed., sec. National 1A.

Sharma, Deepak. "Hindu Leaders in North America?" *Teaching Theology and Religion* 9.2 (2006): 115–20.

Smith, Timothy. "Religion and Ethnicity in America." *American Historical Review* 83 (1978): 1155–85.

U. S. Bureau of the Census. 2008.

Waghorne, Joanne Punzo. "The Hindu Gods in a Split-Level World: The Sri Siva-Vishnu Temple in Suburban Washington, D.C." *Gods of the City: Religion and the American Urban Landscape.* Ed. Orsi, Robert A. Bloomington: Indiana University Press, 1999.

Williams, R. B. *Religions of Immigrants from India and Pakistan.* New York: Cambridge University Press, 1988.

Williams, Raymond Brady. *An Introduction to Swaminarayan Hinduism.* Cambridge, U.K.: Cambridge University Press, 2001.

Wilson, Charles Reagan. *Southern Missions: The Religion of the American South in Global Perspective.* Waco, Tex.: Baylor University Press, 2007.

PART III

Performing Race, Region, and Nation

CHAPTER 8

Southern Eruptions in Asian American Narratives

Jennifer Ho

Introduction

> Hank Hill: "So are you Chinese or Japanese?"
> Kahn Souphanousinphone: "I live in California last 20 years but first come from Laos."
> Hank Hill: "Huh?"
> Kahn Souphanousinphone: "Laos—we Laotian."
> Bill Dauterive: "The ocean, what ocean?"
> Kahn Souphanousinphone: "We Laotian, from Laos, stupid! It's a landlocked country in Southeast Asia. It's between Viet Nam and Thailand, OK. Population 4.7 million."
> Hank Hill: "So are you Chinese or Japanese?"
> *King of the Hill*

During the first season of the popular animated television sitcom, *King of the Hill*,[1] the exchange above takes place among white Texans Hank Hill and Bill Dauterive, and their newly arrived Laotian American neighbor Kahn Souphanousinphone.[2] Meant to elicit laughter at the expense of ignorant white southerners, the exchange is an apt introduction to the ways in which Asian Americans in the South erupt in unpredictable ways. The conversation highlights the ethnic myopia of Hank and Bill, yet it also repeats (with a difference) a well-worn stereotype within Asian American life: the misunderstood foreigner.[3] And yet the very presence of Kahn and his family within the fictional Arlen, Texas, announces that Asian Americans in the South exist, even in seemingly white neighborhoods and regions. Indeed, the Souphanousinphone family is an integral part of the *King of the Hill* world that Mike Judge created, just as Asian Americans in the South have been an integral part of the southern landscape and American and Asian American narratives.

Asian American literature has historically been set on either the East or West Coasts, following the trajectory of most Asian American immigration and settlement. Yet there have always been small pockets of Asians in the American South. Filipino sailors jumped shipped from Spanish galleons in the eighteenth century and settled in Louisiana (and their descendants are still proud to claim that heritage to this day), and nineteenth-century Chinese laborers came to work on plantations during the post–Emancipation era, eventually settling into a middle-man shopkeeper economy in the Mississippi Delta. In our contemporary period, Indian motel owners proliferate around Mississippi and the entire southern region.[4] Vietnamese, Laotian, and Hmong refugees from the American war in Viet Nam[5] have settled around southern states in the Gulf of Mexico and make up one of the largest Asian American populations in Atlanta, Georgia.[6] And within the Triangle region of North Carolina, Asians and Asian Americans with various national and ethnic affiliations—Korean, Chinese, Indian, Pakistani, Japanese, Malaysian, Taiwanese, and many others—have settled in the area lured by high-tech jobs and the area's research universities. Currently, Asian American immigration to the South has risen at exponential rates, in many cases doubling their numbers from the 1990 to the 2010 census.[7]

As Asian Americans populate the South, stories about Asians in America begin to reflect this demographic shift. From novels like Susan Choi's *The Foreign Student* to Mira Nair's feature-length film *Mississippi Masala*, the South takes center stage, reorienting Asian American narratives away from West Coast Chinatowns or East Coast suburban subdivisions and reminding audiences of the global and transnational composition of southern communities. Used as setting, character, and symbol, the South erupts within Asian American literature as a force of violence, shame, and the redemption inherent in change. Although eruptions are often associated with devastation, the eruptions that occur in Asian American literature set in the South have both destructive and ameliorative effects; in other words, these eruptions cause damage but lead to growth.[8] In particular, within the last essay of writer and poet Paisley Rekdal's creative nonfiction collection of autobiographical essays, *The Night My Mother Met Bruce Lee: Observations on Not Fitting In*, the southern eruptions interrupt both southern and Asian American narratives about what it means to be in the South and to be Asian American. The South is synonymous with an American past associated with violence and racism and a population polarized into segregated black or white communities. Yet the Asian and Asian American people who intersect with representations and representatives of "the South" in Rekdal's narrative, as in those of Choi and Nair, trouble this binary with their seemingly "foreign" presence and their position as being both within and without this southern history. Furthermore, an Asian and Asian American presence within southern landscapes ties the local region to a larger global community, disrupting an entrenched provincialism typically associated with the South. Analyzing the intersections of Asian Americans with the southern region and history allows for not only a more diverse understanding of both southern and Asian American Studies, but also a truer conception of race in the American South that extends beyond a pure black-white paradigm into a more nuanced vision of American pluralism in all its mixed-race and transnational manifestations.

Part I: Asian American Eruptions in the New South and Southern Eruptions in Asian American Literature

"The South is an idea, I know. But then, so is the Orient. They are not places, but sites of elaborate mythologies, of longing, of profound feelings of repulsion and desire. If they did not exist, they would have to be invented, to borrow a catch-phrase. They serve as the self's negative image, the projection of difference necessary for self-definition" (Leslie Bow, "Meditations on the Partly Colored").[9]

Traditionally, Asian American narratives have followed the trajectory of Asian American immigration: recording and representing the experiences of Asian American immigrants to predominantly West Coast (and some East Coast and Hawaiian) geographic spaces. Maxine Hong Kingston's novels chart Chinese American life as experienced in California and other West Coast locations.[10] Milton Murayama writes a fictionalized version of his Japanese American family's life working on a sugar plantation in Hawaii.[11] And contemporary authors Chang-rae Lee and Jhumpa Lahiri have depicted, respectively, Korean American and Indian American immigrant life post-1965 on the East Coast.[12] All of these writers are fairly canonical within Asian American literary and academic circles, and their works have, at one time or another, become representative of an Asian American experience within Asian American literature. These texts, read either in the privacy of one's home or in the semipublic space of the classroom, place Asian Americans within the United States as largely coastal or metropolitan people.

Despite the fact that Asian Americans have long been part of the southern landscape (even if in the background and forgotten), it is only in the "new" New South[13] that an "eruption" of Asian American narratives have begun to proliferate, keeping pace with the growing number of Asian Americans living in this region. A brief sample of contemporary Asian American works with Southern settings include Monique Truong's short story, "Kelly," and her novel *Bitter in the Mouth*; Abraham Verghese's *My Own Country: A Doctor's Story* and *The Tennis Partner*; the documentary film *Daughter from Danang*; Cynthia Kadohata's *The Floating World* and *Kira-Kira*; and the narratives under consideration in this essay: Susan Choi's *The Foreign Student*, Mira Nair's film *Mississippi Masala*, and Paisley Rekdal's essay "Traveling to Opal."[14] Each of these stories presents a different perspective on an "Asian American" experience, reflecting a diverse range of ages, ethnicities, experiences, and politics—a diversity in keeping with the expansive Asian American community in the United States. These stories about Asian Americans in the South, whether in filmic or literary text, depict the tension between the lingering effects of the "Old South" and the more diverse social climate of the New South;[15] highlight the ambiguity of being neither black nor white; portray Asian Americans experiencing the South as uniquely different from life on either the East or West Coasts; and demonstrate southern-transnational connections, making the South a more cosmopolitan and global space than is typically shown in canonical southern narratives.

Moreover, Asian American narratives set in the South challenge and change the story of what it means to be a southerner and what southern literature looks like, as well as challenge and change the genre of Asian American literature and the kinds of stories that are told about an Asian American experience. Asian American narratives set in the South remind readers that Asian Americans have been part of a truly American national landscape and not simply ghettoized into urban Chinatowns and ethnic enclaves. And Asian American southern narratives remind readers that "the South" isn't merely a location of regional color but is part of the larger national fabric and an even larger global network of the transnational flow of people, making the South a site of international immigration and labor. Furthermore, Asian American southern narratives question the nature of both regional and ethnic literature by acknowledging that Asian American narratives set in the South are both southern and Asian American and irreducibly American. These narratives complicate simple boundaries of region and race, advancing a more syncretic vision of what it means to live in the South and what it means to experience life as an Asian American—that both can be representations of American culture and society.

As noted in the introduction to this essay, the first significant settlement of Asians in America occurred in the eighteenth century when a crew of Filipino sailors jumped ship off of a Spanish galleon in the port of New Orleans in 1763.[16] In subsequent years, other Filipino men working on Spanish ships would also escape from brutal Spanish employment, disembarking in New Orleans or making their way from Acapulco, Mexico, to various settlements around the Louisiana Bayou. Saint Malo, Manila Village, Alombro Canal, Camp Dewey, Bayou Cholas, Leon Rojas, and Bassa Bassa supported the new Filipino American community in the early stages of the formation of the United States. These communities propagated through interracial marriage between the Manilamen and local Cajun, Indian, and African American women.[17] Thus, Asian American immigration history begins in the South amid an escape from violence at the hands of an international colonial oppressor and continues through a perpetuation of racial amalgamation.

I provide this extended description of the first settlement of Asian Americans because the themes of the Manilamen's adoption and adaptation to American society—rebellion, global diasporic connections, interracial romance, racial mixing, an atmosphere of violence, and the intertwining of all these themes—erupt throughout Asian American literature set in the South; both the initial Asian American community as well as the stories surrounding Asian Americans in the

South begin with a history of violence and transgressive sexuality. Indeed, the history of southern literature, as of the southern region, is a history of violence and racial tension, one typically rendered in black and white terms.[18] In many ways the South has served as a magnifying lens for the anxieties and fears of the nation as a whole, enlarging them to a grotesque degree. For example, the history of black-white interracial sex, and the violence tied into it, is one bound up with a racial and sexual politics that go back to the days of slavery. The rape of enslaved black women by white slave masters for purposes of increasing human chattel is part of this legacy of interracial sex and violence.[19] So too is the postbellum period of racial and sexual politics that led to the lynching of black men for even the hint of alleged impropriety (in many cases a charge of impropriety that stemmed from false allegations of molesting white women that emerged from racist impulses) as both the cases of the Scottsboro Boys[20] and Emmett Till[21] demonstrate. Although the rest of the nation in the pre–civil rights era showed intolerance and prejudice toward varying types of interracial unions, the extreme forms of condemnations used to prevent these romantic pairings in ex-confederacy states points to a particular history of violence connected with the intertwining of sexual and racial politics in this region.

Amid this backdrop of race, sex, and violence, narratives of Asian Americans set in the South feature eruptions that signal a connection to this legacy. But as noted earlier, these eruptions are not simply indications of destruction; rather, they signal the growth and rise of new perspectives, new relationships, and a new understanding of what it means to live in the South and to be Asian American. Eruption, as I am using the term and applying it to these Asian American works, becomes a means of sudden change, one associated with violence, sometimes physical, oftentimes ontological and emotional. In particular, the narratives under examination in this essay (which span three different genres as well as three different southern locales and Asian ethnicities) all demonstrate that interracial eruptions interrupt social, cultural, ethnic, and historic assumptions about intimate relationships—who counts as Asian American and who counts as a southerner. In choosing to examine these three narratives, I focus on the ways in which the various eruptions in these stories occur precisely as a means of forward progress, racially speaking, because eruptions, while sudden and violent, also lead to new beginnings, potential paradigm shifts, and new perspectives.

As a population that is neither black nor white in a region that codifies law and people according to this binary, Asian Americans[22] exist in what literary critic Leslie Bow calls "racial interstitiality," a place between white privilege and black abjection, an interstitial racial space in which Asian bodies act as a screen for the racial anxieties between blacks and whites, and who, in turn, enact these same anxieties through their choice of affiliation, thus contributing to a discourse within the South of either racial degeneracy or progress: "[W]hat remains constant from the 1920s through the 1990s are the narratives in which this interstitial community was placed: they were represented as either backsliding into blackness or extolled as exemplary citizens 'accepted' by southern whites."[23] The stories told from the perspective of Asian Americans living in the South and taking part in southern culture and customs erupt this commonly held narrative of Asian Americans having to choose between abject blackness and white privilege. Asian American narratives in the South, told from an Asian American point of view, create an alternative space that recognizes racial interstitiality to be negotiated in Asian American rather than black or white terms, or more importantly, through creating other perspectives to think about the intersections of race and gender through interracial intimacies that erupt old narratives of miscegenation and segregation. In particular, the eruptions in these three narratives demonstrate the ways in which Asian Americans in the South are both exceptional and ordinary; their presence as an interruption to a black and white hierarchy signals the need to rethink racial politics along different axes.

Part II: Transracial Eruptions in
Asian American Narratives of the South

"This narrative of Chinese American settlement in the American South is a kind of historical extension of the California narrative of Chinese working on the railroads, though the story takes interesting and distinctive turns as soon as the 'triangle' among Yellows, Blacks, and Whites takes shape and then persists through three, four, and more generations in the Mississippi locale, its economy, and its formations of race, all of which Chinese Americans of Mississippi have had a part in constructing" (Sumida, "East of California").[24]

As Sumida points out, an Asian American presence in the South has connections with a larger, national history of Asians across the Americas and among black as well as white citizens.[25] Chinese arrived in the Mississippi Delta region by way of Cuba as well as California—the community they have formed continues from the late nineteenth century to the present day.[26] Yet the ways in which Asian Americans continue to be read as a distinctly foreign (and hence unassimilable) and unplaceable third group within a black-white binary of southern racial politics—to triangulate race relations as Sumida's quote observes—is, in part, what works such as *The Foreign Student* and *Mississippi Masala* complicate through their respective portraits of Asian Americans in the South and the sometimes surprising global networks that they are tied to. Specifically, the specter of violence that accompanies the sexual transgressions of their protagonists erupt old ideas of race and racial intimacy.

The history and residue of violence is a recurring theme that threads its way throughout the twin stories of Chang Ahn and Katherine Monroe in Susan Choi's debut novel *The Foreign Student*. Set in 1955 at Sewanee, the University of the South, Chang (or Chuck as he is known in Tennessee), the newly arrived and eponymous "foreign student" from Korea, carries with him the physical, emotional, and psychic scars of the recent Korean war,[27] all of which are hidden from almost all he encounters, since the veneer of southern gentility facilitates his own reticence. Chang is a survivor, and in his budding friendship and eventual romance with Katherine, he finds an intimacy borne out of similar scars that are a result of violence: in his case, physical; in hers, sexual; for both, mental and emotional.[28] Their romance, which does not culminate until the final chapters of the novel, erupts the polite veneer of southern decorum, particularly since the novel is set in the Jim Crow era of southern race relations at a time when public interracial intimacy was nearly impossible.

Chang's racial position in the novel is one of "racial interstitiality," for he is neither black nor white and therefore cannot exist comfortably in any social milieu within Sewanee of the 1950s. Drinking a soda with Katherine at a roadside café, Chang observes of the dozen white patrons whose stares are impossible to ignore, "They don't know what to make of me."[29] Indeed, this comment applies to almost all characters, white as well as black, whom Chang encounters. His first attempt at friendliness with Louis, an African American steward at Sewanee's dining hall, results in Chang's white housemate, Crane, admonishing him about the inappropriateness of Chang shaking Louis's hand and greeting him in a friendly manner.[30] Even later, when Chang finds himself dining with the African American kitchen help during the winter break, his overtures at polite conversation with these men falls flat, causing Chang to realize that he cannot penetrate their wall of deference to him because the racial hierarchy of Sewanee made impossible any real friendship between them.[31] As for his white southern housemate Crane, the two form a tentative bond through the first term, but when Crane realizes that Chuck has received better grades than he has, during the second term his grudging friendship with the misfit Chang turns into hostility toward a foreigner who outstrips him academically. Left in the lonely position of Asian foreigner, of outcast, Chang is discouraged from camaraderie with the African American hired help yet he is never fully embraced by the white elites who attend Sewanee either.

Given the social restrictions that Chang faces at Sewanee, his interracial romance with Katherine literally erupts the rigid color lines that have placed him in the position of racial indeterminacy as well as the placidity he has maintained in an effort to keep at bay the memories and hauntings of his violent past.[32] And as his relationship with Katherine grows and becomes public, the early scene at the café where Chang observes that the white patrons "don't know what to make me," is repeated in a Nashville restaurant and a New Orleans sidewalk—both times the gaze of white men causes Chang to tense himself and react bodily to the latent hostility: "Chuck's scalp prickled, and his armpits. He sat with his eyes trained ahead but feeling the man's gaze on him like a wash of unpleasant heat,"[33] Chang must prepare himself for possible attack; he understands, intuitively, that the sight of an interracial pair is enough to unleash a violence that lies just beneath the surface of social relations in the South. Moreover, Chang as Asian foreigner is a visual reminder of the global conflict in Korea and the changing demographics of the United States and the American South. In other words, he represents both the violence from the most recent overseas war in Asia and the future violence of the civil rights movement because his very presence in the South challenges the social and racial norms predicated on a black-white binary. As a "foreign student" Chang's stay in the United States signals a temporality that can be deemed palatable by those at Sewanee. But his relationship with Katherine shatters his image as temporary sojourner and, instead, provokes a reaction by others, particularly white others, to see him as a threat, both to white womanhood as well as to the nation through his Asian, foreign presence.

Beyond the harsh reaction that Chang and Katherine receive from onlookers, however, Choi renders their relationship in explosive terms; their first embrace occurs during the tail end of a hurricane. Furthermore, the week they spend clandestinely entwined in a hotel room is contrasted with memories of Chang's torture: his most violent and traumatic experience during the war. The coincidence of setting Chang, a Korean survivor of an Asian civil war living in the diaspora, in the dawning age of the civil rights movement in the South—where the U.S. Civil War was fought and lost from the standpoint of many southerners—can only point to the ways in which Asians in the South erupt the veneer of gentility in order to expose the reality of race relations and the violence that has been suppressed beneath the surface. Chang and Katherine are two damaged individuals who find comfort and intimacy through their cross-cultural and transracial and transnational romance. Choi does not present their relationship in sentimental terms but rather demonstrates how both, as survivors of their respective traumas, learn to heal in the presence of one another. Their interracial relationship stands as a testament to the types of growth that can occur in the aftermath of eruptions.

The stigma of transracial sexual relations, while violently stigmatized in the Jim Crow era, does not enjoy automatic approval or easy acceptance in the post–civil rights era of the South. But rather than focus on the tensions between a white majority and Asian minority, filmmaker Mira Nair depicts cross-racial love involving an African American man and an Indian American woman in *Mississippi Masala*. The film begins with the Loha family's exile from Uganda due to dictator Idi Amin's expulsion of the Indian community from the African nation. The film's protagonist, Mina, born and bred in Uganda, arrives in Greenwood, Mississippi, with her parents Kinnu and Jay by way of Great Britain. The entire family lives and works with their extended relatives at the Monte Cristo motel, and it is after an auto accident that Mina meets and begins a romance with Demetrius Williams, a local entrepreneur who owns a carpet cleaning business. Mina exists as somewhat of an anomaly from the Asian American protagonists of East and West Coast Asian American narratives: she chooses not to attend college, and her parents, while disappointed, do not pressure her to do so;[34] she chooses an interracial relationship with a man neither of her own race nor of the dominant race; and while there seems to be a sizable South Asian American community in Greenwood,[35] she feels like an outsider among them, perhaps largely due to her global and diasporic existence. Mina and Demetrius's love affair highlights the racial divisions within Greenwood through Mina's racial identity as neither black nor white and yet still not acceptable as a romantic counterpart for an African American man—their affair upsets all racial codes: black and Indian as well as white.

Though critics of the film find fault with Nair's depiction of the interracial relationship between Mina and Demetrius, citing its lack of attention to institutional forms of discrimination in favor of privileging individual romance as a panacea to racial prejudice,[36] my own interpretation of this particular Asian American southern narrative sees Mina and Demetrius's relationship as one that interrupts a multitude of narratives within Indian, African American, and southern contexts in order to provide a redemptive if not entirely realistic vision of race relations in a post–civil rights southern landscape. By exploring an African American–Asian American interracial romance in a small southern town, Nair's film questions the construction of race and the nature of white privilege and racism to dictate social codes even after the codification of legal civil rights. Although, as Kum-Kum Bhavnani observes, "[w]hiteness is not at the center of this film, and the nature of the relationship between Mina and Demetrius demonstrates the intertwining of their personal and political histories," *Mississippi Masala* does reveal tensions within both the Indian and African American community toward color—noting a preference toward lighter skin tone within the Indian community that represents an alignment with the dominant white society. Noting the colorism inherent in both communities, Binita Mehta writes: "Attitudes toward skin color in the film likewise show that the Indians identify with the whites rather than the blacks; the preference for light skin color is frequently stressed. . . . The concern with gradations of skin color is something Indian cultures share with African American culture, but it serves to drive them apart rather than bring them closer."[37] In depicting this concern with "color," the film draws attention to the ways in which the residue of racism and its legacy of violence, in this case psychic and emotional, continues to guide various characters. Yet by decentering the film away from whiteness and between two minority communities, the film also shows how both Mina and Demetrius refuse to be defined through white privilege and the cultural constraints of their respective racial groups.

Although Nair could have set her interracial romance in any other setting in which a critical mass of Indian Americans and African Americans coexist (Manhattan Masala perhaps?) the South is an apt setting for a tale of transracial romance that literally erupts unexpectedly and through violent means (the weekend Mina and Demetrius consummate their relationship is also the same weekend that Mina's cousin physically attacks Demetrius after discovering them secretly tucked away in a motel room in Biloxi, Mississippi).[38] Though the restrictions on their relationship may have been the same in Glenwood, California, as in Greenwood, Mississippi, the institutional force of racism and its lingering effects appear to have greater force in ex-confederacy states than in other parts of the nation, perhaps due to the sensational and extreme nature of the civil rights confrontations in the region. As stated earlier, the South does not have a monopoly on prejudice and discrimination but rather acts as a magnifying lens to enlarge the anxieties and fears of the nation-state within a particular locale.[39] Although Mina and Demetrius's relationship does not upend white supremacy, it does interfere with the status quo within Greenwood in which blacks know their place and Asians serve in a middleman economy. By erupting this social and racial color line, Mina and Demetrius defy everyone's expectations within the film of knowing their place. According to critic Urmila Seshagiri, "*Mississippi Masala* asserts that in Uganda's colonial past as well as in the present-day American South, Indian people have mediated between a white ruling class and a black underclass; as Nair puts it, the film's dual Uganda-Mississippi narratives demonstrate 'history repeating itself, with the Asians coming between black and white people.'"[40] By the film's end, with Mina and Demetrius lighting out for new territory like their American literary precursor, Huck Finn, the image of their interracial union does not stand as a mediation between white and black but acts as a buffer; their transracial romance and the promise of their mixed-race children erupts the racial hierarchy of the South.

Mina and her family disrupt not only the racial binary of the South but also the Asian American narratives of immigration from an Asian locale to the United States by their transnational migrations from India (within the grandparents' generation) to Uganda, and then briefly to England and finally to the United States. The Loha family's intimate connection with Uganda, in particular, reminds viewers of the many different transnational flows that have erupted out of past histories of colonialism, as well as the cross-racial affiliations and affections that such flows inspire.[41] The Lohas are not simply a newly arrived Asian immigrant family seeking to assimilate; the ties they have to Uganda—their birthplace and homeland—signal a global consciousness that contrasts strongly with their present circumstances and location in the South. Their cosmopolitan[42] journeys indicate displacement rather than luxury, a theme within the film that highlights the continual displacement of Asians in the South as people who conform neither to southern nor Asian American narratives. Furthermore, as part of the Indian Diaspora, Nair's film also helps to push the boundaries of Asian American narratives by including South Asian Americans within the category of Asian American stories. As the recent proliferation of works of literature and anthologies by and about South Asian Americans attests to, the presence of South Asian Americans, whether in the South or other locales within North America, signals their eruption of a previously East Asian American canonization of Asian American narratives.[43]

In both Mira Nair's *Mississippi Masala* and Susan Choi's *The Foreign Student*, Asian and Asian American characters within southern settings serve as catalysts for change. They erupt the seemingly tranquil surfaces of southern society by being a visual sign of a larger global society that the South must acknowledge. Asian immigrants like Chang and the Lohas force the southerners they encounter, whether white or black, to recognize the transnational forces that have propelled these Asian bodies into southern spaces. These Asian American narratives, in turn, create global connections, signaling to readers and viewers that the South is a space that is part of a larger transnational history extending beyond the region of the American South and into international territories around the globe. Additionally, these Asian bodies erupt the binary of race in the South by introducing their Asian American characters and their non–Asian American romantic partners as an alternative to black-white race relations and the purity of the color line. These transracial couples force others to consider the meaning of race, even tacitly and subconsciously, through their very presence as people who are neither black nor white and most especially through the absent presence of the mixed-race yet-to-be-born children of these interracial pairs. Yet the southern eruptions within the narratives of this study, as shall be particularly demonstrated in the following analysis of Paisley Rekdal's essay "Traveling to Opal," occur not to reinforce racial hierarchies of the past but to literally explode and thereby alter the shape and scope of both southern and Asian American literature. Only through such a change in the landscape can progress begin.

Part III: The Place of Asian Americans in the South in Paisley Rekdal's "Traveling to Opal"

"We were simply passing through, Chinese told researchers who asked. Only after decades passed and they and their children still had not gone did they realize they were stuck. Actively or not, they had chosen to remain" (Rekdal, "Traveling to Opal").[44] Paisley Rekdal's collection of creative nonfiction *The Night My Mother Met Bruce Lee, Observations on Not Fitting In* contains Rekdal's recordings and reflections about her life as a biracial Chinese-Norwegian American woman. Although the majority of the essays take place in either Seattle (her childhood home) or various Asian locales (the places she travels to as a young adult), the last essay, "Traveling to Opal," is set in the South. The quotation above summarizes Rekdal's understanding of how the Chinese came to Mississippi. In "Traveling to Opal" Rekdal leaves her new hometown of Atlanta in the mid-1990s for Natchez, Mississippi, looking for traces of her great-aunt Opal's life in that southern town. Opal, born in Seattle, Washington, in the early part of the twentieth century, married a Chinese grocer and moved to Natchez in the 1930s, where she raised a family and eventually left her abusive husband to return West. These are the bare facts that Rekdal weaves into the essay, but her depiction of her trip to Natchez is more than a simple recording of a road trip: it is an observation about difference and an acknowledgment of the uneasy relationship of Asian Americans in a southern racial landscape.

"Traveling to Opal" opens with a torrential rainstorm, one so fierce that Rekdal must take shelter at a gas station mini-mart with other sodden motorists, both black and white. As the only Asian American traveler, Rekdal describes sideways glances and hard stares, noting that "more than a few looks get shot at me, the foreigner. I clearly don't belong here with my accent and outfit."[45] Here Rekdal upends what the word "foreigner" typically connotes since what is "foreign" about Rekdal is not only or simply being an "Asian" other but being someone who is not local to a southern locale, as demonstrated through her lack of southern accent and her different attire. Additionally, Rekdal begins her essay with a theme that will continue throughout her narrative (one which is echoed in both Choi's and Nair's works): displacement. To return to Bow's concept of "racial interstitiality," Rekdal's Asian American presence is in-between black and white and hence unplaceable in many ways. "In reading Asian Americans through the lens of racial interstitiality—between black and white" writes Bow, "I am reminded why they are such a significant cultural site: they are uneasily positioned in American culture as American but not quite; as middle class—almost; as minority but not one of "those" minorities; as like us but not like us."[46]

As a biracial woman, Rekdal's very existence is the physical product of transgressive sexuality in the form of interracial intimacy; she is the material mixed-race person that both Choi and Nair's narratives hint at—the future of race relations and the new face of the new New South. Rekdal, in seeking shelter with her fellow motorists, is like them and yet distinctly unlike them because she does not fit into the racial conception of who should belong in this landscape. Whether it is an eruption of rain from the sky or an eruption of herself in southern space, neither the torrential rain nor her sodden biracial Asian American presence was expected, nor as Rekdal's description of her reception would have us believe, welcomed.

Indeed, Rekdal's trip South causes concern among her friends and lover, as they fear that harm will befall Rekdal as one so out of place. The South has long been coded through racialized violence, most especially for those whom others believe don't belong there. Her boyfriend worries she will be killed or hurt during the trip to Natchez, and a friend who grew up in Louisiana sends Rekdal "slightly hysterical, cryptic messages about the dangers I would face."[47] Clearly for Rekdal, as well as her friends, the South is a place with a legacy of violence, especially for someone neither black nor white, whom one Georgia friend describes as "somewhere inbetween [*sic*]. People won't know what to do with you."[48] In many ways the fears of Rekdal's friends are not unwarranted since a few years before her trip to Natchez, 16-year-old Japanese exchange student Yoshihiro Hattori was killed in a suburb of Baton Rouge, Louisiana, while looking for a Halloween party at the wrong address. Supposedly confusing Hattori for a trespasser, Rodney Peirs shot Hattori and was later acquitted for his death under a Louisiana statue called "Kill the burglar."[49] Violence as part of a southern landscape is not just a thing of the past, and violence as a reaction to fear of a foreign "other" still predominates in southern locales, erupting without warning even in the late twentieth century.

Although Rekdal does not encounter any physical harm during her stay in Natchez, she does recount an incident at a restaurant with three white men, who stare at Rekdal throughout their meal, never wavering in their gaze: "Half an hour passes; they are still looking. Each of the men has gone either to the bathroom or to the cashier for matches during this time and each has walked by my table, deliberately close and slowly."[50] The description of this unwanted attention as menacing and vaguely threatening is one that Rekdal connects to the way that she is being perceived as a woman of color traveling alone, perhaps someone, as her Georgia friend noted, who is in-between and therefore hard to place. Rekdal's perception of herself is reflected and refracted back to her through the gaze of these southern white men. Her encounter with these men hints at a violence lurking beneath the surface, one in which she, as a woman of color, is placed in peril, the potential object of an eruption of violence. Furthermore, the violence of the men's gaze reflects the attitudes in the new New South toward Asian Americans, ones that Rekdal believes also reflect attitudes of the Old South toward her great-aunt Opal, because what follows from this encounter is Rekdal's speculation on the loneliness her aunt must have felt:

> She has children she can't get into the right schools, almost no friends, lives above the rancid meat and powdered-milk smells of a grocery store. Maybe her husband beats her, maybe he doesn't. Maybe her neighbors snub her when she walks outdoors or are friendly. Regardless, she's dependent on her husband and isolated and unhappy.[51]

Both Rekdal and her aunt experience isolation, displacement, and discomfort; their situation as Asians in the American South renders them without a place where they can belong. And yet, the sense of belonging, of the place of Asian Americans in the South, is one that Rekdal cannot leave alone. Throughout the piece Rekdal makes multiple attempts to abandon her search for Opal and return north to Atlanta because she believes her search for traces of Chinese in

Natchez to be pointless or voyeuristic; however, she does not abort her search and instead continues to interrogate several Natchez locals—a Visitor Center's staffer, a museum tour guide, the town librarian, a local doctor, and a City Hall clerk—about the Chinese community of Natchez, Mississippi. These locals answer Rekdal's question about Chinese in Natchez in a variety of ways: with puzzlement, defensiveness, curiosity, skepticism, and surprise. None of them has any concrete answers to provide her about the whereabouts of Chinese in Natchez, past or present, and none of them can give her any specific information about her great-aunt Opal.

However, the response of the Visitor Center staff person, the first person Rekdal queries upon entering Natchez, echoes throughout the essay, for when Rekdal asks her about a Chinese community in Natchez, the woman bluntly informs her that "There's just us. Just Natchez. . . . Everyone—blacks, white, Chinese, we're all in here together."[52] Initially, Rekdal has difficulty interpreting her comment, wondering, "does she mean Natchez was simply too small to have distinct communities, or that Natchez is not—has not ever been—segregated by the virtue of being free-thinking, liberal Natchez?"[53] The staff person's response—"we're all in here together"—becomes a refrain for Rekdal, one she returns to throughout the piece, mulling over what "we're all in here together" truly means, as she searches for traces of her great-aunt Opal and of other Chinese in Natchez.

More tellingly, this refrain, "we're all in here together," erupts the narrative that Rekdal both constructs for herself while she is in Natchez and imagines others have also constructed of Asians in the South. After a fruitless day of being referred from one civil servant to another, of spying on Chinese tourists at a riverboat casino, and ogling an Asian American attorney in the window of his law firm, Rekdal returns to the Visitor Center clerk's response and wonders "Was that pride in her voice? What did she think I meant by the question? As a northerner, what did I mean by this question? Why was it so important that I find Chinese in Natchez, Mississippi?"[54] Moving from a stance of questioning and scrutinizing others to questioning and scrutinizing her own pursuit for traces of a Chinese American community and, specifically, remnants of Opal, the refrain ruptures Rekdal's previously unexamined motivations and social position as an outsider not only by virtue of race but region. Rekdal realizes, at this moment, that her search for Chinese and her relentless quest and questioning of the local citizens about a Chinese community creates a narrative of separation and exclusion—one in which she assumes the Chinese to be an abject presence in keeping with a racist and violent southern past, which Rekdal, and others, have constructed about the South. And yet, the lack of physical harm (the restaurant scene notwithstanding) that Rekdal finds herself in, the unrelenting helpfulness (though largely unhelpful) exhibited by the locals, and Rekdal's own gaze pointed outward at others, particularly any Asian others she finds in Natchez, forces Rekdal to question her assumptions about her reception as an outsider, about Opal's treatment as an outsider, or about the mythical Chinese community of Natchez and what they may or may not feel. The narrative of the Chinese in Natchez as simply an op-pressed and marginalized group is but one narrative possibility of the Chinese American condition in Natchez, Mississippi, which also leads Rekdal to reflect that "Like it or not, I am here too, among the black and white and Chinese. I am one of the people thrown simply into the mix."[55]

Rekdal's admission that she is also part of the southern landscape has as much to do with her present location in Natchez as it does with her relocation from the West to the southern metropolis of Atlanta. As an Asian American in the new New South, Rekdal's ambivalence about her living situation is exacerbated by her joblessness and subsequent financial dependence on her boyfriend, her biracial status, the distance from her family in Seattle, and her discomfort with the his-tory of violence and racial hierarchies of the Old South. Her search for Opal is, perhaps, a search for proof of Asian American existence in the South—proof that Asian American communities have lived in the South and are part of southern history. Looking for traces of Opal and other Chinese in Natchez may affirm that there is a place for the "inbetween" [*sic*], especially one as in-between as Rekdal's own biracial and West Coast status leaves her to feel in Atlanta and Natchez.

Directly after this admission, Rekdal makes a last ditch attempt to find Opal by going to the Historic Natchez Foundation. There, she finally finds the evi-dence she has long been searching for: a reference to Opal in a phone book and a photograph of Opal's first husband and two children, the absent photographer perhaps being Opal herself. The Wangs are the only Chinese surname listed in the Natchez phonebook from 1928–1940, leading Rekdal to understand that Opal's family "was the Chinese community in Natchez,"[56] thus making her pursuit of finding a Chinese community here truly fruitless since unlike the urban enclaves of San Francisco and New York, Natchez never had a critical mass of Chinese to create a Chinatown. The narrative of Chinese or other Asian Americans in the South does not correspond to the stories of Asian immigrants on the East and West Coasts.[57] Their numbers are too small, their presence scattered among small towns, their race a third space where neither whites nor blacks fully accepted them, and where they, in turn, never fully accepted their black or white neigh-bors.[58] Rekdal's discovery of textual evidence of her great-aunt Opal confirms that Opal did, indeed, live once-upon-a-time, for a brief time, in Natchez, Mississippi, but it also confirms, for Rekdal, the shape of her great-aunt's life—the type of person her great-aunt was. A self-described black sheep of the family, Opal was the one who told secrets, who said the things that others did not wish to hear, who aired the dirty laundry of the family, leading Rekdal to acknowledge that "Opal's great difference from her family was that she would talk about the ugly things in life, the strangeness, the race."[59]

To talk about race is to talk about the ugly and strange things in life: the un-acknowledged discourse surrounding race of racism, white privilege, and white supremacy. To talk about race in the South is to confront a legacy of violence and hatred—to acknowledge the magnification of the ugliness and strangeness of race/racism/white supremacy. And for Rekdal, a biracial Asian American recently transplanted West Coast northerner, to come into the new New South of Natchez in search of remnants of a Chinese community is to be, like Opal, willing to talk about the ugly and strange—to talk about race, racism, and its lingering residue:

> And now I realize what a perfect place I have come to for
> resuscitating the past, this shame of race and meaning, violence,
> history. Everywhere are signs of it. Horse carriages, posters
> for old time dances, the occasional Confederate bumper sticker
> and gun rack. What would it be like to live in an area that
> represents the glory of the Confederate past seen suddenly
> through the eyes of a northerner? And a northerner looking for,
> of all things, Chinese? How can the past help but sound
> grotesque, fabulous? This is what Po Po knows, sitting by
> herself at home, refusing to talk about her life. This is what
> the woman at the Visitors' Center hopes, giving help to people
> like me while insisting I am just like her. I cannot exoticize
> her town into an anecdote. These are people's lives. No one
> wants to be victim to someone else's storytelling.[60]

"We are all in here together" is the fiction of the new New South—an insistence that the racial problems of the past are simply that: part of a bygone era. And yet, the violence of the Old South persists—in prosaic and mundane signs, like the advertisement for the dance, or racially controversial symbols, like the Confederate flag. It persists in the hard gaze of the people Rekdal encounters and most especially in the persistent question of where she is from, a question she is asked, routinely, as she ventures from site to site looking for evidence of Chinese in Natchez.[61] Yet even though it may be a fiction, "We are all in here together" is also a reality of the new New South. As Jigna Desai observes of this refrain, "it replies that we are linked but do not necessarily operate on equal terrain."[62] And it reminds Rekdal, as it does her readers, that the story we have previously been told about the Old South—one of violence and racial hatred, one of racial hierarchies and binaries between white and black—is no longer the only story that should be told about the South. "We are all in here together" erupts both the South's narrative of its past as well as Rekdal's narrative of the South, a reminder that exoticization can work both ways and that each of us wants the opportunity to tell our own stories, to create our own realities, to speak our own truths.

Conclusion

"We are 'all in here together,' if 'here' is the predicament of defining identity. But once 'here' becomes as specific as a place on a map, an ethnicity, the truth of the phrase breaks down" (Paisley Rekdal, "Traveling to Opal").[63] "Traveling to Opal" serves as a culmination for the many observations and reflections Rekdal has made about being a biracial Chinese Norwegian American woman, one who grew up in Seattle, Washington, and who spent much of her young adult life traveling around various Asian locales: the Philippines, Taiwan, Korea, China, and Japan. It is the only essay set in the present-day United States and set in the American South; all other essays in the collection focus on Rekdal's excursions in Asia or memories of her childhood in Seattle. Her choice of ending the collection with a trip South, searching for family connections in a place that would seem to hold no trace of Asians in America, aptly concludes her myriad observations of being different and not fitting in. This southern literary side trip erupts Rekdal's narration as well as any preconceived notions she has of the South and of Asian Americans, particularly the ones who comprise her Chinese American family.

In the quotation above, Rekdal leaves readers with a final rumination on the refrain that echoes throughout her essay and her ultimate understanding of where "here" is—a place where one is fixed into a racial hierarchy. Rekdal's observation that "Race was not a choice for Opal in Mississippi. It was not a place we could enter or leave at will,"[64] leads her to reject the "here" of both the South and the American understanding of race as existing as "white" or "other." As a biracial woman, Rekdal differentiates herself from Opal and from a binary understanding of race, not just a binary of black versus white but monoracial versus multiracial: "ethnicity, for me, is not Chinese American versus white American. Unlike Opal, I cannot choose one identity without losing half of myself."[65] Rekdal's ultimate southern eruption is not only to explode racial binaries and to expose the layers of the Old South among the new in order to create racial progress; it is to reject the one-drop rule of the Old South altogether, to assert her own multiracial, multiethnic subjectivity—to create a new category of both Asian American and American southern narrative, one not rooted in either location or identity but in truly being an indeterminate person—one of the "inbetweens" that people, southern and not, Asian American and not, may not know what to do with.

The line that separates the Old from the new "New South" is the imaginary line of the contemporary civil rights movement, one that divides lynchings and legalized segregation from racial enfranchisement and equal opportunity for all. Rekdal's narrative, as well as those of *The Foreign Student* and *Mississippi Masala*, do not allow for such easy revisionist demarcations of a racist past and an equitable present. Asian American stories set in the South erupt the myth of imaginary lines between the past and present, reminding us that the inclusion of Asian American voices signals not simply a pluralistic affirmation of racial harmony but the complications of understanding race beyond a black-white paradigm. Or further, that race relations in the South always extended beyond a simplistic black-white binary. A true understanding of southern race relations crosses the geographic borders of the U.S. South into not only Europe and Africa but the Caribbean, Latin America, and Asia as well, because the South, like the rest of the United States, is a space that is implicated in larger transnational and global flows. The "foreigners" who comprise Choi, Nair, and Rekdal's narratives embody these transnational histories of war, colonialism, and immigration and erupt the provincialism of the South through their international ties around the globe. Asian American narratives of the South force a reconsideration of these lines of affiliation and difference that have become sedimented in southern history and southern narratives. Rekdal's essay, like Choi's novel and Nair's film, neither revels in the racial hope of the new "New South" nor laments the racism of the Old; instead, these Asian American narratives allow us to reinterpret the South from the vantage point of outsiders who are within, which is, in essence, the paradoxical position of being an Asian in America. Perhaps through these various eruptions, new paradigms and perspectives can emerge so that the narratives of Asian Americans set in the South and southern narratives that feature Asian Americans will ultimately be understood to be simultaneously southern and Asian and ultimately and uniquely American.

Notes

1. Judge, "Westie Side Story."
2. Since Kahn and his family had lived in Anaheim, California for twenty years, and his only child, Kahn Jr., also known as "Connie" was born there, despite his assertion that his family is "Laotian," it is more accurate to describe them as Laotian American.
3. The difference in this exchange is not that Kahn is incomprehensible, for despite his thick "fake" accent, he is rendered as articulate and intelligent in comparison to his white Texan neighbors; instead, the misunderstanding is on the part of Hank and Bill, whose own not-so-internalized racism creates the joke at the heart of this exchange.
4. Although a considerable number of motels in the South are owned by Indian Americans, Indian motel owners actually proliferate around the United States, forming what journalist Tunku Varadarajan calls " a nonlinear ethnic niche: a certain ethnic group becomes entrenched in a clearly identifiable economic sector" and owning about 37 percent of all hotels in the United States.
5. Although I realize that the convention in the United States is to refer to the war in Southeast Asia of the 1960s and 1970s as "the Vietnam war," people in Viet Nam refer to that conflict as the "American" war. Additionally, I will be using the convention of spelling Viet Nam as two separate words—again, in keeping with how people within Viet Nam refer to their country. For more on the nomenclature of both the American war in Viet Nam and the use of "Viet Nam" versus "Vietnam," see Renny Christopher's *The Viet Nam War/The American War* and Eben Muse's *The Land of Nam*.
6. See Carl Bankston's "Immigrants to the New South" and the documentary *Displaced in the New South*.
7. The increased numbers of Asians in America can be seen from the 1970 census through to the 2010 census because the passage of the 1965 Immigration Acts bill allowed for a great number of Asian immigrants to come to the United States and the end of the war in Viet Nam in the mid-1970s also heralded a great number of Southeast Asian refu-

gees to the United States, causing the Asian American population to rise significantly in the last thirty years. Indeed, taking just one small sample, in North Carolina, the 1990 census lists the Asian population at .8 percent, the 2000 census at 1.4 percent, and data from the 2010 census has the Asian population in North Carolina at 2.0 percent.

8. To better understand how "eruption" can be understood as productive and generative, one need only look to the *Oxford English Dictionary*. The etymology of the word "erupt" comes from the Latin participial stem "erumpere" meaning "to break out, burst forth." The *OED* further lists definitions of "eruption" as pertaining to the bursting forth of water (breaking out from a dam or coming out from a firehose); an outburst of "passion, eloquence, or merriment"; and in plants, the bursting forth of new growth (leaves, buds, shoots, and so forth).

9. Bow, "Meditations on the 'Partly Colored'," 94.

10. Kingston, *Woman Warrior, China Men*, and *Tripmaster Monkey*.

11. Murayama, *All I Asking for Is My Body, Five Years on a Rock*, and *Plantation Boy*.

12. Chang-rae Lee's novels include *Native Speaker, A Gesture Life*, and *Aloft*, and Jhumpa Lahiri's works include *Interpreter of Maladies* and *Namesake*.

13. I will be referring to the new "New South" to refer to a post–civil rights era in the South and a sea change that saw the end (or the systematic and institutionally beginning of the end) of Jim Crow segregation and the enactment of civil rights legislation (for example, the end of miscegenation nationwide).

14. These narratives are not meant to be comprehensive but are merely a select sampling of Asian American works that are set in the South.

15. Typically, the "Old South" refers to life in the ex-confederacy states prior to and perhaps even during the Civil War; the "Old South," in other words, reflects antebellum values and a way of life that was swept away with the surrender at Appomattox and the era of Reconstruction. The *New South* typically refers to the period after the Civil War and the social and cultural changes that the loss entailed and the end of slavery augured.

16. For more on the history of early Manilamen, see Bautista's *Filipino Americans*.

17. Although I'm sure it goes without saying, the Manilamen engaged in interracial marriages because there were no Filipino women in the United States for them to marry. Indeed, significant numbers of Filipino women did not come to the United States until the early part of the twentieth century. For more on a history of Filipino migration and settlement to the United States, see Bautista's *Filipino Americans* and Takaki's Chapter 9 on Filipino Americans, "Dollar a Day, Dime a Dance," in *Strangers from a Different Shore*. And for a more contemporary account of the descendants of the eighteenth-century Manilamen, see Rena Tajima-Pena's excellent documentary, *My America or Honk if You Love Buddha*, in which she interviews a pair of Filipino sisters in New Orleans descended from the Manilamen.

18. Although it is beyond the scope of this article to discuss the history of violence in the South or within southern literature, the following works do record such a history, whether explicitly within their analysis and/or their content or implicitly in their handling of racial tensions and intimate relationships. For works focusing on southern history, see Franklin's *The Militant South, 1800–1861*; Ayers's *Promise of the New South*; Daniels's *Standing at the Crossroads*; and Brundage's *Southern Past*. For examples of southern literature, see William Faulkner's *Sound and the Fury* and *Absalom, Absalom!*; Smith's *Strange Fruit*; Angelou's memoir *I Know Why the Caged Bird Sings*; and Toni Morrison's *Beloved*.

19. For a more complete history of this legacy, see Angela Davis's *Women, Race and Class*.

20. The case of the Scottsboro Boys originated in 1931 when nine African American men were falsely accused of raping two white women in a train boxcar. Although one of the women recanted her accusation, and although various Northern civil rights attorneys attempted to overturn the initial judgment that would have resulted in the execution of all nine men, the charge of rape stuck and while the men did receive a stay of execution, all nine served varying degrees of incarceration, ranging from a minimum of six years to a maximum of twenty. The case of the Scottsboro Boys demonstrates the rampant and institutional racism in the South and the connection of violence with a politics of race and sex designed to cause terror among the African American population in this region.

21. Emmett Till was a teenager from Chicago visiting a relative in Monroe, Mississippi, when he was murdered by two white men for allegedly whistling at or making a suggestive comment to a white woman in August 1955. The two white men were brought to trial but were quickly acquitted by the all-white jury. The Till case, like the case of the Scottsboro Boys, became a symbol of rampant and violent racism associated with the hint of miscegenation. Furthermore, it galvanized the African American community and other people agitating for social justice and civil rights.

22. Although Bow is writing specifically about the Chinese community in the South, I believe her analysis can be broadened to include consideration of other Asian-ethnic groups and thus Asian Americans in the South, because whether it's Chinese Americans in the Mississippi Delta or Indian motel owners or Korean foreign exchange students, all of these nonwhite, nonblack, "yellow" and/or foreign bodies are read as neither black nor white and hence are given the place of racial interstitiality.

23. Bow, "Racial Interstitiality," 12.

24. Sumida, "East of California," 92.

25. For a historic examination of Asian, African, and Latin American connections to the South, see Jung's very thorough work, *Coolies and Cane*, and Guterl's engaging essay, "After Slavery."

26. For more on the history of Chinese in the Mississippi Delta, see Loewen's *Mississippi Chinese*; Quan's *Lotus among the Magnolias*; and *Mississippi Triangle*, directed by Choy, Long, and Siegel.

27. Chang's war scars result from the displacement of fleeing the invading Northern forces (he was a translator for U.S. news agencies), depravation of various sorts, and torture.

28. As noted above, Chang's scars result from the trauma of war; Katherine's scars come by way of an early sexual violation—at the age of fourteen she began an affair with a Sewanee English professor, Charles Addison, who was the best friend and peer of Katherine's father. Although Choi takes pains to describe the relationship as consensual—noting Katherine's crush on Addison and the development of their mutual attraction, Addison and Katherine's relationship is also described, by Choi, in violent terms. And the discovery of the affair leads to a split between Katherine and her family—one that is slow to heal and, again, is described violently. Furthermore, even though Katherine is tied to Addison at the beginning of the novel at age twenty-eight, in the words of one Sewanee resident, "she was just a child when he started with her. And he ruined her." Choi, *Foreign Student*, 162.

29. Ibid., 37.

30. Ibid., 15–16. What Crane tells Chang after observing his friendliness to Louis is "You can't be casual with them," which further confuses Chang about Sewanee social protocol but also alerts him to the racial differences and hierarchies in the South.

31. Ibid., 166–167. Actually, at the end of the novel, Chang is able to achieve a type of friendship with these men after he joins their ranks as a member of the kitchen staff, having been expelled from Sewanee and thus fallen in social status. However, Choi does not demonstrate any true interracial intimacy between Chang and anyone else but Katherine.

32. Additionally, there are several metaphors and analogies to "war" within the novel, enhancing the bellicose and violent tone of the scenes of Chuck's life during the Korean war. For instance, describing the older white housekeeper who cooks and cleans for Chuck and the other boys in the guest house, Katherine says: "This is Mrs. Wade's fortress, where she protects herself from you. It has to be that way. She loves you all and she lives for you, she has nothing else, and so she must feel a little embattled by you. She must feel she's at war." Choi, *Foreign Student*, 175.

33. Ibid., 281. Although this quote occurs right as the man first catches sight of Chang alone in Katherine's car, the man's gaze hardens and he cannot help but turn around and continue staring at Chang and Katherine, as Chang watches the man "turn slowly and begin walking, frequently looking back," a further indication that when he's alone, Chang is the recipient of hostility but paired with Katherine, they are both potential targets of racial violence.

34. Although Mina's father, Jay, tries to persuade Mina to attend college because she is too intelligent to remain a cleaning lady, Mina reminds her father that there is no shame in cleaning rooms and that despite his assertion that he has failed her as a father, she will think about attending college once his law suit against the Ugandan government is settled. In this manner, Nair shows true intimacy between father and daughter, both recognizing the aspirations of the other and attempting to bridge their current financial and social circumstances through their mutual love.

35. A scene from Mina's cousin's wedding reception shows a number of South Asian people, particularly younger people, in attendance; additionally, from the gossip surrounding Mina's dating life among the South Asian community in Greenville, it would appear that there isn't a shortage of eligible men for Mina to date, should she choose to date one of them. The eligibility of Indian American men is further enhanced by Mina's rejection of one potential suitor, Harry Patel.

36. Kum-Kum Bhavnani does an excellent job of summarizing the major reservations that critics have of the film by dividing the critiques into three major areas of concern: lack of racial consciousness, overly romanticized interracial relationship, and critique of gender. The critics whom Bhavnani most frequently cites are R. Rhadakrishnan, bell hooks, and Anuradha Dingwaney. For more, see the respective works of each of these critics on *Mississippi Masala*.

37. Mehta, "Emigrants Twice Displaced," 224–225.

38. As further evidence for the importance of understanding the particular connections between African and Indian diasporas, see Desai's work *Beyond Bollywood*, in particular Chapter 3, "When Indians Play Cowboys." Desai opens her chapter by reading W. E. B. Du-Bois's *Dark Princess* and its interracial romance that echoes the one in *Mississippi Masala*. Both narratives invoke the global South in order to highlight the diasporic connections

of the transatlantic slave trade—which are made all the more obvious in a U.S. southern locale like Mississippi, rather than in a cosmopolitan, urban location like Manhattan.

39. I'd like to thank the editors of this collection for pushing me to think about the significance of the South in this particular tale of interracial romance.

40. Seshagiri, "At the Crossroads of Two Empires," 187.

41. Indeed, both the South Asian and African diasporas are formed through networks of global labor. The transatlantic slave trade in fact paved the way for other forms of racialized labor, particularly from the Indian subcontinent, to Africa and the Caribbean—the global South if you will.

42. I use the adjective *cosmopolitan* to suggest the worldliness of Mina's family rather than their current economic situation. The fact that Mina's family has connections in both Great Britain and the United States that allow them to live a relatively comfortable lifestyle (in the sense that they can entertain the possibility of Mina going to college). Additionally, their educational capital, or Jay's at least, supports the sense of understanding the world beyond provincial borders that the word *cosmopolitan* also resonates with.

43. The issue of East Asian American concerns dominating Asian American Studies has been discussed at the annual meeting of the Association of Asian American studies, at least from the late 1990s to the present day, as is anecdotally evidenced by remarks made during the conference presentations I attended during the times I went to the annual meeting (and I have missed only two conferences since first attending in 1999). The number of Southeast Asian and South Asian studies that have emerged since the new millennium suggests a break in the East Asian American monopoly. For example, recent works of South Asian American narratives include the previously cited novels of Jhumpa Lahiri, as well as Chandra's *Red Earth and Pouring Rain*, Mukherjee's *Holder of the World*, and Nigam's *Transplanted Man*; the anthologies *Contours of the Heart* by Maira and Srikanth and *A Part Yet Apart* by Shankar and Srikanth; and *World Next Door* by Srikanth.

44. Rekdal, "Traveling to Opal," 192.

45. Ibid., 185. It is also important to note that the "accent" that marks Rekdal as a "foreigner" is her non-Southern accent, her "Yankee" voice rather than an "Asian"-inflected speech pattern.

46. Bow, "Racial Interstitiality," 26.

47. Rekdal, "Traveling to Opal," 186.

48. Ibid., 187.

49. For more details about Hattori's tragic death and the subsequent criminal and civil trials that followed, see Christine Choy's documentary *The Shot Heard Round the World* and a series of *New York Times* articles about the case: "Grief Spans Sea as Gun Ends Life Mistakenly," October 21, 1992; "After Gunman's Acquittal, Japan Struggles to Understand America," May 25, 1993; and "Judge Awards Damages in Japanese Youth's Death," September 16, 1994.

50. Rekdal, "Traveling to Opal," 198.

51. Ibid., 199.

52. Ibid., 188.

53. Ibid., 189.

54. Ibid., 201.

55. Ibid., 202.

56. Ibid., 205.

57. For more on the immigration and settlement histories of Chinese in America, see Kwong and Miscevic, *Chinese America*.

58. The prohibitions against racial intermarriage and even interracial friendships can be seen in the film *Mississippi Triangle*, where Chinese American young adults talk about their parents' prejudices against their dating (let alone marrying) black or white southerners, and the adults dodge the question of how they feel about their black neighbors and white neighbors. When the question of interracial dating and marriage is raised, it leads to uncomfortable laughter and a changing of the subject. For more on an analysis of the prejudices within the Chinese American community, particularly against African American interracial marriages, see Bow's "Racial Interstitiality and the Anxiety of the 'Partly Colored.'"

59. Rekdal, "Traveling to Opal," 206.

60. Ibid., 207.

61. This question, "Where are you from?," can be seen as a standard query of any visitor to a tourist site, but leveled at an Asian American person, it becomes the interrogative that evokes a weariness and wariness because one is never sure whether it is an innocent question about current residence or an attempt to find out ancestral origins. As law professor Frank Wu notes, "Where are you really from? Is a question some of us tend to ask others of us very selectively. . . . More than anything else that unites us, everyone with an Asian face who lives in America is afflicted by the perpetual foreigner syndrome. We are figuratively and even literally returned to Asia and ejected from America," 79.

62. Quotation taken from personal correspondence and commentary provided by anthology editor Jigna Desai, April 20, 2011.

63. Rekdal, "Traveling to Opal," 207–208.

64. Ibid., 208.

65. Ibid., 208.

Bibliography

Angelou, Maya. *I Know Why the Caged Bird Sings*. New York: Random House, 1969.

Ayers, Edward. *Promise of the New South: Life after Reconstruction*. New York: Oxford University Press, 1993.

Bankston, Carl. "Immigrants to the New South: An Introduction." *Sociological Spectrum* 23, no. 2 (April 2000): 123–128.

Bautista, Veltisezar. *The Filipino Americans From 1763 to the Present: Their History, Culture, and Traditions*. Farmington Hills, Mich.: Bookhaus Publishers, 1998.

Bhavnani, Kum-Kum. "Organic Hybridity or Commodification of Hybridity? Comments on *Mississippi Masala*." *Meridians: Feminism, Race, Transnationalism* 1, no. 1 (2000): 187–203.

Bow, Leslie. "Racial Interstitiality and the Anxiety of the 'Partly Colored': Representations of Asians under Jim Crow." *Journal of Asian American Studies* 10, no. 1 (February 2007): 1–30.

———. "Meditations on the Partly Colored." *Southern Review* 43, no. 1 (Winter 2007): 89–95.

Brundage, W. Fitzhugh. *The Southern Past: A Clash of Race and Memory*. Cambridge, Mass.: Belknap Press, 2005.

Chandra, Vikram. *Red Earth and Pouring Rain*. Boston: Little, Brown and Company, 1995.

Choi, Susan. *The Foreign Student*. New York: Harper Flamingo, 1998.

Christopher, Renny. *The Viet Nam War/The American War: Images and Representations in Euro-American and Vietnamese Exile Narratives*. Amherst: University of Massachusetts Press, 1995.

Daniel, Pete. *Standing at the Crossroads: Southern Life in the Twentieth Century*. Baltimore: The Johns Hopkins University Press, 1996.

Daughter from Danang. DVD. Directed by Gail Dolgin and Vincente Franco. Public Broadcasting System, 2002.

Davis, Angela. *Women, Race & Class*. New York: Vintage, 1983.

Desai, Jigna. *Beyond Bollywood: The Cultural Politics of South Asian Diasporic Film*. New York: Routledge Press, 2004.

Displaced in the New South. VHS. Directed by David Zeiger and Eric Mofford. Displaced Films, 1995.

DuBois, W. E. B. *Dark Princess*. New York: Harcourt Brace, 1928.

Faulkner, William. *The Sound and the Fury*. 1929. New York: Vintage, 1991.

———. *Absalom, Absalom!* 1936. New York: Vintage, 1991.

Franklin, John Hope. *The Militant South, 1800–1861*. Cambridge, Mass.: Belknap Press, 1956.

Guterl, Matthew Pratt. "After Slavery: Asian Labor, the American South, and the Age of Emancipation." *Journal of World History* 14, no. 2 (June 2003): 209–241.

Hart, Dave. "East Meets South." *Chapel Hill News*. April 21, 2004, and April 25, 2004.

hooks, bell, and Anuradha Dingwaney. "Sisters of the Yam: *Mississippi Masala*." *Z Magazine* 5 (July/August 1992): 41–43.

Jung, Moon-Ho. *Coolies and Cane: Race, Labor, and Sugar in the Age of Emancipation*. Baltimore: The Johns Hopkins University Press, 2006.

Kadohata, Cythnia. *The Floating World*. New York: Viking, 1989.

———. *Kira, Kira*. New York: Atheneum Books for Young Readers, 2004.

Kalnis, Arturs, and Wilbur Chung. "Social Capital, Geography, and Survival: Gujarati Immigrant Entrepreneurs in the U.S. Lodging Industry." *Management Science* 52, no. 2 (February 2006): 233–247.

Kim, Kwang Chung, Won Moo Hurh, and Marilyn Fernandez. "Intra-Group Differences in Business Participation: Three Asian Immigrant Groups." *International Migration Review* 23, no. 1 (Spring 1989): 73–95.

Kingston, Maxine Hong. *The Woman Warrior: A Childhood among Ghosts*. New York: Knopf, 1976.

———. *China Men*. New York: Knopf, 1980.

———. *Tripmaster Monkey: His Fake Book*. New York: Knopf, 1989.

Kwong, Peter, and Dusanka Miscevic. *Chinese America: The Untold Story of America's Oldest New Community*. New York: The New Press, 2005.

Lahiri, Jhumpa. *The Interpreter of Maladies*. Boston: Houghton Mifflin, 1999.

———. *The Namesake*. Boston: Houghton Mifflin, 2003.

Lee, Chang-rae. *Native Speaker*. New York: Riverhead Books, 1995.

———. *A Gesture Life*. New York: Riverhead Books, 1999.

———. *Aloft*. New York: Riverhead Books, 2004.

Lew, Bonnie. "'I always felt out of place there': Growing Up Chinese in Mississippi (1982)." In *Chinese American Voices: From the Gold Rush to the Present*, edited by Judy Yung, Gordon H. Chang, and Him Mark Lai, 281–291. Berkeley: University of California Press, 2006.

Loewen, James W. *The Mississippi Chinese: Between Black and White*. Cambridge, Mass.: Harvard University Press, 1971.

Maira, Sunaina, and Rajini Srikanth. *Contours of the Heart: South Asian Map North America*. New York: Asian American Writer's Workshop, 1996.

Mehta, Binita. "Emigrants Twice Displaced: Race, Color, and Identity in Mira Nair's *Mississippi Masala*." In *Screening Asian Americans*, edited by Peter Feng, 217–234. New Brunswick, N.J.: Rutgers University Press, 2002.

Mississippi Masala. DVD. 1992. Directed by Mira Nair. Columbia TriStar Home Video, 2003.

Mississippi Triangle. VHS. Directed by Christine Choy, Worth Long, and Allan Siegel. New York: Third World Newsreel, 1987.

Morrison, Toni. *Beloved*. New York: Knopf, 1987.

Mukherjee, Bharati. *The Holder of the World*. New York: Ballantine Books, 1994.

Murayama, Milton. *All I Asking for Is My Body*. San Francisco: Supa Press, 1975.

———. *Five Years on a Rock*. Honolulu: University of Hawaii Press, 1994.

———. *Plantation Boy*. Honolulu: University of Hawaii Press, 1998.

Muse, Eben. *The Land of Nam: The Vietnam War in American Film*. Lanham, Md.: Scarecrow Press, 1995.

My America or Honk if You Love Buddha. VHS. Directed by Renee Tajima-Pena. Sai Communications 1998.

New York Times. "Grief Spans Sea as Gun Ends Life Mistakenly." October 21, 1992.

Nigam, Sanjay. *Transplanted Man*. New York: HarperCollins, 2002.

Nossiter, Adam. "Judge Awards Damages in Japanese Youth's Death." *New York Times*. September 16, 1994.

Oxford English Dictionary. Second edition. Oxford: Oxford University Press, 1989.

Quan, Robert Seto. *Lotus among the Magnolias: The Mississippi Chinese*. Jackson, Mich.: University Press of Mississippi, 1982.

Radhakrishnan, R. "Is the Ethnic 'Authentic' in the Diaspora?" In *The State of Asian America: Activism and Resistance in the 1990s*, edited by Karin Aguilar-San Juan. Boston: South End Press, 1994.

Rekdal, Paisley. "Traveling to Opal." *The Night My Mother Met Bruce Lee: Observations on Not Fitting In*. New York: Pantheon Books, 2000. 182–209.

Sanger, David. "After Gunman's Acquittal, Japan Struggles to Understand America." *New York Times*. May 25, 1993.

Seshagiri, Urmila. "At the Crossroads of Two Empires: Mira Nair's *Mississippi Masala* and the Limits of Hybridity." *Journal of Asian American Studies* 6, no. 2 (June 2003): 177–198.

Shankar, Lavina, and Rajini Srikanth. *A Part Yet Apart: South Asians in Asian America*. Philadelphia: Temple University Press, 1998.

The Shot Heard Round the World. VHS. Directed by Christine Choy. New York: Filmmakers Library, 1997.

Smith, Lillian. *Strange Fruit*. New York: Harcourt Brace and Company, 1944.

Srikanth, Rajini. *The World Next Door: South Asian American Literature and the Idea of America*. Philadelphia: Temple University Press, 2006.

Sumida, Stephen. "East of California: Points of Origin in Asian American Studies." *Journal of Asian American Studies* 1, no. 1 (February 1998): 83–100.

Takaki, Ronald. *Strangers from a Different Shore*. Boston: Little Brown, 1989.

Truong, Monique. "Kelly." *Amerasia Journal* 17, no. 2 (1991): 41–48.

———. *Bitter in the Mouth: A Novel*. New York: Random House, 2010.

Varadarajan, Tunku. "A Patel Motel Cartel?" *New York Times*. July 4, 1999.

Verghese, Abraham. *My Own Country: A Doctor's Story*. New York: Vintage Books, 1995.

———. *The Tennis Partner*. New York: Harper Collins, 1999.

"Westie Side Story." *King of the Hill—The Complete First Season (1997)*. Created by Mike Judge. DVD. March 3, 1997. 20th Century Fox DVD, 2003.

Wu, Frank. *Yellow: Race in America beyond Black and White*. New York: Basic Books, 2002.

CHAPTER 9

"A Tennessean in an Unlikely Package"
The Stand-Up Comedy of Henry Cho

Jasmine Kar Tang

> "My name is Henry Cho. I am full-blooded Korean. I was born and raised here in Knoxville, Tennessee. So I'm South Korean."

> "I'm an Asian with a Southern accent. To a lot of people, that right there is funny."

I first heard Henry Cho over ten years ago at a Seattle comedy club. When Cho, who is Korean American, started his set, I was doubly struck by the sound of his voice—first because of his thick southern accent, and second because of its very familiarity. The setup to his opening joke then revealed that we shared the same hometown, and I was completely floored.[1] When I later introduced myself, Cho immediately asked, "What's your last name?" a reflection of how few Asian American families there were in east Tennessee during our respective upbringings. Years later, Cho released a comedy special, and his stand-up material continues to make me think about how Asian Americans from the U.S. South are seen as strange or out of place in the cultural imaginary and even among other Asian Americans.[2]

Drawing from the comedy special *What's That Clickin' Noise?* and news publications about his work, this essay takes seriously the comedy of Henry Cho, examining how he performatively manages his social location as a racialized Asian American of the U.S. South. While Leslie Bow examines "the intermediate space between white normativity and black abjection" occupied by Asian Americans in the South during Jim Crow,[3] the Asian American southerner like Henry Cho is caught in a contemporary web of liberal multiculturalism and discourses of colorblindness in a region of the country that is not typically associated with Asian bodies. Moving away from *anomaly* and *aberration* as a framework for viewing racialized subjects in cultural representation, Philip Deloria calls for a shift toward *frequency* and *unexpectedness*.[4] Something is unexpected when it has not happened that often; some*one* is unexpected when she or he seems to be a numerical minority. Cho's performance operates as a representation that refuses to be dismissed as an anomaly in the South and in Asian America.

Although Cho has been performing as a stand-up comedian since the 1980s, his career has especially been gaining ground over the last few years.[5] *What's That Clickin' Noise?*—his debut DVD comedy special—was filmed in Knoxville and released by Warner Brothers in 2006, premiering on the Comedy Central network. Cho regularly brings his stand-up comedy on tour to various cities around the country and has been featured on late night television shows.[6] He has also signed a deal with a major television network to produce a sitcom about a Korean American man from Tennessee in which "the pilot . . . will center on Cho's status as a Southerner who still sometimes feels like an outsider in the South."[7] Known for his "rare family-friendly" comedy,[8] Cho's style is based on observational humor about his family and friends, alongside his "Southern-fried humor" and brief jokes concerning his racial subjectivity.[9] As he has stated, "My act revolves around my life."[10]

A self-described "Tennessean in an unlikely package,"[11] Cho was once told by the creator of *The Tonight Show*, "Henry, . . . you know the old saying that there's no such thing as a new joke, well, Kid, you've got about 12. No one has ever come from your angle, no one, ever. They'll show up down the road now that you've established yourself, but you are an original."[12] This notion of being "original" can be predicated on Cho's anomalousness, but originality can also rest on un-expectedness. Framing Cho's performance in this way is not only grounded in geographic unexpectedness but also in the unexpected coupling of the physical body and the vocal sounds coming from it—that is, his accent. Additionally, moving Cho from anomaly to unexpectedness signals a focus on agency. Cho's performances as a stand-up comedian and as an actor, in addition to his remarks in numerous interviews, insist on dismantling the dichotomous constructions that render him as Asian and as southern. As one article notes, "By birth, he's Korean-American, but he's also a dyed-in-the-wool Southerner raised in Tennessee."[13] Moreover, while Cho's performance reflects a simultaneity around the articulation of Asian southerner identity, *What's That Clickin' Noise?* also troubles the black/white racial binary that is often attached to how we imagine the U.S. South. Thus, Cho's material speaks to a racial inbetweenness that pushes the boundaries and master narratives of not only what is American, but also what is southern and, notably, what is Asian American. Cho's management of his racial positionality is also quite fraught and full of contradictions, revealing the messiness of this negotiation. This essay considers the implications of the Asian American in the "unexpected places" of the South, particularly with respect to the formation of Asian southerner identities.[14]

"Just to Get Past the Obvious": The Function of Expected and Unexpected "Asian Jokes"

Cho begins and ends his comedy special with relatively predictable jokes that are explicitly related to his racial and ethnic social identities; his comedy often refutes stereotypes of Asian Americans through his Asian southerner identity, one that is inextricably embedded in the jokes themselves.[15] For example, Cho's first joke is about being Korean in the South and therefore, "South Korean."[16] Cho appears to use "Asian" and "Korean" interchangeably,[17] as he then sarcastically launches into how he "loves the Asian stereotypes," sharing his childhood experiences: "It's different growing up here [in east Tennessee], man. A lot of Asian people live here now. When I was growing up, I was it. I was the only one, man. Made it kind of tough when I was a little kid. Do you guys remember playing army when you were a kid? Pretty much hated that game, man." At this point the comedy special cuts to a shot of the audience, where it is hard not to notice a white male viewer laughing heartily. Cho then finishes the joke with, "All my buddies [were] goin', 'K, Henry, it's the neighborhood against . . . *you*." Yet this finishing statement is unnecessary: the man and his fellow audience members already know why Cho "hated that game."

What is happening in the editorial choice to feature a spectator's reaction to the army joke? The force of the man's unchecked laugh throws his head and upper body back into his seat. In the predominantly white audience of the Tennessee Theatre, this army joke appears to be very well-received, provoking widespread general laughter. It is perhaps a laughter of white guilt—of the audience members' discomfort about their own assumptions of Asians as foreigners, perhaps even a recognition of the absurdity of how racial differences and hierarchies are rendered in a children's game. Cho, born in the 1960s, grew up in a Vietnam War and post–Vietnam War era where Asians were visibly portrayed in U.S. popular culture not just as foreigners, but as enemies.[18] If it's a painful memory, then Cho masks it effectively. As sounding southern is a distinct way of sounding "American," Cho exposes the absurdity behind the idea that he could be an enemy, begging the question, how could someone with a southern accent be a foreigner, much less an enemy?

In this regard, the chuckle that results from watching Cho in action is fraught with many layers of meaning that ultimately speak to Cho's agency in the context of both Asian southerner identity and in deconstructing and further complicating the Asian American's state as a "forever foreigner" in dominant discourses. Deloria troubles the phenomenon of laughing—of "the chuckle": what makes people laugh, and who is laughing? Especially as it relates to minoritized subjects, the chuckle reveals the hierarchies of power inherent in the chuckler and the one being chuckled at. When it comes to cultural productions, the chuckle in response to Cho and other Asian American performers often draws upon Orientalist practices that render Asians as racial others. Deloria underscores the connection between the chuckle and a "history [that] contains a full share of malice and misunderstanding,"[19] but in *What's That Clickin' Noise?*, Cho is in control of the chuckle, creating it, provoking it, and ultimately using it in a way that articulates his identity as an Asian southerner. The genre of stand-up comedy also ensures this sense of control. Sometimes, the chuckle comes at the expense of Asian Americans, and at other times, it involves a recognition of racial stereotypes. While he inevitably speaks from his social locations as an Asian or Korean southerner, Cho's performance does not feature many stories that are explicitly concerned with him as a Korean American. As he states through the Comedy Central website, "I'll do some Asian jokes up front . . . just to get past the obvious. Then I move on—maybe throw in another one in the middle—and then I close with a story about my dad and me."[20] Transitioning to other, less "obvious" (read: less "Asian") jokes, Cho manages his social locations on his own terms while disrupting essentialist readings of his work.

"It's Not a Character, It's Me": The Incongruity of Body and Accent

From the moment he steps on stage, Cho's performance exhibits a seemingly mismatched embodiment of sight and sound. Aesthetically, the stark simplicity of the physical setting highlights Cho's Asian body.[21] *What's That Clickin' Noise?* features a bare stage with red curtains in the background; Cho is in a black dress shirt and blue jeans. His microphone and a glass of water on a stool are the only other noticeable objects. With a skillful comedic timing that is extremely measured yet effective, he is comfortable on stage, and his slow-paced delivery and lack of physical humor also signal how laid-back he is. This relaxed style, coupled with his accent, marks him as southern, and the focus is on his body and his voice. Thus, Cho's Asian body and the southern accent that comes from it force the audience to visually and aurally recognize his positionality as an Asian southern comedian. In the context of race, voice, and the body, Shilpa Davé and Sean Brayton, in their respective work, look for ways to decenter the privileging of the visual, pointing to the implications of considering both sight and sound in race and representation.[22] Henry Cho's stand-up comedy illuminates the inseparability of the body and voice. One California-based news article describes how Cho's southern accent in combination with his Asian body provokes a type of laughter that is predicated on the imagined corporeal dissonance of the visual and the aural:

> A Korean comic with a Southern accent released an album on a Country label [Warner Brothers Nashville]. Sound unlikely? Not to Henry Cho. Having grown up in East Tennessee, this fast-rising standup comic hasn't met a stereotype he couldn't debunk. Onstage and off, Cho has made a career of defying expecta-

tions. . . . [T]he combination of his Asian countenance and distinctly Southern way of speaking has been surprising people and making them laugh since his college days.[23]

Cho's "distinctly Southern way of speaking" does not reflect a "style shift," which, in Brayton's formulation, can involve the act of donning Asian ethnic accents in performance.[24] Thus, unlike English-speaking Asian comedians who affect accents in their humor,[25] Henry Cho's southern accent is his own, raising new questions about sound and authenticity in the study of Asian American performance and racial formation.[26]

For instance, upon hearing (and perhaps chuckling at) Cho's accent in the comedy special, one might wonder whether Cho's distinct accent is "real." This act of questioning the authenticity of Cho's accent accentuates his status as a racially in-between subject. As Cho once remarked, "We met these girls from Michigan and they thought I was mocking my buddies with my southern accent."[27] The question to ask is not whether Cho's accent is an affectation or a style shift. Rather, *why* do we pose this question in the first place? This is particularly compelling when we compare Cho to the enormously successful comedian Larry the Cable Guy, who fits every stereotype of the southerner: with his standard attire of a baseball cap and plaid flannel shirt with cut-off sleeves, his accent is extreme—the archetypal country accent. Yet Larry the Cable Guy is actually Dan Whitney, and in one stand-up comedy performance from years ago, Whitney has no distinctive southern accent and is introduced as himself, a native of Nebraska.[28] Indeed, "Larry the Cable Guy" is a character who comes alive on stage or in the movies: he is a persona developed and perfected by Whitney. This fact is well known, and in an interview with the news program *60 Minutes* where he reflects on his success as a comedian, Whitney's accent is still distinctly southern but less pronounced than "Larry's":[29] Whitney's use of a stereotypical and suggestively derogatory "redneck"-sounding southern accent for "Larry" marks a careful distinction that also implicitly evokes questions around the southern working class. I am not necessarily calling into question the authenticity of Whitney's accent. It's more about the quizzical look of disbelief that many experience in reaction to Cho's southern accent: as Cho explains, "A lot of people say, 'You've got a great character.' Well, it's not a character, it's me."[30] This disbelief clearly comes from the unexpectedness of a southern accent attached to an Asian body. Cho is invested in making clear that even when he is on stage, he should be read as "authentic."

"I'm a Southern Boy All the Way": The Implications of Identifying with the South

The inextricability of being simultaneously Asian and southern leads Cho to moments of uncertainty that emerge in multiple forms often around class and gender, beginning as early as the thematic choices in the comedy special's DVD menu. In its attempt to connect Cho to Blue Collar Comedy, the menu reveals a moment where, to cite Bow, "the need for reassurance [of Cho's southern-ness] unveils tenuousness."[31] The DVD menu takes as its theme the prototypical cowboy, an image that implicitly sets in motion normative constructions spe-cifically around American masculinity. The menu features a still shot of Cho set in a country-themed background with corresponding font and an instrumental country song titled "Guns of Laredo." Thus, the art direction situates Cho in this regionally ambiguous conflation of the South, the Southwest, and the Wild West; the net effect is that Cho is in an unexpected place for Asians.

Another section of the DVD menu then draws a connection between Cho and other purportedly southern comedians, specifically those of Blue Collar Comedy fame. Placed shortly after the opening credits of Cho's performance, an animated sequence begins with still headshot photographs of Blue Collar Comedy headlin-ers Larry the Cable Guy, Jeff Foxworthy, and Bill Engvall. In this short sequence, the trio is giving Cho a ride to the theater: incorporating his trademark phrase, Foxworthy proclaims, "If you're late for your own comedy special, you might be a redneck." Cho then steps out of his (animated) car, and the scene switches to the actual lobby of the Tennessee Theatre. This brief animated sequence legitimizes Cho's credibility with mainstream audiences (especially those familiar with Blue Collar Comedy). With comedy "so clean even grandma would approve," Cho, however, seems distinctly out of place.[32]

Originally featuring four white comedians (including the trio in the se-quence),[33] the Blue Collar Comedy brand, given its literal identification with the working class, evokes a sense of southernness among its audiences through the comedians' southern accents and "'redneck' humor."[34] The brand, especially with respect to Larry the Cable Guy, is marked by its crassness (e.g., "fart jokes") and deliberate lack of "political correctness" featuring uncouth humor through the hypermasculinity of heterosexist and misogynistic jokes.[35] Blue Collar appears to resonate with audiences that feel slighted by the multiculturalist turn in main-stream discourse, especially in such liberal phenomena as "political correctness." Furthermore, by aligning itself with whiteness, the racial politics of Blue Collar Comedy come through in how its comedians—"four good ol' boys"[36]—have performatively positioned themselves in contrast to the extremely successful tour and motion picture, *The Original Kings of Comedy*, which is based on the stand-up comedy of a team of four African American male veteran comedians, including Steve Harvey and Cedric the Entertainer.[37] In one racially coded segment of *Blue Collar Comedy Tour: The Movie*, the four white comedians, in a brazen attempt to mock "the Kings," don flashy suits, an exaggeration of what Steve Harvey and his colleagues wear in their own film. Thus, the two films share the same genre, but the similarities end there. *Blue Collar Comedy Tour: The Movie* has also been described in contrast to *Kings*: "Along the same lines as *The Original Kings of Comedy*, but marketed toward a radically different crowd, this comedy concert headlines the top names in so-called 'redneck' humor."[38] Through their marketed juxtaposition to the Original Kings of Comedy and through the stand-up material itself, Blue Collar Comedy caters to southern white male audiences.

What does Henry Cho's stand-up comedy have in common with the Blue Collar comedians? In preparation for the night that the comedy special was filmed, one article notes, "The Blue Collar/Jeff Foxworthy–type comedians have won over both the red and blue states. Cho says comedy is cyclical, and, at the moment, audiences are yearning for something less racy and more relatable."[39] In terms of comedic style, the connection between Cho and Blue Collar is not quite convincing: if Cho's comedy is marked as "family-friendly," Blue Collar is quite the opposite.[40] As one of Cho's longtime friends has remarked, "He has found a way to be successful without going the blue-[collar] comedy route."[41] Blue Collar's identity as not "clean," though, surpasses "fart jokes," and is directly related to its politics: it is difficult to overlook the misogynistic musings featured in Blue Collar Comedy performances by Bill Engvall, for example, or the overt heterosexism that Larry the Cable Guy relies on. Blue Collar Comedy and Henry Cho do at times participate in constructing various images of southerners, a common thread that persists alongside Blue Collar Comedy's intense misogyny and heterosexism. The Blue-Collar–Cho link appears to situate Cho's comedy in southernness, reflecting the need to establish his southernness in the first place and speaking to the unexpectedness of Cho's identification with the South. As he has also made clear elsewhere, "I'm a southern boy all the way."[42]

In *What's That Clickin' Noise?* Cho's identification with the South among non-Asian southerners can be contradictory: while he critiques racial stereotypes through what he calls "Asian jokes" (e.g., playing army), at other times Cho paradoxically employs stereotypes about Asians. Cho wrestles with his state of racial inbetweenness in a performative back-and-forth that also brings to light his discomfort as an Asian southerner among Asians. For example, Cho tells a story in which he ridicules someone who ignorantly assumed that all Asians must know—or want to be friends with—one another. Yet later in the comedy special, he jokes about his first trip to Korea: "Here in Knoxville, when I was growing up, we were the only Asian people. My dad's the only Asian man I'd ever seen before I went to Korea. So I'd always pick him out of any crowd like *that* [snaps fingers]. Well, this reversed on me in Korea. We got off the plane, he walked twenty feet away, and I just *lost* him." In this joke, perhaps a sense of Cho's insecurity is revealed and projected on the Asian body. While the joke may truly speak to his felt experiences of being part of a numerical minority in the U.S. South (he jokes about being the "only Asian guy in, like, four states"[43]), it also appeals and plays to the predominantly white audience at the Tennessee Theatre. A double move is performed: white audiences are relieved of their guilt in not making the effort to tell Asians apart, speaking to a "myth of interchangeability."[44] The joke also allows Cho to implicitly proclaim to his southern audience, "I'm one of you," as though he is insecure about where he stands. As he has shared elsewhere, "I don't really have any water. People always say you're a fish out of water. I don't fit in 100 percent with my southern buddies, and I don't fit in 100 percent with Korean people so I'm kind of an enigma with no water. People always say, 'Are you Korean or Tennessean' and I always say 'I'm a Tennessean in an unlikely package.'"[45] The "I lost my dad in Korea" joke, where Cho performatively acknowledges how he is more comfortable around whites than other Koreans, reveals a contradictory moment of tenuousness where Cho straddles and augments the false dichotomies constructed around his Asian southerner and Korean southerner social locations.

At the same time, when Cho clearly imitates his father's accent, the messiness ultimately ends with a joke that does contest the Korean/southerner binary. In one such instance of style-shifting, the joke lands well—almost too well, as Cho, shaking his head, puts his hand up with his palm toward the audience. As if to both cut short the laughter and move the joke forward, he says, "I'm not making fun of my dad. My dad is a brilliant man. He speaks five languages. He just dudn't speak any of 'em any good."[46] Through the use of a local and perhaps regional version of the word "doesn't," combined with the idiomatic phrase "any good," the joke also brings the South back into the picture when it comes to language, suggesting that "speaking well" goes both ways—for Koreans as well as southerners. For a brief moment, the Korean accent and southern accent are aligned: Cho's status as a Korean southerner is at the heart of the joke.[47]

"I Was a Bachelor My Entire Life before I Got Married": The Model Minority in the South

In Cho's move to claim the South, narratives around masculinity and the model minority converge. Using his male privilege, Cho tells many wife-and-kids jokes that articulate his overstated role as a domesticated husband to his spouse. Although these seemingly run-of-the-mill jokes are not unique in the world of comedy, Cho's performed status as the all-American "family man" serves a different purpose if we consider his social location as a straight Asian American man.[48] It is not simply that Cho's jokes about his relationship with his southern white wife suggest the possibility of the Asian American man as a masculine, sexual being in the U.S. cultural imaginary.[49] Invariably interpellated as a model minority, Cho remains a "safe" and more desirable alternative to black/white interracial marriage to the mostly white audience, and whether he wishes to or not, his positionality serves to alleviate southern white guilt. With his "suave southern accent,"[50] Cho is clean-cut, physically appealing, and his jokes are distinctly not "racy," earning him the nickname "Mr. Clean."[51] In the face of historic antimiscegenation sentiment in the United States, Cho is far from a threat to the sanctity of the white woman and is in fact an ideal partner, and this is further achieved by the fact that he often jokes about his deference to his wife. As one reviewer has remarked, "Everybody likes relationship jokes and stand-up material about being married."[52] Cho muses, "I want to win one argument before I die, one argument with my wife, just one. . . . They could just put that on my headstone, you know, 'He won one. This was it.'" Clearly, his wife is the dominant partner. To revisit Blue Collar Comedy, the *New York Times* has noted, "The comedian Jeff Foxworthy's Southern shtick operates on the assumption that masculinity is an endangered commodity, under threat from feminists, gays and contemporary life in general, and that relationships between men and women are based on deceit and manipulation."[53] If Foxworthy works from a notion of an "endangered" masculinity, Cho's brand of masculinity takes a racialized turn through his wife-and-kids jokes in which he consistently praises his wife and the value of marriage: in short, Cho's palatable, downtrodden form of masculinity satisfies audiences. Cho is an Asian American of the South in a contemporary moment where mainstream racial discourse lies in colorblindness, when white audiences watching performers of color want to "see past race." Although this is complicated by the fact that stand-up comedy often relies on jokes that do point out difference, the racially in-between Cho is posited as "innocent, approachable, and everyman,"[54] embodying a comparatively "safe" site of difference.

The model minority narrative is inevitably attached to Cho's image, appearing in popular news sources and in his performance. As he jokes in a question-and-answer bonus track of the comedy special, "There are sixteen doctors in the family. I hate the family reunion." If the notion of the model minority involves the idea of excelling in the educational system through arduous years of hard work based on some notion of Asian cultural values and work ethic, Cho's success as a stand-up comedian puts a different spin on the narrative. Instead of being an overachiever in school, Cho opted for a completely different route. He is not only funny, but he is a college dropout. As a sixth-year college undergraduate in the 1980s, Cho entered a local comedy club competition:[55] "When Cho walked off the stage, the owner of the Funny Bone Comedy Clubs offered him a spot hosting the show for the rest of that week. By Friday, he had decided to drop out of college."[56] Cho has also acknowledged the unexpectedness of his career choice, citing his father as one of his "heroes": "He [Cho's father] came to this country as an eighteen year old who spoke no English, earned two doctorates . . . one generation later I get to do comedy!!"[57] News features also often stress how Cho broke away from family expectations: an article entitled, "They Couldn't Dub Him Dr. Comedy," states, "He was without much of a career direction when he was a college student. Once he became a comedian, though, he says he was the first member of his traditional Korean family not to be a doctor."[58] Thus, buried in the notion of how Cho is the anomaly of a "traditional Korean family," another narrative emerges: the overachieving, dual-doctorate father enables the son to pursue his own American dream. In the end, these articles and interviews suggest that Cho, in departing from his "sixteen doctors in the family" background, is perhaps more "American," different from his "traditional Korean family." Cho, the college dropout, and his father, the dual-doctorate dad, are frequently referenced in news sources, a moment that exposes the persistence of both the model minority and forever foreigner narratives in Cho's career.[59]

Assuming a southern in-group posture, Cho performatively brushes off this model minority narrative by unexpectedly evoking its southern counterpart: the stereotype of the southern-accented southerner as dumb and uneducated. Later in the performance, he affectionately pokes fun at a southerner named J. B., notably as a cultural insider and as a friend to J. B., *not* as a nonsoutherner looking down on a southerner. Cho's embodied racial difference, in combination with the fact that he is at ease and commanding in his own skin, refuses the notion of "the Asian/Southern contradiction," as one newspaper calls it.[60] His body will be read as intelligent ("Asians are smart"), but his accent will not ("southerners sound dumb"). When a kindergarten teacher predicts that one of Cho's sons will attend an Ivy League university one day, Cho quips to the audience, "Well, I can't afford that. I've gotta keep him down. 'Here's a Gameboy. Go learn a skill.'" Thus, this joke and other lines such as, "I was a bachelor my entire life before I got married," merge the smart-Asian/dumb-southerner juxtaposition, simultaneously drawing attention to and refuting the model minority stereotype through the performance of dumbness.

In-group humor also takes an unexpected turn, demonstrating how Cho aligns himself with the South in the midst of class stratification. Cho's stories about his friend J. B. further underscore this point. He talks at length about how "stupid" J. B. is, joking that because J. B's initials stand for no underlying referent names (it is his birth name), J. B. formally wrote "J. only, B. only" on his driver's license application, earning himself the nickname "Jonly" (pronounced "Jone-lee"). Thereafter, Cho refers to J. B. as "Jonly" or "Jonly Bonly" ("Jone-lee Bone-lee"), and Jonly jokes are interspersed throughout the performance. Cho comfortably claims the South through Jonly, who is in fact a primary character in the show, and when channeling what Jonly says, Cho noticeably uses a heavier accent in imitation. Moreover, in a live recording, the sound of the nickname's syllables articulated through Cho's own southern accent has the inexplicable effect of provoking bigger laughs: we hear "the southern" come through loud and clear in what will lead to arguably the most well-received joke of the night, one that people frequently refer to on Cho's fan sites: given *Star Trek*'s famous line, "To boldly go where no man has gone before," Jonly is so "stupid" that he assumed "boldly go" is a place, a proper noun. He is now "Jonly Bonly from Boldly Go." The joke is well executed and shows Cho at his best: he is not making fun of southerners as an outsider. Rather, he is poking fun at and chuckling with his own—with fellow southerners. In a moment of unexpectedness, audiences anticipate his "Asian jokes" but instead, they get southern jokes from an insider. While Cho turns anomaly into unexpectedness, he achieves this shift by relying on a classist stereotype that seems to match his voice more than his body. As he has noted, "My main audience is college kids and college-educated adults,"[61] and the imagined dissonance of his body and voice emerges again, as Cho asserts his southern status by incorporating and sometimes actually assuming the image of the dumb southerner—the southern "redneck." Embodying a conflation of class status and the South, this figure further reflects Cho's performative resistance to the Asian/southerner dichotomy. Reinforcing Cho's status as a Korean southerner, one of the final jokes of the night is Jonly's response to Cho's trip to Korea: "That's just like going to a different country." "Jonly Bonly from Boldly Go" is so central that the DVD is named after him: "What's that clickin' noise?" is what Jonly asked when Cho used the turn signal in his car one day. The fact that the DVD title comes from Jonly cannot be missed: Cho's hook is being "south Korean" because he's a "full-blooded Korean" from the South. The "Jonly Bonly" jokes drive home this point: the South is home. Through the use of a southern stereotype, Cho's performance reconfigures dominant narratives of the South and of southerners.

"Bless Her Heart": Performing the Simultaneity of Asian Southerner Identity

Like Deloria, who looks "to make a hard turn from anomaly to frequency and unexpectedness,"[62] Cho is able to use his visibly and aurally anomalous status as an Asian American from the South to counter the stereotypes and expectations placed on Asian Americans, carving out a space for himself as an unexpected Asian southerner. For example, once in Arab, his wife's Alabama hometown (pronounced, "A'-raab," as he makes clear), Cho recalls, "So just for fun, I took my whole family to Wal-Mart. And we just started walking around. 'What are you staring at? We just bought this place.'" We might read Cho's performance as somewhat self-exotifying; however, fully aware of his interpellated forever foreigner status, Cho breaks through in this Wal-Mart joke, as he turns it around on the white southern subject. Similarly, Cho relays that when ordering from the menu at a restaurant back in the United States, his father inadvertently mispronounces "quiche" as "quickie," and the audience erupts with laughter. Noticeably, though, Cho trails off saying his dad now does it on purpose: "Of course to this day he still knows what it means, but he orders it the same way." Like his son, the Korea-born father understands how he is interpellated and now plays with it, deliberately ordering "quickies" at restaurants. The sexual undertones are completely unexpected by the waitress and by the audience, particularly in light of the father's own status as an elderly Asian male.

Cho's unexpected articulation of his place as an Asian southerner reaches its performative height in a joke that concerns his southern mother-in-law. He prefaces the story by sharing that his mother-in-law taught him how the phrase "bless your heart" can be used to shield the abrasiveness of insults. Displaying a mastery of what might be marked as a southern expression,[63] Cho jokes that following an insult about someone with "bless his heart" excuses the meanness: "Look at that ugly baby. Bless its heart." The story begins when he brings his father to Arab, Alabama, to meet the in-laws for the first time. (Throughout the performance, Cho references his wife's hometown, Arab, characterizing it as "a little bitty town. All white people. All the time. Except the day we got married.") As Cho tells the story, when the mother-in-law met Cho's father, she haltingly shouted, "HEL-LO. MIS-TER. CHO! HOW. ARE. YEEW?!" Cho, without losing his southern accent, relays that his father then asked him, "What is she doin'?" speaking to the narrow-mindedness of the mother-in-law's assumptions about the father's English skills. Cho responds, "Well, she thinks she's speaking Korean." Amid the audience's laughter, Cho then walks across the stage and takes a sip of water, shaking his head and punctuating the applause with his finishing line: "Bless her heart." The audience explodes, and like the childhood army joke, Cho has exposed the absurdity of the situation (this time of his mother-in-law's ridiculous affectations) to an appreciative audience, using the very expression that his mother-in-law supposedly taught him. As Cho concludes, "It's a true story. . . . She still yells at the man." The success of the "bless her heart" joke demonstrates how Cho's Asian and Korean identities are inextricable from his southern identity.

The final joke of the comedy special involves Cho's trip to Korea, one that ultimately relies on Cho's status as a Korean southerner. He recounts that an American woman asked him at the bus stop, "Is this the bus-EE that goes-EE down-EE town-EE?" Cho's enunciation makes clear that the woman, perhaps in a stronger manner than the mother-in-law, spoke in a loud, infantilizing way. The woman's question also exudes characteristics of what linguist Elaine Chun calls *Mock Asian*, "an imagined variety of American English" that involves "a stereotypical Asianness that unambiguously mocks Asians, rather than being characteristic of 'realistic' impersonations of Asian speech."[64] Cho then performatively refutes this condescending manner of speaking, responding, "I reckon so . . . bless your heart." In this instance, Cho's "bless your heart" subtly calls out the American woman's silly and insulting way of speaking English to someone who, in her mind, would not understand her otherwise. Thus, Cho's response may simultaneously express his unease about how he is not usually associated with southernness ("I reckon so"), as well as his control over the situation ("Bless your heart"). This Tennessee Theatre audience nods and claps heartily with approval. They appreciate his identification with the South: he not only responds to the woman in English (and in his own accent, of course), but he also uses what is arguably marked as a southern expression. Though we do not know if this woman is a southerner, it doesn't matter for this hometown crowd: in this story, Cho is their man—the southerner—and that's all that matters. With this, Cho thanks the audience and leaves the stage. The audience is left with the lasting impression of Cho as the southern-twanged Korean from the South.

Though it is his hook ("the best hook since Rodney Dangerfield," he's been told[65]), Cho does not wish to be known only as "the Asian southern comic. I wanted to be a comic."[66] Cho has mentioned that his jokes about his so-called Asianness have decreased over time as he has gained popularity: "When I first started out I had many jokes and made many references to my upbringing. Nowadays I'll do an hour show and not do any Asian jokes."[67] He spends the first two minutes of *What's That Clickin' Noise?* on "Asian jokes," distinctly ending this segment with, "There you go. There's your three Asian jokes. Take 'em home with ya." It is not that Cho avoids or minimally plays into Asian American subjectivity, however: his racial/ethnic subjectivity (as his performance often conflates the two) is embedded even in his anecdotal jokes, giving rise to a performance predicated on being an Asian southerner on his own terms. Cho also resists being typecast as a "country comic," as well.[68] Thus, in his interviews, Cho consistently has to contend with either/or constructions of being an Asian southerner.[69]

Cho's resistance to this simplistic construction also surfaces in his work beyond stand-up comedy. For example, Cho turned down an acting role that demanded "broken English," but he also accepted one that called for an exaggerated country accent. On a panel discussion on race and humor, Cho remarked:

> I've been pitching shows for years, and I've heard networks say, "Why don't you write a character like Ms. Swan into your show [played by a white actor in yellowface and speaking in Mock Asian, Ms. Swan was an Asian racial caricature on *MadTV*[70]]?" I've left the table every time. A few years ago, I had this great script in which Pat Morita would play my dad, a widower that I would teach how to date again. It was very funny. They said it'd actually be funnier if I spoke broken English. No it wouldn't. It has nothing to do with it. So I walked. Pat called me and said, "I would have done it." Trust me, if I was waiting tables and I had to do it to make a living, I may have sold out a decade ago. Fortunately, I was very successful at standup comedy, and I make a living doing what I love.[71]

Conversely, Cho plays a character in another film in which he speaks in an accent that is a distinct exaggeration of his own in real life: in *Say It Isn't So*, Cho has a minor role playing a southern stereotype. His character, "Freddy," is a troublemaker with an exaggerated country accent that easily and derogatorily marks him as uneducated and "redneck."[72] Why is "broken English" off limits to Cho while a stereotypical country accent is acceptable? Cho's avoidance of Asian stereotypes at least in film and television comes through, but so does an implicit insistence on being seen as Asian and southern, all at once. When playing southern-accented characters, the interpellation of Cho as an Asian southerner is a given: his body is a site of racial difference. Unlike a role with "broken English," Cho's over-the-top character in *Say It Isn't So* reflects the performed simultaneity of the Asian southerner that the comedy special also demonstrates.[73]

Conclusion: "Every Show I Create, I Have Control"

Seeing and hearing Henry Cho in the flesh so many years ago has since become a fun memory for me. It would complete my anecdote to say that our families have known each other for years, but we never met in the east Tennessee landscape. The presence of Asian bodies in the South continues to evoke double-takes figuratively (and sometimes literally), and amid the perceived strangeness of Asian Americans in the region, Cho's material in *What's That Clickin' Noise?* reveals that he is in control of his image through his performance: he has the last laugh, an agential chuckle that relies on his Asian southerner identity. He has remarked, "Every show I create, I have control."[74] Cho's representation of his racial subjectivity reveals how he carefully manages others' expectations of him. The audience's chuckling, which is simultaneously with *and* in response to Cho, bridges the interpellated foreignness of his body with the demonstrated domesticity of the southern accent. The resulting tension that is produced by the unexpected coupling is alleviated by Cho's chosen performance genre—stand-up comedy—that actually facilitates the chuckle and encourages outbursts of laughter. The use of humor by a racialized subject in performance can mitigate discomfort about racial difference among mainstream white audiences.[75] Thus, the stand-up comedy of Henry Cho presents an especially rich site of study when we consider how accents and jokes operate as markers and articulations of belonging.

Cho's comedy—and the messy contradictions that come with it—attest to the challenges in pulling away from what Jon Smith and Deborah Cohn describe as the "pernicious either/or habit common in the formation of imagined communities" especially in constructions of the South, as they push for ways "to talk about region without talking about essential identities or 'heritage.'"[76] My claims here represent a counterargument to the facile conclusion that Cho's identification with the South is overall in excess, is somehow inauthentic, or that it represents a forced sense of American and/or southern identity. It would also be too convenient to conclude that Cho's identification with the South signifies an escape from "Asianness," so to speak. Cho's performative choices in *What's That Clickin' Noise?* reflect a "both-and" (not an "either/or") approach to understanding his positionality. Cho's performance does not work to establish what it definitively means to be an Asian southerner: he does nothing to claim a representative voice for Asian Americans in the South. Thus, rather than argue for an Asian southerner subjectivity or authenticity, I hope this analysis speaks to a more productive site of inquiry: how the stand-up comedy of Henry Cho complicates and challenges dominant narratives of the U.S. South and Asian America.

Notes

I thank Jigna Desai and Khyati Joshi for their helpful feedback and the opportunity to contribute to this anthology. I am also deeply appreciative of Lauren Curtright, Juliana Hu Pegues, Josephine Lee, Emily Smith Beitiks, and especially Darren Lee for their encouragement and critique on multiple drafts.

1. *What's That Clickin' Noise?* DVD, dir. Alan C. Blomquist (Nashville: Warner Brothers, 2006).

2. "Henry Cho: Actor, Comedian, Rancher," Cho Industries, 2006, http://www.choindustries .com (accessed April 1, 2008).

3. Leslie Bow, "Racial Interstitiality and the Anxieties of the 'Partly Colored': Representations of Asians under Jim Crow," *Journal of Asian American Studies* 10, no. 1 (2007): 6.

4. Philip J. Deloria, *Indians in Unexpected Places* (Lawrence: University Press of Kansas, 2004).

5. Cho has been doing stand-up comedy since 1986. H. Y. Nahm, "Comedy's Southern Squire: Henry Cho's Jaw-Dropping Accent was the Springboard for a Roaring Comedy Career," *Goldsea: Asian American Daily*, November 19, 2007, http://goldsea.com/Personalities/ Chohenry/chohenry.html (April 1, 2008) (accessed March 18, 2013).

In September 2011, the Great American Country network premiered *The Henry Cho Show*, a sketch comedy show featuring Cho hosting and starring in a production reported to be "a modern day version of 'The Carol Burnett Show' and a clean take on 'Saturday Night Live.'" At the time of this essay's publication, there have been no additional episodes. The inability for the show to continue beyond the pilot can arguably be attributed to several factors (for example, perhaps Cho's forte lies more in stand-up, not sketch, comedy), and while *The Henry Cho Show* is beyond the scope of this essay, its articulation of Asian southerner identities is worth further examination. Terry Morrow, "Henry Cho to Headline Pilot for GAC Series," *Tele-Buddy's Tinseltown Tales*, Scripps Interactive Newspapers Group, August 8, 2011, http://blogs.knoxnews.com/telebuddy/archives/2011/08/knoxville-celebrities-henry- cho-standup-comedy-tv-series.shtml (accessed March 29, 2012).

6. Henry Cho, Home page, Myspace.com, http://myspace.com/henrycho (November 19, 2007) (accessed March 18, 2013).

7. "Henry Cho Presents Comedy for Everyone," *Chattanooga Times Free Press*, October 25, 2009, http://www.timesfreepress.com/news/2009/oct/15/henry-cho-presents-comedy -for-everyone/ (accessed June 15, 2010).

8. David Jeffries, "What's That Clickin' Noise? Henry Cho," Review of *What's That Clickin' Noise?* dir. Alan C. Blomquist, *All Music*, http://www.allmusic.com/cg/amg.dll?p =amg&sql=10:fzfixqwdldfe~To (accessed July 15, 2008).

9. Terry Morrow, "Hometown Comic Says His Humor's So Clean Even Grandma Would Approve," *Knoxville News Sentinel*, November 4, 2005, 17.

10. Terry Morrow, "A Clean-talking Cuss: In 19-year Career, Knox Comic Says He's Never Relied on Racy Material," *Knoxville News Sentinel*, December 2, 2005, 4.

11. Christina Shams, "Stand-Up Sit-Down: Henry Cho," *NBC Dallas-Fort Worth*, June 4, 2010, http://www.nbcdfw.com/around-town/events/Standup-Sit-Down-Henry -Cho-95630584.html (accessed June 15, 2010).

12. Steve Allen, as quoted in Nahm, "Comedy's Southern Squire," 2.

13. Anthony Sclafani, "Columbia Arts Fest Has Henry Cho, for Starters," *Howard County Times*, May 7, 2009, http://www.explorehoward.com/news/61815/columbia-arts-fest-has -henry-cho-starters (accessed June 15, 2010).

14. Deloria, *Indians in Unexpected Places*.

15. I am choosing to use "Asian" and not "Asian American" because Cho describes himself in this way. I am also using "southerner" as well, based on how he describes his background and how news sources describe him.

16. In numerous recordings of him online, Cho uses this as his first joke. For example, see Sonia Baghdady, Interview with Henry Cho, *Wtnh.com*, October 5, 2007, http://www.wtnh.com/Global/story.asp?S=7174360 (accessed November 19, 2007).

17. When the joke has to do with Korea or the Korean language, he mentions his ethnicity. In most other jokes he uses "Asian." Hereafter I will base my usage on Cho's own articulation of his experiences as an Asian southerner and/or Korean southerner.

18. See Robert G. Lee, *Orientals: Asian Americans in Popular Culture* (Philadelphia: Temple UP, 1999).

19. Deloria, *Indians in Unexpected Places*, 4.

20. Comedians A-Z, "Henry Cho," Comedy Central, http://www.comedycentral.com/comedians/browse/c/henry_cho.jhtml (accessed April 1, 2008).

21. Recognizing that the notion of an "Asian body" is a social construction, I use this term to point out how Cho is racialized because of his physical appearance. Cho's stand-up comedy performance perhaps speaks to Josephine Lee's discussion of the "borders of the body": analyzing plays by Asian American playwrights, she notes how the "characters wrestle with the perceived limits of the body and its inability to pass beyond the barriers of race and ethnicity as categories defining and confining the body" (215). In this essay, I also employ the term *body* in a way that is distinct from "voice" and "accent" (i.e., other forms of embodiment) because descriptions of Cho's stand-up comedy frequently suggest a juxtaposition of his southern accent to his Asian body. Josephine Lee, *Performing Asian America: Race and Ethnicity on the Contemporary Stage* (Philadelphia: Temple UP, 1997).

22. Shilpa Davé, "Apu's Brown Voice: Cultural Inflection and South Asian Accents," in *East Main Street: Asian American Popular Culture*, eds. Shilpa Davé, LeiLani Nishime and Tasha G. Oren (New York: New York UP, 2005), 313–336. Sean Brayton, "Race Comedy and the 'Misembodied' Voice," *Topia* 22 (2009): 97–116.

23. Peter Cronin, "New Artist Spotlight: Henry Cho," *California Chronicle*, October 14, 2006, http://www.californiachronicle.com/articles/viewArticle.asp?articleID=14855 (accessed April 1, 2008).

24. Brayton, "Race Comedy and the 'Misembodied' Voice," 97.

25. For example, Brayton analyzes the style shifting of Margaret Cho and Russell Peters.

26. For example, Krystyn Moon has noted how language, including accent, was one of the "theatrical practices" that Chinese and Chinese American vaudevillians used to manage white expectations of their performances (151). Krystyn R. Moon, *Yellowface: Creating the Chinese in American Popular Music and Performance, 1850s-1920s* (New Brunswick, N.J.: Rutgers UP, 2005).

27. Nahm, "Comedy's Southern Squire," 1.

28. "Larry the Cable Guy, also known as Dan Whitney," 2006, http://youtube.com/watch?v=VROn7ZvVoW8 (accessed April 1, 2008).

29. Bob Simon, Interview with Larry the Cable Guy, *60 Minutes*, April 15, 2009, http://www.cbsnews.com/video/watch/?id=4948849n (accessed February 24, 2013).

30. Glenn Doggrell, "Comedy: Henry Cho: Never out of Character," *Los Angeles Times*, April 28, 1994, http://articles.latimes.com/1994-04-28/news/ol-51374_1_henry-cho (accessed June 15, 2010).

31. Bow, "Racial Interstitiality," 17.

32. Morrow, "Hometown Comic Says His Humor's So Clean."

33. The fourth is Ron White, who eventually left the group. This discussion refers to the first (and most well known) generation of Blue Collar Comedy, a brand that involved a highly successful tour; the *Blue Collar TV* sketch comedy television show, which lasted two seasons; and three films, including the 2003 *Blue Collar Comedy Tour: The Movie*.

34. Andrea LeVasseur, "Blue Collar Comedy Tour: The Movie," *All Movie*, http://www .allmovie.com/work/the-blue-collar-comedy-tour-movie-270865 (accessed June 15, 2010). Blue Collar Comedy is often perceived to reflect a southern identity, whether or not this is made explicit in the comedy itself. For example, one review states, "While Cho's reflections on his Tennessee upbringing might endear him to the Foxworthy and Larry the Cable Guy crowd, he's not nearly as obsessed with Southern living." Although I would contend that "Southern living" is a central component of Cho's performance, this review nonetheless makes clear that Cho, Foxworthy, and Larry the Cable Guy, for example, are distinctly associated with the South. See Jeffries, "What's That Clickin' Noise?"

35. As Larry the Cable Guy has remarked, "The only people who are uptight at my shows are politically correct white people." Regarding his fan base, "Larry" notes, "My crowd is good, honest, hard-working Americans. . . . They don't hate anybody, they just want to enjoy themselves, and they're not into that PC crap." "Larry's" act has included intense, no-holds-barred displays of homophobia, in addition to mocking other minoritized subjectivities such as people with disabilities. See Gavin Edwards, "Larry the Cable Guy Bared: The New King of Comedy Plugs into Red-State Fervor," *Rolling Stone*, April 26, 2005, http://www .rollingstone.com/news/story/7277749/larry_the_cable_guy_bared (accessed April 2, 2008).

36. Rodney Ho of *Atlanta Journal-Constitution*, as quoted on the DVD front cover of *Blue Collar Comedy Tour: The Movie*.

37. Bernie Mac and D. L. Hughley are the other two. The movie was released in 2000.

38. Andrea LeVasseur, "Blue Collar Comedy Tour: The Movie."

39. Morrow, "A Clean-talking Cuss."

40. Jeffries, "What's That Clickin' Noise?"

41. Morrow, "A Clean-talking Cuss."

42. "Meet Henry Cho: America's Favorite Comedian," *Georgia Asian Times*, September 20, 2007, http://gasiantimes.com/sept07/q&asept15.07.htm (accessed December 18, 2007).

43. Doggrell, "Comedy: Henry Cho."

44. Lee, *Performing Asian America*, 17.

45. Shams, "Stand-Up Sit-Down."

46. Like many Tennesseans, Cho generally pronounces "doesn't" as "dudn't" in his show, but I spell out Cho's pronunciation here to demonstrate that a southern pronunciation of an English word may not be "correct," either.

47. Cho has also stated, "I've turned down countless roles where they wanted me to speak broken English as a stereotypical derogatory character." Thus, Cho adamantly refuses "broken English" roles but also imitates his father's accent in his stand-up comedy. Although performing "broken English" may be different from affecting his father's accent, a contradiction remains in Cho's decision about whether to use accents that are interpellated as Asian or Korean. Shams, "Stand-Up Sit-Down." For a closer look at the implications of the performance of accents that are marked as Asian, see Elaine W. Chun, "Ideologies of Legitimate Mockery: Margaret Cho's Revoicings of Mock Asian," *Pragmatics* 14, no. 2/3 (2004): 263–289.

48. Emily Steele, "Henry Cho—Funny Man, Family Man," *Dream Row Magazine*, June 1, 2010, http://dreamrow.com/2010/06/henry-cho-funny-man-family-man (accessed June 15, 2010).

49. I attended a performance where Cho directly stated that his wife is white. Performance, *Henry Cho*, by Henry Cho, South Point Casino, Las Vegas. March 17, 2012. Also, in one interview, Cho is directly asked about whether his wife is also Korean American. He does not answer directly but notes, "She is from Arab, Alabama, which is a town of zero color—of any kind. . . . People ask occasionally how it is in a mixed marriage. I say it's tough [']cause she's an Alabama fan and I'm a Tennessee fan—big college football rivalry. That's the only part of our marriage that is 'mixed.'" See Nahm, "Comedy's Southern Squire," 5.

Also, Cho's performance reveals that he is aware of the emasculation of Asian men in the United States, as revealed in an early joke about his childhood: "We used to play a lot of 'Cowboys and Indians.' Didn't we, guys? Cowboys and Indians. You guess I hated this game, too, man. I was always the cook."

50. Shams, "Stand-Up Sit-Down."

51. "Meet Henry Cho," *Georgia Asian Times*.

52. Review of *What's That Clickin' Noise?* dir. Alan C. Blomquist. The Serious Comedy Site, July 15, 2008, http://www.theseriouscomedysite.com/showreview.php?r_id=690 (accessed March 18, 2013).

53. Susan Stewart, "Just a Good Old Boy, Traversing Familiar Old Comic Territory," *New York Times*, October 20, 2006, E29.

54. Jeffries, "What's That Clickin' Noise?"

55. "Meet Henry Cho," *Georgia Asian Times*.

56. Comedians A-Z, "Henry Cho."

57. Henry Cho, Home page. Myspace.com.

58. Terry Morrow, "They Couldn't Dub Him Dr. Comedy," *Knoxville News Sentinel*, December 2, 2005, 4.

59. The forever foreigner narrative so often experienced by Asian Americans is not lost on Cho, following him into his career as a comedian. Cho has recalled that in one performance for a corporate audience in Tennessee, he was asked about his Korean language fluency before entering the stage. After responding that he is American-born and not bilingual, Cho then found out "that the audience was all Koreans and none of them spoke English." Saved by a translator, the performance was still a success. The forever foreigner narrative seems inescapable, but Cho manages to make do. See Henry Cho, "I Said What?" *I Killed: True Stories of the Road from America's Top Comics*, eds. Ritch Shydner and Mark Schiff (New York: Crown, 2006), 166–167.

60. Doggrell, "Comedy: Henry Cho."

61. Morrow, "A Clean-talking Cuss."

62. Deloria, *Indians in Unexpected Places*, 6.

63. For example, one article about Cho begins with, "If you've lived in the south . . . for more than five minutes, you are familiar with the cardinal rule; you can say anything about anybody, no matter how rude or insulting, as long as you follow it up with the phrase, 'Bless his heart.' Seriously! As a bonafide Yankee . . ., I was used to verbally bashing people and leaving it at that. I had no idea that those three little words could absolve you of any guilt you might experience after having said such disparaging things. . . . [N]o one explains this protocol better than stand-up comedian, Henry Cho." See Steele, "Henry Cho—Funny Man, Family Man."

64. Chun, "Ideologies of Legitimate Mockery," 263, 269.

65. Cho has stated, "As far as comedy though, being Asian and from Tennessee is the best hook since Rodney Dangerfield. That's been said by many people in the industry." Nahm, "Comedy's Southern Squire," 4.

66. "Meet Henry Cho," *Georgia Asian Times.*

67. Ibid.

68. Morrow, "A Clean-talking Cuss."

69. As he also notes in another interview, "I never wanted to be the Asian comic or the Southern Corean comic." Nahm, "Comedy's Southern Squire," 2. Note: the spelling of "Corean" is the website's editorial choice, not Cho's. See "Corea and Korea?" *Goldsea: Asian American Daily,* http://www.goldsea.com/Air/Issues/Corea/corea.html (accessed June 30, 2010).

70. I use the term *yellowface* to also speak to how this *MadTV* character inherits a particular historical context concerning the portrayal of Asian Americans in U.S. popular culture. See Moon's discussion about the contemporary uses of this term (Moon, *Yellowface,* 164–165).

71. Neil Justin, "Can Race Be a Laughing Matter?" *YellowWorld,* 2004, http://yellowworld .org/arts_culture_media/172.html (accessed June 15, 2010).

72. Starring Heather Graham, *Say It Isn't So* (2001) is a comedy about a man and a woman who fall in love, only to find out that they may be long-lost siblings.

73. In the 2006 film *Material Girls,* Cho plays Ned Nakamori, a character who does not have a southern accent and is therefore not read as southern. The film is set in southern California.

74. Shams, "Stand-Up Sit-Down."

75. For example, Moon analyzes how Lee Tung Foo, the Chinese American vaudevillian of the early 1900s, employed humor that in turn "soften[ed] the racial maneuvers" he was making in his performance. Krystyn R. Moon, "Lee Tung Foo and the Making of a Chinese American Vaudevillian, 1900s-1920s," *Journal of Asian American Studies* 8, no. 1 (2005): 38.

76. Jon Smith and Deborah Cohn. *Look Away! The U.S. South in New World Studies* (Durham, N.C.: Duke University Press, 2004), 8.

CHAPTER 10

"Like We Lost Our Citizenship"

Vietnamese Americans, African Americans, and Hurricane Katrina

Marguerite Nguyen

In a convocation speech given at Tulane University on April 23, 1975, President Gerald Ford tied the history of New Orleans to the history of Vietnam, pointing toward a postwar future in which the Crescent City could serve as "the beacon light of the past" and "illuminate a boundless future for all Americans and a peace for all mankind." Just as America's 1815 victory at the Battle of New Orleans restored a national pride that was lost with the War of 1812, so could 1975 New Orleans take the lead in recuperating "the sense of pride that existed before Vietnam." Famously diverse New Orleans—"a melting pot," "the very, very best of America's evolution"—could remind America of its best possibilities, but with the condition of accepting the war as a "finished" chapter in U.S. history.[1] Ford's speech positioned New Orleans as an exemplary American city, one that could show the nation how to put military defeat behind it and set America back on track as a nation committed to diversity and global peace.

Of course "Vietnam" was all but finished. If the war was folded into history on April 23, 1975, what was to become of the South Vietnamese who weren't mentioned in Ford's speech but would become objects of worldwide interest as they were rendered stateless on April 30? Ford's rhetoric may have established narrative closure to Vietnam, but even as he spoke to Tulane graduates the story of Vietnam continued as Attorney General Edward Levi used discretionary powers to grant former Indochinese asylum in America. By the time of Ford's speech, Levi had already waived immigration restrictions, and in a process that would eventually result in fourteen changes to America's parolee and refugee policy, Levi declared on April 22 that the United States would accept up to 132,000 Vietnamese and Cambodians.[2]

Approximately one thousand of this initial wave of refugees arrived in New Orleans in 1975.[3] Their entry made headlines and generated heated discussions about what their impact on New Orleans might be. The press often framed Vietnamese arrival as straining the local economy and already tense racial relations, an acknowledgment of the more general sense of urban disfranchisement that was permeating the city. The Vietnamese diasporic community itself struggled to cultivate internal leadership and confront anti-Vietnamese sentiment coming from other marginalized populations. Occasional shootings of Vietnamese shop-owners, charges of a Vietnamese takeover of housing and jobs, perceptions of Vietnamese as the new inassimilable aliens, and a postwar culture that drove America to "move past" Vietnam—these all shaped the early formation of Vietnamese diaspora in New Orleans.

The recuperation of American political and military might in the 1980s—perhaps most evident in Vietnam War movies of the Reagan era—marked a transition in representations of Vietnamese, as the New Orleans media began to focus on stories of Vietnamese American economic and educational "success." This model minority rhetoric suggested that the community was a healthy contribution to New Orleans's already diverse population and culture, but it neither alleviated interracial tensions nor addressed significant needs within the refugee population. Nevertheless, as some community members claimed, Vietnamese lived more or less under the radar until about thirty years later, when they were once again thrust into the media limelight because of their quick return and recovery after Hurricane Katrina. Once potential objects of New Orleans exclusion, Vietnamese Americans now represented the city at its best, with national and international media outlets upholding the community's efforts as a story of hope and achievement in the aftermath of disaster. Afro-Asian alliances also formed in the face of city, state, and national abandonment, indicating a panethnic solidarity quite different from the charges of interracial tension of the 1970s and '80s.

This essay examines representations of Vietnamese Americans in post-Katrina New Orleans, but insofar as they relate to representations of Vietnamese as refugees in pre-Katrina New Orleans. By tracking the central themes and tropes across discourses of New Orleans Vietnamese spanning 1975–2005, this essay shows how shifts in Vietnamese American–African American relations tie local histories and politics to transnational flows. In particular, I will show that while the status of refugee subjects as stateless persons bolstered some African American claims that Vietnamese should not be given U.S. aid in the 1970s, in 2005 refugee discourse implicitly related Vietnamese Americans and African Americans, as Katrina exposed all New Orleans marginalized as "others" who were denied local and federal aid. Utilizing English and Vietnamese language sources, this paper shows that examining the refugee category in New Orleans provides a historical context and figurative language for understanding not only the nature of racial discourse after the hurricane but also how interracial antagonism became interracial cooperation in the Crescent City. The refugee-citizen continuum, I suggest, can complement current models of race. My paper thus contributes to scholarship that posits New Orleans, one of America's most famously hybrid cities, as a fertile example for understanding the possibilities and constraints underpinning Afro-Asian alliances in the U.S. South. Moreover, it hopes to advance discussions concerning Asian American politics and activism in the region.

Pre-Katrina

The anxiety over Vietnamese refugees crossing borders generated intense discussions in the news in 1975 New Orleans. Mid-April articles assessing the financial costs and political damage of the Vietnam War transitioned into late-April discussions about an impending mass migration. *Times-Picayune* readers hashed out the expected anxieties about whether New Orleans should respect the "humanitarian dimension"[4] to admit refugees or whether the city should stay out of it, as an economy in recession would not be able to handle more people "[looking] to the government for food stamps or welfare."[5] These sentiments concerning what to do about the refugees revealed an intermingling of local and global frames: how would New Orleans respond to a world humanitarian crisis, one resulting from a history of French colonialism and American militarism in the Pacific now looping its way to the Crescent City?

The Catholic Church spearheaded efforts to resettle Vietnamese in New Orleans.[6] New Orleans archbishop Phillip M. Hannan visited the former Republic of Vietnam after the fall of Saigon in hopes of bringing back individuals who had American passports but were still stuck in the country; he reassured the public that this did not mean an influx of refugees for New Orleans.[7] At the same time that he was assuaging public concerns however, Hannan also visited Fort Chaffee, one of four Vietnamese refugee camps in the United States, to find possible candidates for resettlement.[8] Elise Cerniglia, Associated Catholic Charities' (ACC) director of Resettlement and Immigration Services, scoped out possible housing sites for these newly displaced persons.[9] While Ford's administration had put forth a policy of dispersal, or scattering the Vietnamese population across the United States so as to discourage ethnic enclaving, ACC's vision was one of collective housing for refugees.[10] The ACC chose Versailles Arms Apartments, a housing complex located in the easternmost suburban residential area of New Orleans, as the refugees' new home.[11]

Catholic Charities relocated the Vietnamese to Versailles Arms because the area was not densely populated, and the complex qualified as low-income, section-eight housing.[12] New Orleans East had experienced a brief period of development in the 1960s, in part because the Michoud NASA facility was expected to bring highly skilled employees and their families to the neighborhood. But this anticipated boom and demand for housing never happened. As Carl Bankston notes, "activities at the plant declined, the flight of the white middle class out of Orleans Parish removed a major source of housing demand, and homeowners in the drained swamp began to discover that their houses, sidewalks, and garages were sinking unevenly."[13] Partly bound by the Bayou Sauvage National Wildlife Refuge—the nation's largest urban National Wildlife refuge—New Orleans East is on the outskirts of the city. As Eric Tang notes, it "is located so far to the east that it is often jokingly referred to as 'Mississippi.'"[14] Yet in some ways this disconnect from the city center worked favorably for Vietnamese. Many of them came from the North Vietnamese Catholic villages of Phat Diem and Bui Chu, which had been one of North Vietnam's largest dioceses. When the State of Vietnam was divided at the 17th parallel in 1954, these Catholics moved to South Vietnam and reestablished their all-Catholic subparishes from the North.[15] Collective resettlement in New Orleans enabled yet another transplantation of Catholic community, this time across the Pacific.[16]

Whether for or against admitting refugees, Vietnamese resettlement in New Orleans happened, and their presence profoundly transformed the Gulf Coast's social and cultural landscape. A particularly salient fact is that many went into fishing and shrimping around the region; Bankston notes that by the end of the twentieth century, "close to one of every ten Louisiana Vietnamese men worked as fishers or shrimpers and the Vietnamese accounted for one out of every twenty workers in the Louisiana fishing industry."[17] Especially in the early years, confrontations between Vietnamese and non-Vietnamese fishermen occurred in Empire, Plaquemines Parish, Louisiana, and Seadrift, Texas, manifesting in territorial claims couched in terms of uneven and unfair competition and Ku Klux Klan intimidations. Nicholas Spitzer, former Louisiana state folklorist, notes that Vietnamese success in the Gulf Coast waters was due to specific social and material strategies. First, Vietnamese would use their extended families to divide the labor related to all aspects of fishing, from the catching to the bookkeeping. Second, they often built their own boats and nets and also used an efficient, eco-conscious technique called "plowing," whereby, as Spitzer explains, two telephone poles are placed "on the bow end of the boats and lowered" to form one large catch net. This approach taps a much deeper source while minimizing the chances of catching extraneous materials and animals.[18] Nevertheless, stereotypes of Vietnamese labor emerged that were removed from these particularities. In addition to accusing Vietnamese fishermen of illegal fishing practices[19] and receiving federal money to purchase boats, white fishermen portrayed Vietnamese as ominously resourceful and efficient—"SOB" fisherman who "[could] live on practically nothing," "rugged" as they worked "day and night, dragging the bay."[20] Evoking stereotypes of Asian labor found in late-nineteenth–early-twentieth-century "Meat versus Rice" discussions, here Asian laborers' perceived minimal subsistence and superhuman efficiency posed a threat to America's labor pool. America's humanitarian impulse seemed to be backfiring, quickly destroying the local economy and lifestyle; Vietnamese were a force encroaching from the outside in, "an alien horde that swept into the area and ruined a way of life."[21]

African American leaders were also concerned about the aid given to Vietnamese refugees and demanded to know why more was not being done for New Orleans's own struggling citizens.[22] There is no definitive answer to the question of whether or not Vietnamese refugee resettlement in Versailles Arms displaced African Americans and thus furthered the latter's marginalization. Scholarly sources note that many units in Versailles were empty until the first one thousand Vietnamese moved in,[23] while the Urban League of Greater New Orleans (ULGNO) asserted that Vietnamese arrival put African Americans out of homes.[24] In any case, the ULGNO adopted and distributed "Indo-China Refugee Issue: An Urban League Position Paper" to local and national leaders on May 25, 1978, after a series of meetings between African American community leaders and ACC to discuss the refugee question. In these documents, leaders expressed worry that support for Vietnamese was getting excessive and eclipsed the immediate needs of African Americans already suffering in the bleak context of global recession. The Position Paper held ACC responsible for setting a precedent that attracted 5,400 more refugees in addition to the original two thousand,[25] for supporting the creation of "homogeneous neighborhoods, turned inward and apart from the larger communities," and for not preparing refugees for "the harsh racial and economic realities of a region that was sorely pressed to solve its own problems before taking on the added burden of another troubled minority." Referencing the racial tensions in the Gulf Coast waters, the document cited local fishermen who shared the ULGNO's belief that Vietnamese refugees were using up benefits and taking over jobs: "As one irate fishermen put it, 'the fish supply is like an apple. The more fishermen, the smaller each slice becomes.'" The citation awkwardly resonated with KKK statements that also accused Vietnamese of using up limited resources in a tight economy and remaining foreign, failing to assimilate. To prevent a Vietnamese displacement of New Orleans's black residents, the ULGNO document concluded with a final recommendation to suspend the Catholic Charities Refugee Program.[26]

We can read these representations as attempts on the part of New Orleanians to negotiate the presence of a newly displaced group within existing structures of economic and social relations. Put another way, casting Vietnamese refugees as a problem indicated how New Orleanians were understanding and shaping Vietnamese racial formation within an existing racial structure, but one that took a black-white model as its starting point. In her study of the Jim Crow South, Leslie Bow offers the notion of "racial interstitiality" to show that Asians were often considered to be a third term in the segregated south—foreigners and strangers "who did not fit into a cultural and legal system predicated on the binary distinction between black and white."[27] Claire Jean Kim refers to "racial triangulation" to describe the process whereby Asian American racialization is one of "civic ostracism" that derives from a model of race defined by slavery; Asian ostracism inserts into an embedded racial logic wherein white supremacy has rested on antiblackness and African American inferiority, such that Asian American racialization follows an assimilationist model, or a striving for whiteness as a way to achieve upward mobility.[28]

But is there a way to think about Asian American racialization in New Orleans in terms other than an interracial hostility rooted in a black-white model? As Colleen Lye puts it, is there a way to conceive of Asian racialization as something other than "a third term to trouble binary habits of racial classification and analysis"?[29] Here we can think about black othering of Vietnamese refugees as not just about representing Vietnamese as a third term or as simply another Asian group on its way to model minority status, but also about the material conditions relating what Helen Heran Jun calls the problem of "black surplus" in the American city. In an attempt to move away from model minority paradigms that position "virtuous Asian American mobility as evidence of the pathological failure of the black poor," Jun suggests that post-1965 expressions of black dispossession demonstrate "a yearning for national redemption from the very spaces violently ghettoized by the state, a fantasy of black citizenship felt to be displaced by the metanational forces of globalization."[30] As deindustrialization, the rise of the prison industrial complex, and other forms of de facto segregation arose alongside a post–1965 neoliberal logic that redefined access to state resources as dependence rather than a matter of rights, African American discourses of Asian Americans cannot be read simply as examples of "Asian scapegoating," but rather an attempt to center attention on "the abandonment and disenfranchisement of the black urban poor." Particularly in a late twentieth century heralded as the Pacific Century, the mobility of Asians within an imagined U.S.-Asian cooperation brought into starker relief the position of African American citizens as institutionally and experientially outside "the national citizenry"—denied mobility and prosperity, resulting in a black surplus without the rights and resources of U.S. citizenship.[31]

If we incorporate Jun's innovative argument, an interesting subtext emerges in discourses of Vietnamese refugee—African American relations in New Orleans. African American critiques of Vietnamese refugee aid can be clarified as an effort on the part of the ULGNO to sustain attention on longer-standing problems not directly tied to refugees. This makes sense when we consider that African Americans in New Orleans have experienced de facto segregation in particularly devastating ways. In 1966, the construction of I-10 cut right through North Claiborne Avenue, destroying oak trees, eliminating important African American historical and gathering spaces, and decimating the African American residential and retail backbone of the Sixth Ward (Treme) and the Seventh Ward. Louisiana incarceration has increased 272 percent since 1982 and now has the highest incarceration rate in the country.[32] As historian Larry Powell writes: "We are last, or nearly so, in every category in which we should be first; and first in every category where we should be pulling up the rear. Children in poverty. Illiteracy. Infant mortality. School dropout rates. Blighted housing—it's a depressing litany."[33]

Thus while we've seen how the ULGNO Position Paper was wary of Vietnamese refugees as potentially moving upward with state support without integrating into local culture and society, it is not quite sufficient to say that these representations followed a model minority or racial triangulation paradigm wherein the insertion of Vietnamese in a black-white structure established a black-Asian American distance that highlighted black "failure" in turn. Rather, the document rooted problems of refugee arrival in the ACC's lack of preparedness and foresight. The Paper chastised Rev. Michael Haddad, head of ACC New Orleans, for his "refusal to participate in any committee" to discuss the refugee issue with other community leaders (though he would deny this in a personal letter to the ULGNO).[34] The Paper also censured Haddad for his lack of transparency, adding that Catholic Charities needed to employ black Catholics in proportion to the number that lived in New Orleans, that more efforts needed to be made to assist African Americans with jobs and housing, and that the city needed to pursue more sustained and adequate studies of urban problems.[35] Long-standing inequities and poor leadership outlined a structural explanation for the unequal distribution of resources, bringing into focus the continued dispossession and strife of urban African Americans.

But what do we make of the fact that, despite the ULGNO's emphasis that "this [was] not a 'Black vs. Vietnamese' issue," the Position Paper's final recommendation was to suspend all forms of assistance to Vietnamese refugees in New Orleans? After all, 27 percent of local African American leaders surveyed disagreed with the ULGNO's stance, one citing the League's misplaced blame: "the Urban League should be fighting white folks."[36] Further, a full-page ad signed by a number of prominent local and national African American leaders—including President of the National Urban League, Vernon Jordan—was taken out in the March 19, 1978, *New York Times* to express nationwide African American support for giving aid to recently displaced Southeast Asians.[37] In other words, there was substantive disagreement in African American communities about the Vietnamese refugee issue, particularly between the local and national levels.

In Lye's critique of models that situate Asian racialization as derivative of and subsequent to black and white racialization—shaped by rather than constitutive of existing black-white racial structures—taking a long historical lens is one way to work toward a more nuanced understanding of race. Recently, scholars including Moon-Ho Jung and Lisa Yun have studied the coolie's nineteenth-century global routes, in turn illuminating how unexamined Asian circuits have organized ideas, laws, and practices tied to enslavement and freedom in the antebellum South; Asians and Asian histories have transformed notions of race in ways that are coeval with rather than derivative of black-white relations. This doesn't do away with the fact that popular and scholarly discussions do often *represent* Asians as a by-product of black-white relations, which in New Orleans gets complicated with the strong presence of Creoles and Cajuns.[38] The point is that Jung and Yun suggest that one way of opening up discussions about race is to not only go more historical but also to go more global—to link the local or nation-based model more strongly to a long historical lens and transnational scale.

Marguerite Bryan, then sociologist at Xavier University in New Orleans, helps us think about how the historical and transnational scales of New Orleans discourses about Vietnamese refugees inflects the construction of race. At a March 24, 1980, hearing held in New Orleans by the U.S. Select Committee on Immigration and Refugee Policy,[39] Bryan noted that "race relations studies have indicated that because of the Indochinese association with an unpopular war (Vietnam) mixed feelings of guilt and resentment about the war by Americans could be rekindled by the migration." Offered out of national guilt, Vietnamese asylum had proved only that African Americans were "still discriminated against," increasingly displaced despite their "painful history for over 300 years."[40] Bryan questioned how American humanitarian globetrotting could trump adequate action for African Americans in a city still bearing the costs of its slave history. In referencing the Vietnam War's many wrongs, she evoked the disproportionate percentage of minority males drafted during the war. The negativity that Bryan suggested Vietnamese presence generated was thus not only linked to the abstract shame of a lost war, but also to the disposability of black bodies that has spanned slave history to the Vietnam War draft and beyond. If Bryan portrayed South Vietnamese refugees as not only bringing the war back home but also threatening the survival of blacks, the message was that African American men had become dispensable not only at home, but also abroad. Black othering of and grievances against Vietnamese were also calls to action against further black dispossession and against the devaluation of black bodies in the city and the world.

To put it another way, when Bryan and the ULGNO document described Vietnamese as beneficiaries of more than what refugees should be entitled to, they drew from the notion of citizenship as a legal category to claim rights and belonging. Yet as Renato Rosaldo points out, citizenship exists along a continuum, ranging from first-class citizen to second-class citizen to noncitizen.[41] Blacks in New Orleans might have been legal U.S. citizens, with the right to state aid and resources, but their claims in the post–Vietnam War moment spoke to continued social and political dispossession. Their claims recentered the issue of full belonging that legal citizenship is supposed to guarantee, but in turn they cast Vietnamese as outsiders without the rights, responsibilities, protection, and belonging of legal citizenship. At work was a taxonomy of belonging that opposed the rights of a legal citizen to the perceived lack of rights of a refugee, which in turn achieved a racialization that ended up opposing dispossessed black to dispossessed Vietnamese rather than centering a shared dispossession at the hands of multiple levels of governance.

In her call for critical refugee studies, Yen Le Espiritu critiques the tendency of mainstream media and scholarship to portray Vietnamese refugee bodies within such rigid frames—as unproductive, depoliticized receivers of charity rather than productive subjects of the world compelled to flight because of political circumstances.[42] Examining the United Nations High Commission on Refugees (UNHCR) 1951 definition and 1967 Protocol compels us to recognize that statelessness is the very condition that guarantees a refugee rights: "A refugee as someone who, 'owing to a well-founded fear of being persecuted for reasons of race, religion, nationality, membership of a particular social group, or political opinion, is outside the country of his nationality, and is unable to or, owing to such fear, is unwilling to avail himself of the protection of that country.'"[43] The UNHCR further stipulates that governments must provide refugees physical safety; legal protection;[44] material aid for survival; and ways to resettle, educate, and integrate refugees over time.[45] In short, states must coordinate their own concerns with international protocol in order to guarantee stateless persons the same social, economic, and political rights "as any other foreigner who is a legal resident" of the participating state.[46]

A document published by the Vietnamese Nationals Association in New Orleans follows this logic. Le Thanh Trang, vice president of the Association, had attended the 1980 meeting at which Bryan was present. In response to the gathering, Le penned an appeal to the Vietnamese refugee community that appeared in the Association's special journal issue titled *Dau Thuong* ("hurt" or "sorrow"), issued on April 30, 1980, in commemoration of the five-year anniversary of the fall of Saigon. Le's appeal noted that at the meeting, representatives from the African American and Latina/o communities[47] expressed "unfriendliness" and "negative reactions toward Asian refugees" and protested the financial and social aid that they believed Vietnamese had received.[48] Declaring that five years of silence on race matters needed to come to an end, Le wrote that it was time for the "community to speak out." He argued that the community's most crucial task was to correct erroneous assumptions about refugee benefits in order to facilitate daily interactions with other minorities. The piece concluded with an urgent appeal for individuals to take leadership positions, with the hope that any "skepticism" in the community would be transformed into "deep feeling" galvanized toward collaborative action so that refugees could live equally and with "self-determination."[49]

This document is important because the effort to define Vietnamese diaspora in relation to other racial groups in the immediate post–Vietnam War period—particularly with regard to Latina/o communities—is something we know very little about. In contrast to the united voice in the ULGNO document, the voice in this document shows that Vietnamese were still in the throes of postmigration and did not yet have a political voice. Le's rhetorical flourishes and appeals to affect suggest that encouraging community members to assume leadership roles and assist in facilitating intercultural understanding was a challenge in a charged racial environment. The public may have read stories of Vietnamese refugee desperation and otherness that Vietnamese themselves did not publicly reject. But

Le's Vietnamese-language appeal, directed to Vietnamese audiences, revealed a different side to the public story, instead highlighting the long process of diasporic community building needed to garner political presence and collective feeling for Vietnamese in post–Vietnam War America—a far cry from model minority paradigms that naturalize Asian American achievement while ignoring the long and difficult process of transcultural community building and politicization. Le's attempt at self-definition and self-determination for the community engaged the long-term goal of integration that the UNHCR ensures is the right of refugees and the responsibility of the state.

Placing these sources in conversation, we are reminded that the relocation of Vietnamese refugees is very much entangled in imperial legacies that have driven mass migrations across African American and Asian American histories. We can understand the ULGNO document as more complicated than an example of localized anti-Asianism or anti-refugeeism when we pay attention to its global themes. Consider how the ULGNO Position Paper begins:

> With the fall of Saigon to the North Vietnamese in 1975, numerous international agencies of goodwill began a mammoth effort to accommodate the fleeing South Vietnamese. Fearing loss of life and abdicating all ties to property and position, those Indo-Chinese unable to accept the incoming Communist ideology abandoned Vietnam by the thousands under conditions resembling nothing less than panic. Their exodus on foot, through water, and by air was guided by an unshakable conviction in the promise of freedom that they strove to embrace. Their struggle captured the sympathies of the West; and it is those sympathizers that assumed responsibility in aiding the dislocated in the resolution of their ordeal.

This passage takes us on a journey through multiple shifts in postcolonial subject formation. Vietnamese forced displacement is initially cast as an external affair—the effect of a Southeast Asian civil war. But as "Indo-Chinese unable to accept the incoming Communist ideology," the refugees are then recognized as products of French colonialism who now find themselves facing an implicitly unfree postcolonial state. South Vietnamese emerge as objects of Western sympathy and humanitarianism, but the West itself has shaped the very crisis it seems to alleviate. America inherits this history and is hence implicated in the current crisis: "Because of its involvement in the unpopular and ill-fated war, the U.S. government committed itself to relocating more than 120,000 homeless Vietnamese." The South Vietnamese national turned refugee enacts what Espiritu describes as the narrative of U.S. militarism revised as one of U.S. rescue.[50] More broadly, a narrative of colonial division cedes to a narrative of the Cold War division of the globe, with America now assuming responsibility for refugee subjects that it, like old world colonialism, has helped to create.

Thus while the ULGNO's recommendation to end the ACC refugee program was clear, what stands out more is the document's representation of the Vietnamese as seeming cause but ultimate effect—that the increased strain in local resources, exacerbated racial tensions, and Catholic Charities' misdirection were "caused by Vietnamese influx,"[51] but its acknowledgment that Vietnamese refugees themselves were ultimately not to blame as their migrations, like those of the African diaspora, have been shaped by Western aggression and exploitation in the global South. Interestingly, any sentiments of "guilt and resentment" Bryan noted were folded into a statement of panethnicity in the ULGNO document, suggesting that the Vietnamese experience was also the African American experience, and that both groups had been those desperate, displaced subjects in need of aid: "The plight of the Vietnamese refugees, though derived from different circumstances, is like the black struggle, complicated by similar backgrounds of relocation and suffering."[52] Similarly, Le made clear that his call for leadership in response to racial antagonism was not meant to oppose other ethnic groups, but to clear up misunderstandings in the service of interracial cooperation. The hardships of each community stemmed from histories that were different but that shared the suffering and involuntary displacement borne of imperial systems.

The question at hand might have been framed in simple terms—should New Orleans offer asylum to Vietnamese refugees or not—but the presentation of Vietnamese refugees as a problem was really a consolidation of multiple anxieties emerging from the interface between local concerns and post–Vietnam War transpacific migration. The ULGNO and Vietnamese National Association documents remind us of America's implication in not only the building of empires, but also in the ongoing process of decolonization. African Americans saw U.S. rescue as a self-interested corrective to a war that was unfocused, disorganized, and detrimental to marginalized U.S. citizens. It not only accelerated the accumulation of laborers without available labor—a black surplus—but also alleviated national guilt at the expense of New Orleanians' rightful access to resources of U.S. citizenship. For Vietnamese, the postcolonial time and space that Ford's speech relegated to memory was ever present within America but contained by more powerful American self-imaginings. African Americans and Vietnamese thus juggled—rather than only dichotomized—the perception of refugees as furthering urban strife in New Orleans and as fellow sufferers and displaced persons in a world driven by Western power. And at the center of this discourse was an othering of Vietnamese that aligned Vietnamese refugees and African Americans based on a shared outsiderism relative to western hegemony, but finally that denied resources to Vietnamese based on their construction as foreign, stateless persons not entitled to aid. Such a logic would take a slightly different turn after Katrina, when direct and indirect Afro-Asian alliances emerged out of the limits of claiming legal citizenship, as the devastation of the hurricane exposed widespread local and national abandonment of New Orleans's marginalized persons, rendering them all less than U.S. citizens.

Post-Katrina

Fast forward to post-Katrina New Orleans in 2005. Images of New Orleans residents desperate for assistance and the basics of survival are by now familiar, as is the notion that Hurricane Katrina's destruction lay bare the city's deep and historical inequality. From this picture one of the stories of hope that emerged placed New Orleans Vietnamese Americans at its center. This time they were not the hungry and desperate refugees seeking U.S. asylum after a bitter war, but figures who had established New Orleans roots so deep that they returned and rebuilt faster than any other community. National and international media outlets paid attention to the story of intergenerational Vietnamese Americans organized around the Mary Queen of Viet Nam Catholic Church (MQVN), whose parishioners pooled together resources and manpower under the leadership of its pastor, Father Vien Nguyen, as if to prove that New Orleans would rebuild better than before. Perhaps the first instance of cross-racial outreach that occurred right after the flood was when MQVN helped rescue about 300 African Americans from New Orleans East by going door-to-door in boats.[53] Vietnamese American visibility in the Crescent City was no longer viewed as a threat, but rather a model of citizenship and exemplified the city at its best.[54]

As Eric Tang and S. Leo Chiang reveal, the image of African Americans and Vietnamese Americans celebrating together at MQVN's first post-Katrina mass signaled a new era in race relations in New Orleans; no longer perceived antagonists, Vietnamese Americans and African Americans worshipped side by side in the face of government neglect. Tang offers a way to understand this moment of Afro-Asian solidarity, noting that two things paved the way for the interracial activism that emerged after the hurricane—resilient, "'usable pasts' that community members summoned to explain their unlikely return and rebuilding efforts," and "class heterogeneity in both communities: each consists of the business owners, the home owners, the working poor, the welfare-dependent, and the jobless."[55] Tang shows that Vietnamese Americans and African Americans in New Orleans East were not cut off from each other because of disparate histories and class antagonisms, but actually shared a narrative arc of survival and coexistence across economic tiers. These factors helped facilitate their post-Katrina cooperation, which drew from both groups' strategies for survival in the face of state neglect.[56]

How did this story of Afro-Asian cooperation emerge from the 1970s narrative of interracial division? After all, as Father Vien noted, the community before Katrina had remained "quiet," staying "below the radar."[57] However, after Katrina experiences of outsiderism and political silence characterized not only the Vietnamese American community but all those who resided in New Orleans East. According to the 2010 Census, within the 70129 zip code that Vietnamese Americans and African Americans share, 33.3 percent are Asian and 50.8 percent are African American. Far from the city center and flanked by marsh, swamp,[58] and landfills, New Orleans East's geographical marginality meant minimal access to "evacuation, transportation, public safety, food, and water" for substantial communities of color during the hurricane.[59] While in 1975 Vietnamese refugee arrival caused concerns over African American displacement, in 2005 Katrina exposed their shared victimization as residents of a neglected space. When the storm surge broke the Intracoastal Waterway levees protecting New Orleans East, flooding began there hours before the storm surge reached the city's core and ended up impacting this area more than any other large-scale space in New Orleans;[60] this is significant considering New Orleans East comprises two-thirds of the city's space.[61]

United by their shared position on the wrong side of town, Vietnamese American and African American cooperation superseded the 1970s-1980s story of their opposition. But how might we explain these moments of Afro-Asian alliance, besides through a narrative of "coming together" after natural disaster, or the fact that Vietnamese acquired naturalized citizenship and thus could be said now to "belong?"[62] Here a look at terminology proves useful. Just days after the hurricane news outlets and many New Orleanians referred to Katrina victims as refugees. Discussions soon erupted concerning whether or not the term "refugee" adequately described those that Katrina displaced. One observer noted that one could not help but conjure a refugee situation given realities of individuals "[scrounging] for diapers, water, and basic survival."[63] Aaron Brown, with CNN at the time, expressed discomfort with the category but couldn't think of another term that adequately captured the experiences of evacuation, homelessness, and material loss.[64] Mike Pesca of NPR described a city of third-world dimensions in which hurricane victims wandered around, "dirty and foul-smelling." Pesca noted the parallels between uprooted hurricane victims and refugees, as many New Orleanians, particularly the city's poor, did not have proper documentation, did not even know "what state they'd be bused to," and were reined in by barricades separating them from "armed men in fatigues."[65] The use of refugee in these cases amplified the plight of refugees by portraying a scrounging for necessities in the "nightmarish experience" of Katrina—not unlike portrayals of Vietnamese refugees thirty years earlier.[66]

It was not long before use of the term refugee became highly contentious because of its racial connotations and legal implications. While media outlets including the Associated Press and the *New York Times* defended their use of the term, others rightly pointed out that refugee was not the correct legal term to use. An interesting combination of individuals and organizations rejected its usage, including President George W. Bush, Reverend Jesse Jackson, Reverend Al Sharpton, *Washington Post*, and NPR. Adeline Masquelier wrote that "*refugee* became the 'R-word': an ethnic slur,"[67] while another person stated that refugee evoked assumptions about "a Third World country, the babies in Africa that have all the flies and are starving to death."[68] Al Sharpton made clear the importance of terminology in his appeal to legal rights when he famously stated that Katrina victims "are not refugees. They are citizens of the United States. . . . They are victims of neglect and a situation they should have never been put in the first place." He further added that they were "not refugees wandering somewhere looking for charity."[69] These quotes amplify the plight of Katrina victims by distancing the refugee figure's desperate, third-world associations, suggesting the pejorative connotations that *refugee* as a term has acquired over the years—its "demeaning"[70] if not "racist" turns.[71] If "displaced person" emerged during World War II as a category to describe Europeans fleeing Communism, refugee has been stamped with a racialized shame particularly after the Vietnam War, one that manifested in the New Orleans context in images of dirty, leeching figures of color.

Kaleema H. Nur emphasizes that it is important to identify the legal status of Katrina victims correctly because rights and access to resources are at stake. Nur iterates that the appropriate category for Katrina victims is internally displaced persons (IDPs),[72] defined by the United Nations as those displaced by "conflict, situations of generalized violence, violations of human rights or natural or human-made disasters" but who "have not crossed an internationally recognized State border." An IDP's own government is responsible for protecting and ensuring rights for IDPs both during and after displacement.[73] Yet Hannah Arendt offers a useful way to think about what disagreement over terminology might mean in itself as opposed to focusing too narrowly on which terms do or do not fit shifting national and international definitions. Arendt notes that political and public language often ignore a core issue in our era of mass displacement—that of the *condition* of statelessness, whether recognized (de jure) or not (de facto), whether within or outside one's own national borders. For Arendt, the rhetorical turn to "displaced persons" suggests our willingness to ignore the material conditions of statelessness, which in turn disavows that stateless persons "[require] international agreements for safeguarding their legal status" because their own governments no longer protect them.[74] In emphasizing that Katrina victims were not refugees, those who rejected using the term understood the importance of semantics in making legal claims; but they also fixed the word with negative connotations by opposing the figure of entitled citizen to the figure of unentitled, noncontributing refugee. Yet refugee also had potential as a metaphor to approximate and force the recognition of the experience of statelessness, regardless of whether one was or was not a legal U.S. citizen. As Arendt suggests, contestations over terminology can also be a way for states to absolve themselves from responding to the condition of statelessness where it exists.

State neglect of Vietnamese Americans and African Americans during and after Katrina strongly emerged in the Bring New Orleans Back (BNOB) rebuilding plans. Father Vien noted that "the Bring New Orleans Back commission brought in the Urban Land Institute to do a recommendation on land use. The majority

of New Orleans East was recommended to be green space. . . . I remember looking at, on the screen and asked the people around me, 'Where are we?' The map
ended. Right on our border."[75] A nonprofit organization providing research and
education services regarding land use and development, the Urban Land Institute (ULI) was charged with the task of making rebuilding and redevelopment
recommendations to African American Mayor Ray Nagin's BNOB commission.
Most experts serving on the ULI "run major corporations and municipalities,"[76]
and Mayor Nagin's BNOB commission consisted of three real estate developers
out of its seventeen members.[77] The initial ULI report that Father Vien referred
to deemed New Orleans East a flood prone area unfit for rebuilding and at risk
of becoming one of post-Katrina's "shanty towns."[78] ULI-city alignment basically
ignored the voice, needs, and legal status of eastern New Orleanians as it appropriated their space in its plans for a greener Crescent City. The city essentially
subordinated New Orleans East residents to an agenda of development and profit.

Under Father Vien's leadership, the MQVN church helped spearhead a cross-
racial challenge to the ULI's report. At a BNOB commission meeting on November
21, 2005, Father Vien confronted the commission about its discriminatory practices
that had the veneer of environmentalist concern: "When we saw this Urban Land
Institute Report, I, we were shocked. We were never invited to the table. We have a
right to be part of the community-driven process." In front of variously interested,
frustrated, and distracted members of the commission, Father Vien proceeded:
"I'm speaking here not only for just my parish. I believe I speak for the people in
New Orleans East as well on this matter." After Father Vien's comments, applause
erupted from the interracial, standing-room-only crowd.

Among those who joined Father Vien in criticizing the commission's report
were African American community members, the New Orleans East Business
Association, Louisiana ACORN, and the NAACP.[79] Cynthia Willard-Lewis, then
African American City Council member representing District E in New Orleans
(which includes Versailles), said of the gathering: "It was actually a very painful and divisive discussion that said to almost 40% of the city's population, 'We
don't want you back.' That 60% of the city's land mass was going to be eliminated
from redevelopment."[80] That Willard-Lewis could provide a unified public voice
as a policy maker for cross-racial constituents was essential to charging the city
with silencing Vietnamese Americans and African Americans. The BNOB plans
denied New Orleans East inhabitants the right to return and rebuild as well as
government aid and protection during and after Katrina—an effective rendering
of eastern New Orleanians as abandoned by the government.

By Spring 2006, Nagin began regularly to reiterate the need to include New
Orleans East in the city's recovery. The cross-racial solidarity of the outcry against
the ULI report established precedent for future Vietnamese American and African
American collaborations. Thus when Mayor Nagin exercised state of emergency
powers to grant Waste Management (WM) a permit on February 14, 2006, to con-

struct and open a landfill in New Orleans East at 16600 Chef Menteur Highway, another opportunity for cross-racial activism emerged. The landfill site occupies one hundred acres and has a capacity of six and a half million cubic yards, and it is a half-mile away from the Vietnamese American community. While the sign in front of the site still states that WM will accept only construction and demolition (C and D) materials and prohibits "hazardous waste," post-Katrina waste was undoubtedly moldy and toxic.[81] Further, the landfill connects to three main waterways: the Maxent Canal, the Intracoastal Waterway, and Lake Borgne. Vietnamese community members water their gardens and farms with water from the Maxent Canal.[82] The unlined landfill opened on April 26, and on May 5, Vietnamese Americans protested at City Hall[83] after consultations with African American leaders and alongside the interethnic and interfaith Citizens for a Strong New Orleans East, the Presbyterian Church of USA, Willard-Lewis (who had initially supported the landfill), and Southern Christian Leadership Conference representatives including National President Charles Steele.[84] They demanded a meeting with Mayor Nagin who, though initially closing the landfill on May 10 only to reopen it on May 21, signed an affidavit on July 13, stating he would not renew the permit that opened the Chef Menteur landfill.

Not only did the eastern New Orleans community help force a rewriting of redevelopment plans and stage an environmental battle, Versailles in particular became a model for the city's future and a site for cutting-edge design. The Viet Village Urban Farm, a collaboration between the Mary Queen of Viet Nam Community Development Corporation (MQVNCDC) and Tulane City Center and in partnership with the LSU School of Architecture and the University of Montana's Environmental Studies program, became a much talked-about project of post-Katrina rebuilding. Its original blueprint included a large community garden on a twenty-eight-acre site, a large organic open market, chicken and duck farms, a lagoon, and a play area for children. It also relied on low-tech forms of sustainability and innovative, green designs[85] to help Vietnamese Americans maintain gardening and farming as cultural practices and means of subsistence, as well as ways to provide organic, healthier products for New Orleans residents, local schools, and restaurants.[86] The Urban Farm design received major awards, including 2008 landscape architecture awards given by the American Society of Landscape Architecture and the Australian Institute of Landscape Architects.[87] Given these accomplishments, it would appear that the layers of Ford's 1975 speech—that the country could forget the Vietnam War even as it brought Vietnamese refugees to America—rang true decades later, as globally displaced persons appeared to thrive in the local, contributing to and enlivening local economies and communities rather than simply being displaced postwar charges of the state. We might say that the Viet Village project reflects what Rosaldo calls a "vernacular [notion] of citizenship" wherein cultural practice not only claims space and belonging but also makes a political statement in the public sphere.[88] This momentum seemed to crystallize on the national stage with the election of Republican Joseph Cao to Congress in 2008—the first Vietnamese American Congressman and the first Republican to hold the seat of the strongly Democratic 2nd congressional district.[89] Over time, Cao variously voted with and against his party and was also instrumental in addressing language barrier problems within the Vietnamese diasporic community in the wake of the BP oil spill.

In addition to the community's post-Katrina rebuilding and landfill protests, Cao's election could easily be taken as an example of Vietnamese American model minority successes.[90] But the sustainability of the best parts of these gains remains to be seen, particularly given that the government continues to fail these communities in many ways. Even in the case of Cao's election, while he undoubtedly had significant public support, to some his win was also partly luck. The scope and focus of this essay cannot treat the details of Cao's election, but it is useful to note that when Cao was elected, his opponent, incumbent Democrat William Jefferson, had been caught in 2005 with $90,000 in supposed bribe money in his freezer[91] and had been indicted in 2007 with sixteen counts of corruption.[92] The election had also been delayed due to Hurricane Gustav, which pushed the election date to December 8th from the original November 4th and may have contributed to low voter turnout. 164,000 Democrats cast ballots on November 4th—when President Barack Obama was elected—compared to a cross-party *total* of 66,846 voters on December 8th.[93] Furthermore, the Viet Village Urban Farm project is no longer a go, as high levels of benzine, likely from Katrina, have been detected in the site's soil, and most of the area has been identified as wetlands by the Army Corps of Engineers.[94] MQVNCDC decided to abandon the large site and shift the focus to sustainable aquaculture.[95] The aquaponics systems are meant to serve the community cross-racially, but the degree to which their planning and construction will be interracial is not yet known. Additionally, while the landfill protest succeeded, local black church leaders noted that few African Americans responded to their recruitment efforts because they wanted to stand beside African American Mayor Nagin. Waste continues to sit in the Chef Menteur landfill, all below water and thus not visible to the passerby. The Vietnamese American community continues to face a significant language barrier, contributing to low voter registration, Father Vien has been transferred and now works for the church tribunal, and Cao lost his reelection bid in 2010.[96] Vietnamese American mobilization and Cao's victory actually demonstrate the precariousness and contingent nature of marginalized communities' exercise of interracial cooperation and cultural and political agency.

Lye notes that the recent scholarly upsurge in Afro-Asian linkages suggests a somewhat nostalgic desire for a "third stage of ethnic studies" that hearkens Bandung Afro-Asian solidarities over the divisiveness of the model-minority structure to meet the challenges of contemporary forms of empire.[97] The New Orleans example shows that Asian American and African American cooperation can indeed gain traction in the face of development interests that would wipe residents off a map. But this traction ebbs and flows.[98] To Lye's point regarding how we can think about Afro-Asian linkages in ways fitting to specific historical contexts, the example discussed in this essay foregrounds how categories of *citizen* and *refugee*, with all their gradations, inflect our understanding of race. Masquelier notes that the use of refugee to describe displaced Katrina victims takes away individuals' particularity—their history, culture, and sense of home.[99] And as Alisa Solomon puts it, if you take away one's history you take away one's humanity.[100] But as the narrative about Vietnamese Americans in New Orleans shows, refugee's meanings vary and can effectively relate cross-racial conditions of state neglect when "refugee" is freed from its strict legal definition and its perceived character of passivity and shame.

Kimberly Rivers Roberts in the documentary *Trouble the Water* perhaps highlights the comparative value of the refugee category best, stating that the treatment she and others received in the days after Katrina was one of displacement from the nation, rendering them "un-American"—it was "*like* we lost our citizenship [emphasis mine]."[101] Positioned at odds in the 1970s, in 2005 citizen had become like, rather than opposed to, refugee, revealing how shifting social, political, and ecological landscapes can generate creative narrative moves that contest the unmet ideal of U.S. citizenship.

Notes

My thanks to Wesleyan University and the Mellon Postdoctoral Fellowship in the Humanities at Tulane University for various forms of support that allowed me to complete this project. My thanks also to the Amistad Research Center, the American Studies Workshop at Tulane University, Carl Bankston, Kathy Carlin, T. R. Johnson, Amy Lee, Jana Lipman, Daniel Nguyen, Minh Nguyen, Nicholas Spitzer, Mark Vanlandingham, the editors of this volume, and two anonymous reviewers for their assistance and feedback.

The quotation in this essay's title is from *Trouble the Water*, dirs. Tia Lessin and Carl Deal, Zeitgeist Films, 2008.

1. Gerald Ford, Convocation Speech, Tulane University, April 23, 1975. http://www.ford .utexas.edu/library/speeches/750208.htm (accessed March 18, 2013).

2. Initially, about five thousand evacuees were transported by air on a daily basis, and in the first wave of refugees between ten and fifteen thousand people were able to flee seven to ten days before Thiệu's government fell. In a second wave about eighty-six thousand evacuees left by air, and in a third wave forty to sixty thousand Vietnamese left by both air and sea in early May. See William T. Liu and Alice Murata, "The Vietnamese in America: Refugees or Immigrants?" *Bridge: An Asian American Perspective* 5.3 (1997): 13–14; Sucheng Chan, *Remapping Asian American History* (Walnut Creek, Calif.: Alta Mira Press, 2003), 175. The Indochina Migration and Refugee Assistance Act of 1975 appropriated $455,000,000 for refugee evacuation and assistance. The period for aid was extended with H.R. 7769 on October 28, 1977. Section 212(d)(5) of the 1952 Immigration and Nationality Act (also known as the 1952 McCarran-Walter Act) gives the attorney

general discretion to give aliens U.S. parolee status beyond allowable quotas under crisis situations—for "urgent humanitarian reasons or if there is a significant public benefit." Discretion was initially used for individuals but was later applied to groups, for example, Hungarians, Chinese, Cubans, and then those from former Indochina. Up until 1977, refugees were considered parolees, whose stay was temporary as the McCarran-Walter Act of 1952 stipulated. Senator Edward Kennedy sponsored a bill in 1977 to change the status of a refugee from parolee to permanent resident. The bill also provided Southeast Asian refugees with, in Carter's words, "additional opportunity for language training, for vocational training, for basic education principles, for counseling, for job placement," as well as resident alien status after two years.

3. Another two thousand arrived in 1976. See Carl Bankston, "Education and Ethnicity in an Urban Vietnamese Village," in *Beyond Black and White: New Faces and Voices in U.S. Schools*, eds. Maxine Seller and Lois Weis (Albany: State University of New York Press, 1997), 211.

4. "Managing Viet 'Crisis,'" *New Orleans Times-Picayune*, May 18, 1978: 1.18.

5. Denise Fiegle, "Treatment of Refugees," *New Orleans Times-Picayune*, May 5, 1978: 1.18.

6. An interesting but undocumented story circulates in New Orleans about a Cuban American Catholic woman living there who felt a shared sense of anticommunism and Catholicism with Vietnamese refugees after watching footage of them during the fall of Saigon in 1975.

7. Russell Goodman, "Viet Emigration to U.S. Delayed, Hannan Says," *New Orleans Times-Picayune*, August 14, 1978: 1.3. Hannan papers remain classified.

8. Karen Leong et al., "Resilient History and the Rebuilding of a Community: The Vietnamese American Community in New Orleans East," *Through the Eye of Katrina: The Past as Prologue? Special issue of Journal of American History*, eds. Lawrence N. Powell and Clarence L. Mohr, 94.3 (2007): 775.

9. Carl Bankston, "Vietnamese-American Catholicism, Transplanted and Flourishing," *U.S. Catholic Historian* 18.1 (2000): 45.

10. Agendas to disperse Asian populations in the United States have a long and complicated history tied to both conservative and liberal projects. For example, dispersal of Japanese Americans after internment was portrayed by the liberals as an antiracist maneuver; if Japanese Americans could be prevented from living in clusters as they did before internment, they would face less racism. See Colleen Lye, *America's Asia: Racial Form and American Literature, 1893–1945* (Princeton, N.J.: Princeton University Press, 2005), 141–203.

11. Christopher Airriess, "Spaces and Places of Adaptation in an Ethnic Vietnamese Cluster in New Orleans, Louisiana," in *Immigrants outside Megalopolis: Ethnic Transformation in the Heartland*, ed. Richard C. Jones (Lanham, Md.: Lexington Books, 2008), 167.

12. Ibid., 168.

13. Bankston, "Vietnamese-American Catholicism," 45–46.

14. Eric Tang, "A Gulf Unites Us: The Vietnamese Americans of Black New Orleans East," *American Quarterly* 63.1 (2011): 125.

15. Peter Hansen, "Bac Di Cu: Catholic Refugees from the North of Vietnam, and Their Role in the Southern Republic, 1954–1959," *Journal of Vietnamese Studies* 4.3 (2009): 178–180. When the French were defeated at Dien Bien Phu on May 7, 1954, church leadership quickly learned of secret plans for French withdrawal, and the Catholic exodus south

soon began (bac di cu). In October 1955, the RVN reported that 676,348 Catholics, 209,132 Buddhists, and 1,041 Protestants had migrated to the South.

16. It is estimated that 80 percent of Vietnamese residents in New Orleans East are Catholic. See Christopher Airriess et al., "Church-Based Social Capital, Networks and Geographical Scale: Katrina Evacuation, Relocation, and Recovery in a New Orleans Vietnamese American Community," *Geoforum* 39:3 (2008): 1334.

17. Bankston, "Vietnamese-American Catholicism," 47; Bankston and Min Zhou, "Go Fish: The Louisiana Vietnamese and Ethnic Entrepreneurship in an Extractive Industry," *National Journal of Sociology* 10:1 (1996). Eventually, many Vietnamese in New Orleans East would become entrepreneurs, operating ninety-three businesses in the area and leading to a more diverse and independent economy relative to other Gulf Coast areas more reliant upon the fishing industry.

18. Nicholas Spitzer, correspondence with the author, New Orleans, La., April 22, 2011.

19. Paul D. Starr, "Troubled Waters: Vietnamese Fisherfolk on America's Gulf Coast," *International Migration Review* 15.1/2 (1981): 230. My conversations with New Orleans natives and longtime residents have revealed a variety of explanations for hostility against Vietnamese Gulf Coast fishermen, including Vietnamese use of gill nets, which were legal in Vietnam but not in the United States, and Vietnamese fishers' willingness to stay at sea for longer periods of time. Explanations for friendliness among Gulf Coast fishermen include admiration for what locals perceived as a Vietnamese work ethic and a shared cross-racial preference for drinking and conversation after work.

20. Paul Taylor, "Vietnamese Shrimpers Alter Texas Gulf Towns; Natives' Economy and Pride Wounded," *New Orleans Times-Picayune*, December 26, 1984: A1.

21. Gayle Ashton, "Shrimping: A Small Revolution on the Water," *New Orleans Times-Picayune*, April 22, 1985: A-13.

22. Carl Galmon of the A. Phillip Randolph Institute asked for much more sensitivity to the black community from Associated Catholic Charities, while Ron Chisolm of the Citywide Housing Coalition called for more affordable housing for African Americans. Representative Louis Charbonnet pointed out the negative impact of unemployment on African American families. See Therese L. Mitchell, "Vietnamese Take Jobs from Blacks in Charge," *New Orleans Times-Picayune*, April 14, 1978: 1.9.

23. Bankston, "Vietnamese-American Catholicism," 46.

24. Urban League of Greater New Orleans, "Summary of the Analysis of Housing Conditions in New Orleans," *Urban League of Greater New Orleans Records, 1978–1988*. New Orleans: Amistad Research Center, Box 81, Folder 9.

25. While scholarly sources note that many units in Versailles were empty until the 1,000 Vietnamese moved in, the Urban League document states that Catholic Charities admitted to resettling refugees in 700 units in Versailles; if one takes the average family household to be five to six persons, this would mean that 3,500–4,200 Vietnamese were actually resettled by ACC. The document also asserts that a large number of white and black families were displaced from Versailles Arms I and II. There are a number of ways to parse out the possible discrepancy here, if there is one. Regardless, the point is that the Urban League identifies a much longer-standing problem of unavailable affordable housing in New Orleans. See Urban League of Greater New Orleans, "Summary."

26. Urban League of Greater New Orleans, "Recommendations," *Urban League of Greater New Orleans Records, 1978–1988*. New Orleans: Amistad Research Center, Box 81, Folder 5.

27. Leslie Bow, *Partly Colored: Asian Americans and Racial Anomaly in the Segregated South* (New York: New York University Press, 2010), 1.

28. Claire Jean Kim, "Racial Triangulation of Asian Americans," *Politics & Society* 27.1 (1999): 105–138.

29. Colleen Lye, "The Afro-Asian Analogy," *PMLA* 123.5 (2008): 1733.

30. Helen Heran Jun, *Race for Citizenship: Black Orientalism and Asian Uplift from Pre-Emancipation to Neoliberal America* (New York: New York University Press, 2011), 9.

31. Ibid., 100.

32. Tim Morris, "Louisiana's Incarceration Rate is No. 1 in the Country," *New Orleans Times-Picayune*, March 2, 2009, April 29, 2011. http://www.nola.com/news/index.ssf/2009/03/louisianas_ incarceration_rate.html. Statistics are taken from the Pew Center for the States 2007 study (accessed March 18, 2013).

33. Larry Powell, "New Orleans: An American Pompeii?" in *Satchmo Meets Amadeus*, ed. Reinhold Wagnleitner (Innsbruck, Austria: Studien Verlag, 2007), 143.

34. In his letter, Haddad states that he had expressed refusal to join such a committee because it had been stipulated that Vietnamese displaced persons would not be invited to the table.

35. Urban League of Greater New Orleans, "Recommendations."

36. Urban League of Greater New Orleans, "Survey of Black Leadership," *Urban League of Greater New Orleans Records, 1978–1988*. New Orleans: Amistad Research Center, Box 81, Folder 9.

37. "Black Americans Urge Admission of the Indochinese Refugees," *New York Times*, March 29, 1978: E9.

38. Creoles historically occupied lower New Orleans and adopted a "three-tiered" racial structure, while English speakers occupied upper New Orleans and relied on a "two-tiered," black-white racial structure. See Richard Campanella, "An Ethnic Geography of New Orleans," *Journal of American History* 94.3 (2007): 706.

39. The committee's task was to visit various cities in the country to evaluate immigration and refugee resettlement and provide final recommendations to the U.S. administration for improving refugee policies. At the meeting on March 24, 1980, organization and community leaders, scholars, a few refugees, and others were invited to provide research, responses, and testimony. Cities visited by the committee included Albany, Baltimore, Boston, Chicago, Denver, Los Angeles, Miami, New Orleans, New York, Phoenix, San Antonio, and San Francisco. The U.S. Select Committee on Immigration and Refugee Policy's final report reiterated that the goals of refugee resettlement were "self-sufficiency" and "survival training," and, contrary to the administration's initial policy of dispersal, it endorsed "refugee clustering." See *Papers of the Select Commission on Immigration and Refugee Policy*, ed. Randolph Boehm (Frederick, Md.: University Publications of America), 1984.

40. Andrea Stahl, "Blacks Rap Indochinese 'Invasion,'" *New Orleans Times-Picayune*, March 25, 1980: 16.

41. Renato Rosaldo, "Cultural Citizenship, Inequality, and Multiculturalism," in *Latino Cultural Citizenship*, eds. William V. Flores and Rina Benmayor (Boston: Beacon Press, 1997), 27.

42. Yen Le Espiritu, "Toward a Critical Refugee Study: The Vietnamese Refugee Subject in US Scholarship," *Journal of Vietnamese Studies* 1:1–2 (2006): 410–433.

43. United Nations High Commissioner for Refugees, *Protecting Refugees & Role of UNHCR* (Geneva: UNHCR Media Relations and Public Information Service, 2008–09), 4. PDF file. http://www.unhcr.org/4034b6a34.html (accessed March 18, 2013).

44. Ibid., 14.

45. Ibid., 21.

46. Ibid., 25. It is also important to note that the refugee category did not always require the crossing of international borders. In various historical moments, "refugee" has included those we now call IDPs. See Luke T. Lee, "Internally Displaced Persons and Refugees: Toward a Legal Synthesis?" *Journal of Refugee Studies* 9.1 (1996): 27–42; Andreas Zimmermann, *The 1951 Convention Relating to the Status of Refugees and its 1967 Protocol: A Commentary* (New York: Oxford University Press, 2011).

47. New Orleans's long history with Latinos began with Spanish imperial rule from 1763–1801. Around 1800, Creoles with Francophone/Hispanic backgrounds "were spatially intermixed" in New Orleans, with masters living close to slaves. See Campanella, "Ethnic Geography of New Orleans," 705. When the United States acquired New Orleans through the Louisiana Purchase in 1803, the city was the ninth largest port in the nation, and its trade networks included Europe, North America, the Caribbean, and Latin America. In 1866, the state's commissioner of immigration began recruiting laborers from a number of nations including Mexico, but it was not until the mid–twentieth century that Latin American migrants began to settle in New Orleans. The number of these migrants, mostly from Honduras (fruit trade) but also from Cuba (Cuban Revolution), Mexico, and Nicaragua, was relatively small. See Anita I. Drever, "New Orleans: A Re-Emerging Latino Destination City," *Journal of Cultural Geography* 25.3 (2008): 289–290; Elizabeth Fussell, "Constructing New Orleans, Constructing Race: A Population History of New Orleans," *Journal of American History* 94.3 (December 2007): 848–849. Vietnamese refugee arrival triggered some Vietnamese-Latino tensions, including a 1979 protest at the New Orleans Services Employment and Redevelopment office where Latina/os claimed federal language and job programs were servicing more Vietnamese than Latinos. See Millie Ball, "N.O. Hispanics Picket SET Office," *New Orleans Times-Picayune*, April 3, 1979: 10. Latina/o migration to New Orleans declined by 1980, though it increased in other southern cities. According to Drever, pre-Katrina Latinos in New Orleans were among the most diverse in the country, were mostly U.S. citizens, and were "economically integrated." After Katrina, about fifty thousand Latina/os, mostly from Central America, have moved to New Orleans to clean and rebuild the city and are the only ethnic group to experience an increase in the Crescent City; actual numbers are likely much higher. Many work and live in New Orleans East. See Sara Catania, "From Fish Sauce to Salsa—New Orleans Vietnamese Adapt to Influx of Latinos," *Gambit*, October 24, 2006. The press's portrayal of post-Katrina Latina/os as a new phenomenon elides the fact that New Orleans has had long historical ties with Latin America. See Drever, "New Orleans," 287–303.

48. Le Thanh Trang, "Please Join Us," *Dau Thuong: Dac San Ky Niem Ngay Viet Nam*, April 30, 1980: 7, my translation. Included in Le's list of rumors circulating about Southeast Asian refugees are beliefs that Vietnamese are exempt from taxes and are beneficiaries of subsidized employment, housing, cars, and shrimping boats.

49. Ibid.

50. Espiritu, "Toward a Critical Refugee Study," 410.

51. Urban League of Greater New Orleans, "Recommendations."

52. Urban League of Greater New Orleans, "Indo-China Refugee Question: An Urban League Position Paper," *Urban League of Greater New Orleans Records, 1978–1988*. New Orleans: Amistad Research Center, Box 81, Folder 9.

53. S. Leo Chiang, dir., *A Village Called Versailles*, New Day Films, 2009.

54. The 2010 U.S. Census shows that Vietnamese comprise 42 percent of Louisiana's Asian population and 35 percent of Orleans Parish's Asian population.

55. Tang, "A Gulf Unites Us," 120–121.

56. Airriess et al. note that "social capital and networking" were critical to Vietnamese American rebuilding in New Orleans East. Taking L. A. Ritchie and D. A. Gill's definition of social networks as "[facilitating] a flow of information providing a basis for action and assisting an individual and community goal attainment," the authors importantly argue that human and technological networks established since mass Vietnamese migration to the United States helped "rescale" the community's capital to encompass ethnic media and organizations on a scale beyond New Orleans East's particular location ("Church-Based Social Capital," 1336–1338).

57. Chiang, *Village Called Versailles*.

58. Wei Li et al., "Surviving Katrina and Its Aftermath: Evacuation and Community Mobilization by Vietnamese Americans and African Americans," *Journal of Cultural Geography* 25.3 (2008): 272.

59. Ibid.

60. Richard Campanella importantly notes that the press and the public have misunderstood the relationship between elevation and hurricane devastation in New Orleans. He writes that the "technological neutralization of topography" has actually driven New Orleanians across race and class into geographically vulnerable areas. For example, "middle-class whites in the 1910s-1950s moved enthusiastically *into* the lowest-lying areas," while "working-class African Americans [have settled] along some of the *highest* land in New Orleans—the riverfront." Additionally, some wealthier neighborhoods, such as Lakeview, are actually lower than the Lower Ninth Ward ("Ethnic Geography of New Orleans," 715).

61. Airriess et al., "Church-Based Social Capital," 1333.

62. See Cathy Schlund-Vials, *Modeling Citizenship: Jewish and Asian American Writing* (Philadelphia: Temple University Press), 2011, for a deft treatment of citizenship and belonging in relation to naturalization.

63. Joseph Treaster and Deborah Sontag, "Despair and Lawlessness Grip New Orleans as Thousands Remain Stranded in Squalor," *New York Times*, September 2, 2005: A1.

64. Adeline Masquelier, "Why Katrina's Victims Aren't *Refugees*: Musings on a 'Dirty' Word." *American Anthropologist* 108:4 (2006): 735.

65. Mike Pesca, "Are Katrina Victims 'Refugees' or 'Evacuees?'" NPR.org. http://www.npr.org/templates/story/story.php?storyId=4833613 (accessed March 18, 2013).

66. Masquelier, "Why Katrina's Victims Aren't *Refugees*," 735.

67. Quoted in ibid., 742.

68. Quoted in ibid., 737.

69. John M. Broder, "Amid Criticism of Federal Efforts, Charges of Racism Are Lodged," *New York Times*, September 5, 2005: A9.

70. Masquelier, "Why Katrina's Victims Aren't *Refugees*," 737.

71. Nina Bernstein, "Refugee Groups Reaching Out to Victims of Hurricane," *New York Times*, September 18, 2005: 37.

72. Kaleema H. Nur, "Drowning in the Rhetoric: Reconceptualizing New Orleans as a Human Rights Issue," PDF File, May 13, 2011, 2–3. http://www.northeastern.edu/law/academics/institutes/phrge/rights-katrina.html (accessed March 18, 2013).

73. United Nations, *Guiding Principles on Internal Displacement* (Washington, D.C.: The Brookings-Bern Project on Internal Displacement, 1998), 1.

74. Hannah Arendt, *The Origins of Totalitarianism* (New York: Harvest, 1973), 279–280.

75. Chiang, *Village Called Versailles*.

76. Leslie Williams, "Starting Over Is Nothing New for Thousands of New Orleanians with Roots in Vietnam, but Many Feel They Are Not Given a Voice in the Process," *New Orleans Times-Picayune*, November 27, 2005: 1.

77. Bruce Eggler, "Lower 9th Ward, East N.O. Endorsed; Rebuilding Panel Says They Must Be Included," *New Orleans Times-Picayune*, October 25, 2005: 1.

78. Williams, "Starting Over Is Nothing New."

79. Gordon Russell and Frank Donze, "Rebuilding Proposal Gets Mixed Reception," *New Orleans Times-Picayune*, January 12, 2006: 1.

80. Chiang, *Village Called Versailles*.

81. Juliet K. Choi, Avani Bhatt, and Frankie Chen, "In the Aftermath of Hurricane Katrina: The Chef Menteur Landfill and Its Effects on the Vietnamese American Community," Washington, D.C., Asian American Justice Center, August 2006, 6.

82. Daniel Nguyen, Interview by the author, New Orleans, May 26, 2011.

83. Susan Finch, "SCLC Joins Protest against Landfill," *New Orleans Times-Picayune*, May 6, 2006: 1.

84. Choi et al., 9.

85. Bruce Nolan, "Vietnamese Church Resowing Tradition: Project Aims to Replace Gardens Lost in Storm," *New Orleans Times-Picayune*, November 25, 2007: 1.

86. Nguyen, Interview.

87. "Viet Village Urban Farm," Mary Queen of Viet Nam Development Community Development Corporation, Inc. http://www.mqvncdc.org/page.php?id=18 (accessed March 18, 2013).

88. Rosaldo, "Cultural Citizenship, Inequality, and Multiculturalism," 38.

89. The 2nd congressional district in Louisiana consists of almost all of New Orleans and some suburbs in neighboring Jefferson Parish. Cao defeated nine-term incumbent William Jefferson in 2008 in an election delayed by Hurricane Gustav amid charges of Jefferson's corruption. Hamilton D. Coleman was the last Republican to represent the 2nd congressional district in 1891.

90. For critical treatments of the model-minority rhetoric in the New Orleans Vietnamese American example, see Leong et al., "Resilient History," 770; and Tang, "A Gulf Unites Us," 119–120.

91. Terri Troncale, "The William Jefferson Verdict," *New Orleans Times-Picayune*, August 5, 2009, April 20, 2012. http://blog.nola.com/editorials/2009/08/the_jefferson_verdict.html (accessed March 18, 2013).

92. Keith I. Marszalek, "Jefferson Indicted for Bribery, Racketeering," *New Orleans Times-Picayune*, June 4, 2007, April 20, 2012. http://blog.nola.com/updates/2007/06/jefferson _indicted_for_bribery.html (accessed March 18, 2013). Jefferson was convicted of 11 of those 16 charges in 2009. See Tim Morris, "William Jefferson Verdict: Guilty on 11 of 16 Counts," *New Orleans Times-Picayune*, August 5, 2009.

93. Michelle Krupa, "Anh 'Joseph' Cao Beats Rep. William Jefferson in 2nd Congressional District," *New Orleans Times-Picayune*, December 12, 2008, April 17, 2012, April 19, 2012. http://www.nola.com/news/index.ssf/2008/12/jefferson_cao_in_dead_heat.html (accessed March 18, 2013).

94. Nguyen, Interview. This meant that MQVNCDC had to purchase "environmental credits" worth $300,000 in order to develop the land.

95. Nguyen, Interview.

96. My research has yielded only anecdotal rather than definitive explanations for this change in Father Vien's position.

97. Lye, "The Afro-Asian Analogy," 1732.

98. One important example of the complexity of Afro-Asian alliance in Louisiana is the case of Harry Lee, self-declared Chinese cowboy and six-time sheriff of Orleans Parish's neighbor, Jefferson Parish. He first rose to power in David Duke's district in 1979, but my research shows he had no comment on Vietnamese refugee arrival. Further, when individuals attempted to get out of New Orleans after Katrina by crossing the Crescent City Connection, Jefferson Parish police were told to turn them away at gunpoint. Karen Carter, then Louisiana state Representative for New Orleans, says in Spike Lee's *When the Levees Broke: A Requiem in Four Acts*, HBO Home Video, 2006: "I thought that I lived in America until shortly after Katrina, and the Crescent City connection was blocked off from people being able to walk freely on United States soil. . . . It was unjust. It was inhumane."

99. Masquelier, "Why Katrina's Victims Aren't *Refugees*," 737.

100. Alisa Solomon, "Who Gets to Be Human on the Evening News?" *PMLA* 121.5 (2006): 1590.

101. Dirs. Tia Lessin and Carl Deal, *Trouble the Water*, Zeitgeist Films, 2008. Film.

CONTRIBUTORS

VIVEK BALD is a documentary filmmaker and associate professor of Writing and Digital Media at the Massachusetts Institute of Technology. He is the author of the book *Bengali Harlem and the Lost Histories of South Asian America* (Harvard University Press, 2012), and director of the documentary film *In Search of Bengali Harlem* with actor and writer Alaudin Ullah.

LESLIE BOW is Mark and Elisabeth Eccles Professor of English and Asian American Studies at the University of Wisconsin, Madison. She is the author of *Betrayal and Other Acts of Subversion: Feminism, Sexual Politics, Asian American Women's Literature* (Princeton University Press, 2001) and *"Partly Colored": Asian Americans and Racial Anomaly in the Segregated South* (New York University Press, 2010).

AMY L. BRANDZEL is assistant professor of American Studies and Women Studies at the University of New Mexico. Her work utilizes postcolonial queer and feminist theories to examine citizenship, law, history, and knowledge production. She is finishing her manuscript, *Against Citizenship: Queer Intersections and the Violence of the Normative*, which exposes how discourses of citizenship work to reify normative knowledge systems and enact violence (rhetorical, emotional, corporeal, social, and institutional) on nonnormative bodies, practices, behaviors, and forms of affiliation.

DANIEL BRONSTEIN is an independent scholar. He is currently living in South Korea teaching English.

JIGNA DESAI is an associate professor in the Department of Gender, Women, and Sexuality Studies and Asian American Studies Program at the University of Minnesota. Her research interests include transnational feminist, Asian American, diasporic, queer, and disability cultural studies. She is the author of *Beyond Bollywood: The Cultural Politics of South Asian Diasporic Films* (Routledge, 2004), coeditor of *The Bollywood Reader* (Open University Press, 2008), and coeditor of *Transnational Feminism and Global Advocacy in South Asia* (Routledge, 2012).

JENNIFER HO is an associate professor in the Department of English and Comparative Literature at the University of North Carolina at Chapel Hill. Her first book, *Consumption and Identity in Asian American Coming-of-Age Novels* examined the connection between food and subjectivity. Her current research project explores racially ambiguous Asian Americans in contemporary culture.

KHYATI JOSHI is an associate professor in the School of Education at Fairleigh Dickinson University. She is the author of *New Roots in America's Sacred Ground: Religion, Race and Ethnicity in Indian America* (Rutgers University Press, 2006) and numerous publications on religious oppression and Christian Privilege.

CHANGHWAN KIM is associate professor of Sociology at the University of Kansas. His areas of interest include labor market inequality, race and ethnicity, Asian American Studies, and quantitative methodology. His recent research appears in, among other outlets, *American Sociological Review*, *Social Forces*, *Social Science Research*, and *Sociological Methods and Research*.

MARGUERITE NGUYEN is assistant professor of English at Wesleyan University. She specializes in American literature, with an emphasis on Vietnamese American literature and transnational Asian American studies. Her current book project examines the impact of Vietnamese decolonization on the making of twentieth-to twenty-first–century American culture. She received her PhD in English at U.C. Berkeley.

ARTHUR SAKAMOTO is professor of Sociology at the University of Texas at Austin. His research interests include racial and ethnic relations, demography, and social inequality. He served as the first interim director of the Center for Asian American Studies at the University of Texas at Austin.

PURVI SHAH's *Terrain Tracks* (New Rivers Press, 2006), which explores migration as potential and loss, won the Many Voices Project prize and was nominated for the Asian American Writers' Workshop Members' Choice Award. She is the winner of the inaugural SONY South Asian Social Services Award in 2008 for her work fighting violence against women. In 2011, she served as artistic director for "Together We Are New York," a community-based poetry project to highlight the voices of Asian Americans during the tenth anniversary of 9/11.

ISAO TAKEI is an assistant professor in International Relations at Nihon University. He received his PhD in sociology from the University of Texas at Austin. He has published several articles on Japanese culture and Asian American issues.

JASMINE KAR TANG is a PhD candidate in American Studies at the University of Minnesota. Her dissertation explores post-1965 Asian American racial formation in the U.S. South. Her research interests also include comparative race and ethnic studies, performance studies, and writing center theory and practice.

ROY VU is a professor and Coordinator of History at North Lake College in Irving, Texas. He earned his BA (1998) in History at Texas Christian University and his MA (2001) and PhD (2006) in History at the University of Houston. He and his wife, Ngoc, reside in Irving.

INDEX

Abhedananda, Swami, 36
activism, community, 22, 33, 76, 166, 196,
    208–209, 266; civil rights, 69; cross-racial,
    275, 279; nativist and anti-immigration,
    18–19; online, 205–206; religious organiza-
    tions, 275, 278, 279, 286n56
African Americans: as common denominator
    in conflicts between immigrants and jobs,
    58; emancipation of, 8–9; Hurricane Katrina
    and, 276–281; Jim Crow laws and, 118–119;
    relationship with Asian Americans, 10–11,
    169–170, 268–271; slavery and, 4, 7, 8; Viet-
    namese relationships with, 169–170, 268–281
Afro-Asian(s): alliances, 25, 265–266, 274–
    276, 280–281; South, 10–11
Afro-Orientalism, 10–11
After Whiteness, 58
Ahn, Chang, 224–226
Alabama, 3, 9, 19, 133; Bengali peddlers in, 40;
    Henry Cho and, 255–256
Ali, Mushareef, 37
Alley, Ahmed, 39
Alley, Kamieth, 39
Alli, Mobarak, 37
Alli, Muhioadeen, 37
Ally, Abad, 37
Almost White, 55
Aly, Sohboth, 37
ambivalence, 72–73
American Community Survey, 132, 134–135
American Religious Identification Survey,
    27n19
Anderson, Benedict, 206
Angel Island, California, 114
antimiscegenation laws, 17, 62, 120, 122
antisemitism, 16–17
Aplin, Billy Joe, 167
Arendt, Hannah, 277
Arizona SB 1070, 19
Arkansas, 3, 9, 19, 67–68, 133, 165
arts and entertainment: Asian American lit-
    erature, 221–224; film portrayals of, 57, 59,
    62–65, 68; Oriental themed, 35–36, 42–43,

52–53n38; portrayals of Asians in, 57, 59,
    62–65, 68, 219; television, 259n5
Asian American and Pacific Islander Policy
    Research Consortium, 21; migration statis-
    tics, 156–159
Asian American Journalists Association, 98
Asian Americans: antimiscegenation laws and,
    17, 62, 120, 122; biracial, 138–140, 229–234,
    235; in the Black/White binary, 13–18, 29n59,
    71–73, 80, 81–85, 108, 235–236; California
    centric paradigm of, 23, 82, 100n3, 161; citi-
    zenship of, 15, 271, 281; as coolies, 7–9, 107;
    demographic data sources and definitions,
    132–134; education of, 16–17, 59, 69, 122, 124,
    145–146; government categorization of, 14,
    123, 132–133, 162–163n2; household socioeco-
    nomic characteristics, 150–151, *152*; identify-
    ing with the South, 249–252; incongruity of
    body and accent in, 248–249, 260n21; inter-
    stitiality, 59–62, 71–72, 223, 225, 268–269; in-
    troduction to scholarship on the South and,
    1–3; jokes about, 247–248; labor force and
    related socioeconomic characteristics, 147–
    150; literary portrayals of, 61–62; mass media
    and, 98–99, 271–272; as middleman mi-
    norities, 56–57; migration statistics, 156–159;
    migration to the South, 7–9; military draft
    and, 40–41; as model minorities, 54–55, 84,
    171–172, 252–255; multiracial and ethnic di-
    versity of, 138–144; political participation by,
    174–176; postracial South and, 96–97; as ra-
    cial and religious "others," 194–196; racializa-
    tion of, 59–62, 71–72, 81–85, 98–99, 166–172,
    184, 194–196, 223, 225, 268–269; racialized
    masculinity and, 77–80, 89–96; refugees,
    165, 167, 173, 236–237n7, 264–267, 273–274;
    relationships with African Americans,
    10–11, 169–170, 268–281; religious, linguis-
    tic, and social service institutions, 181–183;
    scapegoating of, 269; social communities,
    176–178, 186n11; violence against, 77, 119, 167;
    violence by, 77–80, 89–96, 98–99, 170. *See
    also* demographics of Asian Americans

THE ASIAN AMERICAN EXPERIENCE